W9-CLG-285

THE INFIDEL AND THE PROFESSOR

COPYRIGHT © 2017 BY PRINCETON UNIVERSITY PRESS

PUBLISHED BY PRINCETON UNIVERSITY PRESS
41 William Street, Princeton, New Jersey 08540

IN THE UNITED KINGDOM: PRINCETON UNIVERSITY PRESS
6 Oxford Street, Woodstock, Oxfordshire OX20 1TR

press.princeton.edu

Jacket art: (Left) *David Hume*, Scottish National Portrait Gallery, (right) *Adam Smith*, The Miriam and Ira D. Wallach Division of Art, Prints and Photographs: Print Collection; The New York Public Library, Astor, Lenox and Tilden Foundations

Frontispiece: statues of Hume and Smith. Original photo taken by staff. Scottish National Portrait Gallery

ISBN 978-0-691-17701-4

Library of Congress Control Number: 2017936619

British Library Cataloging-in-Publication Data is available

This book has been composed in Adobe Caslon and The Fell Types
The Fell Types are digitally reproduced by Igino Marini.
www.iginomarini.com

Printed on acid-free paper. ∞

PRINTED IN THE UNITED STATES OF AMERICA

1 3 5 7 9 10 8 6 4 2

Upon the whole, I have always considered him, both in his lifetime and since his death, as approaching as nearly to the idea of a perfectly wise and virtuous man, as perhaps the nature of human frailty will permit.

—ADAM SMITH ON DAVID HUME*

Without doubt you have read what is called the Life of David Hume, written by himself, with the letter from Dr. Adam Smith subjoined to it. Is not this an age of daring effrontery? My friend Mr. [John] Anderson . . . paid me a visit lately; and after we had talked with indignation and contempt of the poisonous productions with which this age is infested, he said there was now an excellent opportunity for Dr. Johnson to step forth. I agreed with him that you might knock Hume's and Smith's heads together, and make vain and ostentatious infidelity exceedingly ridiculous. Would it not be worth your while to crush such noxious weeds in the moral garden?

—JAMES BOSWELL TO SAMUEL JOHNSON**

* Adam Smith, *Letter from Adam Smith, LL.D. to William Strahan, Esq.*, in David Hume, *Essays, Moral, Political, and Literary*, ed. Eugene F. Miller (Indianapolis: Liberty Fund, [1777] 1987), xlix.
** James Boswell, *The Life of Samuel Johnson, LL.D.* (London: William Pickering, [1791] 1826), 104–5.

CONTENTS

CONTENTS

ILLUSTRATIONS

PREFACE

D
AVID HUME IS widely regarded as the greatest philosopher ever to write in the English language, and Adam Smith is almost certainly history's most famous theorist of commercial society. Remarkably, the two were best friends for most of their adult lives. This book follows the course of their friendship from their first meeting in 1749 until Hume's death more than a quarter of a century later, examining both their personal interactions and the impact that each had on the other's outlook. We will see them comment on one another's works, support one another's careers and literary ambitions, and counsel one another when needed, such as in the aftermath of Hume's dramatic quarrel with Jean-Jacques Rousseau. We will see them make many of the same friends (and enemies), join the same clubs, and strive constantly—though with less success than they always hoped—to spend more time together. We will also see them adopt broadly similar views, but very different public postures, with respect to religion and the religious; indeed, this will be a running theme throughout the book.

Although I am a professor and hope that this book will contribute to the scholarly study of Hume and Smith, it was written not just for academics but for anyone interested in learning more about the lives and ideas of these two giants of the Enlightenment, and about what is arguably the greatest of all philosophical friendships.

ACKNOWLEDGMENTS

THIS BOOK WAS an absolute joy to write, and I am glad to have an opportunity to express my appreciation to some of those who helped to make it so. I must begin with a general word of thanks to Tufts University, particularly to the Department of Political Science for providing a congenial academic home and to the Faculty Research Awards Committee for generous funding. I am grateful to Bill Curtis, Emily Nacol, Rich Rasmussen, Michelle Schwarze, and two anonymous reviewers for reading a draft of the book and providing helpful comments, and to Felix Waldmann for pointing me toward useful resources. I have benefited enormously from the conversation, encouragement, and insight of many other scholars of Hume, Smith, and the Enlightenment more broadly. It would be impossible to name all of these individuals here, but I must single out Sam Fleischacker, Michael Frazer, Michael Gillespie, Ruth Grant, Charles Griswold, and Ryan Hanley. I am grateful for the assistance provided by the staffs of the Tisch Library at Tufts University, the Widener and Lamont Libraries at Harvard University, the Beinecke Library at Yale University, the Morgan Library and Museum in New York, the British Library and Dr. Williams's Library in London, the Edinburgh University Library and the National Library of Scotland in Edinburgh, the University of Glasgow Library, and the Public Record Office of Northern Ireland in Belfast. I would also like to thank my editor, Rob Tempio, and the whole team at Princeton University Press for all of the effort and care that went into making the book as good as it could be.

As always, my deepest thanks go to my wife, Emily, and now also our son, Sam. Given that this book focuses on a friendship, however, this one is dedicated to my friends. I can think of few better wishes for Sam than that he be as fortunate in his friends as I have been.

THE INFIDEL AND THE PROFESSOR

INTRODUCTION

DEAREST FRIENDS

A S DAVID HUME lay on his deathbed in the summer of 1776, much of the British public, both north and south of the Tweed, waited expectantly for news of his passing. His writings had challenged their views—philosophical, political, and especially religious—for the better part of four decades. He had experienced a lifetime of abuse and reproach from the pious, including a concerted effort to excommunicate him from the Church of Scotland, but he was now beyond their reach. Everyone wanted to know how the notorious infidel would face his end. Would he show remorse or perhaps even recant his skepticism? Would he die in a state of distress, having none of the usual consolations afforded by belief in an afterlife? In the event Hume died as he had lived, with remarkable good humor and without religion. The most prominent account of his calm and courageous end was penned by his best friend, a renowned philosopher in his own right who had just published a book that would soon change the world. While *The Wealth of Nations* was, in Adam Smith's own words, a "very violent attack . . . upon the whole commercial system of Great Britain," it was on the whole quite well received.[1] Smith was to suffer far more opprobrium on account of a short public letter that he wrote later that year describing—even flaunting—the cheerfulness and equanimity of Hume's final days. He concluded the letter by declaring that his unbelieving friend approached "as nearly to the idea of a perfectly wise and virtuous man, as perhaps the nature of human frailty will permit."[2] It was the closest that Smith ever came to openly antagonizing the devout, an act for which he would pay dearly but that he would never regret. It was, moreover, a fitting conclusion to a friendship that had played a central role in the lives of two of history's most significant thinkers. This book tells the story of that friendship.

I

It must be admitted that the two main protagonists of this book might have objected to its very existence. Though Hume and Smith attained fame and relative fortune during their lifetimes, they were both averse to having their unpolished writings and their private lives made public. Hume worried that his correspondence might "fall into idle People's hands, and be honord with a Publication," and Smith remarked that "I never suffer my name to appear in a Newspaper when I can hinder it, which to my sorrow, I cannot always do."[3] Their solicitude was not just for their privacy, but also for their posthumous reputations. After Hume's death their mutual publisher, William Strahan, contemplated issuing a collection of Hume's letters, but Smith quickly thwarted the idea, fearing that others "would immediately set about rummaging the cabinets of those who had ever received a scrap of paper from him. Many things would be published not fit to see the light to the great mortification of all those who wish well to his memory."[4] As they approached their ends Hume and Smith both enjoined their executors to burn all but a select few of their papers, a request that was fulfilled in Smith's case though not in Hume's.[5]

Smith was well aware, however, that "the smallest circumstances, the most minute transactions of a great man are sought after with eagerness," and he himself seems to have shared in the fascination.[6] The inventor of the modern biography, James Boswell, who was a student of Smith's for a brief time, justified the exhaustive detail of his memoirs of Samuel Johnson on the grounds that "everything relative to so great a man is worth observing. I remember Dr. Adam Smith, in his rhetorical lectures at Glasgow, told us he was glad to know that Milton wore latchets in his shoes instead of buckles."[7] Even more significantly, Hume called attention to his life story by composing a short autobiography during his final illness. Titling it *My Own Life*, Hume asked Strahan to use it as the preface for all future collections of his writings. Smith evidently approved, as he supplemented it with a narration of Hume's last days in the form of a *Letter from Adam Smith, LL.D. to William Strahan, Esq.*—the public letter that provoked such an outcry. (Both of these delightful works are included in the appendix of this book.) This is the closest thing we have to a joint work by the two of them, and Smith's contribution conspicuously calls the reader's attention to their friendship; he uses the word "friend" no fewer than seventeen times in the space of around a half dozen pages. Furthermore, even geniuses are seldom the best judges in their own cases. While Hume and Smith worried that the publication of their letters might tarnish the reputations that they had earned through their more carefully composed works, in fact a greater appreciation of their characters and their friendship with one another can only heighten our sense of admiration. Nor, finally, does this book draw exclusively on their unpublished writings. As philosophers and men of letters, much of their lives were dedicated to thinking and writing, and one of the primary forms their friendship took was engagement with one another's ideas and works. These ideas and works will, accordingly, play a major role in our story.

Given their stature and influence, it is remarkable that no book has heretofore been written on Hume and Smith's personal or intellectual relationship.[8] One likely reason for this is that their lives—especially Smith's—are not as well documented as one could wish. Hume was not a particularly prolific writer of correspondence, though his surviving letters make up for in wit and charm what they lack in length and number. His published corpus, on the other hand, is vast, including not just his many philosophical treatises but also a six-volume *History of England*, essays on seemingly every conceivable topic, a few pamphlets on current events, and of course *My Own Life*. Smith was an even more negligent correspondent than Hume, apparently due in part to the fact that he found writing physically painful.[9] His aversion to putting pen to paper was a habit for which Hume sometimes chided him, as when he opened his letters, "I can write as seldom and as Short as you . . ." or "I am as lazy a Correspondent as you. . . ."[10] Smith also published only two books, *The Theory of Moral Sentiments* and *The Wealth of Nations*. We have a set of essays that his executors published after his death and student notes from some courses that he taught, but the sum total is still dwarfed by Hume's output. Indeed, Smith's biographers frequently lament that he seems to have gone out of his way to make things difficult for them. In addition to composing few letters, releasing only two books, and ensuring that most of his papers were burned before he died, Smith also avoided writing about himself to an unusual degree. As one scholar has commented, in terms of self-conscious self-revelation he was about as far from his contemporary Jean-Jacques Rousseau as it is possible to be.[11]

Happily for our purposes, Smith was a slightly less inattentive correspondent with Hume than with others, especially in the later years of their friendship. There are a total of one hundred seventy known letters that Smith either wrote or received dating from the period between when he met Hume and Hume's death. Of these, we have fifteen letters from Smith to Hume and forty-one from Hume to Smith—far and away the most for any of Smith's correspondents during this period. (Hume, for his part, wrote more letters to Smith than to anyone except his publishers, William Strahan and Andrew Millar, at least among those that survive.) The fifty-six extant letters between Hume and Smith cover all manner of topics, including their ideas and arguments, the fortunes and misfortunes of their publications, current events and recent books, and their families, friends, adversaries, health, job prospects, travels, and future plans. Some are fairly short and mundane, but others are quite humorous, intellectually substantial, or revealing about their characters. The growing warmth of their relationship can be traced not only in the contents of the letters but also in the salutations themselves. The earliest of the letters open with a formal "Dear Sir," but it was not long before they transitioned to the more affectionate "Dear Smith" or "My Dear Hume," then "My Dear Friend," and finally "My Dearest Friend"— an epithet that neither of them used with any other correspondent during the course of their friendship.[12]

There are also numerous references to Hume, both explicit and implicit, throughout virtually all of Smith's writings. The reverse is less true, as Hume had composed almost all of his works before Smith's first book appeared, though Hume did publish an anonymous review of *The Theory of Moral Sentiments* soon after its release. As a result of their renown during their lifetimes, moreover, many of their contemporaries recorded stories about them. One can thus find comments and reminiscences relating to their friendship in a number of contemporaneous and near-contemporaneous sources, including Dugald

Stewart's biography of Smith; the myriad writings of James Boswell; the autobiography of the Moderate minister Alexander Carlyle and the journal of the playwright John Home, both of whom traveled in the same circles as Hume and Smith; the private correspondence of a number of their acquaintances; the periodicals, book reviews, and obituaries of the day; and the anecdotes collected by Henry Mackenzie and John Ramsay of Ochtertyre, among others. This book draws on all of the available evidence to provide the fullest possible account of Hume and Smith's friendship.

Another likely reason why Hume and Smith's friendship has not received sustained analysis is that friendships are more difficult to bring to life than feuds and quarrels: conflict makes for high drama, while camaraderie does not. It is perhaps not surprising, then, that there have been many books written on philosophical clashes—think of David Edmonds and John Eidinow's *Wittgenstein's Poker* and *Rousseau's Dog*, Yuval Levin's *The Great Debate*, Steven Nadler's *The Best of All Possible Worlds*, Matthew Stewart's *The Courtier and the Heretic*, and Robert Zaretsky and John Scott's *The Philosophers' Quarrel*, to name only a few recent titles—but far fewer on philosophical friendships.[13] Even biographies of Hume tend to devote less attention to his long friendship with Smith than to his brief quarrel with Rousseau, which, sensational as it may have been, was not nearly as central to Hume's life and thought.

The relative lack of attention paid to philosophical friendships, while understandable, is unfortunate. Friendship was understood to be a key component of philosophy and the philosophical life from the very beginning, as even a cursory reading of Plato or Aristotle should remind us. The latter famously claimed that friendship is the one good without which no one would choose to live even if he possessed all other goods, and Hume and Smith clearly concurred.[14] Hume held that "friendship is the chief joy of human life," and Smith proclaimed that the esteem and affection of one's friends constitutes "the chief part of human happiness."[15] Indeed, Hume proposed a small thought experiment to prove Aristotle's point. "Let all the powers and elements of nature conspire to serve and obey one man," he suggests. "Let the sun rise and set at his command: The sea and rivers roll as he pleases, and the earth furnish spontaneously whatever may be useful or agreeable to him. He will still be miserable, till you give him some one person at least, with whom he may share his happiness, and whose esteem and friendship he may enjoy."[16] The notion of friendship plays a surprisingly large role even in Hume's *History of England*, where, as a leading Hume scholar notes, he treats the "capacity for friendship . . . almost as an acid test of character."[17]

Aristotle divides friendships into three types: those motivated by utility, those motivated by pleasure, and—the highest and rarest of the three—those motivated by virtue or excellence. Smith draws a similar distinction in *The Theory of Moral Sentiments*, though he insists that the latter alone "deserve the sacred and venerable name of friendship."[18] Smith's relationship with Hume represents a nearly textbook model of this kind of friendship: a stable, enduring, reciprocal bond that arises not just from serving one another's interests or from taking pleasure in one another's company, but also from the shared pursuit of a noble end—in their case, philosophical understanding. An examination of Hume and Smith's personal and intellectual relationship thus allows for a different kind of reflection on friendship than is found in the works of Plato, Aristotle, Cicero, Michel de Montaigne, Francis Bacon, and the like.[19] Whereas these leading philosophers of friendship tend to analyze the concept in the abstract—the different forms that friendship takes, its roots in human nature, its relationship to self-interest, to romantic love, and to justice—a consideration of Hume and Smith allows us to see that rare thing, a philosophical friendship of the very highest level in action: a case study, as it were.

Indeed, there is arguably no higher example of a philosophical friendship in the entire Western tradition. It takes some effort, in fact, to think of who the closest rivals would be. Socrates and Plato? Given the four-decade age disparity between them, their relationship was probably more one of teacher and student, or perhaps mentor and protégé, than one of equals, and in any case the record of their personal interactions is scant. Ditto for Plato and Aristotle. John Locke and Isaac Newton admired one another, but could hardly be said to be close friends. Martin Heidegger and Hannah Arendt had more of a (stormy) romantic relationship than a friendship, as did Jean-Paul

Sartre and Simone de Beauvoir (with somewhat less drama). As for Michel de Montaigne and Étienne de La Boétie, Gotthold Lessing and Moses Mendelssohn, Jeremy Bentham and James Mill, G. W. F. Hegel and Friedrich Schelling, Karl Marx and Friedrich Engels, and Alfred North Whitehead and Bertrand Russell, in each of these cases at least one member of the pair falls considerably below Hume and Smith in terms of impact and originality. Ralph Waldo Emerson and Henry David Thoreau approach closer to their level, if we choose to count them as philosophers rather than literary figures. The leading contenders among philosophers are probably Erasmus and Thomas More, but in terms of influence and depth of thought most would give the clear nod to Hume and Smith.[20]

The context in which Hume and Smith's friendship took place was just as remarkable as the friendship itself. The Scotland into which they were born, in the early eighteenth century, had suffered for untold generations from poverty and disease, ignorance and superstition, incessant religious conflict and occasional military occupation. Hume himself remarked that Scotland had long been "the rudest, perhaps, of all European Nations; the most necessitous, the most turbulent, and the most unsettled."[21] Yet Hume's and Smith's lifetimes saw the arrival of a vibrant new age of economic prosperity and cultural achievement, a transformation that was palpable—indeed, startling—to contemporary observers. Hume once again captured the feeling well. "Really it is admirable how many Men of Genius this Country produces at present," he commented to a friend in 1757. "Is it not strange," he asks, "that, at a time when we have lost our Princes, our Parliaments, our independent Government, even the Presence of our chief Nobility, are unhappy, in our Accent & Pronunciation, speak a very corrupt Dialect of the Tongue which we make use of; is it not strange, I say, that, in these Circumstances, we shou'd really be the People most distinguish'd for Literature in Europe?"[22] Dugald Stewart, Smith's first biographer, marveled at "the sudden burst of genius, which to a foreigner must seem to have sprung up in this country by a sort of enchantment, soon after the [Jacobite] Rebellion of 1745."[23] Writing in the early nineteenth century, Walter Scott looked back with nostalgia on the days of Hume, Smith, and their compatriots, "when there were giants in the land."[24] Nor was it only Scots themselves who noticed this development. Perhaps the most "enlightened" Englishman of the age, Edward Gibbon, admitted in 1776 that he had "always looked up with the most sincere respect towards the northern part of our island, whither taste and philosophy seemed to have retired from the smoke and hurry of this immense capital [i.e., London]."[25]

The Scottish Enlightenment is now widely regarded as an intellectual golden age, the rival of Periclean Athens, Augustan Rome, and Renaissance Italy. There is even a best-selling book recounting *How the Scots Invented the Modern World*.[26] Some of the leading men of letters of the period, in addition to Hume and Smith, included Hugh Blair, Adam Ferguson, Henry Home (Lord Kames), Francis Hutcheson, John Millar, Thomas Reid, William Robertson, and Dugald Stewart. This Scottish renaissance also comprised natural scientists such as the founder of modern geology, James Hutton, the chemist Joseph Black, and James Watt of steam engine fame, as well as artists like the painter Allan Ramsay, the playwright John Home, and the architect Robert Adam. Hume and Smith knew all of these figures personally, and they will each play a role in our story. The Scottish "literati," as they were often dubbed, were not disaffected intellectuals at war with the establishment and the elite of their society, as their counterparts in France so often were, but rather widely admired and deeply engaged members of their communities. With only a few exceptions—the most notable being Hume—they were employed in one of the learned professions: the university, the law, the church, or medicine. In part as a result, perhaps, their outlooks generally lacked the subversive edge that was so conspicuous among the Parisian *philosophes*, causing the more radical side of Smith's and especially Hume's thought to stand out in starker relief.[27]

How did a nation that began the eighteenth century as a poor, backward outpost on the fringe of Europe manage to become such an intellectual powerhouse by the middle of the century? There were a variety of factors involved, including the innovative system of parish schools that had made Scotland one of the most literate societies in the world; the universities of Glasgow, Edinburgh, Aberdeen, and

St. Andrews, which grew to be some of the very best in Europe; the emergence of numerous clubs and debating societies; the thriving publishing industry; and the progressive Moderate ministers who eventually came to lead the Kirk (the Church of Scotland).[28] Also crucial, surely, was the union of 1707 that created Great Britain.[29] Scotland had not had a separate monarchy since the Union of the Crowns in 1603, but the merger of its parliament with England's near the outset of the eighteenth century bound the nation still closer to its powerful southern neighbor, offering the promise of greater security, greater stability, and greater access to the markets of England and its colonies. The Scots gave up much of their political power in the bargain—they held only 45 of the 558 seats in the newly constituted House of Commons—but they retained a great deal of control over their legal, religious, and educational establishments. Though it took longer than its supporters hoped it would, the union did eventually lead to the promised economic boom, along with increased personal freedoms and opportunities. To be sure, not all Scots were pleased with the new order, as the Jacobite rebellions of 1715 and 1745 amply demonstrated. Yet few of the leading Scottish literati ever questioned the benefits of the union. Hume and Smith, in particular, embraced it with open arms, even as they resented the continued prejudices of the English toward all things Scottish.

All in all, Hume and Smith's friendship took place during a period of political stability in Britain. In fact, it fell neatly in between the more turbulent eras that preceded it and followed it: they first met in 1749, a few years after the last of the major Jacobite uprisings, and Hume died in 1776, just as the conflict with the American colonies began to escalate. The only real political disturbances during this period were the Seven Years' War with France (1756–63) and the "Wilkes and Liberty" riots of the late 1760s and early 1770s. While the latter, in particular, alarmed Hume at the time, these episodes were both fairly tame by most standards—certainly compared to the upheavals that opened and closed the century, those connected with the Glorious Revolution and the union of 1707, on the one hand, and the American and French Revolutions, on the other.

Also relevant to our story is the religious climate of the time. One result of the Glorious Revolution settlement was that the Presbyterian

Kirk was reinstated as the established church of Scotland in 1690, while England retained its Anglican establishment. The character and practices of the Kirk were, however, to be a source of continual and often bitter conflict throughout much of the eighteenth century. During Hume's and Smith's youths the Kirk was "as rigid and intolerant as any church in Europe," as one scholar puts it.[30] It promulgated a particularly grim and unforgiving form of Calvinism, including belief in predestination and the utter depravity of human nature, and it forbade such activities as dancing, merriment at weddings, and walking idly on the streets on Sundays. Voltaire, after visiting Britain in the late 1720s—when Hume was a teenager and Smith a young boy—described the typical Presbyterian minister as one who "affects a serious gate, puts on a sour look," and harangues his flock with "grave and severe exhortations."[31] Only a few decades earlier, in 1697, an eighteen-year-old student at Edinburgh University named Thomas Aikenhead was hanged for some blasphemous remarks that he had boastingly made to friends.[32] The judicial murder of alleged witches continued well into the century: the last woman to be convicted for witchcraft in Scotland was burned alive in 1727 for having turned her daughter into a pony (always a dead giveaway).[33]

As the eighteenth century wore on, a group of progressive clergymen known as the Moderates made a concerted effort to drag the Kirk, kicking and screaming, into the modern, polite, enlightened world.[34] They preached a softer brand of Calvinism, emphasizing conduct over creed, and insisted on the importance of tolerance and humanistic learning. The Moderates included many of Edinburgh's preeminent literati: they were led by William Robertson and Hugh Blair and also included Adam Ferguson and John Home among their ranks. These individuals were all friends with Hume and Smith, although in Hume's case, in particular, this was more a testament to their mutual civility than a sign of a genuine meeting of the minds: no minister, however liberal-minded, could altogether approve of Hume's more or less open irreligiosity. The Moderates' agenda was opposed, at every step along the way, by a rival faction within the Kirk known alternately as the Popular Party, the Evangelicals, or the High-Flyers.[35] This latter group attached great importance to the maintenance of strict orthodoxy and sought to retain or restore the more severe—some would say repressive—doctrines and practices that had characterized the Kirk since the days of John Knox and the Reformation. Their intransigence and broad base of support among the populace ensured that the process of liberalization was a slow and fitful one. Even after the Moderates gained the upper hand within the Kirk in the second half of the century, the Popular Party could (and did) continue to make life uncomfortable for nonbelievers and nonconformists. As we will see throughout the book, Hume and Smith took rather different approaches to living and writing in this atmosphere.

That Hume and Smith adopted such contrary stances toward their more pious contemporaries is all the more striking in view of the fact that the similarities between their outlooks were so broad and so deep on so many other fronts. Hume was the older of the two by a dozen years, and he got off the blocks quickly, composing almost all of his works before Smith even began to publish his. As a result, Smith's thought was shaped by Hume far more than Hume's was by Smith. Smith certainly drew on many thinkers besides his close friend—he has been described as "*the* great eclectic"—yet almost all Smith scholars recognize the pervasive influence of Hume on nearly everything he wrote.[36] Nicholas Phillipson's recent biography of Smith, for instance, dubs him "a committed Humean" and even "a perfect Humean" whose "task would be to develop the implications of Hume's philosophy and extend its reach into territories he was to make his own."[37] None of this is to say, however, that Smith simply adopted Hume's views wholesale. On the contrary, we will see that he modified almost everything he touched. The noted Smith scholar Samuel Fleischacker describes their intellectual relationship well: "Smith's thought circles around Hume's: there is virtually nothing in either *The Theory of Moral Sentiments* or *The Wealth of Nations* without some sort of source or anticipation in Hume, although there is also almost no respect in which Smith agrees entirely with Hume."[38] Fleischacker reiterates the point elsewhere, remarking that "to fail to see Smith's debt to Hume is to miss the sources of many of his major doctrines. But to fail to see Smith's *revisions* of Hume—his incessant, almost obsessive refusal to accept anything Hume says as is—is to miss what is distinctive, and most interesting, in Smith."[39]

The idea that the intellectual affinities between Hume and Smith were this broad and deep might seem to be belied by a series of common caricatures of the two. According to the caricatures, Hume was a philosopher interested primarily in abstract metaphysical and epistemological questions, while Smith was a hardheaded economist focused on more practical matters; Hume was a conservative Tory in his politics, while Smith was a liberal Whig; and Hume was a skeptic with regard to religion or perhaps even an atheist, while Smith was a confirmed believer. The first of these three supposed divergences is easily disposed of. It is true that Hume began his career by investigating metaphysical and epistemological questions, and it is this part of his corpus that still receives the lion's share of attention from academic philosophers. Yet even within the pages of his first book, *A Treatise of Human Nature*, Hume transitioned from these fairly abstract issues to more practical discussions relating to psychology and morality. Moreover, he then proceeded to write essays on a huge range of subjects, from politics to polygamy and from economics to eloquence, as well as several works on religion and a monumental *History of England*. Indeed, Hume was regarded for much of his lifetime and for many generations thereafter as a historian first and a philosopher second.

Similarly, while Smith is often hailed as the "founding father" of capitalism, he was in fact, as his modern interpreters never tire of pointing out, far more than an economist who theorized the invisible hand and championed free trade. Instead, he was a professor of moral philosophy who included political economy as just one of his many intellectual interests, and he recognized—to a greater degree than Hume, as a matter of fact—a number of potential dangers and drawbacks associated with commercial society. Smith taught courses on ethics, jurisprudence, and rhetoric, and he wrote essays on the development of language and the history of astronomy, among other topics. When one moves beyond Book 1 of Hume's *Treatise* and the most famous handful of passages from *The Wealth of Nations*, then, it becomes clear that Hume's and Smith's interests overlapped a great deal, in part because they were both interested in, well, pretty much everything.

For much of the twentieth century Smith's philosophical writings were deemed to be little more than a series of footnotes to Hume's, and as an economist Hume has long been regarded as a minor predecessor of Smith, insofar as he is taken notice of at all. Ironically, we will see that putting the two side by side serves to highlight the importance of Smith's contributions to moral philosophy and Hume's to political economy. Smith followed Hume in developing a moral theory based on human sentiments, but his version of moral sentimentalism incorporated several significant improvements on Hume's. Conversely, Hume argued for free trade and stressed the moral, social, and political benefits of commerce several decades before *The Wealth of Nations* appeared, and it is striking how much of that work builds on Hume's insights.

The second purported dichotomy between the two is similarly misleading. Hume's political thought does have its conservative aspects, and Smith is unquestionably a key member of the liberal tradition, but the reverse is equally true: Hume too is a liberal in the broadest sense of the term, and Smith's liberalism too has a distinctly conservative bent. More concretely speaking, both of these thinkers embraced the core ideals associated with the liberal tradition, stressing the benefits of the rule of law, limited government, religious toleration, freedom of expression, private property, and commerce. They were thus both generally supportive of the modern, liberal, commercial order of the Britain of their time. On the other hand, they both distrusted large and sudden innovations in politics. Given the fallibility of human reason and the complicated, variable nature of the political world, they held, we should be wary of grand schemes for radically restructuring society. Hence, while they advocated certain reforms to the society of their day—freer trade and greater religious toleration, for instance—they always insisted that these changes should be implemented in a gradual, measured way.

As for terms like "Tory" and "Whig," neither Hume nor Smith can accurately be described as a partisan in any straightforward sense: neither had much faith in either of the main political parties of eighteenth-century Britain. One prominent scholar of the Scottish Enlightenment, taking his cue from one of Hume's letters, labels them both "sceptical Whigs": Whigs because they supported the constitution that resulted from the Glorious Revolution, judging that it did a reasonable job of providing individual liberty and security, but "sceptical" because they pointedly eschewed the ideological baggage that so often attended Whiggism.[40] They might be even better described as pragmatic liberals, given that they embraced the core ideals of the liberal tradition but also emphasized the importance of moderation, caution, flexibility, and attentiveness to context in applying these ideals.[41] At any rate, the political divergences between the two were relatively minor, matters of detail and emphasis rather than general outlook.

The third and final dichotomy implied by the common images of these two thinkers—that concerning their religious views—is worth pausing to consider a bit more carefully, especially as it will play a major role in our story. Religion was one of Hume's primary preoccupations. Nearly everything he wrote touched on the topic in one way or another: the credibility of the arguments in its favor, its psychological origins and consequences, its history, its effects on morality and politics. While there is naturally debate at the margins, the basic outlines of his stance are relatively clear: Hume was neither a believer nor an out-and-out atheist, but rather what we might call an agnostic, or what in the eighteenth century was called simply a skeptic (the better term in any case).[42] He never denied outright the existence of a higher power, but he deemed the principal arguments on behalf of one highly implausible, and he considered the effects of religion to be mostly pernicious. As one scholar has written, "Hume's critique of religion and religious belief is . . . subtle, profound, and damaging to religion in ways that have no philosophical antecedents and few successors."[43] Hume sometimes presented his arguments in an artful or oblique manner—by attributing them to a character in a dialogue, for instance, or by clothing skeptical conclusions in the garb of fideistic wonder at the mysteries of God's ways—but the smoke screens were usually fairly transparent. His contemporaries were not fooled, nor did he particularly mean them to be. On the contrary, Hume often delighted in the prospect of eliciting "a murmur among the zealots."[44]

Smith preferred to play his cards much closer to the vest. In both his writings and his personal life he generally went to great lengths to avoid revealing his religious beliefs—or lack thereof—and to steer clear of confrontations with the pious. Contemporaries frequently noted that Smith was "very guarded in conversation" when the topic of religion came up.[45] He also wrote far less than Hume did on the subject, and the little that he did write points in multiple directions. On the one hand, in *The Theory of Moral Sentiments* Smith periodically invokes the idea of a providential order, and he generally describes the religious impulse in fairly sympathetic terms. Far more than Hume, he depicts the belief in a higher power as having important practical benefits, above all in providing consolation and buttressing morality. On the other hand, none of Smith's core arguments about morality, politics, or economics ultimately depend on religious premises; in every instance in which he has recourse to "the author of Nature" to explain a point, he also offers a more worldly explanation as well. Indeed, one of the central purposes of his moral theory, like Hume's, was to show that morality comes from human beings themselves rather than from the word or will of God, and hence that religion is not a precondition of virtue. The revisions that Smith made to *The Theory of Moral Sentiments* later in life served to soften the religious undertones of the early editions, but even the first edition was sufficiently ambiguous to leave many readers unsure of his ultimate convictions. For instance, one of Smith's former students, the Reverend James Wodrow, recommended the book to a friend soon after its publication, commenting equivocally that "the Author seems to have a strong detestation of vice & Love of Virtue & perhaps a regard for Religion at least it does not appear to me that the book has any licentious tendency like the most part of David Hume's writing on those subjects tho' perhaps the Principles are at the bottom the same."[46] Moreover, Smith's other book, *The Wealth of Nations*, is strikingly secular in language and outlook, and some of his posthumously published essays are deeply skeptical in character.

There is no more consensus today than there was in Smith's own time as to his religious views. The conjectures range from sincere Christian belief to closet atheism, though the majority of scholars come down somewhere in the middle, reading Smith as a deist of some kind.[47] Long reflection on Smith's friendship with Hume cannot help but push one's interpretation toward the skeptical end of the spectrum. Emma Rothschild rightly remarks that their correspondence reveals a sense of "intimacy and complicity" that seems "difficult to reconcile with the presumption of serious religious differences."[48] They frequently joked about religion in their letters to one another, and Smith's irony on the subject was just as pronounced and transparent as Hume's. It is true that Smith refused to take on the responsibility of posthumously publishing Hume's *Dialogues Concerning Natural Religion*, thereby creating some discord between the two during Hume's final days. This is often taken as an indication that Smith disagreed with or disapproved of Hume's skepticism, but we will see in chapter 10 that this episode was in fact less acrimonious and philosophically charged than is generally assumed. Moreover, Smith's glowing praise of Hume's wisdom and virtue in the *Letter to Strahan*, written only a few months later, should be sufficient to gainsay the idea that he was disturbed by his friend's lack of belief.

It is impossible to determine, at a remove of well over two centuries, what prompted Smith to be so much more reticent than Hume on this score, though it is easy to imagine a number of possibilities. For instance, it is possible that Smith was simply temperamentally predisposed to be more circumspect; or that he had greater concern for his reputation and for career and professional success; or that he saw religion as less important, or less dangerous, of a phenomenon; or that he believed the dangers of religion are better combated through quiet neglect rather than open confrontation; or that he wanted to avoid offending his pious mother, with whom he was especially close; or that he had learned a lesson from Hume's unhappy encounters with the devout.[49] (These possibilities are not, of course, mutually exclusive.) Regardless, as a result of his caginess it is difficult to avoid a degree of speculation when considering Smith's personal faith. If forced to apply a label to Smith's religious views this observer would describe him as a skeptical deist (as opposed to an outright skeptic like Hume).[50] Smith was almost certainly not a believing Christian—he showed no sign of having accepted the divinity of Jesus, for example—and he seems to have been suspicious of most forms of religious devotion. Yet it is distinctly possible that he retained a belief in a distant, perhaps benevolent, higher power.

Of course, this would not have mattered a whit to the pious of Smith's time: atheism, skepticism, and deism—all of which implied disbelief *in Christianity*—were considered to be of a piece, and all of these terms were used regularly as marks of opprobrium. With regard to how Hume and Smith were viewed and treated by their contemporaries, the subtle theoretical distinction between Hume's skepticism and Smith's skeptical deism was far less consequential than the much bigger practical divergence between Hume's forthrightness and Smith's studied reticence. These contrary postures led to equally contrary reputations: Hume was christened "the Great Infidel" and was deemed unfit to teach the young—he twice sought professorships, but in both cases the clergy opposed his candidacy decisively—while Smith became a respected professor of moral philosophy. All of this, we will see, occasioned much teasing and bantering between them, but did not dampen their esteem and affection for one another in the slightest.

THE CHEERFUL
SKEPTIC
(1711-1749)

D AVID HUME IS, it seems fair to say, among the most loved
of philosophers, widely cherished for his affable personality,
his clearheadedness, and his unflinching yet humane worldview. A recent survey of thousands of academic philosophers around
the world found that more identified themselves with Hume than
with any other figure in the history of philosophy.[1] During his own
time too Hume was adored by virtually everyone who knew him well.
He was a favorite among the Edinburgh literati, even the ministers,
and the high society of Paris bestowed on him the honorific *le bon
David.* Outside of these relatively confined circles, however, Hume's
controversial views earned him plenty of fierce detractors. He told
a friend in 1764, "I do not believe there is one Englishman in fifty,
who, if he heard that I broke my Neck last night, woud not be rejoic'd
with it. Some hate me because I am not a Tory, some because I am
not a Whig, some because I am not a Christian, and all because I am
a Scotsman."[2] Even in our own more hardened age, and notwithstanding all of Hume's engaging good humor, the seemingly relent-
less nature of his skepticism leaves many readers disconcerted, even
alarmed. Isaiah Berlin spoke for many when he opined that "no man
has influenced the history of philosophical thought to a deeper and
more disturbing degree."[3]

Hume was born on April 26, 1711, the third and final child of a relatively
prosperous farmer and country laird.[4] The Home family—Hume
changed the spelling of his last name to match the pronunciation

while in England in 1734—lived at Ninewells, south of Edinburgh, near the border with England. Hume was still a small child when his father, Joseph, died of tuberculosis, so he was largely raised by his mother, née Katherine Falconer, who was the daughter of one of the leading judges in Scotland. As the oldest son Hume's brother, John, eventually inherited the family estate. Like Hume himself his sister, named Katherine like their mother, never married, and so she remained attached to her brothers throughout their lives; she would become an integral part of Hume's household in his later years.

Hume entered Edinburgh University at the decidedly tender age of ten.[5] The universities of eighteenth-century Scotland were in many respects more reminiscent of modern boarding schools for high school students than today's colleges and universities, but Hume's entrance was early even by the standards of the day, likely because he began at the same time as his older brother. At Edinburgh Hume studied Latin, Greek, logic, metaphysics, and "natural philosophy," or natural science as we would call it today. He would have been able to attend public lecture series on moral philosophy and "pneumatics" (i.e., philosophy of mind) as well, though we do not know if he did. All of the courses were thoroughly infused with religious precepts for the edification of the young students. Judging from his later comments Hume seems to have found his university education emphatically lacking in interest and usefulness, with the possible exception of the natural philosophy course. In 1735 he counseled a young friend that "there is nothing to be learnt from a Professor, which is not to be met with in Books. . . . I see no reason why we shou'd either go to an University, more than to any other place, or ever trouble ourselves about the Learning or Capacity of the Professor."[6] Hume attended classes for four years without, however, taking a degree—a fairly common practice at the time.

After leaving the university Hume's real education began. He spent most of the next eight years—ages fourteen to twenty-two—in independent study, immersing himself in works of philosophy and literature. He did attend law lectures at the university for a time, but he found the subject less than congenial. Hume reports in *My Own Life* that "my studious disposition, my sobriety, and my industry, gave my family a notion that the law was a proper profession for me; but I found an insurmountable aversion to every thing but the pursuits of philosophy and general learning; and while they fancied I was poring upon Voet and Vinnius"—that is, legal works—"Cicero and Virgil were the authors which I was secretly devouring."[7] The central role that friendship would come to play in Hume's life too was evident quite early on: in his first extant letter, written when he was only sixteen, he declares that "the free Conversation of a friend is what I would preferr to any Entertainment."[8] During this period he continued to live with his family, mostly spending the winters in Edinburgh and the summers at Ninewells.

Hume was, as far as we can tell, given a typical Christian up-bringing in a God-fearing family. His mother, brother, and sister were all pious Presbyterians, and his uncle was a minister at the local kirk in the village of Chirnside, which was strict enough to conduct heresy trials and put sinners in the pillory. As a boy Hume too was religious. He later recalled using the catalogue of vices in *The Whole Duty of Man*, a popular seventeenth-century devotional tract, to test his moral character. Among the breaches of duty highlighted in the text are "not assigning any set or solemn times for humiliation and confession, or too seldom"; "making pleasure, not health, the end of eating"; and "wasting the time or estate in good fellowship"—all injunctions that the adult Hume would find difficult to observe indeed.[9] During his teenage years, however, doubts persistently crept into his mind. As he later told a friend, he began "with an anxious Search after Arguments, to confirm the common Opinion: Doubts stole in, dissipated, return'd, were again dissipated, return'd again."[10] Near the end of his life Hume disclosed to James Boswell that he "never had entertained any belief in Religion since he began to read Locke and Clarke."[11] In other words, Hume's encounter with the defenses of theism in the works of John Locke and Samuel Clarke had the effect of undermining his faith rather than bolstering it. (He thereby unwittingly made good the quip of Clarke's contemporary Anthony Collins that no one had doubted God's existence until Clarke tried to prove it.)[12]

By the time of his eighteenth birthday Hume had determined what course he would pursue in life: "I cou'd think of no other way of pushing my Fortune in the World, but that of a Scholar & Philosopher." Yet the road from his early studies to the (still early) writing of *A Treatise of Human Nature* was not an entirely straight one. After a period of intense, solitary reading Hume found himself suffering from a psychosomatic illness that his doctor dubbed "the Disease of the Learned." Upon moderating the pace of his studies, spending more time in society, eating better, and taking some exercise—walking and riding virtually every day—his health began to improve. One result of this change in lifestyle was that Hume was transformed from a "tall, lean, & rawbon'd" youth into the "most sturdy, robust, healthful-like Fellow you have seen, with a ruddy Complexion & a chearful Countenance."[13] In the process of recovering from his malady Hume made a brief stab at a life of commerce, working as a merchant's clerk in Bristol, but he soon found the post "totally unsuitable."[14] He seems to have been found equally unsuitable by his employer: he was fired for correcting his master's grammar.

In September 1734 Hume departed for France with an eye to composing a projected work on the broad topic of human nature. After a brief period in Paris he spent a year in the university city of Rheims and then another two at La Flèche, a sleepy town in the Loire Valley whose Jesuit college was famous as the site of René Descartes's education and was still, in the eighteenth century, a hotbed of the Cartesian philosophy that Hume was seeking to upend. The first two volumes of the *Treatise*, "Of the Understanding" and "Of the Passions," were largely written during this three-year stay on the Continent. Filled with anticipation, Hume returned to London in September 1737 to publish the work, which finally appeared in January 1739. Rather naïvely expecting that a long, dense, difficult philosophical tome would produce an immediate revolution in thought, Hume was bound to be disappointed in the work's reception. In *My Own Life* he lamented that it "fell *dead-born from the press*, without reaching such distinction, as even to excite a murmur among the zealots."[15] (The italicized phrase derives from Alexander Pope's declaration that "All, all but Truth, drops dead-born from the Press, / Like the last Gazette, or the last address.")[16] The *Treatise* was reviewed a bit more often, and more favorably, than Hume's lament suggests, but it is true that it did not sell particularly well. Soon after the work's release Hume returned to Scotland and persevered in adding a third volume, "Of Morals," which met with even greater public indifference when it was published in November 1740. While Hume's first book failed to find much of an audience at the time, the intervening years have more than made up for this failing: contemporary philosophers are nearly unanimous in deeming the *Treatise* Hume's philosophical masterpiece. In the nineteenth century Thomas Henry Huxley, aka "Darwin's Bulldog," went so far as to claim that "it is probably the most remarkable philosophical work, both intrinsically and in its effects upon the course of thought, that has ever been written."[17]

For a first book by a young man still in his late twenties, the *Treatise* certainly did not lack for ambition. Hume's stated goal was nothing less than to propound a new science of human nature that would in turn serve as the basis for every other branch of knowledge. He opens the work by bemoaning the "ignorance, which we still lie under in the most important questions, that can come before the tribunal of human reason," and he proposes that the only effective strategy for remedying the deficiency is "to leave the tedious lingring method, which we have hitherto follow'd, and instead of taking now and then a castle or village on the frontier, to march up directly to the capital or center of these sciences, to human nature itself; which being once masters of, we may every where else hope for an easy victory."[18] Hume sought to erect his science of human nature using what he called, in the subtitle of the work, "the experimental method." Whereas Descartes, for instance, had aimed to base his conclusions as much as possible on pure, abstract reason, Hume insisted that the "only solid foundation" for knowledge about human beings and the world around us is to be found in "experience and observation."[19] He was far from the first philosopher to propose relying on experience in this way—he himself names John Locke, the Third Earl of Shaftesbury, Bernard Mandeville, Francis Hutcheson, and Joseph Butler as his predecessors in this regard—but Hume sought to push this method further, and to draw out its consequences more uncompromisingly, than anyone ever had.[20]

The consequences turned out to be revolutionary. Hume concluded that if we rely entirely on experience—that is, if we reject the

inflated, unwarranted faith in the powers of human reason that previous philosophers had shown—then we can know exceedingly little
about the world or ourselves with absolute certainty. Indeed, we cannot even know that there *is* an external world, beyond our immediate
senses, or that we *are* selves, meaning discrete individuals who persist
stably over time. Pretty much the only things that we *can* know with
certainty, according to Hume, are the propositions of mathematics
(2 + 2 = 4) and pure logic (all bachelors are unmarried). However, he
does not suggest that we should therefore live in a perpetual skeptical
fog, constantly doubting everything that we see and think. On the
contrary, he insists that human nature itself prevents this: universal
doubt is simply unsustainable in the course of everyday life. Just as
importantly, Hume allows that we can attain a great deal of *probable*
knowledge about the world and ourselves through the experimental method—hence the possibility of formulating a new "science of
man." His most famous example is that of causation: even if abstract
reason cannot demonstrate that one billiard ball striking another
will produce movement—and it cannot—all of our past experience
suggests that it will do so, and it would be foolish to disregard the
guidance that experience provides. Hume's stunning diminution of
the role that reason plays in human life is thus matched by a great
expansion of the roles played by custom, habit, the passions, and the
imagination.

The *Treatise* includes very little explicit discussion of God or religion, but this very omission was sufficient to make the work scandalous: by exploring human nature in painstaking detail without appealing to any kind of higher power, Hume was implying that no such
appeal is needed. Human beings are neither innately sinful nor created in God's image, for Hume, but rather comparatively intelligent,
if passion-driven, animals. Moreover, the idea that experience is the
only reliable basis of knowledge suggests that we are on our own, with
nothing beyond our frail and error-prone powers of understanding
to guide us. That the work was irreligious in nature was not lost on
Hume's contemporaries, although it was originally intended to be
still more so.[21] The version that Hume penned in France had included a section casting doubt on the reality of miracles and perhaps
also a section questioning the immortality of the soul.[22] Fearing that

these passages would "give too much Offence even as the World is dispos'd at present," Hume decided that it would be worth his while to spend some time "castrating my Work, that is, cutting off its noble Parts, that is, endeavouring it shall give as little Offence as possible." He declared that "this is a Piece of Cowardice, for which I blame myself. . . . But I was resolv'd not to be an Enthusiast, in Philosophy, while I was blaming other Enthusiasms."[23] While Hume would later lament that the work failed even to excite a murmur among the zealots, then, he had in fact taken some pains to prevent it from doing so.

The third volume that Hume added in 1740 was just as resolutely secular in its account of morality as the first two had been in their account of human nature more generally. Hume argues that morality derives not from any transcendent source but rather from common human sentiments, specifically our feelings of approval and disapproval. Hume did not believe, as Francis Hutcheson did, that we possess a kind of "sixth sense," a moral sense, that perceives good and evil in the way that our eyes perceive colors and our ears perceive sounds. Rather, in Hume's view we simply find certain character traits—say, industriousness and cheerfulness—to be useful or agreeable, and we therefore approve of them. Similarly, other character traits—say, generosity and modesty—are useful or agreeable to others, as we recognize by means of the faculty that Hume calls "sympathy," which transmits feelings between people. Our sympathy with the pleasure other people gain from these character traits leads us to approve of these traits, as well. This is all morality is, for Hume: an eminently practical human convention whose entire purpose is to make people's lives go better. The virtues are the qualities that we collectively find to be either useful or agreeable, either for ourselves or for others; they have nothing to do with God's will, a divine plan, or an afterlife.

By this point, Hume had clearly left his childhood religiosity far behind. As he told Hutcheson, "I desire to take my Catalogue of Virtues from *Cicero's Offices*, not from the *Whole Duty of Man*." Still, he ended up amending this volume of the *Treatise*, as he had the earlier volumes, to minimize the offense it would give to the pious, though he did so rather grudgingly. "I intend to follow your Advice," he told Hutcheson, "in altering most of those Passages you have remarkt as defective in Point of Prudence; tho' I must own, I think you a little delicate. Except a Man be in Orders, or be immediatly concern'd in the Instruction of Youth, I do not think his Character depends upon his philosophical Speculations, as the World is now model'd."[24]

Like most first-time authors Hume was exceedingly proud of his work at the time of its release, but it was not long before he came to rue having ever published it. As early as the spring of 1751 he was telling friends that "I was carry'd away by the Heat of Youth & Invention to publish too precipitately. So vast an Undertaking, plan'd before I was one and twenty, & compos'd before twenty five, must necessarily be very defective. I have repented my Haste a hundred, & a hundred times."[25] A few years later he admitted that "the positive Air, which prevails in that Book, & which may be imputed to the Ardor of Youth, so much displeases me, that I have no Patience to review it."[26] Nor did he ever change his mind on the matter. Every version of Hume's collected writings published during his lifetime left the *Treatise* out altogether, and near the end of his life he wrote an advertisement for a new edition in which he requested that the philosophical writings that he published after "that juvenile work . . . may alone be regarded as containing his philosophical sentiments and principles."[27] This is, of course, a request that modern scholars have persistently and brazenly ignored; Hume's advertisement has even been dismissed as "the posthumous utterance of a splenetic invalid."[28] While this seems patently unfair, it is true that Hume never quite disavowed the *ideas* contained in the *Treatise*. On the contrary, he always allowed that "most of the principles" contained in his mature philosophical works were the same as those of the *Treatise* and that the later works merely remedied "some negligences in [the] reasoning and more in the expression."[29] While Hume came to regret the abstruse style and "positive Air" of his first book, he remained a skeptic to the end.

———————

Reconsidering his literary strategy in the wake of the disappointing reception of the *Treatise*, Hume soon turned to essay writing. He abandoned the dense, complex argumentation of his first work and endeavored to serve as a self-appointed "Ambassador from the Dominions of Learning to those of Conversation," bringing the fruits of philosophy, literature, and history to a wider audience.[30] It was not simply a desire for fame or fortune that led to this shift in approach: the topics Hume addressed in his essays, and the views he expressed in them, would have been poorly chosen indeed if his aim had been to attain maximum popularity. Rather, he believed that scholars and the educated public would both benefit from more open lines of communication. Just as philosophy could furnish meaningful substance to the conversation of the drawing room, the club, and the tavern, he felt, so too "Learning has been as great a Loser by being shut up in Colleges and Cells, and secluded from the World and good Company." If real-world experience is the only reliable basis of knowledge about human beings and the world around us, after all, then philosophy cannot simply divorce itself from "common life and Conversation."[31] The essay form, popularized by Joseph Addison and Richard Steele earlier in the century, seemed like a perfect vehicle for Hume's bridge-building effort, though he transformed this typically anodyne genre by bringing to it his characteristic philosophical depth and controversial edge.

The first volume of Hume's *Essays Moral and Political* appeared in 1741. The majority of the pieces focused on political questions, with the dangers of partisan zeal serving as the underlying theme. In Hume's view, "factions subvert government, render laws impotent, and beget the fiercest animosities among men of the same nation, who ought to give mutual assistance and protection to each other." Accordingly, throughout the essays he challenged partisan views and arguments of all stripes—Court and Country, Whig and Tory, even republican and monarchist—in hopes of thereby imparting "a lesson of moderation in all our political controversies."[32] Perhaps predictably, zeal of the religious variety too earned Hume's ire. In several of the essays he highlighted the ways in which religious "superstition" (essentially, Catholicism) "renders men tame and abject, and fits them for slavery," while religious "enthusiasm" (essentially, the more rigorous strands of Protestantism) "produces the most cruel disorders" as it makes its way into the world. Together, he claims, the various Christian sects had "engendered a spirit of persecution" that had proved to be "the poison of human society, and the source of the most inveterate factions in every government."[33] Not content with simply showing that religion is superfluous for philosophy and morality, he had commenced what would become a lifelong effort to highlight its deleterious effects.

The following year Hume brought out a second volume of essays, the highlight of which was a series of pieces titled "The Epicurean," "The Stoic," "The Platonist," and "The Sceptic." Rather than a dry discussion of the ancient philosophical sects named in the titles, these essays provide lively explorations of the attractions and shortcomings of four conceptions of the good life: the life of pleasure, the life of virtue, the life of religious devotion, and the life of the skeptic.[34] The essay on the skeptical life is longer than the other three combined, and it is clearly the one with which Hume shows the most sympathy. While skepticism is often associated with nihilism and paralysis, Hume suggests that it actually tends to lead to inner tranquility, intellectual humility, and a passion for ever-further inquiry. The essay also explores how one might *attain* the moderate, balanced, humane disposition of the skeptic, and to this end it recommends "a serious attention to the sciences and liberal arts."[35]

Hume had drawn a similar lesson in the first essay of the first volume, "Of the Delicacy of Taste and Passion," which is one of the underappreciated gems of his corpus. The basic argument of this piece is that the cultivation of the liberal arts is quite simply the secret to happiness. This is true, in the first place, because a person of refined taste is able to "place his happiness on such objects chiefly as depend upon himself," since "we are pretty much masters of what books we shall read, what diversions we shall partake of, and what company we shall keep." Those who find genuine happiness in a good book or a conversation with a good friend, for instance, are far more likely to find it within their reach than those who desire immense fame or fortune. Hume argues, further, that "a delicacy of taste is favourable to love and friendship, by confining our choice to few people," since "one that has well digested his knowledge of both books and men, has little enjoyment but in the company of a few select companions."[36] In other words, people of refined taste are better able to discern who truly shares their sentiments and preferences and thereby to form deeper, more meaningful relationships with those select few, as Hume would do with Smith in due course. The *Essays* were more favorably received than the *Treatise* had been, which eventually led Hume to contemplate recasting the arguments of the latter work in a more accessible form.

First, though, from the summer of 1744 through the spring of 1745 Hume sought an appointment to the Chair of Ethics and Pneumatical Philosophy at Edinburgh University.[37] His interests and expertise would have fit the position nicely, but it was not to be. A "popular Clamour" was raised against his candidacy, he complained, "on account of Scepticism, Heterodoxy & other hard Names," and he failed to obtain the post.[38] The zealots had started to do far more than just murmur. In this instance even some of Hume's erstwhile friends, such as Francis Hutcheson, stood against him. In truth, their opposition was not entirely unreasonable. The holder of this chair was expected to instruct his students about "the being and perfections of the one true God, the nature of Angels and the Soul of man," and to lecture every Monday "upon the truth of the Christian religion"—tasks that Hume was not particularly well suited to perform. According to the university's job description, if any text that the professor used were to contain, by accident, "any thing contrary to the Scriptures or the [Westminster] Confession of faith or to good manners," he would naturally be obliged to "confute the Same to prevent the youth's being corrupted with errour or immorality."[39] Given these requirements, it would have taken an impossibly blind eye on the part of the university to appoint Hume, not to mention quite a bit of barefaced hypocrisy on Hume's part for him to accept the position. Recall that when Hume had insisted to Hutcheson that an individual's character does not depend on his philosophical beliefs "as the World is now model'd," he himself had made an exception for those who had taken holy orders or were "immediatly concern'd in the Instruction of Youth."[40]

Later evidence suggests, however, that Hume was not overly troubled by this kind of hypocrisy where religion is concerned. In 1764 a friend asked Hume for advice about the case of a young clergyman whose religious beliefs had started to waver and who was deliberating about whether to give up his orders. Hume counseled him not to, given that reliable occupations were so difficult to come by for men of letters. As for the young man's scruples, Hume acidly responded: "It is putting too great a Respect on the Vulgar, and on their Superstitions, to pique oneself on Sincerity with regard to them. Did ever one make it a point of Honour to speak Truth to Children or Madmen? . . . I wish it were still in my Power to be a Hypocrite in this particular: The common Duties of Society usually require it; and the ecclesiastical Profession only adds a little more to an innocent Dissimulation or rather Simulation, without which it is impossible to pass thro the World."[41] Given the outcome of the search for the Edinburgh chair, Hume clearly had not done nearly enough to simulate the right kind of belief. Smith, we will see, was far more adept at keeping his real views quiet.

In any event, in the wake of his failure to obtain a professorship Hume moved near London to serve as a tutor to the "mad" Marquess of Annandale, who was declared legally insane a few years after Hume left his employ. He was dismissed from the tutorship after a year as a result of the machinations of the marquess's supervisor. Hume's occupational peregrinations then took yet another interesting turn as he took part in a minor military expedition to the western coast of France as a secretary to a distant relation of his, Lieutenant-General James St. Clair. (The expedition's original destination was Canada, but this transatlantic adventure was thwarted by administrative delays and contrary winds.) St. Clair's expedition must rank, by any measure, as one of the more inconsequential events in the War of the Austrian Succession. It was little more than a diversion designed to draw off French troops from the heavier fighting in Flanders, the logistics were badly bungled by the ministry in London, and the incursion took place too late in the campaign season to have much real effect in any event. Still, the future historian surely benefited from the opportunity to witness the conduct of war up close.

At this point Hume was thirty-six years old and still had no settled career by which to financially support his passions of philosophizing and writing. In a letter to Henry Home he eliminated the most obvious candidates, one by one: he was now too old to enter the law or the army, he found the idea of a traveling tutorship disagreeable, he deemed political positions too precarious, he would make a poor courtier, and, he told Home bluntly, "the Church is my Aversion." Thus, after some hesitation he decided that he had little choice but to "continu[e] a poor Philosopher for ever."[42]

———————————

After returning to Ninewells in the autumn of 1747 Hume set about completing a work that he had begun during his time as a tutor to Lord Annandale, the *Philosophical Essays Concerning Human Understanding* (later retitled *An Enquiry Concerning Human Understanding*, and now commonly known as the *First Enquiry*). This work was, in essence, a rewriting of the first book of the ill-fated *Treatise*—the one on the limits of human reason—into a more accessible form. Whereas in the *Treatise* Hume had reveled in every minute detail and difficulty that he could uncover, in the *Philosophical Essays* he cuts to the philosophical chase in clear, engaging language. He was pleased with the result, judging that "by shortening & simplifying the Questions, I really render them much more complete."[43] It was also in many respects a more daring work than the *Treatise*, perhaps because Hume felt he had little left to lose after his failure to attain the Edinburgh chair. If he was going to have a reputation for impiety, he seems to have reasoned, he might as well earn it.[44] Whereas Hume "castrated" the *Treatise* by removing the passages most likely to give offense to the pious, then, in the *Philosophical Essays* he left his ideas intact. The inflammatory essay on miracles in the latter work is almost certainly the most famous discussion of that subject in the entire history of philosophy; there is probably no other passage in Hume's corpus that has provoked as much commentary and abuse.

The argument, in a nutshell, is as follows. Hume defines a miracle as a violation of the laws of nature, by which he means our uniform experience of how nature works. Examples of a miracle in this sense might include the parting of a sea or a person walking on water or being resurrected from the dead. When we hear or read of such a miracle having occurred, he says, we should proportion our belief to the evidence, as we would for any kind of report concerning a matter of fact. Since the purported miracle (by definition) violates all of our past experience, the evidence in its favor would have to be incredibly strong in order to establish its credibility. In weighing the testimony, we would need to consider the intelligence, the character, and the motives of the person making the report, as well as the circumstances under which the alleged miracle was witnessed. Did the person observe the supposed miracle directly? How much knowledge and experience does he have in these kinds of matters? Is he honest, impartial, and a sober judge? Does he have any interested reasons for deceiving us? Does he relate the testimony with hesitation, or on the contrary does he protest too much? How many people observed the supposed miracle? Is there any other testimony that contradicts the testimony on its behalf? Particularly once we have added up all of these considerations, Hume suggests, the evidence in favor of a purported miracle will always be dwarfed by that against it, namely our uniform experience of how nature works. A skeptic to the end, Hume never claims that miracles are impossible; to insist on their impossibility would be nearly as dogmatic as to insist on their reality. Rather, he "merely" argues that it is never reasonable to believe a report of a miracle having occurred.

As if this devastating attack on a key foundation of revealed religion were not enough, Hume turned his sights, in the next essay, on the foremost philosophical argument for God's existence in his time, namely the argument from design. The essence of this argument is that the world is sufficiently complex, and that its parts fit sufficiently well together, that it must have had a designer, and that this designer must be a supremely wise, powerful, and benevolent God. This line of reasoning was so commonplace in eighteenth-century Britain that its soundness was simply taken for granted among most intellectuals. Hume suggests, however, that the inference from the apparent order in the world to such a designer goes considerably beyond the evidence. In the mouth of Epicurus, he argues that when we infer a cause from its effect we should proportion the one to the other; we should not infer anything greater in the cause than we can see in the effect. Thus, we should attribute only that degree of intelligence, power, and benevolence to God that we see in his workmanship. Given the innumerable disorders and evils in the world, then, there is no reason to believe that its designer must have been terribly wise, powerful, or benevolent. Nor can we turn around and use the inferred cause to infer any few effects. For instance, there is no reason

---

to suppose, on the basis of experience, that God's apparent goodness requires an afterlife in which the virtuous are rewarded and the wicked punished. The only experience that we have is the experience of this world, and there is nothing in this world from which we can infer anything beyond this world. Here again Hume avoids coming to a dogmatic conclusion: he does not claim that there *is* no God, or that the world has no designer. The upshot of his argument, however, is that the argument from design cannot tell us anything new about the world or give us any reason to think or act differently than we would based on our own experience. It is essentially a useless hypothesis.

This work was Hume's most daring to date not just in terms of its content but also in that it included his identity as the author; the *Treatise* and the first two volumes of *Essays* had all been published anonymously, as was common at the time.[45] Some of Hume's friends, including Henry Home, thought the work too "indiscreet," but by this point Hume professed that he could "see not what bad consequences follow, in the present age, from the character of an infidel; especially if a man's conduct be in other respects irreproachable."[46] At first the *Philosophical Essays* received little more attention than the *Treatise* had, but responses started to pick up in the 1750s, including a string of attempted refutations of Hume's argument regarding miracles—an enterprise that has continued unabated to this day.

That same year Hume, continuing to court controversy, brought out another small volume of essays—with his name attached this time—in which he persisted in grappling with the sacred cows of both political parties. Drawing on his earlier arguments in the *Treatise*, he challenged the popular Whig notion of an "original contract," according to which all legitimate political authority rests solely on the consent of the people expressed in the form of a social contract, as well as the Tory doctrine of "passive obedience," according to which political authority is sacred and thus inviolable.[47] Given the intellectual predominance of the Whigs at the time, Hume took special pride in the former essay, describing it as "a short, but compleat Refutation of the political Systems of [Algernon] Sydney, [John] Locke, and the Whigs, which all the half Philosophers of the Nation have implicitely embrac'd for near a Century; tho' they are plainly, in my humble Opinion, repugnant to Reason & the Practice of all Nations."[48] To cap it off, he planned to include an essay on the Protestant succession, or the exclusion of the Stuart line from the British throne after the death of Queen Anne. This was still a highly loaded topic only three years after the Jacobite uprising of 1745, but Hume sought to "treat that subject as coolly and indifferently, as I would the dispute betwixt Caesar and Pompey. . . . Some people would frighten me with the consequences that may attend this candour . . . but I own I cannot apprehend any thing."[49] In the end, however, Hume's friends succeeded in persuading him to hold back this particular essay, at least for the time being; it was incorporated into his *Political Discourses* a few years later.

In its place Hume added the essay "Of National Characters," which has brought him far more infamy among modern readers than "Of the Protestant Succession" did in the eighteenth century. The former essay investigates the divergences in character that are often observed among the peoples of different nations and seeks to show that "moral causes" such as a nation's government, economy, and religion have a greater impact than "physical causes" such as climate and terrain. In a later version of the essay, in the context of discussing the possible influence of climate on people's characters, Hume included a footnote that has rightly become notorious. He remarks there that he is "apt to suspect the negroes to be naturally inferior to the whites. There scarcely ever was a civilized nation of that complexion, nor even any individual eminent in either action or speculation"—a potent demonstration of the dangers of relying on personal suspicion rather than actual experience, straight from the pen of one of history's greatest empiricists.[50] This was a blunder that Smith, for one, avoided, writing for instance that "there is not a negro from the coast of Africa who does not . . . possess a degree of magnanimity which the soul of his sordid master is too often scarce capable of conceiving. Fortune never exerted more cruelly her empire over mankind, than when she subjected those nations of heroes to the refuse of the jails of Europe."[51] There is no record of any discussion or open disagreement between Hume and Smith on the subject of race, but in any event from a modern standpoint this footnote marks one of the few real stains on Hume's character.

———————

As he was completing these works Hume was called away from his literary pursuits once again in order to serve a second stint as St. Clair's secretary, this time on a military embassy to Vienna and Turin. While Hume insisted to his friend James Oswald of Dunnikier that the life of a man of letters remained "the sole object of my ambition," he believed that the "opportunity of seeing Courts & Camps" might in fact further that ambition, given that he had "long had an intention, in my riper years, of composing some History."[52] The glimpse of the diplomatic side of international affairs that this trip provided served as a perfect complement to the military action that Hume had witnessed during his first mission with St. Clair. Hume's account of his travels, related in the form of a journal sent home to his brother, still makes for highly entertaining reading. The story of his encounter with Maria Theresa, Holy Roman Empress, will have to stand in for the whole:

> You must know, that you neither bow nor kneel to Emperors and Empresses; but Curtsy: So that after we had had a little Conversation with her Imperial Majesty, we were to walk backwards, thro a very long Room, curtsying all the way: And there was very great Danger of our falling foul of each other, as well as of tumbling topsy-turvy. She saw the Difficulty we were in: And immediatly calld to us: Allez, Allez, Messieurs, sans ceremonie: Vous n'etes pas accoutumés a ce mouvemen et le plancher est glissant. ["Go on, go on, sirs, without ceremony: you are not accustomed to this movement and the floor is slippery."] We esteemed ourselves very much oblig'd to her for this Attention, especially my Companions, who were desperately afraid of my falling on them & crushing them.[53]

Needless to say, by this point Hume had acquired the hefty frame for which he is now so famous.

As Hume recalled in *My Own Life*, the pensions that he received from these secretarial appointments left him more or less financially secure—he had managed to attain "a fortune, which I called independent, though most of my friends were inclined to smile when I said so"—and he was thus able to devote the lion's share of his energy to his literary career from that time forward.[54] While he had been far from idle to this point, the next decade would be the most productive of his life. Between 1749 and 1759 Hume would compose a draft of the *Dialogues Concerning Natural Religion* and publish *An Enquiry Concerning the Principles of Morals*, a substantial volume of *Political Discourses*, yet another collection of essays that included *The Natural History of Religion*, and the first four volumes of *The History of England*. Together, these works would make him the most famous writer in Britain—or the most infamous, depending on one's vantage point. This would also be the first decade of his friendship with Smith.

CHAPTER 2

ENCOUNTERING HUME

(1723-1749)

F OR ALL OF Hume's nearly unparalleled influence and prominence within the history of philosophy, Smith is probably the better known of the two outside of academia. His profile adorns banknotes and neckties, his name has become synonymous with the idea of free market capitalism, and *The Wealth of Nations* is one of the most famous—though certainly not most read or understood—books of all time. It is unlikely that any prime minister of the United Kingdom ever carried around a copy of Hume's *Treatise* in her handbag, as Margaret Thatcher reportedly did with Smith's second great work. That said, Smith's life was not a terribly glamorous one. His personality did not sparkle as Hume's did, nor were his writings as controversial. He was, however, widely liked and respected among his contemporaries; for many, his friendship with Hume was the only real strike against him. And his ideas have had as much real-world impact as those of almost any thinker before or since. The great economic historian Robert Heilbroner overstates the case for effect, but does not misrepresent it entirely, when he proclaims that "after Smith . . . displayed the first true tableau of modern society, all the Western world became the world of Adam Smith: his vision became the prescription for the spectacles of generations."[1]

Smith was born in June 1723 in the small port town of Kirkcaldy, across the Firth of Forth from Edinburgh, where the twelve-year-old Hume was studying at the university.[2] His father, also named Adam

Smith, had been a modestly affluent customs officer, a position that the younger Smith would likewise come to occupy in his later years. The older Smith died before the younger was born, however, so our Smith, like Hume, grew up fatherless. He was thus raised by his mother, née Margaret Douglas, who was, like's Hume's mother, a deeply pious Presbyterian. Smith was an only child and, yet again like Hume, a lifelong bachelor.[3] (Incidentally, the number of canonical philosophers who never married is startling: Plato, Thomas Aquinas, Thomas Hobbes, René Descartes, John Locke, Benedict Spinoza, Isaac Newton, Gottfried Leibniz, Voltaire, Immanuel Kant, Edward Gibbon, Arthur Schopenhauer, Søren Kierkegaard, Friedrich Nietzsche, and Ludwig Wittgenstein are some of the other prominent names that could be added to the list—hence Nietzsche's remark that true philosophers never marry and that Socrates did so only ironically.)[4] Without siblings or a family of his own, Smith relied on his mother for a sense of domestic stability well into his adulthood. He ended up surviving her by only six years, and upon her death he averred that she "certainly loved me more than any other person ever did or ever will love me."[5]

After attending Kirkcaldy's excellent burgh school Smith entered Glasgow University in 1737, at the age of fourteen. His Latin being sufficiently advanced by that point to bypass the first year of instruction, he took up the rest of the standard fare of the day: Greek, logic, metaphysics, mathematics, natural philosophy, ethics, and jurisprudence. Smith studied the latter two subjects, both of which were to be central to his career, with none other than Francis Hutcheson, whom he later called "the never to be forgotten Dr Hutcheson."[6] Scholars quote this tribute to Hutcheson almost compulsively, but in fact Smith first coined the epithet to describe Hume, his "never to be forgotten friend," soon after the latter's death, and only later applied it to his teacher.[7] Moreover, it is not entirely clear that Hutcheson was even the professor whom Smith regarded most highly at the time, as his "favourite pursuits" at Glasgow were said to be mathematics and natural philosophy.[8] He studied these subjects with Robert Simson and Robert Dick, respectively, both widely seen as excellent teachers. Simson later became a colleague and friend, and Smith considered him to be one of the "greatest mathematicians . . . that have lived in my time."[9]

After three years at Glasgow Smith went on to spend another six, from 1740 to 1746, as a student at Oxford University's Balliol College. In stark contrast to his experience at Glasgow, Smith found his classes at Oxford exceedingly uninspiring. He later remarked that the professors there had "given up altogether even the pretence of teaching," and he was also clearly thinking of Oxford when he wrote that the best endowed universities often served as "sanctuaries in which exploded systems and obsolete prejudices found shelter and protection, after they had been hunted out of every other corner of the world."[10] The mature Smith regarded the Scottish universities, by contrast, as "in spite of all their faults, without exception the best seminaries of learning that are to be found any where in Europe."[11] Their recent progress, even since Hume's time at Edinburgh, was indeed astounding. In the early eighteenth century the universities of Glasgow, Edinburgh, Aberdeen, and St. Andrews were still small and little known, dedicated mostly to teaching an outdated theology in Latin, but by the middle of the century they had grown in both size and stature and had begun to teach a wide range of cutting-edge subjects, mostly in English.[12] In the 1750s and 1760s Smith himself would do a great deal to further Glasgow's development, both as a teacher and as an administrator.

"It will be his own fault," Smith commented dryly in August 1740, in the first of his letters that survives, "if anyone should endanger his health at Oxford by excessive Study, our only business here being to go to prayers twice a day, and to lecture twice a week."[13] Accordingly, he spent much of his time there in self-instruction, much as Hume did in his post-university years. Ironically enough, Smith *did* endanger his health at Oxford by excessive study: the rigor of his self-imposed work habits led to a sort of nervous breakdown in 1743–44, not dissimilar to the one Hume had suffered in the pursuit of his own studies.[14] It appears that it was during this period that Smith's main interests shifted from math and science to "the study of human nature in all its branches, more particularly of the political history of mankind."[15] He left Oxford in August 1746, perhaps because of the anti-Scottish feeling at the university in the wake of the Jacobite uprising of the previous year; in any event, he apparently departed "in disgust."[16]

Smith had attended Oxford as a Snell Exhibitioner, meaning that his spot at Balliol was earned through a scholarship whose original intent was to support Scottish youths who intended to be ordained in the Anglican Church and then return to Scotland to propagate its teachings.[17] This requirement—or at least the penalties for violating it—had been dropped by Smith's time, however, and in the end he showed no inclination to enter the ministry, despite his mother's wish that he would do so.[18] We know next to nothing about how religious Smith was during his youth. Whereas Hume was candid about his early loss of belief, at least among his friends, Smith was always reticent on the matter, and no letters survive from before his time at Oxford. As we will see shortly, however, Smith's first piece of polished writing, which dates from his Oxford days, displays markedly skeptical tendencies.

It was also during Smith's time at Oxford that the paths of our two protagonists first crossed, in a sense. While Hume's *Treatise* found a much smaller audience than he had hoped, it did manage to find at least one attentive reader in the early 1740s: none other than Smith himself. Smith apparently said or did something to arouse the suspicions of his orthodox Balliol dons, for they entered his room unannounced one day to find him, to their horror, poring over Hume's work. Naturally, "the reverend inquisitors seized that heretical book, and severely reprimanded the young philosopher."[19] The story sounds almost too good to be true, but it is reasonably well attested. The first report, which appeared in the *Monthly Review* in 1797, came from John Leslie, a mathematician and scientist who had known Smith well. Indeed, Smith held Leslie in such high regard that he hired him to tutor David Douglas, Smith's nearest living relative (a cousin's son) and his eventual heir.[20] The anecdote was related again in the mid-nineteenth century by John Ramsay McCulloch, an economist and editor of *The Wealth of Nations*, who promised that it rested "on the best authority," as well as by John Strang, an expert on the history of Glasgow, according to whom Smith himself frequently told the tale in the clubs of that city.[21] Strang also suggests that the "unceremonious manner" in which Smith was treated by the Balliol faculty in this instance helped to convince him not to enter the ministry.[22] Certainly this episode cannot have endeared his professors to him, or discouraged his interest in Hume's thought.

We do not know how Smith came to possess, or even to be aware of, the scandalous book. Hume published the *Treatise*—and corresponded with Smith's teacher Hutcheson about it—during the latter part of Smith's time as a student at Glasgow, so it is possible that Smith became acquainted with the work before even arriving at Oxford.[23] Perhaps more likely is that he first read Hume's *Essays Moral and Political*, which were published during Smith's first years at Oxford, and then found his way from them back to the earlier *Treatise*. The *Essays* were, after all, far more popular than the *Treatise*, and they could very well have been brought to Smith's attention by his and Hume's mutual friend James Oswald of Dunnikier, who recommended Hume and his essays far and wide upon their publication.[24] Nor do we know what exactly Smith made of Hume's ideas upon this first encounter. It is probably too much to say, as Nicholas Phillipson does, that "Smith became at Oxford as he remained, the perfect Humean," but there is strong evidence to suggest that his views came to resemble Hume's in several important respects around this time (evidence that, oddly, Phillipson does not bring to bear): Smith's earliest surviving work.[25]

⬩

During his years at Oxford Smith composed a remarkable work titled *The Principles Which Lead and Direct Philosophical Enquiries*, which consists of three related essays.[26] The first, longest, and most polished of the three examines the history of astronomy from primitive societies to modern times. The second considers the study of physics in the ancient world: the nature of and relationship between earth, water, air, and fire. The third is on "ancient logics and metaphysics," in this case meaning the question of how and why we categorize things, with a particular focus on Plato's Forms. The work was not published until five years after Smith's death, when his close friends and literary executors, Joseph Black and James Hutton, included it as part of a posthumous collection of Smith's *Essays on Philosophical Subjects*.

The bulk of the *Principles* was, however, completed before Smith was twenty-three—even younger than Hume was when he wrote the *Treatise*. Smith later described it as "a juvenile work," just as Hume did the *Treatise*, and admitted suspecting that there may be "more refinement than solidity in some parts of it."[27] Yet unlike Hume, Smith never disavowed his first work. On the contrary, he carefully preserved the *Principles* and ensured that it was one of the very few unpublished writings to survive his death. He also continued to tinker with it for many years, adding a section on Newton to the first essay sometime between 1749 and 1758 and perhaps revising the work again near the end of his life.[28]

The *Principles* constitutes an excellent entry point into Smith's thought, not only chronologically but also in terms of its subject matter and argument. As the title of the work indicates, Smith's real interest was less in the nominal topics of the essays themselves—astronomy, physics, and logic—than in human nature and the workings of the human mind, just as Hume's was in the *Treatise*. Smith too plays down the role of reason throughout, in terms of both its motivating force and its capacities. The first essay, in particular, goes to some lengths to highlight what we might call the "subjective" side of the scientific enterprise. Smith argues that human beings engage in science primarily in hopes of "sooth[ing] the imagination" by accounting for the "chaos of jarring and discordant appearances."[29] That is to say, when we come across unusual or perplexing phenomena—the irregular movements of the stars and planets, for instance—the tranquility of our minds is disrupted. Our inability to comprehend such phenomena frustrates our craving for a sense of order and coherence. Science is, in Smith's view, a way of allaying our bewilderment by explaining the apparently inexplicable. In this sense, all scientific theories are "mere inventions of the imagination," as Smith calls them: they do not penetrate the secrets of nature or reveal ultimate reality to us so much as make us feel better.[30] We mentally bestow order on the natural world rather than discovering it there. The view that Smith espouses here, of course, casts doubt on the notion that any scientific finding will ever constitute the last word on its subject. Every theory must remain forever subject to revision—even

Newton's laws of motion and gravity, which in Smith's time had, as he notes, "prevail[ed] over all opposition, and . . . advanced to the acquisition of the most universal empire that was ever established in philosophy."[31] In Smith's view, then, science is a permanently open-ended activity, one that is prompted by our passions and forged by the imagination.

While the focus of the *Principles* is narrower than that of Hume's *Treatise*, there is a certain parallel between them: Smith's and Hume's first works both convey deeply skeptical assessments of the power and scope of human reason, and both served as prolegomena of sorts to their more constructive works. Moreover, there are unmistakable allusions to the *Treatise* within the *Principles*, further confirming that Smith was familiar with Hume's work during his time at Oxford. The clearest and most extended reference is a textbook restatement of Hume's argument about the roles of custom and the imagination in inferring cause and effect and filling in gaps in our experience. In the midst of this discussion Smith speaks of the "connection, or, as it has been called, th[e] association of . . . ideas"—a nearly verbatim repetition of one of the *Treatise*'s first chapter titles.[32] As in his later writings, however, Smith does not simply adopt Hume's views, but rather builds on them. Hume's theory of the association of ideas in the *Treatise* was directed primarily at explaining our everyday beliefs about the external world, such as the interaction of billiard balls, but Smith extends it to explain scientific inquiry, as well. The reason why Ptolemy's views were superseded by Copernicus, and Copernicus's by Newton, according to Smith, is that the newer theories were able to account for the movements of the firmament with fewer "breaks" or "gaps" in the corresponding movements of our minds. That the *Principles* drew on Hume's thought has been amply demonstrated by modern scholars, and it was also recognized almost immediately after Smith's death. When John Millar, Smith's friend and former colleague (and before that his student), learned that Smith had allowed the work to survive the flames he expressed his eagerness "to see his [Smith's] powers of illustration employed upon the true old Humean philosophy."[33]

The argument of the *Principles* also bears very directly on questions of religion. In a section of the astronomy essay titled "Of the

Origin of Philosophy," Smith suggests that while religion predates science, it arose in a similar way and for similar reasons. In the most primitive ages, he conjectures, the "awful or terrible" irregularities of nature—thunder and lightning, eclipses, and the like—must have overawed people, invoking "a reverence that approaches to fear." Similarly, the more "beautiful and agreeable" irregularities of the natural world, such as rainbows, would have produced uncomprehending "transports of gratitude." Unable to situate such phenomena within their narrow understanding of nature's operations, primitive peoples would instinctively attribute them to "the direction of some invisible and designing power."[34] In Smith's view, then, the first religions were, like later scientific theories, inventions of the imagination designed to explain the inexplicable and thereby satisfy the human mind. Gods were created by human beings rather than the other way around, and they were created as a direct result of human ignorance. Nor was it solely, or even primarily, positive passions such as gratitude that produced belief in willful deities, according to Smith's account; rather, it was mostly a combination of terror and cowardice that led to "the lowest and most pusillanimous superstition."[35]

Eventually, society advanced and life ceased to be so precarious. According to Smith's conjectural history, increased security and leisure allowed people to indulge their curiosity by searching for a chain linking the various phenomena of the natural world. Rather than turning to a separate "invisible being" to explain each event or appearance, they sought an overarching explanation, and thus gave birth to philosophy or science—and to monotheism. It was the desire to explain the world as a coherent whole, on Smith's telling, that first led to "the idea of a universal mind, of a God of all, who originally formed the whole, and who governs the whole by general laws."[36] Although he does not stress the point, it appears that Smith considers this belief—that is, the belief that the world is a coherent whole in need of a unified explanation—to be just as much of an invention of the imagination, driven by human desires, as earlier polytheistic superstitions and later scientific theories were. He writes, for instance, that the first philosophers "discovered, or imagined they had discovered" that a single chain must bind all of nature together.[37] Once again, the order is not so much observed in the world as imposed on it, by us and for the sake of our own mental comfort.

It is not hard to see why Smith might have soft-pedaled this last step in his argument. Polytheism was a safe enough target, but the idea of a ordered world created by an intelligent designer was a staple of eighteenth-century religious belief, both deist and Christian. It appears that Smith did not feel comfortable casting doubt on this idea too openly even within the confines of his private notebook, though naturally he may have originally intended to publish the *Principles*. Indeed, it has plausibly been suggested that such "considerations of prudence" are precisely what prevented him from releasing these essays until after his death.[38] Nothing that Smith says rules out the possibility of there actually being an ordered world or an intelligent designer, of course, but the whole work has a distinctly deflationary character, providing unflattering psychological and sociological explanations for beliefs that were widely assumed to emanate from reason if not from God himself.

Curiously, Smith's treatment of religion in the *Principles* anticipates, to an almost eerie degree, the argument of Hume's *The Natural History of Religion*, which was published in 1757 and probably composed in the early 1750s—several years after Smith had completed the bulk of the *Principles*.[39] That work too searches for the origins of religion in human nature; it too locates the roots of religious belief not in reason but rather in a combination of ignorance and passions such as hope and fear; it too posits that the earliest religions were polytheistic, and that only later did philosophers develop the idea of a single God who governs the world through general laws. Indeed, the two works contain a number of analogous passages that articulate similar ideas using different words.[40] It is doubtful, however, that Smith influenced Hume on this score, as Hume did not learn of the existence of the *Principles* until 1773.[41] It is possible that they discussed these issues in conversation or in now-lost correspondence, of course, but it seems more likely that this is simply an instance of kindred minds running on parallel tracks. One wonders, though, what Smith made of these conspicuous parallels when Hume shared *The Natural History of Religion* with him prior to its publication.[42]

On leaving Oxford, Smith, still only twenty-three, returned to Kirk-caldy to stay with his mother. Whereas the young Hume made brief forays in a number of different occupations—working as a merchant's clerk, a tutor to an aristocrat, and a personal secretary on both military and diplomatic missions—Smith trod a much straighter path to the life of a man of letters. In the autumn of 1748 he was invited, partly at the instigation of Hume's neighbor, patron, and friend Henry Home, to deliver a series of public lectures in Edinburgh on rhetoric and belles lettres. The initial lectures were well received and well subscribed, so Smith continued his freelance lecturing in the city for two more years, adding a series on jurisprudence and perhaps one on the history of natural science as well.[43]

It was during this period, probably in the autumn of 1749, that Smith met Hume for the first time. Hume had returned to the Edinburgh area in the summer of that year after completing his mission to Vienna and Turin, at which point he continued to split his time between the city and Ninewells. Alas, there is no record of exactly when, or under what circumstances, the first encounter between the two took place. The only near-contemporaneous documentation we have on this point is a set of notes by the antiquarian George Chalmers, probably written soon after Smith's death, which suggests that it was during the time of Smith's lectures in Edinburgh that "he first became acquainted w[ith] D. Hume: The friendship between them continued thro' Life"—but of course this is not terribly informative.[44] Presumably Smith would have been eager to meet Hume, given his familiarity with Hume's works and his interest in Hume's ideas, and by this point they already had a number of mutual friends who could have facilitated a meeting, including Henry Home and James Oswald of Dunnikier. It is also possible that Hume attended some of Smith's lectures. Indeed, it is quite likely that he did so if the lectures were, as W. R. Scott plausibly suggests, hosted by the Edinburgh Philosophical Society, since Hume was an active member of the society and would soon become one of its two joint secretaries.[45] This conjecture is further strengthened by a letter that Hume wrote to

Smith almost a decade later in which he reminds Smith how popular his Edinburgh lectures had been.[46] While we cannot know for certain, then, the likeliest time of their first meeting would seem to be the first lectures that Smith gave after Hume's return to Scotland, which were delivered in the autumn of 1749.

Let us pause here, at the time of this first meeting, to consider what kind of impression Hume and Smith must have made on one another. At thirty-eight years of age Hume had already attained a reputation as a thinker and writer of some note—and of impious principles— through the *Treatise*, several volumes of essays, and the *First Enquiry*. Tall and stout, he was a fairly imposing physical presence. An observer who encountered Hume in Turin, just before he met Smith, claimed that "his face was broad and fat, his mouth wide . . . and the corpulence of his whole person was far better fitted to communicate the idea of a turtle-eating Alderman, than of a refined philosopher . . . wisdom, most certainly, never disguised herself before in so uncouth a garb."[47] This portrait seems a bit harsh, however: many found Hume's ungainliness rather charming, and he was always the first to crack a joke about his girth. Though Hume worked hard to rid his writings of Scotticisms, he also admitted that his spoken burr was "totally desperate and irreclaimable."[48] As for his character, Hume seems to have been one of the best-natured philosophers who ever lived. Although his good temper was not unbreakable, in general he was open, kindly, and cheerful, so much so that even those who were scandalized by his writings—which Smith was not—were often disarmed when they met him in person. He was fond of food, drink, games (his favorite being whist), and above all good company. Like many others who knew Hume well, Alexander Carlyle found his conversation "irresistible," commenting that "for innocent mirth and agreeable raillery I never knew his match."[49]

The twenty-six-year-old Smith was, of course, just embarking on his career and had not yet published anything of his own.[50] We have little information about Smith's physical appearance until somewhat later in life and, unusually for someone of his prominence in the eighteenth century, he never sat for his portrait. Judging from later descriptions, however, he was of average build and slightly above average height, with prominent teeth and heavy-lidded eyes. Although

FIGURE 2.1 This portrait by Allan Ramsay (1754) is the earliest known likeness of Hume. The conspicuous turban-like cap was on the cutting edge of fashion at the time. Photograph courtesy of the Scottish National Portrait Gallery (PG 3521).

his voice was harsh, he spoke the southern English that was so prized among the Scottish literati "with great purity" thanks to his years in Oxford.[51] Smith's temperament was mild and unassuming and his integrity unquestioned, though his mannerisms were a bit peculiar. He seems to have had a preoccupied air and a habit of mumbling

FIGURE 2.2 This portrait medallion was modeled by James Tassie near the end of Smith's life (1787). Dugald Stewart commented that it "conveys an exact idea of his profile, and of the general expression of his countenance." Photograph courtesy of the Scottish National Portrait Gallery (PG 157).

and smiling to himself, even during church services.[52] The term that resurfaces time and again in descriptions of Smith's demeanor is "absent." James Boswell, for instance, characterizes him as "quite a learned, accurate, absent man," and Dugald Stewart remarks that he was "habitually inattentive to familiar objects, and to common occurrences; and he frequently exhibited instances of absence."[53] In his account of the Scottish literati Carlyle judged that "Smith, though perhaps only second to David [Hume] in learning and ingenuity, was far inferior to him in conversational talents. . . . He was the most absent man in company that I ever saw."[54] (Carlyle does grant, though, that Smith's travels abroad in the 1760s eventually "cured him in part of those foibles.")[55]

The apparently stark contrast between the gregarious, engaging Hume and the more reserved, absentminded Smith has led some to wonder how they managed to get on so well. An early twentieth-century biographer of Hume, J. Y. T. Greig, tried to put a positive spin on the contrast, remarking that "their friendship came as near perfection as their very different natures would permit."[56] Leaving aside the fact that individuals can share similar tastes and outlooks and enjoy one another's company even if they have contrasting personality types, the differences between Hume and Smith on this score should not be overdrawn. After all, Hume too preferred the company of "a few select companions" to large groups, and he too occasionally exhibited a kind of amiable distractedness.[57] He was sometimes observed to stare vacantly into the distance, for instance, a habit that would later unnerve Jean-Jacques Rousseau. Likewise, for all of Smith's oft-noted absence, he also had a decidedly practical side: he would prove to be not just a popular teacher—a role for which a touch of absentmindedness is not always an insurmountable handicap—but also a trusted administrator, a conscientious traveling tutor, and a capable public servant. Smith also made friends exceptionally easily. John Rae, his nineteenth-century biographer, goes so far as to claim that "few men were ever by nature more entirely formed for friendship than Smith," noting that at virtually every stage of his life "we invariably find him surrounded by troops of friends, and deriving from their company his chief solace and delight."[58] Walter Bagehot made the same point in his typically patronizing way, writing that "through life there was about Adam Smith a sort of lumbering *bonhomie* which amused and endeared him to those around him."[59]

Whatever Hume and Smith made of one another at their first meeting, and whatever the differences and similarities in their personalities, they soon became fast friends.

CHAPTER 3

A BUDDING
FRIENDSHIP
(1750-1754)

THE PUBLIC LECTURES that Smith delivered in Edinburgh between 1748 and 1751, in addition to bringing him into contact with Hume for the first time, also marked him as a teacher and scholar of high promise. In January 1751 he was offered a position at his alma mater, Glasgow University, which he eagerly accepted.[1] Smith initially took up the Chair of Logic, whose previous occupant had recently died, but because he was obliged to complete his lecture series back in Edinburgh he did not actually begin teaching at Glasgow until October. Around that time Francis Hutcheson's successor as Chair of Moral Philosophy, Thomas Craigie, was forced to step down on account of ill health, and Smith jumped at the chance to switch to a discipline that he found more congenial, and to earn a slightly higher income to boot. He would occupy the Chair of Moral Philosophy at Glasgow for nearly twelve years, from April 1752 to January 1764. This was arguably the most prestigious academic position in all of Scotland, owing partly to the authority that Hutcheson had conferred on it, partly to the fact that Glasgow had (at least temporarily) surpassed Edinburgh as Scotland's foremost seat of higher learning, and partly to the intrinsic importance of moral philosophy in the curriculum of the day.[2] Occupying as it did the whole final year of the arts syllabus, moral philosophy served as the culmination of the students' collegiate experience, and it was expected to play a central role in shaping the minds and characters of the country's citizens and future leaders.[3]

The typical scope of a moral philosophy course was quite broad in Smith's time. John Millar described Smith's course as consisting of four parts: natural theology, ethics "strictly so called," jurisprudence, and political economy.[4] We have fairly detailed knowledge of the contents of the last three parts of the course: the second part, on ethics, consisted largely of material later published as *The Theory of Moral Sentiments*; the third part, on jurisprudence, was never published by Smith, but we have at least two and possibly three sets of student notes from his lectures on the subject; and the fourth part, on political economy, was largely incorporated into *The Wealth of Nations*.[5] As for the opening lectures on natural theology, Millar reports that they "considered the proofs of the being and attributes of God, and those principles of the human mind upon which religion is founded."[6] Detailed knowledge of the contents of these lectures would clearly add a great deal to our understanding of Smith, but alas we have little more than Millar's bare description of them. Nowhere in Smith's published works or surviving manuscripts is there any explicit consideration of "the proofs of the being and attributes of God." Smith does of course investigate "those principles of the human mind upon which religion is founded" in his *Principles Which Lead and Direct Philosophical Enquiries*, though whether he would have promulgated that work's deeply skeptical perspective to his students is anyone's guess at this point.

We do know, however, that the pious were none too pleased with Smith's approach to this part of the course. John Ramsay of Ochtertyre reports that as a result of Smith's teachings "presumptuous striplings" were induced "to draw an unwarranted conclusion—namely, that the great truths of theology, together with the duties which man owes to God and his neighbours, may be discovered by the light of nature without any special revelation."[7] Smith had signed the required Westminster Confession of Faith before occupying his post at the university, but one of his first actions upon arriving there was to ask to be freed from the customary duty of opening each day's class with a prayer. The request was denied, though the devout were left unsatisfied in any case because the prayers that Smith ended up offering smacked so strongly of "natural religion." He also managed to dispense with Hutcheson's usual practice of convening his students on Sundays to impart "a discourse suited to that day."[8] According to Ramsay, it was widely suspected that Smith's "principles were not sound" both because he was "very guarded in conversation" and because of "the company he kept"—an obvious allusion to his growing friendship with Hume.[9] As time went on, Smith's closeness to Hume seems to have raised red flags among some parents. Théodore Tronchin, a renowned Genevan physician and contributor to Denis Diderot's *Encyclopédie*, sent his son to Glasgow to study with Smith, but he warned him that, as much as he loved him, he would sooner have him die than see him end up adopting Hume's dangerous principles.[10]

Nevertheless, Smith was an extremely popular and effective teacher—"there was no situation," Millar remarked, "in which the abilities of Mr. Smith appeared to greater advantage than as a Professor"—and students were sent to study with him from as far afield as Russia.[11] The student of Smith's who went on to the greatest later fame was none other than James Boswell, who came to Glasgow for a brief time in 1759–60 for the express purpose of taking Smith's course.[12] Boswell was quite fond of Smith for many years, though as we will see his attitude cooled notably in the 1770s, as he came under the sway of Samuel Johnson and as Smith's *Letter to Strahan* had its effects.[13] In consequence of all of Smith's services to the university it conferred on him a Doctorate of Laws in October 1762, which explains why his contemporaries sometimes called him "Dr. Smith." Smith himself was indifferent about such titles and urged his publisher, William Strahan, to "call me simply Adam Smith without any addition either before or behind" on the title page of his publications.[14] In any event, late in life Smith remembered his years on the faculty at Glasgow as "by far the most useful, and, therefore, as by far the happiest and most honourable period of my life."[15]

Smith's move to the Chair of Moral Philosophy opened up Glasgow's Chair of Logic once again, and despite his earlier failure to attain a professorship at Edinburgh Hume allowed his name to be put forward. Among those pressing his case were William Mure of Caldwell and Gilbert Elliot of Minto, both influential politicians as well as close friends of Hume's. Hume traveled to the west of Scotland in the autumn of 1751 to visit some friends, including Mure and perhaps Smith, and it was probably during this trip that the idea of his filling the position was first mooted. Predictably, however, the "violent and solemn remonstrances of the clergy" arose once again, rebuffing Hume in his second and final attempt to join the academy.[16] The commotion occasioned by Hume's nomination prompted the first mention of him in Smith's extant correspondence. The reference occurs in a November 1751 letter to William Cullen, Smith's new colleague at Glasgow, who had recently been appointed Professor of Medicine and who would later serve as a physician for both Smith and Hume. Smith tells Cullen, "I should prefer David Hume to any man for a colleague; but I am afraid the public would not be of my opinion; and the interest of the society [i.e., the university] will oblige us to have some regard to the opinion of the public." Smith suggests, therefore, that they wait to "see how the public receives" Hume's candidacy.[17]

This remark is routinely read by scholars as the first of many instances of Smith's excessive prudence, or even timidity, with respect to Hume and his irreligiosity. J. Y. T. Greig, for instance, scoffs that "Smith had not sat for nothing at the feet of Hutcheson the cautious."[18] Several crucial qualifications should be kept in mind, however. First, we have no information beyond this letter, which was written fairly early in the process of filling the chair, about any further action Smith may have taken with regard to Hume's candidacy. Cullen, the recipient of the letter, ended up backing Hume vigorously, as a letter from Hume himself gratefully acknowledges, and John Rae surmises that since he and Smith acted in concert in the early stages of the process "it is not likely that Smith lagged behind Cullen in the prosecution of the canvass," though he admits that "nothing remains to give us any decisive information on the point."[19] Second, Smith *did* have an obligation to the university, not just to his new friend, and Hume *would* have been an uncomfortable fit for the position, just as he had been for the one at Edinburgh. Smith himself rankled at the myriad religious duties attached to the life of a professor in eighteenth-century Scotland, and presumably Hume would have been even less interested—and less sincere—in performing them. Finally, we should not be too quick to dismiss the first part of Smith's comment: the unequivocal statement that he would prefer

Hume, whom he had met only two years earlier, to *any* man for a colleague provides striking evidence of just how highly he thought of Hume already, both as a thinker and as a friend.

The Chair of Logic was ultimately filled by one James Clow. Like the candidate who bested Hume for Edinburgh's Chair of Ethics, William Cleghorn, Clow could be counted on to fill Scotland's impressionable young minds with the "right" principles, but neither of them seems to have ever published a scholarly work of any kind. As Hume's biographer Ernest Campbell Mossner tartly remarks, "the academic infatuation with respectable mediocrity once more triumphed; and, while Professor Clow of Glasgow remains as insignificant as Professor Cleghorn of Edinburgh, Scotland's most distinguished philosopher never held a philosophy chair."[20] It is astonishing to think what the university would have been like if Hume had, against the odds, been appointed. To have two of the leading philosophical minds of the century on the faculty of a small provincial college with only a dozen professors would have been remarkable indeed.[21] And this is not even to mention the other now-legendary employee of the university: as another Hume biographer notes, if Hume had been selected for the Logic chair, Glasgow would have had the age's greatest philosopher (Hume), greatest economist (Smith), and greatest inventor (James Watt) all working next door to one another.[22]

Happily, almost immediately after this missed opportunity another appealing prospect opened up for Hume. In February 1752 he was appointed keeper of the Advocates' Library in Edinburgh, an office that brought with it a modest salary but also, much more importantly, access to one of the finest libraries in Britain, which would prove a great boon to his labors on *The History of England*. Despite being only "a petty office of forty or fifty guineas a year," as Hume described it, the post had its share of prominent occupants in the eighteenth century: it had once belonged to Henry Home and would eventually pass on to Adam Ferguson. Upon gaining the position Hume felt "ready to burst with vanity and self-conceit," having this time prevailed over the usual "violent cry of Deism, atheism, and scepticism," at least for a time.[23] He worked at the library for five years, resigning in January 1757 for unknown reasons.

Soon after securing this post Hume purchased his first home, an apartment in the oldest part of what is now Edinburgh's Old Town, the Lawnmarket. The building, Riddle's Land, survives to this day in somewhat altered form. The next year Hume moved—heading east down today's Royal Mile—to the Canongate, taking an apartment in a building called Jack's Land that no longer stands. Aside from a couple of visits to London he would live there for the next nine years. Hume was now firmly ensconced in Edinburgh, which he regarded as the acme of Scottish intellectual life. In *My Own Life* he avows that "the town" is "the true scene for a man of letters," and with a midcentury population of just over 50,000 Edinburgh was the biggest town that Scotland had to offer.[24] (Glasgow's population stood at just over 30,000; both were dwarfed by London, which had upward of 650,000 inhabitants.) Although the Scottish Parliament had decamped for London early in the century, Edinburgh remained Scotland's legal and ecclesiastical capital. It was one of the most cosmopolitan cities in all of Britain, boasting a rich cultural life and a close-knit band of prominent literati that prompted the novelist Tobias Smollett to dub it "a hot-bed of genius."[25] It was also shockingly filthy, even by eighteenth-century standards. The inhabitants and their many animals were crowded into an overflowing medieval warren of steep, narrow, dank alleys. Every evening chamber pots were emptied directly onto the streets, where the refuse would remain until it was swept up the next morning, and the omnipresent peat and coal smoke earned the town the nickname "Auld Reekie." For Hume, though, the city's intellectual vitality more than made up for its cramped squalor.

Smith, by contrast, deemed Edinburgh "a very dissolute town" and always preferred Scotland's second city, Glasgow.[26] Eighteenth-century Glasgow was a far cry from the grimy industrial center that it was later to become. In fact, visitors almost unanimously described it as beautiful, clean, spacious, and well-organized—in short, everything Edinburgh was not. Nestled on the northern bank of the River Clyde, the city was dominated by its college, its commerce, and its cathedral. While accounts of the Scottish Enlightenment tend to focus chiefly on the literati of Edinburgh, the intellectual life of Glasgow

FIGURE 3.1 This crowded scene in Libberton's Wynd, a steep lane that ran from the Lawnmarket down to the Cowgate, was painted by George Cattermole in the mid-nineteenth century, but depicts an Edinburgh of an earlier era. The tavern on the right, advertised as Burns' Tavern, is said to have been frequented by Hume under the previous proprietor, when it was known as Johnnie Dowie's Tavern. Image © Edinburgh City Libraries.

FIGURE 3.2 *A View of the Middle Walk in the College Garden*, by Robert Paul (1762), depicts the spacious avenue running behind the main buildings of the University of Glasgow on High Street. The university buildings are visible through the trees on the left, including the library with its distinctive tall windows, while the Glasgow Cathedral dominates the background. Image © The Hunterian Museum, University of Glasgow.

was far from negligible.[27] Centered around its top-notch university and lacking all of the legal and administrative structures of the capital, Glasgow enjoyed a far more collegiate atmosphere. The city was also notable for its bustling, commercial spirit, thanks in large part to the transatlantic trade with the British colonies in North America and the Caribbean, particularly in tobacco. As a result of its booming economy the city expanded continually, with its population surpassing that of Edinburgh by the end of the century. The aspect of Glasgow that left Smith less satisfied was its embrace of a particularly strong form of evangelical Presbyterianism; visitors from the east of Scotland regularly commented on the "gloomy" and "fanatical" nature of the town's populace.[28]

With Hume settled in Edinburgh and Smith in Glasgow as of the early 1750s, the two would be based on opposite sides of the country for the better part of the next dozen years. As we will see, however, their friendship grew ever closer despite this geographical divide.

———————◆———————

Hume's residential and occupational moves did not curtail his literary output in the slightest. The next of his works to appear, in 1751, was *An Enquiry Concerning the Principles of Morals*, which was a recasting of the third book of the *Treatise*, much as the *First Enquiry* had recast the *Treatise*'s first book. Like the *First Enquiry*, the *Second Enquiry* is shorter, more polished, and more to the point than the corresponding volume of the *Treatise*. The basic account of the foundations of morality is the same, though there are a few shifts in tone and emphasis.[29] The *Second Enquiry* is, for instance, more emotionally evocative than the *Treatise* had been. In the earlier work Hume had self-consciously eschewed moralistic language; as he explained to Hutcheson, he tried to think and write as an "anatomist" who studies the "most secret Springs & Principles" of human nature rather than as a "painter" who describes "the Grace & Beauty of its Actions."[30] In the *Second Enquiry* he makes a greater effort to combine the two roles, moving beyond a dry explanation of what morality consists of to also convey some of its attractions.[31] As part of this effort the work includes, as the *Treatise* had not, a rich catalogue of illustrations of the various virtues and vices, often drawn from the Greek and Roman classics.

Book 3 of the *Treatise* had propounded a conspicuously this-worldly account of morality, but the *Second Enquiry* was if anything even more offensive to Christian sensibilities. In the latter work Hume not only reiterates his central claim that morality derives from human sentiments rather than from the word or will of God, but also insists that many of the qualities that the devout took to be the noblest of virtues were in fact vices. After all, if the virtues are simply the traits that we collectively find to be useful or agreeable, for ourselves or for others, then any traits that fail to fit into any of these categories are not in fact virtuous. Hume claims that this is the case with "celibacy, fasting, penance, mortification, self-denial, humility, silence, solitude, and the whole train of monkish virtues." These qualities, he says, "serve to no manner of purpose; neither advance a man's fortune in the world, nor render him a more valuable member of society; neither qualify him for the entertainment of company, nor encrease his power of self-enjoyment." On the contrary, they "cross all these desirable ends; stupify the understanding and harden the heart, obscure the fancy and sour the temper." These qualities should thus be considered vices, he concludes, by anyone whose judgment is not clouded by "the delusive glosses of superstition and false religion."[32] Once again Hume was insisting that religion is not just superfluous but often positively pernicious. Soon after the work's release he admitted that it was his own "favorite Performance," and he maintained that predilection to his dying days.[33] In *My Own Life* Hume proclaims that "in my own opinion (who ought not to judge on that subject)" the *Second Enquiry* is "of all my writings, historical, philosophical, or literary, incomparably the best."[34]

The next year Hume published yet another collection of essays, this one titled *Political Discourses*. The majority of the essays included in the volume—eight of the twelve—focus squarely on issues related to what was then called political economy. The work lacks the comprehensiveness and exhaustive detail of a treatise like *The Wealth of Nations*, but it nonetheless provides an exceptionally cogent set of reflections on commerce and commercial policy, packaged in a clear, easy-to-digest form. The standpoint of the essays is strikingly cosmopolitan. Whereas most economic tracts of the day sought to show how Britain's trading interests might be advanced or—what amounted to the same thing in most eyes—those of France harmed, Hume viewed the world of commerce with the eye of a philosopher and a historian, grandly disdaining petty national prejudices and animosities. He acknowledges at the outset that readers may find his ideas to be "uncommon" or "out of the common road," and indeed the work reads like a sustained attack on the prevailing economic thinking of the time.[35] Many of Hume's arguments anticipate those of Smith's great work: the true source of a nation's wealth is not gold or silver or a positive balance of trade, but rather a productive citizenry; most attempts by politicians to guide or control people's economic choices are either futile or positively counterproductive; free trade works to the benefit of all parties involved—city and country, rich and poor, the government and the populace; free markets are also mutually beneficial in the international sphere, and it is impossible to attain prosperity by beggaring neighboring countries. Hume thus laments "those numberless bars, obstructions, and imposts, which all nations of EUROPE, and none more than ENGLAND, have put upon trade," which "serve to no purpose but to check industry, and rob ourselves and our neighbours of the common benefits of art and nature."[36]

Even greater than Hume's concern to promote *free* trade, however, was his concern to promote trade itself. Two of the most venerable traditions of Western thought, civic republicanism and Christianity, tended to regard commerce, wealth, and luxury as inherently corrupting. For adherents of these traditions, the argument that free trade leads to greater prosperity reads less like a promise than like a threat—a threat to public order, to political liberty, to virtue, to salvation. Against such views, which were quite prevalent in the eighteenth century, Hume insisted that there is nothing particularly noble or redeeming about poverty, nor anything intrinsically objectionable about luxury. On this broader philosophical front the key essay was "Of Luxury" (later retitled "Of Refinement in the Arts"), which amounts to one of the most forceful, comprehensive, yet succinct defenses of the modern, liberal, commercial order ever written. In stark contrast to those who worried that commerce and luxury distract people from their more important duties—to God and to country— Hume posits that "ages of refinement are both the happiest and most virtuous." In his view, commerce encourages industriousness, helps to augment knowledge of all kinds, and renders people more sociable and humane. Indeed, he maintains that "*industry, knowledge*, and *humanity*, are linked together by an indissoluble chain, and are found, from experience as well as reason, to be peculiar to the more polished, and, what are commonly denominated, the more luxurious ages." Hume further argues that commerce is favorable to free government insofar as it helps to create a "middling rank of men, who are the best and firmest basis of public liberty." In stark contrast to the critics, then, Hume holds that commerce *promotes* virtue by making people more industrious, intelligent, and humane and *strengthens* the community by making it not only richer but also freer and more stable and orderly. "Nor are these advantages attended with disadvantages, that bear any proportion to them," he insists.[37] The only real warning bells that Hume sounds in the essays relate to the effects of imperialism and the rapidly mounting public debt, and here too he anticipated the more detailed indictments of his close friend—a point to which we will return in chapter 9.

The *Political Discourses* were widely read and acclaimed throughout Britain and France; Hume later singled this volume out as "the only work of mine that was successful on the first publication."[38] While its fame and influence would later be eclipsed by those of *The Wealth of Nations*, its immediate impact was probably greater than that of any of Hume's other writings. Indeed, according to one economist's judgment "it is doubtful whether any economic composition, with the possible exception of Henry George's *Progress and Poverty*, has ever enjoyed a greater vogue."[39]

As might be expected, the *Political Discourses* caught Smith's attention immediately. In January 1752, just a few months after arriving at Glasgow, Smith helped to found the Literary Society of Glasgow, a group composed largely of professors at the university, along with some local gentlemen and merchants of a literary bent.[40] The group gathered weekly when the university was in session to discuss the members' works in progress or recent publications by others, and at the third meeting, on January 23, Smith read an "Account of some of Mr. David Hume's Essays on Commerce."[41] The *Political Discourses* had appeared no more than a month or two before Smith gave his account of them, and the close timing suggests that Hume may have shared the work with him prior to publication.[42] We do not know what Smith said about Hume's arguments, though Dugald Stewart remarks that "the publication of Mr Hume's political discourses, in the year 1752, could not fail to confirm [Smith] in those liberal views of commercial policy which had already opened to him in the course of his own inquiries."[43] It is worth noting that Smith read his account of Hume's essays right on the heels of the controversy over Hume's candidacy for the Logic chair, just two months after his letter to Cullen on the subject. The fact that Smith chose to focus on Hume's work in his first presentation to the Literary Society may lend support to Rae's conjecture that he ended up joining Cullen in going to bat for Hume. At any rate, it would certainly have been strange for him to call the faculty's attention to the popular new publication of an individual whose candidacy he had just opposed.

Judging from the rough report known as the "Anderson notes," it appears that Smith also discussed Hume's *Political Discourses*—specifically, the essay "Of Interest"—in his jurisprudence lectures beginning quite early in his time at Glasgow.[44] In his later lectures, we know, he showered praise on a concept that Hume outlines in "Of the Balance of Trade" and "Of Money" and that has come to be known as "Hume's specie-flow mechanism." Hume, Smith proclaimed, had "very ingeniously" proven the "absurdity" of the common worry about losing gold and silver through an unfavorable balance of trade. Given that prices and wages adjust automatically to the amount of money in circulation, any attempt to restrict the export of gold and silver would be self-defeating. Smith pronounced to his students that "Mr. Hume's reasoning is exceedingly ingenious," though he also chided Hume for having "gone a little into the notion that public opulence consists in money"—presumably a reference to Hume's strictures on the use of paper money in the early editions of the *Political Discourses*.[45] Based on Hume's "ingenious" argument and a host of others, Smith concluded that "Brittain should by all means be made a free port . . . and that free commerce and liberty of exchange should be allowed with all nations and for all things."[46]

Smith also spent multiple class periods rehearsing Hume's arguments against the notion that a social contract is the only legitimate basis for government. Although he does not invoke Hume by name in this context in the notes that we have, it could scarcely be more obvious that he is drawing on his friend's seminal essay "Of the Original Contract." Smith methodically runs through all of Hume's key points, including the claim that political authority is a convention that emerges gradually and unconsciously over time, rather than through a deliberate agreement made at a single moment; that people obey their rulers out of custom and habit, not because they believe that they or their ancestors promised to do so; that the entire notion of a social contract was virtually unheard of outside of Britain, and yet political obligation was not restricted to their island; that consent cannot be imposed on future generations; and that the idea of tacit consent wrongly presumes that leaving one's country is a feasible option. On the latter point he invokes Hume's famous analogy that an impressed sailor can hardly be said to have tacitly consented to be kidnapped merely because he does not leave the ship and jump into the sea, attributing it to "a very ingenious gentleman."[47] As one scholar remarks, "Smith simply took over Hume's arguments, and the young reporter wrote them down, blow by blow, when he could have saved himself trouble by making a note like 'see Hume's *Essay on the Original Contract.'*"[48]

While these are the only extended, explicit discussions of Hume in the notes we have from Smith's jurisprudence lectures, there are dozens of further allusions to Hume's essays, the *Treatise*, and above all *The History of England* sprinkled throughout the reports.[49] Smith's jurisprudence course was deeply historical in character, tracing the development of various political institutions and forms of law from their rude beginnings to his own time. Much of the course is organized around his famous "four stages" theory, which traces humanity's progress through its hunting, shepherding, agricultural, and commercial stages, and which finds only the briefest of echoes in Hume's works.[50] Yet there are numerous junctures in the narrative where Hume's presence can be felt on matters both big—such as the transition from the feudal era to the commercial age in Europe, a subject that would later play a major role in *The Wealth of Nations*— and small, like the level of crime in Britain during Elizabeth's reign, another point on which Smith mentions Hume by name.[51] Smith seems to have recommended Hume's *History of England* to his students as the only modern history free of "party spirit" in his lectures on rhetoric and belles lettres, as well.[52] For all of Hume's notoriety, then, Smith certainly was not hiding his high opinion of Hume's writings from his students.

The Hume-Smith correspondence that has come down to us commences with a letter that Hume wrote to Smith in September 1752, just before the start of Smith's first full year as the Moral Philosophy chair. (In fact the first ten extant letters between the two were all written by Hume.) We know that this was not the first message between them, as Hume mentions that Smith's previous letter was delayed due to being wrongly directed; apparently Smith had not yet learned of Hume's recent move to the Lawnmarket. But it is appropriate, in some respects, that their surviving correspondence opens in the middle of a conversation about a weighty scholarly question: "I confess, I was once of the same Opinion with you," Hume's letter begins, "and thought that the best Period to begin an English History was about Henry the 7th." This is, of course, a reference to Hume's *History of England*, which he had projected several years earlier but had only recently begun to write, drawing on the resources at the Advocates' Library. He and Smith had evidently been deliberating about which period of English history was the most significant, or would shed the most light on the character of modern Britain, with Smith making a case for the start of the Tudor era (1485), when the absolute monarchy began to come into its own. Hume maintained, however, that "the Change which then happen'd in public Affairs, was very insensible, and did not display its Influence till many Years afterwards." Thus, he argues that the real turning point was the start of the Stuart era (1603): "Twas under James that the House of Commons began first to raise their Head, and then the Quarrel betwixt Privilege and Prerogative commenc'd . . . and the Factions, which then arose, having an Influence on our present Affairs, form the most curious, interesting, and instructive part of our History."[53]

Following this reasoning, Hume began his *History* with a volume on the reigns of James I and his successor Charles I. The work was published in 1754, and eventually became the penultimate volume of the six-volume work. After completing his account of the Stuarts with another volume on the period leading up to the Glorious Revolution, however, Hume found it necessary to go back in time and write the history of the Tudors after all. At that point he admitted that he should have followed Smith's advice and started with the Tudors in the first place. Hume wrote to his bookseller: "At present I begin with the Reign of Henry the 7th. It is properly at that Period modern History commences. America was discoverd: Commerce extended: The Arts cultivated: Printing invented: Religion reform'd: And all the Governments of Europe almost chang'd. I wish therefore I had begun here at first. I shoud have obviated many Objections, that were made to the other Volumes."[54] The objections that Hume here alludes to were the widespread complaints that his treatment of the Stuart "tyrants," especially Charles I, was far too sympathetic, which led many to conclude that he was writing a "Tory" history. Hume's Tudor volumes were designed to show, among other things, that absolute rule had in fact been instituted in England under some of the monarchs most cherished by the Whigs, such as Elizabeth, and that the Stuarts were only following in the footsteps of their predecessors in exercising the broad prerogatives of the crown. As one authority on Hume's *History* puts it, if Hume had begun with the Tudors he would have in effect "spiked the Whig guns in advance."[55] In any case, Hume tells Smith that he was enjoying the work immensely: "I confess, that the Subject appears to me very fine; and I enter upon it with great Ardour and Pleasure. You need not doubt of my Perseverance."

Hume notes further, in this letter, that he was presently "diverted" with correcting his *Essays Moral and Political* for a new edition, and he asks for any suggestions that Smith may have on that front: "If any thing occur to you to be inserted or retrench'd, I shall be obliged to you for the Hint. In case you shou'd not have the last Edition by you, I shall send a Copy of it." He reports that he was prevailed upon, against his judgment, to retain the essays "Of Love and Marriage" and "Of the Study of History" in the most recent edition of the *Essays*. Hume deemed these pieces "too frivolous for the rest," but when his London-based bookseller, Andrew Millar, told Hume "how much he had heard them prais'd by the best Judges . . . the Bowels of a Parent melted, and I preserv'd them alive."[56] (Hume did end up dropping these two essays beginning in the 1760 edition of his collected works.)

The following May Hume wrote Smith again, this time from his new residence in the Canongate. Hume had heard that Smith was ill of late, and he expresses anxiety that "the Fatigues of your Class have exhausted you too much, and that you require more Leizure and Rest than you allow yourself." "Were you not my Friend," Hume says—the first explicit mention of their friendship—"you wou'd envy my robust Constitution. My Application has been and is continual; and yet I preserve entire Health." He informs Smith that his work on the first volume of the *History* was proceeding apace, and that he was now working on the Long Parliament, which sat during the first of England's seventeenth-century civil wars. "Considering the great Number of Volumes I peruse, and my scrupulous method of composing," Hume declares, "I regard [this] as a very great Advance." This letter also contains the first of what would become Hume's regular pleas for Smith to visit him. Smith's classes were ending for the summer in a few weeks, and Hume entreats: "I hope you intend, both for Exercise and Relaxation, to take a Jaunt to this Place [i.e., Edinburgh]. I have many things to communicate to you." Yet a mere jaunt would not ultimately be enough to satisfy him: "I think you shou'd settle in this Town during the Vacation; where there always is some good Company; and you know, that I can supply you with Books, as much as you please." This last reference was to Hume's position at the Advocates' Library, which he put at Smith's disposal during his visits to the capital.[57]

In addition to discussing personal matters and his own books, Hume's letters to Smith often mention recently published works by others. His first letter, for instance, notes that a collection of posthumous writings by Lord Bolingbroke—another author notorious for his anticlerical views—had just been published, though he comments, "I confess my Curiosity is not much rais'd."[58] In February 1754 Hume wrote to Smith to call his attention to the recently published poems of Thomas Blacklock, a blind poet who lived in Edinburgh. Hume was recommending the collection to everyone he could think of, he says, "but especially to those, whose Approbation wou'd contribute most to recommend them [to] the World," and he asks Smith to pass the word along to his friends and colleagues in Glasgow. He expresses pleasure in hearing that Smith was in better health that winter but reproves him once again for failing to visit as often as Hume would like: "We expected to have seen you in Town about this time; but have been disappointed."[59]

In December of that year Hume caught Smith up to speed on a row he was having with the curators of the Advocates' Library. Hume's position as keeper was a public post, and his opponents kept a watchful eye on his activities. In June the curators had pounced, decreeing that three of the volumes he had purchased in the course of fulfilling his duties were "indecent" and "unworthy of a Place in a learned Library," and thus must be removed from the shelves, and further that Hume would have to obtain their approval for all future purchases. Hume understandably took the decree as a personal insult and so was averse to submit to it, but he was equally reluctant to give up his post and the library privileges it entailed.[60] He explained his resolution of the dilemma to Smith: "I retain the Office, but have given Blacklock, our blind Poet, a Bond of Annuity for the Sallary. I have now put it out of these malicious Fellows power to offer me any Indignity; while my Motives for remaining in this Office are so apparent."[61] In other words, the curators could pull rank on Hume all they liked; his own reputation would remain secure as long as it was clear that he was serving in the position for the access to the books and not for the money. As Mossner notes, "by this stroke Hume at once retained his library post, fostered Scottish letters, performed an act of charity—and maintained his honour."[62] "I shou'd be glad that you approve of my Conduct," Hume tells Smith; "I own I am satisfy'd with myself."[63] Sadly, Blacklock would later turn on Hume, joining James Beattie's scurrilous attack on him in the early 1770s.[64] This would not be the last recipient of Hume's good offices to bite the hand that fed him.

The year 1754 saw another connection of sorts between Hume and Smith, though we have no record of them discussing it with one another. That year John Douglas, an Anglican clergyman (and later Bishop of Salisbury), published yet another attempted refutation of Hume on miracles, this one taking the form of a letter to an anonymous friend and titled *The Criterion; or, Miracles Examined, with a View to Expose the Pretensions of Pagans and Papists*. What makes this particular piece relevant for our purposes is that Douglas was a Balliol classmate and friend of Smith's, and it has often been supposed that Smith himself was the work's anonymous addressee. While this may or may not be strictly true, it is very likely that Smith was at least one of the friends whom Douglas had in mind.[65] It is noteworthy, then, that the addressee is said to have "reasoned himself . . . into an unfavourable Opinion of the Evidences of Christianity," in spite of all of his "good Sense, Candor, and Learning," partly as a result of the arguments advanced by Hume but also partly as a result of

"Objections, which are peculiar to yourself and not borrowed from Books." Douglas spends over four hundred pages contending that the miracles of the New Testament are supported by a great deal more evidence than earlier ("pagan") or later ("papist") alleged miracles, in hopes of bringing Smith and perhaps some other friends "back to that Religion which you seem to have forsaken."⁶⁶ It appears that Smith remained on friendly terms with Douglas for many years, but there is no evidence that he ever read *The Criterion* or weighed its arguments; the work is absent from the catalogue of Smith's library.⁶⁷ In typical fashion, Hume too went on to maintain a cordial relationship with Douglas despite the latter's attempted refutation, even going so far as to mention him to William Strahan as someone who might extend Hume's *History of England* beyond 1689 after he himself had declined to do so.⁶⁸

Hume's pleas for Smith to visit him, and complaints about his failure to do so often enough, raise the question of how frequently the two saw each other in person during these years. It is, unfortunately, impossible to answer this question with any precision. Certainly Smith traveled to Edinburgh far more often than Hume did to Glasgow. Initially it would have taken Smith upward of thirteen hours to make the trip, but after the road was improved over the course of the 1750s he could rise in the morning and be in the capital by noon. John Rae writes that "during his residence in Glasgow Smith continued to maintain intimate relations with his old friends in Edinburgh. He often ran through by coach to visit them . . . he spent among them most part of many of his successive vacations; and he took an active share, along with them, in promoting some of those projects of literary, scientific, and social improvement with which Scotland was then rife."⁶⁹ A contemporary account that lends support to the idea that Smith was in Edinburgh with some frequency can be found in the autobiography of Alexander Carlyle. Writing of Edinburgh in the early 1750s, Carlyle recalls wistfully what "a fine time it was when we could collect David Hume, Adam Smith, Adam Ferguson, Lord Elibank and Drs. [Hugh] Blair and [John] Jardine, on an hour's warning." He also reports that when they gathered in the tavern after supper Hume's housekeeper, Peggy Irvine, would insist that he bring the key to his apartment so that she would not have to wait up for him, "for she said when the honest fellows came in from the country, he never returned home till after one o'clock."[70]

As Rae intimates, we also know that Smith came to Edinburgh periodically to attend meetings of various clubs and societies. Easily the most celebrated and influential of these clubs was the Select Society, which was formed in May 1754 and went on to play a key role in the cultural and intellectual life of Edinburgh, and indeed the entire Scottish Enlightenment.[71] The initial idea came from the painter Allan Ramsay, but a number of his friends, including Smith, were vital in bringing the project to fruition. The society gathered leading figures from the university, the law, and the Kirk, along with a few choice aristocrats and gentlemen, for meetings every Wednesday evening at the Advocates' Library. Hume and Smith were both founding members, along with thirteen others including their protégé, the twenty-one-year-old Alexander Wedderburn, who later went on to become Britain's Lord Chancellor.[72] They were soon joined by Hugh Blair, Adam Ferguson, Henry Home (who had now become Lord Kames), John Home (the playwright, not Hume's brother), and William Robertson, among many others.

It was left to Smith to explain the nature and purpose of the club to its members at the first meeting.[73] The format was that at each meeting one member would preside over the debate and then propose a topic for the following week's meeting. All topics were fair game "except such as regard Revealed Religion, or which may give occasion to vent any Principles of Jacobitism."[74] Smith took the chair in the second meeting, on June 19 (posing for the next meeting the question, "Whether bounties on the exportation of corn be advantageous to trade and manufactures, as well as to agriculture?"), and Hume took it on December 4 of that year (posing the question, "Whether the difference of national characters be chiefly owing to the nature of different climates, or to moral and political causes?").[75] Aside from taking their turns as chair Hume and Smith refrained from joining much in the debates, but they were both frequent attendants. Hume was also named the first treasurer, a position to which he was reelected several times. In addition, in 1755 the club formed a sort of practically minded offshoot, the Edinburgh Society for Encouraging Arts, Sciences, Manufacturing, and Agriculture in Scotland. Members of this society too, Hume and Smith were both appointed to the committee on belles lettres and criticism that awarded a prize for the best treatise on taste, which went to Alexander Gerard, Professor of Moral Philosophy at Aberdeen, for his *Essay on Taste*.[76]

As time went on the parent society started to become noticeably less "select," eventually growing to well over a hundred members. Felled by its own success, it collapsed from sheer inertia in the early 1760s. For a time, though, the Select Society was a remarkable institution, hosting hundreds of high-level debates on topics ranging from politics and economics to literature and the arts to manners and customs. The intellectual displays on offer were celebrated far and wide. Hume reported to Ramsay, less than a year after the group's establishment, that it had "grown to be a national concern. Young and old, noble and ignoble, witty and dull, laity and clergy, all the world are ambitious for a place amongst us . . . the House of Commons was less the object of general curiosity at London than the Select Society at Edinburgh."[77] Carlyle, another founding member, credited the society with developing the abilities and characters of the city's intellectual elite: "It was those meetings in particular that rubbed off all corners, as we call it, by collision, and made the literati of Edinburgh less captious and pedantic than they were elsewhere."[78] For "elsewhere," Carlyle might just as easily have substituted "in London."

By the mid-1750s Hume's reputation for irreligiosity had started to catch up to him, and the next few years would see him be excluded from another joint undertaking by the literati—the launch of the *Edinburgh Review*—as well as an attempt to expel him from an even higher profile institution: the Church of Scotland.

CHAPTER 4

THE HISTORIAN AND THE KIRK

(1754-1759)

H UME'S LAST MAJOR literary undertaking was his massive *History of England*. The work would eventually reach six volumes and weigh in at around 1.3 million words, or over 3,000 pages in the modern edition. In a sense, Hume wrote the work backward—just as witches said their prayers, as one critic noted.[1] As we have seen, he started with two volumes on the Stuart era (1603–89), which were published in 1754 and 1756.[2] He then wrote another two on the age of the Tudors (1485–1603), both of which appeared in 1759. The work was completed in 1761 with the release of two more volumes covering the long period from the invasion of Julius Caesar all the way up to the accession of Henry VII in 1485. While the first volume was unfavorably received on its initial release, after Hume finished the last volume the complete set soon became the most popular work of history that had ever been published in Britain. It served as the "standard" history of England for many decades and went through over a hundred editions by the end of the nineteenth century. It was widely translated, abridged, and adapted by others, including one version whose title page promised that it was "revised for family use; with such omissions and alterations as may render it salutary to the young, and unexceptionable to the Christian."[3] The copy money that Hume earned from the work, he noted, "much exceeded any thing formerly known in England," making him "not only independent, but opulent."[4] The most qualified judges of the entire age joined in the applause: Voltaire effused that "nothing can be added to the fame of this *History*, perhaps the best ever written in any language," and Edward Gibbon dubbed Hume the Tacitus of Scotland.[5]

The popular renown and material rewards that the *History* brought Hume were not unexpected or unsought. He recognized, as he embarked on the work, that "there is no post of honour in the English Parnassus more vacant than that of History. Style, judgement, impartiality, care—everything is wanting to our historians."[6] As with his earlier turn from the *Treatise* to the *Essays*, however, Hume was not seeking *only* fame and fortune when he threw himself into writing history, nor did he see himself as abandoning philosophy. On the contrary, the project that he had outlined way back in the *Treatise*— that of developing a science of human nature using "the experimental method"—in fact *demands* a study of history. Given that it is impossible to run controlled laboratory experiments on every aspect of human nature, Hume had noted in the introduction, our only recourse is to "glean up our experiments in this science from a cautious observation of human life, and take them as they appear in the common course of the world."[7] History, of course, provides the largest available reservoir of such observations, making it an indispensable resource. As Hume writes elsewhere, history enables us to see the entire "human race, from the beginning of time, pass, as it were, in review before us . . . if we consider the shortness of human life, and our limited knowledge, even of what passes in our own time, we must be sensible that we should be for ever children in understanding, were it not for this invention."[8]

Hume believed that "the first Quality of an Historian is to be true & impartial; the next to be interesting."[9] It is certain that he attained the second of these goals, as *The History of England* can still be read with great pleasure two and a half centuries after it was written. While the work is very long, its scope is so vast that the narrative hums along at a fairly brisk clip. Hume noted that "I have more propos'd as my Model the concise manner of the antient Historians, than the prolix, tedious Style of some modern Compilers."[10] He strikes a nice balance between narrating specific events and reflecting on broad social, political, economic, religious, and intellectual developments. Rich character sketches pervade every volume, not only of kings, bishops, and generals but also of philosophers, authors, and scientists. Nor does Hume refrain from passing judgment on the actions and beliefs of these figures: he makes no pretense of being a value-free observer. He does, though, resist passing easy judgments. He is a master at sympa-thizing with great historical actors and laying bare their motivations, and at critical junctures in the story he often pauses to give the reader a sort of set-piece debate presenting the strongest arguments on both sides of the question at hand. As one noted Hume scholar observes, throughout the *History* Hume plays the role of "the reporter of all sides, the doubter of exclusive claims, the distruster of systems, the person determined to find some possible truth in a variety of view-points and exclusive and absolute truth in none."[11]

As for whether Hume met his own first criterion of a good histo-rian, that of being "true & impartial," he was sure that he had. "The truth is," he told one friend, "there is so much reason to blame and praise alternately King and Parliament, that I am afraid the mixture of both in my composition, being so equal, may pass sometimes for an affectation, and not the result of judgement and evidence."[12] Hume's claims to be above party bias were not seconded by his contemporar-ies, who saw the first Stuart volume, especially, as a plainly "Tory" tract, with its failure to denounce the power grabs of James and Charles with sufficient vehemence. Yet the Tories were not exactly enamored of Hume's ridicule of the notion of the divine right of kings, his crit-icisms of the Church, his paeans to commerce and free trade, or his embrace of the Glorious Revolution and the balanced constitution that resulted from it. The main objection of the critics, ultimately, was that Hume was not an enthusiastic enough Whig; as he would have been the first to concede, he was insufficiently partisan. He was, he said, "not displeasd to be abusd by the violent of both Parties."[13]

If there is a central, guiding theme of the work as a whole it is the blessings of civilization. As in the *Political Discourses*, Hume takes a stand firmly in favor of the superiority of the modern world and against the idea of a fall from ancient glory. For Hume, most of English history—indeed, most of *human* history—had been a story of dis-order, oppression, poverty, and dependence. He thus finds the ten-dency to romanticize the days of yore and "exalt past times above the present" to be utterly preposterous.[14] Perhaps his most colorful ar-ticulation of this view comes in a later personal letter: "My Notion is," he writes, "that the uncultivated Nations are not only inferior to civiliz'd in Government, civil, military, and eclesiastical; but also in Morals; and that their whole manner of Life is disagreeable and uneligible to the last Degree." He insists that "the English, till near the beginning of the last Century, are very much to be regarded as an uncultivated Nation" and that during the reign of the much-idolized Elizabeth even the castle of a great earl "was no better than a Dungeon: No Chimney to let out the Smoak; no Glass Windows to keep out the Air; a glimmering Candle here and there, which coud scarce keep their Ragamuffins of Servants and Retainers from breaking their Shins or running foul of each other: No Diet but salt Beef and Mutton for nine Months of the Year, without Vegetables of any kind: Few Fires and these very poor ones."[15] That said, Hume did not believe that progress is in any way inevitable. In fact, one of the stated objectives of *The History of England* was to reveal "the great mixture of accident, which commonly concurs with a small ingredient of wisdom and foresight" in the emergence of civilized society.[16] Hume made the notion of unintended consequences one of his great recurring motifs, much as Smith would later do in *The Wealth of Nations*.[17]

A prime example of historical accident in Hume's narrative, interestingly enough, comes in the form of religion playing an unexpectedly beneficial role on several critical occasions. To be sure, throughout the six volumes Hume paints a graphic picture of the manifold ills perpetrated by organized religion, both Catholic and Protestant. The various churches and sects were, in his view, responsible for untold amounts of persecution, oppression, disorder, factionalism, conflict, and war, with England's seventeenth-century civil wars—the subject of the first two volumes—serving as exhibit A. Hume himself admitted, in retrospect, that in composing this work he may have been a bit "indiscreet in some things," namely "my too frank & plain & blunt way of talking of Religion."[18] Yet in *The History of England*, more than in any of his other works, he manages to find some genuine (if largely unintentional) practical benefits stemming from organized religion and even from religious fanaticism. In the earliest ages of English history, for instance, it was often the Catholic Church alone that held society together: "It must be acknowledged," Hume writes, almost against his will, "that the influence of the prelates and the clergy was often of great service to the public. Though the religion of that age can merit no better name than that of superstition, it served to unite together a body of men who had great sway over the people, and who kept the community from falling to pieces, by the factions and inde- pendant power of the nobles."[19] The Church of this era also served as a patron of the arts and performed the invaluable service of pre- serving "the precious literature of antiquity from a total extinction."[20]

Even more surprisingly, Hume claims that during the Tudor and Stuart eras religious fanaticism helped to further the cause of civil liberty. He explains: "so extensive was royal authority, and so firmly established in all its parts, that it is probable the patriots of that age would have despaired of ever resisting it, had they not been stimu- lated by religious motives, which inspire a courage unsurmountable by any human obstacle."[21] In other words, as the monarchs absorbed more and more power into the crown, Puritan zealots, fearing God's judgment far more than anything a mere king or queen could muster, were the only group willing to stand up to them. Hence under the otherwise absolute rule of Elizabeth "the precious spark of liberty had been kindled, and was preserved, by the puritans alone; and it was to this sect, whose principles appear so frivolous and habits so ridiculous, that the English owe the whole freedom of their constitution."[22] This is a remarkable claim for any author, let alone one of Hume's thor- oughly secular outlook, to make: an ordered system of English liberty would not have materialized without religious fanaticism. This has been called "the consummate irony of Hume's career": "Religious fa- natics, whom he detests, many of them intending the wildest excesses, irresponsibly take on imposing odds (as only they would) and destroy the English constitution—and so give birth to the rule of law."[23] Of course, as the Stuart volumes show in some detail, the "precious spark of liberty" that the Puritans managed to keep alive would eventually burst into a decades-long conflagration in the seventeenth century, with a balanced constitution emerging only from the resulting ashes.

Around a month after the first volume of the *History* was released, Hume wrote to Smith to ask about the work's reception. "Pray tell me, and tell me ingenuously," he urges, "What Success has my History met with among the Judges with you [i.e., in Glasgow] . . . ? Dare I presume, that it has been found worthy of Examination, and that its

Beauties are found to overballance its Defects?" The volume had sold well in Edinburgh, he reports, but he had not yet heard how it was faring in the crucial London market; the outcry over the work's alleged Tory bias was still to come. Hume would not have the chance to make corrections any time soon, he knew, given how many copies of the first edition had been printed, but he insists nonetheless that "in all Cases, I am desirous of storing up Instruction, and as you are now idle (I mean, having nothing but your Class to teach: Which to you is comparative Idleness) I will insist upon hearing from you."[24] Although Smith's response is, like all of his early letters to Hume, now lost, we know that he did provide comments on the work, for Hume's next letter, written a few weeks later, responds to some observations Smith had made about the puritanical "bigotry" of Parliament under Charles I and about "the Irish Massacre"—that is, the insurrection against the English in Ireland in 1641, which Hume had described as "the most barbarous [cruelty], that ever, in any nation, was known or heard of."[25]

Hume also seeks, in this letter, to clear up a misunderstanding regarding the Literary Society of Glasgow. Hume had joined the society in 1753, and as a member who did not reside in Glasgow he was expected to send a paper annually in his absence. He had not done so that year, but he suggests that in this case the oversight was in fact Smith's: "I beg you to make my Compliments to the Society, and to take the Fault on Yourself, If I have not executed my Duty, and sent them this time my Anniversary Paper. Had I got a Week's warning, I shou'd have been able to have supply'd them; I shou'd willingly have sent some Sheets of the History of the Commonwealth or Protectorship; but they are all of them out of my hand at present."[26] By this point, it seems, Smith was serving as Hume's representative in Glasgow.

In 1755 the Scottish literati kicked off yet another joint project, the *Edinburgh Review*. The handiwork of a coterie within the Select Society and edited chiefly by Alexander Wedderburn, the *Review* was slated to be a biannual periodical dedicated to reviewing new Scottish literary works. As one scholar notes, though, the contributors ultimately had a grander aim in mind: by announcing and advancing Scotland's place in the international republic of letters, they sought "nothing less than to incite a national Enlightenment."[27] Smith took a leading part in the enterprise: he not only was one of the journal's founders but also contributed to the first two issues—which, as it turned out, were the *only* two issues.[28] For the first, he supplied a critical review of Samuel Johnson's recently published dictionary, focusing on the entries for "but" and "humour." For the second, he wrote a public letter to the editors in which he urged them to broaden the *Review*'s coverage to include works from England and the Continent, providing in the process a wide-ranging overview of the state of learning in mid-eighteenth-century Europe.[29] As an example of the type of works that ought to be considered he included an ambivalent review of Jean-Jacques Rousseau's *Discourse on Inequality*.[30] These occasional pieces, though relatively brief and circulated anonymously, were Smith's first publications. Hume was not invited to join in the undertaking despite his status as Scotland's leading literary figure and his friendship with almost all of the *Review*'s contributors, and his recently published history of the Stuarts went entirely ignored in its pages.[31] Hume's exclusion is not altogether surprising, however, given the intellectual climate in Edinburgh at the time. Even without his inclusion the journal was shuttered after only two issues due to public clamor over its theological content, and Hume's name would have served as a conspicuous red flag to the pious, as he was just then facing potential excommunication from the Kirk.[32]

By the mid-1750s Hume had spent a decade and a half bombarding the public with his skeptical views. In some works, such as the *Treatise*, he had muted his irreligiosity somewhat on prudential grounds, while in others, such as the *First Enquiry*, he had been more outspoken, but the general tendency of his writings was now crystal clear. At times Hume seemed genuinely surprised that his contemporaries were so offended by what he said. On one occasion he complained that he had "written many Volumes, thro'out the whole of which there were but a few Pages that contained any reprehensible Matter, and yet for those few Pages I was abused and torn to pieces." One of his interlocutors responded that Hume reminded him of a notary public he knew who was convicted of forgery and "lamented the Hardship of his Case, that after having written many Thousand inoffensive Sheets, He shou'd be hang'd for one Line." Hume pronounced this retort "the best thing said to me I ever heard. Damn'd cutting indeed, but excellent."[33] Yet in his more honest or self-aware moments Hume knew very well what he was about. Just prior to the excommunication controversy he admitted to a friend that a "Tincture of Deism" often increases the sales of a book since "the Clamor, which it raises, commonly excites Curiosity, & quickens the Demand. The Book is much rail'd at and much read." He notes that a number of authors, including the Third Earl of Shaftesbury, Voltaire, and Montesquieu, "have certainly very much inhancd their Reputation by Liberties of this kind," and he acknowledges that "I myself owe part of that little Reputation I enjoy to some very strong Attempts of that Nature."[34]

The cumulative effect of Hume's broadsides was eventually too much for the pious, and in the mid-1750s the Popular Party within the Kirk mounted a concerted effort to excommunicate him. The campaign was led by a former army chaplain named George Anderson, whom Hume described as "the godly, spiteful, pious, splenetic, charitable, unrelenting, meek, persecuting, Christian, inhuman, peace-making, furious Anderson."[35] Matters first came to a head during the Kirk's General Assembly in 1755. Just as the assembly opened another leading member of the prosecution, James Bonar, published a pamphlet in which he charged Hume with espousing six objectionable views, each illustrated by a string of quotations from Hume's writings. The heresies were as follows:

1. All distinction betwixt virtue and vice is merely imaginary.
2. Justice has no foundation further than it contributes to public advantage.
3. Adultery is very lawful, but sometimes not expedient.
4. Religion and its ministers are prejudicial to mankind, and will always be found either to run into the heights of superstition or enthusiasm.
5. Christianity has no evidence of its being a divine revelation.
6. Of all the modes of Christianity Popery is the best, and the reformation from thence was only the work of madmen and enthusiasts.[36]

As a rap sheet, this was not half bad. Charges 2 and 5 are spot-on, and the fourth too is generally fair, though "always" is a bit strong. Charge

6 is less fair: as with the Whigs and Tories, Hume was fairly even-handed in doling out criticism to Catholic superstition and Protestant enthusiasm. For the first charge "imaginary" is not quite right, though Hume did see the distinction between virtue and vice as a purely human construct, one based on the sentiments rather than reason or any transcendent source. As for charge 3, Hume seems to have believed that the "lawfulness" of adultery depended somewhat on the context: it was less problematic in eighteenth-century France, where promiscuousness was widely accepted—even expected—among the aristocracy, for instance, than it was in Britain, where marital fidelity was the norm.[37] Hume knew that his stances on these subjects, when stated in such a bald form, would prove anathema to most of his contemporaries. He himself joked, a couple of years later, "I believe I shall write no more History; but proceed directly to attack the Lord's Prayer & the ten Commandments and the single Cat [i.e., the catechism of the Anglican Church]; and to recommend Suicide & Adultery: And so persist, till it shall please the Lord to take me to himself."[38]

However objectionable the devout may have deemed Hume's views, though, all of this was certainly a strange business. The prosecutors seem not to have noticed the irony inherent in threatening to kick Hume out of a club to which he did not claim membership. (Hume had not officially renounced his baptism, but it was clear to all involved that he no longer considered himself a member of the Kirk.) It is possible that the Popular Party's real target was less Hume himself than his many friends among the Moderate ministers—Hugh Blair, William Robertson, Alexander Carlyle, John Jardine, and John Home, among others—who were their chief rivals in Kirk politics. Bonar, for instance, concluded his indictment of Hume by reproaching "some of you"—that is, some unnamed ministers within the General Assembly—for living "in the greatest intimacy with one who represents the blessed Saviour as an impostor, and his religion as a cunningly devised fable."[39] In fact, Hume's friendship with the Moderates was the only real loss that he stood to suffer if the excommunication had gone forward. Excommunication carried no civil penalties in eighteenth-century Scotland, and it would no doubt have turned Hume into a martyr in enlightened circles across Europe, adding to his already considerable fame and to the popularity of his books.

Yet the threat to Hume's friendship with the Moderates was both real and important. These were some of his closest friends in Edinburgh, and his relationship with them was already slightly strained by their divergences on religious matters. A few years later Hume broached the subject with Blair, the minister of the biggest and most prestigious church in Scotland, St. Giles' Cathedral. "Whenever I have had the pleasure to be in your company," he writes, "if the discourse turned upon any common subject of literature or reasoning, I always parted from you both entertained and instructed. But when the conversation was diverted by you from this channel towards the subject of your profession; tho I doubt not but your intentions were very friendly towards me, I own I never received the same satisfaction: I was apt to be tired, and you to be angry." Hume thus offers a proposal: "I would therefore wish for the future, wherever my good fortune throws me in your way, that these topics should be forborne between us. I have, long since, done with all inquiries on such subjects, and am become incapable of instruction."[40] It would have proven far more difficult for them to simply agree to disagree if Hume had been officially censured and excommunicated. To remain on intimate terms with an excommunicated Hume would have jeopardized the standing of the Moderates within the Kirk, and they would have found it next to impossible to continue to defend him when the High-Flyers came calling. The Moderates won this battle, however: the General Assembly ended up suspending the charges against Hume and passing instead a general resolution expressing its horror at "the prevalence of *infidelity and immorality*, the principles whereof have been . . . so openly avowed in several books published of late in the country, and which are but too well known amongst us."[41]

The Popular Party sought to renew the inquisition into Hume's writings in the 1756 meeting of the General Assembly, but to no avail. Before the sitting of the 1757 assembly, which Hume assumed would take aim at him again, he wrote to Smith: "Did you ever hear of such Madness and Folly as our Clergy have lately fallen into?" He expects, he says, "that the next Assembly will very solemnly pronounce the Sentence of Excommunication against me," but he blithely declares that "I do not apprehend it to be a Matter of any Consequence. What do you think?"[42] Fortunately for Hume this particular prophecy remained unfulfilled.

The prosecutors must have been sorely disappointed if they were hoping that the threat of excommunication would deter Hume from continuing to speak his mind. In 1757 he brought out a collection of writings titled *Four Dissertations*, the centerpiece of which was *The Natural History of Religion*. The volume also included an abridgement of the second book of the *Treatise*—the one on the passions— and two further essays, one on why we find pleasure in watching tragedies and the other seeking a standard by which to measure taste. The latter was a last-minute replacement for a pair of essays questioning the immorality of suicide and the immortality of the soul. At the urging of friends, perhaps including Smith, Hume decided to withdraw both of these pieces, though during his final illness he would revive the possibility of publishing them posthumously alongside the *Dialogues Concerning Natural Religion*.[43] We do not know what exactly persuaded Hume to retract the essays. In 1772 he recalled having "repented" immediately after sending them to his publisher, declaring that "from my abundant Prudence I suppress'd" these pieces.[44] Yet abundantly prudent the rest of the volume was not: *The Natural History of Religion* is perhaps the most openly hostile of all of Hume's works, published and unpublished, toward Christianity. Witness his brazen declaration in the concluding chapter: "Examine the religious principles, which have, in fact, prevailed in the world. You will scarcely be persuaded, that they are any thing but sick men's dreams: Or perhaps will regard them more as the playsome whimsies of monkies in human shape, than the serious, positive, dogmatical asseverations of a being, who dignifies himself with the name of rational."[45] Once again, then, Hume's response to a charge of impiety was to set about earning it.

The Natural History of Religion, like Smith's *Principles Which Lead and Direct Philosophical Enquiries*, examines how various elements of human nature combine to generate religious belief and devotion. Hume too provides a thoroughly naturalistic—and thoroughly deflating—account of the process, one that revolves primarily around human weaknesses such as fear, cowardice, and ignorance. While Hume agrees with Smith that people turn to the idea of invisible, intelligent powers in hopes of gaining a sense of control over the world around them, he insists that in fact religion tends to *increase* people's fears and anxieties. Once the gods enter the picture, after all, we have to worry not just about the ills of the natural world—storms, droughts, floods, and the like—but also about propitiating powerful and potentially fickle beings, about the state of our souls, and about the possibility of everlasting punishment. Hume also joins Smith in positing that the earliest religions were polytheistic and that the idea of a single God arrived on the scene comparatively late, but he goes on, as Smith had not, to offer an extended comparison of polytheism and monotheism, to the great detriment of the latter. Indeed, almost the entire second half of the work is devoted to showing that polytheistic religions tend to be more tolerant, more conducive to real (as opposed to "monkish") virtue, more reasonable, and more credible.

The penultimate chapter of the work is quite bluntly titled "Bad Influence of Popular Religions on Morality." Hume contends that most religious devotees of all stripes tend to "seek the divine favour, not by virtue and good morals . . . but either by frivolous observances, by intemperate zeal, by rapturous extasies, or by the belief of mysterious and absurd opinions."[46] The reason for this, he submits, is that everyday moral behavior—doing what is useful and agreeable, for ourselves and for others—does not seem to them sufficiently elevated or pure, sufficiently removed from this-worldly concerns. Pious individuals typically seek to go *beyond* ordinary morality, to *suppress* their natural inclinations, in hopes of thereby currying special divine favor. This very effort, however, tends to subvert true morality by impeding the normal operations of sympathy; the mere feelings of others cannot hope to compete, in the minds of the devout, with the will of God. "Hence," Hume writes, "the greatest crimes have been found, in many instances, compatible with a superstitious piety and devotion: Hence it is justly regarded as unsafe to draw any certain inference in favour of a man's morals from the fervour or strictness of his religious exercises." In fact, he argues that "enormities of the blackest dye have been rather apt to produce superstitious terrors, and encrease the religious passion" since the perpetrators of these enormities feel the need to somehow expiate their sins, whereas during the "calm sun-shine of the mind, these spectres of false divinity never make their appearance."[47] This may be Hume's most forthright and uncompromising case for the pernicious effects of religion anywhere in his corpus.

On receiving his copies of the *Four Dissertations* from his bookseller in London Hume promised to send one to Smith "by the first Glasgow Waggon," requesting that he "do me the Favour of accepting this Trifle." He notes that Smith had read each of the pieces in manuscript form but that he "will find that on the natural History of Religion somewhat amended in point of Prudence." (What an even less discreet version of the work might have looked like we can only guess.)[48] Hume optimistically forecasts, for some inexplicable reason, that "I do not apprehend, that it will much encrease the Clamour against me."[49] The usual clamor arose almost immediately, of course, the leading voices coming this time from a pair of friends, William Warburton and Richard Hurd, both of whom were prominent Anglican clergymen; they would eventually become Bishop of Gloucester and Bishop of Worcester, respectively.[50] Hume comments in *My Own Life* that their pamphlet contained "all the illiberal petulance, arrogance, and scurrility, which distinguish the Warburtonian school" and that it "gave me some consolation for the otherwise indifferent reception of my performance."[51]

After the *Four Dissertations* was released Hume was uncertain which direction to turn his pen next, so he asked for Smith's advice: "I am somewhat idle at present; and somewhat undetermin'd as to my next Undertaking. Shall I go backwards or forwards in my History?" Hume had completed both Stuart volumes by this point and was trying to decide whether to go back in time to write on the Tudors or to proceed forward from 1689. "I think you us'd to tell me," he recalls, "that you approvd more of my going backwards. The other woud be the more popular Subject; but I am afraid, that I shall not find Materials sufficient to ascertain the Truth; at least, without settling in London: Which I own, I have some Reluctance to. I am settled here [i.e., in Edinburgh] very much to my Mind; and wou'd not wish, at my Years, to change the Place of my abode."[52] Hume was just forty-six when he wrote this letter; his reluctance to move "at my Years" offers a striking reminder of how just short life expectancies were in eighteenth-century Europe. As we have seen, Hume did end up following Smith's advice at last by tackling the Tudor period next. He told another friend that he began writing these volumes "because I was tir'd of Idleness, & found reading alone, after I had often perus'd all good Books, (which I think is soon done) somewhat a languid Occupation."[53] As for the other question raised in the letter to Smith, Hume would continue to live in Edinburgh for most of the next five years, but he was far from settled for good. He ends the letter, as Smith must have come to expect by this point, with a reproof for failing to visit more frequently: "Pray why did we not see you this Winter?"[54]

Given Smith's reluctance to make the trip from Glasgow as often as Hume wished, Hume decided to see if he could persuade him to move to Edinburgh on a more permanent basis. In 1758 Hume and some of his local friends concocted a scheme to try to induce Smith to take the Chair of the Law of Nature and Nations—essentially, philosophy of law—at Edinburgh University. Smith would have to buy out the current occupant, George Abercromby, but Abercromby was conspicuously negligent in his professorial duties and Hume was certain that the chair could be obtained relatively easily. This was also one of the best-endowed chairs in all of Scotland, so the move would eventually become a financial boon to Smith. "The only real Difficulty is then with you," Hume chides Smith in a letter of June 8. "Pray then consider, that this is perhaps the only Opportunity we shall ever have of getting you to Town." Given Smith's continuing interest in jurisprudence and his presumed desire to live among the Edinburgh literati—"we flatter ourselves that you rate our Company as something," he writes—Hume had high hopes of finally uniting with his friend for good. Lest Smith worry that he would face the kind of opposition from the pious that had sunk Hume's own attempt to obtain a chair at Edinburgh, he assures him that "Lord Milton can with his Finger, stop the foul Mouths of all the Roarers against Heresy."[55] (Milton was an influential judge, a patron of men of letters, and a personal acquaintance of Smith's.) Typically, we do not have Smith's response, but clearly the proposed plan came to naught, as Smith remained in Glasgow; Hume's plans had been foiled once again.

Hume himself left Edinburgh later that year, heading to London in September to see the Tudor volumes of the *History* through the press, though he returned the following summer. When he had last left Scotland nearly a decade earlier Hume was still relatively little known, but he was now one of the foremost men of letters in all of Britain. This trip to London was thus his first—though far from last—opportunity to rub shoulders with some of the other luminaries of the age beyond the Scottish literati; he got along extremely well with Benjamin Franklin, a bit less so with Edmund Burke, and not at all with Samuel Johnson. For all of Hume's talk about being tired of idleness and finding reading alone an overly languid occupation, his writing career was in fact winding down at this point. He would complete the final two volumes of *The History of England* in 1761, but after that he would write only an occasional essay or pamphlet here and there until the posthumous publication the *Dialogues Concerning Natural Religion*. Smith's publishing career, on the other hand, was finally about to begin in earnest.

CHAPTER 5

THEORIZING THE MORAL SENTIMENTS

(1759)

WHEREAS THE FIRST half of Hume's career was prolific by almost any measure, Smith was a far more deliberate writer. He published only two books and refused to rush either of them into print: *The Theory of Moral Sentiments* and *The Wealth of Nations* were published when he was thirty-five and fifty-two, respectively. Smith later admitted, "I am a slow a very slow workman, who do and undo everything I write at least a half a dozen of times before I can be tolerably pleased with it."[1] He also noted Hume's apparently easy prolixity with perhaps a touch of envy. According to Dugald Stewart, "Mr Smith observed to me, not long before his death, that after all his practice in writing, he composed as slowly, and with as great difficulty, as at first. He added, at the same time, that Mr Hume had acquired so great a facility in this respect, that the last volumes of his History were printed from his original copy, with a few marginal corrections."[2]

By 1759, after having occupied Glasgow's Chair of Moral Philosophy for seven years, Smith was finally ready to commit his maiden effort to the presses. He arranged for Andrew Millar to be his bookseller and for William Strahan to do the printing; both had served in the same capacity for most of Hume's books. Millar and Strahan were both Scots based in London and dominant figures in the book industry. Often working in partnership, the two of them—along with Thomas Cadell, Millar's protégé and then successor after Millar retired in 1767—counted among their authors not just Hume and Smith but also William Blackstone, Adam Ferguson, Henry Fielding, Ed-

ward Gibbon, Samuel Johnson, Lord Kames, Thomas Reid, and William Robertson.[3] Johnson commended Millar and Strahan for having
"raised the price of literature," and Hume and Smith were certainly
among those who benefited from their efforts.[4]

In stark contrast to Hume's first book, *The Theory of Moral Sentiments* was an immediate hit. Intelligent and thought-provoking
yet less abstruse than the *Treatise* and less overtly provocative than
most of Hume's other publications, the work found an eager audience
throughout Europe's republic of letters. Its fame was later outstripped
by *The Wealth of Nations* to such an extent that it was nearly forgotten
altogether for much of the nineteenth and twentieth centuries, but
during Smith's lifetime it was quite otherwise. Smith's second great
work did not appear until seventeen years later, so for the majority
of his career it was *The Theory of Moral Sentiments* that secured his
reputation as an important man of letters. Indeed, Smith himself is
reported to have always deemed it "much superior" to *The Wealth of
Nations*.[5]

The Theory of Moral Sentiments is an inquiry into what Smith, bor-
rowing from the title of Hume's *Second Enquiry*, calls "the principles of morals."[6] Virtually the entire inquiry—the questions Smith
takes up, the answers he gives, even the examples he uses—shows
unmistakable signs of Hume's influence. Strikingly, however, Hume
is never mentioned by name anywhere in the text. It has been suggested that Smith refused to invoke Hume's name because of his dis-
comfort regarding his friend's reputation for impiety, but this explanation is not terribly persuasive.[7] First of all, Smith engages not just
with Hume's *Second Enquiry* but also with the earlier presentation
of his moral theory in the *Treatise*, a work that Hume had published
anonymously, and in the eighteenth century it was considered a faux
pas to publicly identify the author of a book if that book did not
actually bear the author's name.[8] Moreover, by this point Hume had
long since regretted having ever published the *Treatise*, and Smith
was presumably well aware of his feelings on the subject. For either
or both of these reasons Smith may have avoided referring to Hume

by name in part for Hume's own sake. Even more decisively, Smith makes a number of unambiguous references to Hume throughout the book, at one point extolling him as "an ingenious and agreeable philosopher, who joins the greatest depth of thought to the greatest elegance of expression, and possesses the singular and happy talent of treating the abstrusest subjects not only with the most perfect perspicuity, but with the most lively eloquence."[9] No pious reader on the lookout for allusions and similarities to the Great Infidel could possibly miss them. A likelier explanation for Smith's avoidance of Hume's name can be found in Smith's understanding of his enterprise and the intended audience of the work. It is not just Hume's name that Smith refrains from citing: he rarely identifies *any* of the philosophers with whom he engages in the text, most likely because he wanted to appeal to the reader's everyday experience rather than to arcane-seeming debates and to keep the work accessible to as broad of an audience as possible.[10]

In Smith's view all moral theories prior to his own were not so much incorrect as one-sided, seeking to base right and wrong too exclusively on a single feature of our moral lives.[11] He regarded Hume's theory as the most accurate yet developed, but still a bit reductive or incomplete.[12] He thus sought to correct and extend Hume's views in order to provide a more comprehensive picture, one that would do full justice to the complexity of our moral lives. The bulk of the present chapter focuses on the areas where Smith diverges from or modifies Hume's views since these are the areas where he engages with Hume most directly, but it should be stressed at the outset that the similarities between their theories are far broader and more fundamental than the differences.[13]

To begin with, Smith joins Hume in viewing morality as an eminently practical and human phenomenon rather than one based on any kind of sacred, mysterious, or otherworldly authority. The distinction between right and wrong does not emanate from God's will, in their view, nor is it somehow written into the fabric of the cosmos; instead, it comes from us. As Smith writes, "What is agreeable to our moral faculties, is fit, and right, and proper to be done; the contrary wrong, unfit, and improper. . . . The very words, right, wrong, fit, improper . . . mean only what pleases or displeases those faculties."[14] Smith departs from Hume, we will see, in maintaining that belief in a providential God often encourages moral behavior, but he does not maintain, any more than Hume does, that right and wrong are in fact established directly by God's providence.

As the title of his book makes clear, Smith also follows Hume in positing that morality derives from the sentiments rather than reason. Whereas Hume devoted a good deal of effort to debunking moral rationalism, however, Smith essentially takes for granted that it had already been thoroughly dismantled by the efforts of Hume and Francis Hutcheson. Smith thus dismisses the rationalist view out of hand rather briskly, writing that "it is altogether absurd and unintelligible to suppose that the first perceptions of right and wrong can be derived from reason."[15] On the main issue separating Hume and Hutcheson, Smith sides with his friend rather than his teacher: in his view, morality springs not from an innate, God-given moral sense but rather from the operations of sympathy.[16] For Smith as for Hume, our moral sentiments are acquired and developed over time, not written directly into human nature.

Still further, Smith agrees with Hume that right and wrong are established by the sentiments that we feel when we adopt the proper perspective, one that corrects for personal biases and misinformation. In other words, they do not claim that whatever "feels right" *is* always right; that I feel like killing my enemy amid a fit of rage does not make it right for me to do so. Hume contends that in order to accurately judge an action or a character trait we must surmount our own circumstances and interests by adopting what he calls the "general point of view" or the "common point of view." That is, we must take into account the effects of a person's actions and character traits not just on ourselves but also on "those, who have any commerce with the person we consider."[17] In a like manner, Smith holds that proper moral judgment requires adopting the standpoint of an impartial spectator, one who knows all of the relevant circumstances and who has "no particular connexion" to any of the individuals involved in a given situation.[18] Smith's central argument in *The Theory of Moral Sentiments* is that the sentiments of an impartial spectator are what set the ultimate moral standard: actions and character traits that would earn such a spectator's approval are morally right and those that would earn his or her disapproval are morally wrong.

Hume's general point of view and Smith's impartial spectator have similar purposes and play similar roles in their respective moral theories. Indeed, Hume occasionally links the concept of the general point of view with the standpoint of "a judicious spectator" or "every spectator" or "every bystander."[19] Smith places greater emphasis than Hume does on how the internalized voice of the impartial spectator allows us to form judgments about our *own* actions and characters, thereby forming the basis for the conscience, but the basic mechanism by which right and wrong are determined is the same for both: morality rests on disinterested sentiments.[20] In fact, they use the same analogy to illustrate the point, comparing the disinterestedness of the moral perspective to the way the human mind naturally corrects for distance when viewing a faraway object. Just as I know that a distant mountain is in fact much bigger than it appears to be in my window, so I know that a given action or character trait is beneficial or harmful, agreeable or disagreeable when considered in itself, regardless of its effects on me personally.[21]

While the structure and underpinning of Smith's moral theory are much the same as Hume's, there are four major topics on which he deviates from or modifies his friend's views: sympathy, utility, justice, and religion.

The first and most fundamental of Smith's divergences from Hume concerns the nature of sympathy.[22] As usual, though, their points of departure are quite similar. First, Hume and Smith both use the term "sympathy" in a rather expansive sense to denote a kind of "fellow feeling" with any emotion, not just with suffering or sorrow. Sympathy is thus broader than compassion or pity, for Hume and Smith; it is closer to what we generally refer to as "empathy," though that term fits Smith's conception of sympathy somewhat better than Hume's. They are also in agreement in regarding this faculty as a fundamental feature of the human makeup. Not for them is the view, often associated with Thomas Hobbes and Bernard Mandeville, that all actions and feelings can ultimately be explained by, or reduced to, self-love. Hume proclaims that "whatever other passions we may be actuated by ... the soul or animating principle of all of them is sympathy," and Smith regards this faculty as so important that he devotes the entire first chapter of *The Theory of Moral Sentiments* to examining it.[23]

Yet their conceptions of this faculty are significantly different. According to Hume's account sympathy simply transmits the emotions of one person to another, more or less vividly depending on the circumstances. I see the joy that you exhibit after being awarded a long-awaited promotion and feel happy myself, for example, or I observe your sorrow on the unexpected death of a loved one and feel a similar sadness. Hume depicts this as a passive, almost mechanical process: he speaks of the way "a chearful countenance infuses a sensible complacency and serenity into my mind; as an angry or sorrowful one throws a sudden damp upon me."[24] He also compares the way sympathy conveys feelings between people to the way vibrating strings convey motion to one another—again, a spontaneous, entirely involuntary operation.[25] Indeed, at several points Hume goes so far as to describe sympathy as a kind of emotional "contagion."[26]

Smith conceives of sympathy as a much fuller, much more active projection into the situation of another person. He accepts that sympathy sometimes seems to operate in the simple, direct manner that Hume describes, such as when a smiling face cheers a spectator or a sorrowful countenance produces a sense of melancholy in someone who observes it—the very examples, of course, that Hume himself had used.[27] He insists, though, that we cannot really enter into the feelings of other people until we have imaginatively placed ourselves in their shoes; the mere observation of their expressions is usually insufficient. This is especially obvious for what Smith calls the "unsocial passions." We do not automatically feel anger when we see an angry person, for instance; rather, we need to know what caused this person's anger in order to "bring his case home to ourselves."[28] Even sympathy with another person's joy or grief, Smith maintains, generally depends on an appreciation of that person's circumstances. Imagine two individuals who exhibit identical signs of anguish, but the lamentations of the first are provoked by a paper cut while those of the second are caused by the death of a loved one; obviously, we would be far more likely to sympathize with the latter than the former. Smith concludes, therefore, that sympathy "does not arise so much from the view of the passion, as from that of the situation which excites it."[29] Smith's view has helpfully been described as a "projection" account of sympathy, as opposed to Hume's "contagion" account, since it involves an imaginative projection into the situation of another person.[30]

Demonstrating the superiority of a "projection" account of sympathy to a "contagion" account is in fact the main burden of the opening chapter of *The Theory of Moral Sentiments*; this place of honor indicates the importance that Smith attached to the topic.[31] That Smith is consciously engaging with Hume in this chapter is clear. In the second paragraph of the book, in the context of arguing that "we can form no idea of the manner in which [other people] are affected, but by conceiving what we ourselves should feel in the like situation," Smith writes that "it is the impressions of our own senses only, not those of his, which our imaginations copy."[32] As any reader of the *Treatise* or the *First Enquiry* knows, this language—the distinction between an "idea" and an "impression," and the "copying" of the latter by means of the imagination—is distinctly Humean. Smith uses this Humean terminology, however, to show that Hume's passive, quasi-mechanical conception of sympathy cannot adequately account for a number of familiar experiences from everyday life, and he tries to show how his own conception enables him to tell a fuller, more accurate story.

Smith concludes the chapter with four examples of sympathetic interaction that his understanding of this faculty handles better than Hume's does. Smith notes that we sometimes cringe on behalf of an individual who is acting rudely even if he is completely oblivious to the offense he is causing; we feel pity for someone who has lost the use of her reason even if she appears perfectly content; we are distressed for an infant who has a terrible disease even if he feels no great pain at the moment; and we can even feel sorry for the dead—who are, of course, no longer around to feel anything at all. In all of these cases we feel an emotion on behalf of others that they do not or cannot feel themselves. Hume would find it difficult to explain such experiences using his "contagion" account of sympathy, since the emotions are not actually present in the other individuals for us to "catch." Smith's "projection" account, on the other hand, explains them easily: we simply project ourselves into these individuals' situations. Here again it is plain that Smith is deliberately taking on Hume, as the first of his examples is drawn straight from the pages of the *Treatise*: Smith writes that "we blush for the impudence and rudeness of another, though he himself appears to have no sense of the impropriety of his own behaviour," while Hume had written that "we blush for the conduct of those, who behave themselves foolishly before us . . . tho' they show no sense of shame, nor seem in the least conscious of their folly."[33] Hume, however, considers this a "pretty remarkable" instance of sympathy and struggles to explain it, whereas Smith deems it relatively clear-cut.

Smith places such great stock in his improvement on Hume's account of sympathy not only because it enables him to provide a better explanation of experiences like these but also because it enables him to formulate a richer moral theory. Hume and Smith both regard sympathy as the starting point of all moral judgment, but once again Smith's account is more complex, and arguably more sophisticated. Hume's conception of moral judgment is grounded firmly in an external or observer's point of view: when considering an action or a character trait I observe its effects—whether useful or harmful, agreeable or disagreeable—by sympathizing with the feelings of all involved and then form my judgment accordingly. This kind of judgment corresponds roughly to what Smith dubs "merit and demerit," which he treats in Part 2 of *The Theory of Moral Sentiments*. Merit and demerit, as Smith uses the terms, relate to "the beneficial or hurtful nature of the effects" that a given action "aims at, or tends to produce."[34] Yet merit and demerit constitute only the second half of moral judgment, for Smith. The first half, which he treats in Part 1, centers on what Smith calls "propriety and impropriety," which relate to "the cause or object which excites" a given action.[35] In other words, Smith insists that complete moral judgment requires that we consider not just the *effects* of an action, but also the *circumstances* in which it occurred, including what *motivated* it. When we assess the moral goodness of a donation to charity, for instance, we care not just about how much good the money does but also about the circumstances and motivation of the donor. Does the donation represent a substantial portion of her income, or just a tiny fraction of a vast fortune? Was she genuinely moved by the plight of the unfortunate, or just looking to get a tax break?

Smith's "projection" account of sympathy allows for these kinds of judgments about context and motivation in a way that Hume's "contagion" account does not. Given that we do not just mechanically "catch" the feelings of others, whatever they happen to be, but instead imaginatively project ourselves into their situation, according to Smith, there is room for us to judge whether their feelings are the right ones, given their circumstances. Again, it matters not just that someone is feeling happy or sad or angry, or even how he acts on his feelings, but also whether his happiness or sadness or anger is *warranted*. Smith's more complex conception of sympathy thus plays a central role in his moral theory. For Smith, we judge the *propriety* of an action through "a direct sympathy with the affections and motives of the person who acts" and we judge the *merit* of that action through "an indirect sympathy with the gratitude of the person who is, if I may say so, acted upon."[36] In other words, moral judgment requires not just an external or observer's point of view, as in Hume's theory, but the active adoption of the perspective of each individual involved in a given situation. While Hume and Smith both place sympathy at the heart of their respective moral theories, then, Smith's richer conception of sympathy allows for a correspondingly richer moral theory.

Smith's most explicit and detailed engagement with Hume in *The Theory of Moral Sentiments* concerns the role of utility in Hume's outlook. This engagement appears principally in Part 4, much of which is directed at Hume. Smith opens this part of the book by discussing the claim of "an ingenious and agreeable philosopher"—obviously, his good friend—that the beauty of physical objects derives in large part from our perception their utility.[37] Hume argues that we admire the beauty of, say, a well-built house because we sympathize with the sense of satisfaction and convenience that we assume its owner must gain from it. "Where any object has a tendency to produce pleasure in its possessor," he writes, "it is always regarded as beautiful."[38] Smith takes it as obvious that the appearance of utility bestows beauty on objects, and he accepts entirely Hume's explanation of *why* it does so, but he quickly moves on to add a further point, one that he claims, with obvious pride, "has not, so far as I know, been yet taken notice of by any body." Smith's insight is that the "fitness" or "happy contrivance of any production of art" is frequently "more valued, than the very end for which it was intended."[39] In other words, we often confuse means for ends and attach greater importance to the "fitness" of an object to produce pleasure—its *appearance* of convenience or efficiency—than we do to the pleasure it actually affords.

Beginning with some "frivolous" illustrations, Smith notes that if a person were to enter his living room and find the chairs sitting all askew he would be annoyed and would set about putting them in their proper order. Yet the only reason why he prefers the "proper" arrangement in the first place is that it is more convenient, and "to attain this conveniency he voluntarily puts himself to more trouble than all he could have suffered from the want of it; since nothing was more easy, than to have set himself down upon one of [the chairs], which is probably what he does when his labour is over." What this person really wanted, then, was not so much ease or convenience itself as "that arrangement of things which promotes it." Similarly, an individual who is "curious in watches" would scorn a timepiece that loses two minutes a day despite the fact that it would serve its real function—preventing her from being late—nearly as well as a more precise watch would. It is not the actual convenience of the better watch that she values, Smith suggests, so much as "the perfection of the machine" itself.[40]

Nor is it only in frivolous cases that we confuse means with ends in this manner: Smith maintains that we make the same mistake in some of "the most serious and important pursuits of both private and public life."[41] He claims, in fact, that the pursuit of wealth and power that drives the economy and indeed the entire process of civilization falls in the same category. The reason why most people strive for these things, Smith holds, is that we instinctively sympathize with the lifestyles of the rich and powerful—their magnificent palaces, their luxurious carriages, their many servants—and assume that these things must make them supremely content.[42] A moment of reflection should easily convince us that this is not the case, that "power and riches" do little to ensure real happiness and in fact leave their possessor "always as much, and sometimes more exposed than before, to anxiety, to fear, and to sorrow; to diseases, to danger, and to death."[43] Yet in hopes of attaining the pleasures that wealth and power appear to afford we voluntarily undergo far more toil and anxiety than we could have ever saved by having them. We not only confuse the means (wealth and power) for the ends (true happiness) but unwittingly sacrifice the ends for the sake of the means. Smith thus builds on Hume's claim about the beauty of utility to make a decidedly un-Humean point, calling attention to an important drawback of the commercial society that Hume admired so unreservedly.[44]

In the second section of Part 4 Smith turns from the beauty that utility confers on physical objects like houses and watches to the beauty it confers on human actions and character traits. This was, of course, a key feature of Hume's moral theory, as Smith immediately observes: "The same ingenious and agreeable author who first explained why utility pleases, has been so struck with this view of things, as to resolve our whole approbation of virtue into a perception of this species of beauty which results from the appearance of utility." He then summarizes Hume's central claim that we naturally approve of—and hence deem virtuous—qualities that are either useful or agreeable, either for ourselves or for others. Smith begins his criticism of this view with a point of agreement, namely that useful qualities are universally approved of while harmful ones are universally disapproved of. Yet he goes on to maintain, in opposition to Hume, that "it is not the view of this utility or hurtfulness which is either the first or principal source of our approbation and disapprobation." In other words, while we approve of useful actions and character traits, in Smith's view, we do not approve of them, at least in the first instance, *because* of their utility. Our feelings of approval may be "enhanced and enlivened" by considerations of utility, he concedes, but he insists that these feelings are "originally and essentially different from" such considerations.[45]

Smith offers two arguments on this score. First, he writes that "it seems impossible that the approbation of virtue should be a sentiment of the same kind with that by which we approve of a convenient and well-contrived building; or that we have no other reason for praising a man than that for which we commend a chest of drawers."[46] That is, if we approved of virtuous actions and character traits solely because of their utility then it would be difficult to see why they *matter* so much to us, why moral considerations *move* us as much as they do.[47] Few people would be willing to risk their lives for a chest of drawers, no matter how useful or beautiful. This criticism of Hume's theory is one that Hume anticipated and in effect sought to rebut in advance. His response is simply that the pleasure we take in the observation of a useful object is, as a matter of empirical fact, different in quality from the pleasure we take in observing a virtuous action or character trait.[48] Here again, though, Hume struggles to explain this fact, noting that "there is something very inexplicable in this variation of our feelings," whereas Smith can account for it much more easily.[49] According to Smith's view, after all, the psychological process by which we evaluate an inanimate object is fundamentally different from that by which we evaluate an action or a character trait. We can sympathize with the owner of a chest of drawers but not with the chest itself, whereas we can and do project ourselves into the situations of both individuals who act and those who are acted upon, thereby allowing us to form judgments about not just the merit of an action but also its propriety.

This leads to Smith's second argument as to why utility is not the first or principal source of moral approval, namely that there is a sense of propriety involved in moral judgment that cannot be reduced to considerations of utility, one that plays a crucial role in our everyday interactions even if it tends to be overlooked by philosophers like Hume.[50] "When a philosopher goes to examine why humanity is approved of, or cruelty condemned," Smith writes, clearly thinking of Hume among others, "he does not always form to himself, in a very clear and distinct manner, the conception of any one particular action either of cruelty or of humanity, but is commonly contented with the vague and indeterminate idea which the general names of those qualities suggest to him." When "men of reflection and speculation" consider character traits in this abstract manner, Smith claims, the effects of these traits on society at large immediately jump out at them, and they invariably conclude that these effects are the ultimate and proper grounds for moral evaluation. Yet when we observe an action in real life, he insists, we naturally consider the circumstances and the motives of the individual who is acting and the specific effects of this action on particular individuals, not just the general effects that this type of action tends to have on society as a whole.[51] Our immediate, everyday moral judgments, that is to say, focus on concrete particulars more than abstract generalities. When we witness an act of benevolence or courage—say, the rescue of a child from a burning building—we do not stop to reflect on the usefulness of this type of action to society before approving of it. Smith admits that abstract considerations of utility may reinforce the moral judgments that we form in this more immediate manner, but he insists that they always enter the picture later, as a kind of afterthought; they are not the original or principal determinants of our judgments.[52] Smith's criticism of Hume here is exactly the kind of criticism that Hume himself frequently levels at others: Hume, Smith suggests, thinks about these matters too rationally or abstractly—too much like a philosopher—and thereby overlooks phenomena that are readily apparent in everyday life.[53]

Smith's reading of Hume's moral theory, it must be admitted, is somewhat oversimplified, at least on the score of utility. Hume's central claim, recall, is that the virtues are not just the qualities that are *useful* for ourselves or others but also those that we or others find immediately *agreeable*. Smith tends to overlook this second part of the equation and so paints Hume as more of a moral utilitarian than he actually was.[54] This error does not affect the main lines of Smith's critique, though it does raise the question of how his understanding of his closest friend's moral theory could have been so one-sided. To be fair to Smith, this misreading is one that Hume almost invites. Hume spends the vast majority of the *Second Enquiry*—sections 2 through 6, a total of fifty-one pages in the modern critical edition—discussing the "useful" virtues and devotes only two later, relatively short sections—sections 7 and 8, comprising thirteen pages—to the "agreeable" ones. He is also willing to state his case in strong, almost exaggerated terms in order to make a point, as when he writes that utility is "a foundation of the chief part of morals."[55] So easy is it to read Hume as a moral utilitarian that this misinterpretation persists to this day among many scholars. The fact that Hume did not correct the mistake before Smith committed it to print, though, would seem to suggest that he did not read *The Theory of Moral Sentiments* until after its publication.[56] This is a bit surprising, given Smith's great esteem for Hume as a thinker and their personal closeness. Perhaps it is an indication of Smith's desire, as he set out on his publishing career, to assert his intellectual independence even from his friend.

———————◆———————

Another, closely related topic on which Smith diverges from Hume is the foundation of justice.[57] Here too they begin from similar premises. Whereas philosophers from Plato to the present have often conceived of justice in a broad way, equating it with notions like fairness or desert, Hume and Smith use the term in a distinctively narrow and entirely negative sense. For both, the virtue of justice entails nothing more (or less) than refraining from harming the life, liberty, or property of others.[58] Hume and Smith also agree that justice is the one virtue that is absolutely necessary for the very survival of society. Hume draws an analogy between justice and "the building of a vault, where each individual stone would, of itself, fall to the ground" unless supported by the others; adherence to the rules of justice is, in other words, necessary to maintain the structure of society.[59] Smith similarly describes justice as "the main pillar that upholds the whole edifice," which, if removed, would cause "the immense fabric of human society" to "crumble into atoms."[60] Finally, Hume and Smith both hold that justice, alone among the virtues, is best enforced through a system of rigid rules. It is impossible to formulate precise guidelines for how to act courageously or generously or modestly, for instance, but it is both possible and necessary to do so for respecting the life, liberty, and property of others.[61]

For all of their agreement about the *content* of justice and its indispensability to society, though, Hume and Smith have very different views of where this virtue comes from. Hume argues at length,

CHAPTER 5

in both the *Treatise* and the *Second Enquiry*, that the virtue of justice is founded entirely on its utility; we approve of just conduct because of our sympathy with the public interest. This is why he notoriously dubs justice an "artificial" virtue in the *Treatise*: rules respecting property rights are human conventions that we develop as we realize how necessary they are for the establishment and maintenance of social order. Smith's view differs from Hume's in two key ways. First, Smith argues that our sense of justice springs not from reflection on its usefulness but rather from the sentiment of resentment. When we witness an act of injustice—the murder of an innocent person or the theft of her life's savings, say—we sympathize with the victim and our feelings of resentment on her behalf lead us to want to punish the wrongdoer. We do not have to sit back and think about the long-term impact of such actions on society in order to form our judgment; a sense of outrage or resentment arises spontaneously within us, "antecedent to all reflection upon the utility of punishment."[62] Justice, that is to say, is a natural rather than an artificial virtue, for Smith. Second, Smith argues that when we witness an unjust action our disapproval derives not principally from sympathy with the interests of society writ large, as Hume claims, but rather from sympathy with the injured party. "When a single man is injured, or destroyed," he writes, "we demand the punishment of the wrong that has been done to him, not so much from a concern for the general interest of society, as from a concern for that very individual who has been injured."[63]

Again, Smith agrees with Hume that rules of justice *are* useful, indeed indispensable, for society as a whole, but he insists that it is not the usefulness of justice that leads us to approve of it. He refers obliquely to his friend on this point, writing that "as society cannot subsist unless the laws of justice are tolerably observed . . . the consideration of this necessity, it has been thought, was the ground upon which we approved of the enforcement of the laws of justice by the punishment of those who violated them."[64] Smith insists, however, that this kind of abstract consideration is not what really animates our disapproval of injustice. After all, "all men, even the most stupid and unthinking, abhor fraud, perfidy, and injustice, and delight to see them punished. But few men have reflected upon the necessity of justice to the existence of society, how obvious soever that necessity may appear to be."[65] Here again Smith turns Hume's own typical mode of argument against him, showing that Hume's view accords too much influence to reason and abstract reflection and not enough to the sentiments that move us in everyday life. Indeed, it has been said that on the subject of justice Smith criticizes Hume "for not being sufficiently Humean."[66]

Smith's attitude toward religion in *The Theory of Moral Sentiments* falls somewhere on the spectrum between ambiguous and ambivalent, but this in itself marks a notable departure from Hume's insistence that it is almost entirely pernicious. To begin with, throughout the book Smith refers periodically to God and the idea of a providential order. These references constitute the primary evidence for those who read him as a committed deist, but several caveats are in order. First, when Smith ventures onto religious terrain his writing is frequently evasive or equivocal; as one scholar observes, his references to a providential God are often "attended with circumlocutions, indirect speech, and frequent use of the verb 'to seem.'"[67] Moreover, these references have the appearance of a supplement or addendum to a self-standing moral theory. As has often been noted, the basic framework of Smith's theory—according to which morality develops from human sentiments and the ultimate standard of right and wrong is determined by the sentiments of an impartial spectator—does not rely in any way on religious premises or a divine will.[68] Finally, Smith rarely invokes "the author of Nature" (his favorite term for the deity) to explain the otherwise inexplicable. On the contrary, he recurrently invokes this-worldly factors like our emotional and intellectual needs to explain our belief in God and an afterlife. As another commentator remarks, "when one goes through all the theological passages in *The Theory of Moral Sentiments*, it stands out as a striking feature in many, if not most, of them that he is really proposing a theory of human nature."[69]

Still, Smith generally describes the religious impulse in fairly sympathetic terms. In a marked divergence from Hume's argument in *The Natural History of Religion*—and to some degree his own argument in *The Principles Which Lead and Direct Philosophical Enquiries*—he suggests that religious beliefs and hopes often spring from what is best in us rather than what is worst. "We are led to the belief of a future state," Smith writes, "not only by the weaknesses, by the hopes and fears of human nature, but by the noblest and best principles which belong to it, by the love of virtue, and by the abhorrence of vice and injustice."[70] (Note, though, that he still sees this belief as motivated *partly* by human weaknesses and fears.) Moreover, Smith insists that religious faith has important practical benefits. It provides comfort in the face of death, for instance, as well as hope and consolation for those who are wronged or wrongly judged here on earth.[71] He also suggests, in stark contrast to Hume, that religion tends to underwrite rather than undermine morality. Religion is neither the ultimate source of right and wrong nor a prerequisite of moral conduct, in Smith's view, but it does commonly reinforce people's adherence to moral norms. After all, people are more likely to respect and obey the "general rules of morality" that their society has formed—more likely to hold them sacred—if they regard these rules as "the commands and laws of the Deity, who will finally reward the obedient, and punish the transgressors of their duty."[72] Put another way, Smith views religion not as a foundation for morality, or even a pillar, but rather a buttress: it provides support from the outside.

Smith's suggestion that belief in God and an afterlife helps to reinforce morality is frequently invoked as proof of his fundamental religiosity. For instance, Lord Brougham, a prominent nineteenth-century commentator, notes that "stern votaries of religion have complained of [Smith's] deficiencies in piety, chiefly because of his letter upon the death of his old and intimate friend Mr. Hume"—that is, the *Letter to Strahan*—but then contends that Smith clearly "regarded his friend as an exception to the rule that religion has a powerful and salutary influence on morals, because he has most forcibly stated his opinion, that whenever the principles of religion . . . are not perverted or corrupted 'the world justly places a double confidence in the rectitude of the religious man's behaviour.' . . . Surely, Dr. Johnson himself could desire no stronger testimony to religion, no more severe condemnation of infidelity."[73] Yet such inferences are not terribly convincing. First and most obviously, the idea that belief in God and an afterlife helps to reinforce morality suggests that religion has salutary effects but not necessarily that it is true. Moreover, Smith's claims on this score are not nearly as unequivocal as is sometimes suggested. The sentence from which Brougham quotes, for example, is hedged with a number of qualifications that can only be described as Humean in character. Smith writes that "wherever the natural principles of religion are not corrupted by the factious and party zeal of some worthless cabal; wherever the first duty which it requires, is to fulfill all the obligations of morality; wherever men are not taught to regard frivolous observances, as more immediate duties of religion, than acts of justice and beneficence; and to imagine, that by sacrifices, and ceremonies, and vain supplications, they can bargain with the Deity for fraud, and perfidy, and violence"—then, and then only, he claims, "the world . . . justly places a double confidence in the rectitude of the religious man's behaviour."[74] Hume himself may not have disagreed with this claim; he would merely point out that these requirements are rarely all met at once. Indeed, some of Smith's wording here recalls Hume's own contention that the pious tend to seek God's favor not through everyday moral behavior but rather "by frivolous observances, by intemperate zeal, by rapturous extasies, or by the belief of mysterious and absurd opinions."[75] In the following chapter Smith goes on to note, once again in a Humean vein, that "false notions of religion are almost the only causes which can occasion any very gross perversion of our [moral] sentiments."[76] While Smith holds that belief in God and an afterlife often supports morality, then, he certainly does not conclude that it always does so. It is also noteworthy that Smith's later revisions of the book served to temper some of the first edition's claims on behalf of religion—a point that will be pursued further in the epilogue.

Hume was in London seeing the Tudor volumes of *The History of England* through the press when *The Theory of Moral Sentiments* was published in the spring of 1759. Smith naturally had a copy sent to him, and Hume's reply must rate as one of the most charming letters in the entire history of philosophy.[77] The letter opens with Hume thanking Smith for "the agreeable Present of your Theory" and reporting that he and Alexander Wedderburn had given copies of the work to a number of highly placed politicians and influential aristocrats, as well as to "an Irish Gentleman, who wrote lately a very pretty Treatise on the Sublime"—Edmund Burke, whose *A Philosophical Enquiry into the Origin of Our Ideas of the Sublime and Beautiful* had appeared two years earlier. (Hume noted in his next letter to Smith that Burke "was much taken with your Book," and this assessment was amply confirmed by Burke's first letter to Smith, written a few months later, as well as by Burke's review of the book in the *Annual Register*.)[78] All of the recipients Hume mentions would be crucial in spreading the word about the book, and perhaps in advancing the career of its author. "I have delayd writing to you," Hume then tells Smith, "till I cou'd tell you something of the Success of the Book, and coud prognosticate with some Probability whether it shoud be finally damnd to Oblivion, or shoud be registerd in the Temple of Immortality. Tho' it has been publishd only a few Weeks, I think there appear already such strong Symptoms, that I can almost venture to fortell its Fate. It is in short this—."

Having thus piqued Smith's interest to the utmost of his ability, Hume then concocts distraction after distraction to delay delivering the news Smith was waiting for. First, he is interrupted by a "foolish impertinent Visit" from a fellow Scot, which leads him to discuss a potential opening for a Professor of Church History at Glasgow University, for which he hopes Smith "will have our Friend, [Adam] Ferguson, in your Eye," and then to dilate on the merits and defects of some recent publications by Scottish authors. After mentioning William Wilkie's epic poem *The Epigoniad*, he writes: "As I doubt not but you consult the Reviews sometimes at present"—a safe assumption, given that Smith was anxiously awaiting the appraisals of *The Theory of Moral Sentiments*—"you will see in the critical Review a Letter upon that Poem; and I desire you to employ your Conjectures in finding out the Author. Let me see a Sample of your Skill in knowing hands by your guessing at the Person." (The author of the anonymous letter was Hume himself.) He also fears that Lord Kames's *Historical Law Tracts* will not be warmly received: "A man

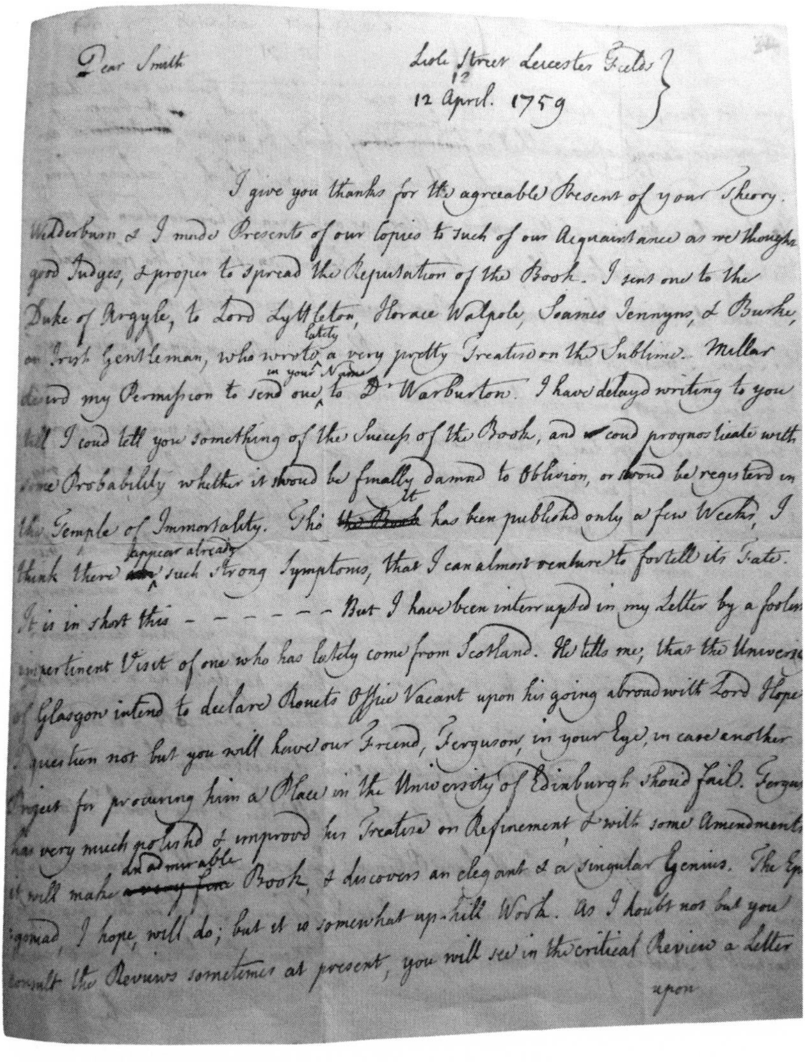

FIGURE 5.1 Hume's congratulatory letter to Smith on *The Theory of Moral Sentiments* must rate as one of the most charming letters in the entire history of philosophy. Photograph by the author, reproduced by permission of the National Library of Scotland (MS 3942).

might as well think of making a fine Sauce by a Mixture of Worm-wood and Aloes as an agreeable Composition by joining Metaphysics and Scotch Law."

Hume then momentarily recovers himself: "But to return to your Book, and its Success in this Town, I must tell you——A Plague of Interruptions! I orderd myself to be deny'd; and yet here is one that has broke upon me again." This time the intrusion is occasioned by a visit from a man of letters, which prompts Hume to discuss the recent works of Claude-Adrien Helvétius and Voltaire. He particularly praises *Candide*, which he says "is full of Sprightliness and Impiety, and is indeed a Saytre upon Providence, under Pretext of criticizing the Leibnitian System"—that is, Leibniz's argument in the *Theodicy* that ours is the best of all possible worlds. It is noteworthy that Hume seems to suppose that *Candide*'s impiety would serve to recommend it to Smith.[79]

Hume continues toying with his friend: "But what is all this to my Book? say you.—My Dear Mr Smith, have Patience: Compose yourself to Tranquillity: Show yourself a Philosopher in Practice as well as Profession: Think on the Emptiness, and Rashness, and Futility of the common Judgements of Men: How little they are regulatd by Reason in any Subject, much more in philosophical Subjects, which so far exceed the Comprehension of the Vulgar. . . . Nothing indeed can be a stronger Presumption of Falsehood than the Approbation of the Multitude." Finally, he lets the penny drop: "Supposing, therefore, that you have duely prepard yourself for the worst by all these Reflections; I proceed to tell you the melancholy News, that your Book has been very unfortunate: For the Public seem disposd to applaud it extremely. It was lookd for by the foolish People with some Impatience; and the Mob of Literati are beginning already to be very loud in its Praises." Hume reports that several bishops had expressed their great admiration of the work and teases, "you may conclude what Opinion true Philosophers will entertain of it, when these Retainers to Superstition praise it so highly." After relating a string of accolades from various friends and influential personages, Hume notes that Andrew Millar, their mutual bookseller, "exults and brags that two thirds of the Edition are already sold, and that he is now sure of Success. You see what a Son of the Earth that is, to value

Books only by the Profit they bring him. In that View, I believe it may prove a very good Book."

The pleasure that Hume took in Smith's success is obvious, and it appears all the more generous when we recall the disappointment that he had experienced in the reception of his own first book two decades earlier. Clearly, he wanted to do his part to ensure that Smith's did not meet a similar fate. Hume concludes the letter with a wry allusion to his own literary fortunes: "In recompense for so many mortifying things, which nothing but Truth coud have extorted from me, and which I coud easily have multiply'd to a great Number; I doubt not but you are so good a Christian as to return good for evil and flatter my Vanity, by telling me, that all the Godly in Scotland abuse me for my Account of John Knox and the Reformation"—a reference, of course, to the Tudor volumes of *The History of England*. In his next letter Hume intimated, not altogether generously, that in fact Smith's book may have benefited from the clamor against his own *History*: "Are the Bigots much in Arms on account of this last Volume?" he asks. "Robertson's Book"—that is, William Robertson's recently published *History of Scotland*—"has great Merit; but it was visible that he profited here by the Animosity against me. I suppose the Case was the same with you."[80] This single, apparently offhand line is the only indication in the surviving record that Hume may have been a bit envious of his younger friend's immediate success.

It was not only in private that Hume sought to further Smith's cause: he also wrote an anonymous review of *The Theory of Moral Sentiments* for the *Critical Review* in May 1759, seeking to call further attention to it.[81] Throughout the review Hume heaps on the praise. He describes how Smith theorizes with "that boldness which naturally accompanies genius"; he predicts that "the ingenuity, and (may we venture to say it) the solidity of his reasonings ought to excite the languid attention of the public, and procure him a favorable reception"; he speaks of the clearness of the principles, the force and vigor of the argumentation and style of "this very ingenious writer"—all in the first few paragraphs.[82] In his concluding remarks Hume refuses to pronounce on the ultimate soundness of Smith's theory, insisting that "time alone [is] the great test of truth," but he extols "the solidity and force of our author's genius" as well as his "lively, perspicuous, manly, unaffected stile," remarking that "though he penetrates the depths of philosophy, he still talks like a man of the world."[83]

At the same time, Hume subtly alludes to some of the philosophical differences between Smith and himself. As was customary at the time, Hume's review consists more of summary and extensive quotation than critical analysis, but the limited commentary that he does offer provides some clues as to his own position. Where he describes the basic features of Smith's moral theory that coincide with his own—its foundation in "fact and experience" rather than abstract reasoning, the central role of sympathy, and so on—Hume gives his full-throated assent. That sympathy is a central feature of human nature, he says, "surely, without the greatest obstinacy, cannot be disputed." Yet on the more specific points where the two diverge, he hedges somewhat. When he comes to Smith's "projection" account of sympathy Hume writes circumspectly that Smith "endeavours to account for" sympathy in this manner and that Smith's account "seems very natural and probable; but whether it be received or not, is not of great importance to our author's Theory." Similarly, Hume notes that it is via this kind of sympathy that Smith "hopes to explain" all types of moral approval and disapproval and then says that "*if* his deductions be as simple and convincing as his first fact or postulatum [i.e., that sympathy is part of human nature] is evident and unquestionable, we may venture to give him the preference above all writers who have made any attempt on this subject."[84] Even as he extols Smith's genius, then, he quietly indicates his disagreements.

The review also includes a number of typically playful touches from Hume. After summarizing Smith's claim that utility plays only a secondary role in generating moral approval, he asserts that Smith "subjoins many irrefragable arguments, by which he refutes the sentiments of Mr. Hume, who founded a great part of his moral system on the consideration of public utility." He does not have the space to expand on this point at length, he says, but "the reader, who will consult the author himself, will find, that philosophy scarce affords any thing more undeniable and conclusive."[85] It is doubtful that Hume really believed his views had been conclusively "refuted" by Smith, of course, not just because their outlooks overlap so broadly but also because, as we have seen, Smith slightly misrepresents Hume's moral theory in the process of contesting it, overstating the degree to which it rests on utility—a misrepresentation that Hume quietly corrects in the review.[86] As David Raynor notes, however, "it is not too difficult to imagine Hume 'diverting' himself with the thought that his enemies would buy [Smith's book] just to see him 'refuted.'"[87]

Hume's tongue is also placed firmly in cheek in the concluding paragraph, where he praises Smith for "the strict regard which [he] every where preserves to the principles of religion." Though some "pretenders to science" may suggest otherwise, he proclaims, it is ultimately impossible to "separate the philosopher from the lover of religion." Indeed, a *true* philosopher will deliberately limit his inquiries to subjects that pose no threat to the Christian faith: "every topic . . . which leads into impiety or infidelity, should be rejected with disdain and contempt." Happily, he declares, "our author seems every where sensible of so fundamental a truth," and he has thereby secured himself "if not against all error, which it is impossible for human nature entirely to avoid, at least against all error that is dangerous or pernicious."[88] This mock-pious harangue is clearly a winking nod to Smith's prudence on this front, and perhaps also an attempt to bolster Smith's efforts at avoiding censure from the devout. In the *Treatise* Hume had made the exact opposite case, writing that "there is no method of reasoning more common, and yet none more blameable, than in philosophical debates to endeavour to refute any hypothesis by a pretext of its dangerous consequences to religion and morality. When any opinion leads us into absurdities, 'tis certainly false; but 'tis not certain an opinion is false, because 'tis of dangerous consequence."[89] In any case, the publication of Smith's first book confirmed that he would be far more cautious than Hume with respect to religion and the religious in his writings, just as he was in his personal life.

In his congratulatory note on the publication of *The Theory of Moral Sentiments* Hume had politely refrained from mentioning any reservations he might have had about Smith's arguments in the work, but a few months later, just before Hume's return to Scotland, he wrote to Smith again to discuss one of the issues on which the two were at odds. "I am told that you are preparing a new Edition, and propose to make some Additions and Alterations, in order to obviate Objections," he writes. "I shall use the Freedom to propose one, which, if it appears to be of any Weight, you may have in your Eye." Interestingly, Hume does not so much as mention Smith's most explicit and extensive criticism of his own moral theory, concerning the role of utility in morality and justice, but instead heads straight for an even more fundamental issue. Hume's query has to do with the nature of sympathy: "I wish you had more particularly and fully prov'd, that all kinds of Sympathy are necessarily Agreeable. This is the Hinge of your System, and yet you only mention the Matter cursorily." In the book's second chapter Smith had argued that mutual sympathy is intrinsically pleasing: we naturally enjoy the feeling of sentimental concord—of being on the same emotional page as someone else—and the sense of approbation that attends this kind of "fellow-feeling." Hume contends, however, in line with his "contagion" account of sympathy, that "there is a disagreeable Sympathy, as well as an agreeable," since "the Sympathetic Passion is a reflex Image of the principal," and so "it must partake of the Qualities, and be painful where that is so." In other words, we feel pain rather than pleasure when we sympathize with a person who is suffering. If we really took pleasure in *all* instances of sympathy, Hume says, "an Hospital woud be a more entertaining Place than a Ball."[90]

While Hume seems to have regarded this difficulty as a deep one, embedded in the very "Hinge" of Smith's system, Smith himself considered it a fairly minor and easily resolved issue. Indeed, in the second edition of *The Theory of Moral Sentiments* he dealt with the problem with the simple addition of a footnote: "It has been objected to me," he writes, "that as I found the sentiment of approbation, which is always agreeable, upon sympathy, it is inconsistent with my system to admit any disagreeable sympathy. I answer, that in the sentiment of approbation there are two things to be taken notice of; first, the sympathetic passion of the spectator; and, secondly, the emotion which arises from his observing the perfect coincidence between this sympathetic passion in himself, and the original passion in the person principally concerned. This last emotion, in which the sentiment of approbation properly consists, is always agreeable and delightful. The other may either be agreeable or disagreeable, according to the nature of the original passion, whose features it must always, in some measure, retain."[91] In short, Smith argues that we can take pleasure in a harmony of sentiments even if the shared sentiment itself is disagreeable. Even while sharing grief over the death of a loved one, for instance, we can appreciate the very fact that we are on the same page as someone else.

It is plainly true that sympathy is often comforting to us when we experience a painful emotion—hence the sense of consolation that mourners generally gain from the presence of visitors. As Smith notes, in such a situation sympathy "alleviates grief by insinuating into the heart almost the only agreeable sensation which it is at that time capable of receiving": the very "sweetness of . . . sympathy" itself.[92] Here Smith's account seems to be on the mark, and it is difficult to see how Hume's "contagion" account of sympathy could account for this phenomenon. It is less obviously the case, however, that the reverse is true—that we ourselves gain pleasure from sympathizing with someone *else* who is experiencing a painful emotion. This seems to have been the core of Hume's objection: we do not choose to spend our days in hospitals and funeral parlors simply in order to sympathize with patients and mourners. Smith was adamant, however, that even in this sort of case the pleasure of mutual sympathy is frequently sufficient to outweigh the pain of the emotion being sympathized with: "We run not only to congratulate the successful, but to condole with the afflicted; and the pleasure which we find in the conversation of one whom in all the passions of his heart we can entirely sympathize with, seems to do more than compensate for the painfulness of that sorrow with which the view of his situation affects us."[93] In any event, Smith was clearly satisfied with his response to Hume's worry. In a letter to Gilbert Elliot he enclosed a draft of his response to the objection Hume had posed, opining that "I think I have entirely discomfited [i.e., rebutted] him."[94]

Altogether, Hume's response to *The Theory of Moral Sentiments*— the mixture of praise, critical engagement, and unconditional support—was entirely characteristic of Hume's interactions with his friends. Smith had paid Hume the ultimate compliment by making him the key (even if unnamed) interlocutor in his first book, and Hume returned the favor by boosting Smith's spirits on its release, helping to publicize his book, and pushing him to refine his ideas. What more could one want from a philosophical friendship?

FÊTED IN FRANCE

(1759-1766)

UME'S JOCULAR LETTER to Smith on the publication and reception of *The Theory of Moral Sentiments* also contained an unexpected overture. The proposal came from Charles Townshend, a leading Whig politician who would later, as Chancellor of the Exchequer, push through a series of taxes on tea and other goods that were to have fateful consequences in the American colonies.[1] Hume reports that Townshend was so taken with Smith's book that he wanted Smith to serve as a traveling tutor to his stepson, the Duke of Buccleuch, then a schoolboy at Eton, and promised that he "woud endeavour to make it worth [Smith's] while to accept of that Charge." Hume tried to call on Townshend to convince him that the best course would be to send Buccleuch to study with Smith at Glasgow, "for I coud not hope, that he coud offer you any Terms, which would tempt you to renounce your Professorship." Hume reminds Smith that Townshend "passes for being a little uncertain in his Resolutions"—indeed, his capriciousness had earned him the nickname "the Weathercock"—and allows that "perhaps you need not build much on this Sally."[2] On this occasion, however, Townshend followed through on his vow, and Smith proved willing to renounce his professorship after all. Townshend visited Smith in Glasgow later that summer and the two worked out an arrangement by which Smith would continue in his position at the university for the next few years while Buccleuch completed his formal schooling, after which Smith would accompany him on a tour of the Continent.[3] Just like that, Smith's vision of his future had changed dramatically.

Hume's own opportunity to relocate across the Channel would open up soon enough, but for the time being he was still immersed in *The History of England*. His next letter to Smith prodded, "My Dear

Mr Smith; You must not be so much engross'd with your own Book, as never to mention mine [i.e., the Tudor volumes]. The Whigs, I am told, are anew in a Rage against me; tho' they know not how to vent themselves: For they are constrain'd to allow all my Facts." Hume found their animadversions preposterous but pledged not to reply to them, reasoning that "if my past Writings do not sufficiently prove me to be no Jacobite, ten Volumes in folio never would." He also reports that he had signed a contract with Andrew Millar to continue the work, moving backward in time once more to cover the period from the Roman invasion of Britain to the accession of Henry VII. This pair of volumes was the last of Hume's major literary projects and the only one for which he secured an advance contract. His plan, he told Smith, was to "execute this Work at Leizure, without fatiguing myself by such ardent Application as I have hitherto employd. It is chiefly as a Ressource against Idleness, that I shall undertake this Work: For as to Money, I have enough: And as to Reputation, what I have wrote already will be sufficient, if it be good: If not, it is not likely I shall now write better."[4] In fact he ended up writing a draft of these volumes in just over a year and a half.

While Hume no longer needed Smith's advice about what subject to tackle next, he did seek his counsel on a question that would occupy their letters for years to come: that of where to live. "I am in doubt," Hume declares, "whether I shall stay here [i.e., London] and execute the Work; or return to Scotland, and only come up here to consult the Manuscripts. I have several inducements on both Sides." On the one hand, he says, Scotland is more affordable than London and is also "the Seat of my principal Friendships." On the other hand, "it is too narrow a Place for me, and it mortifies me that I sometimes hurt my Friends." In other words, Hume worried that the religious bigotry that he often faced in his home country affected not only himself but also those, like Smith, who were closely associated with him. "Pray write me your Judgement soon," he pleads.[5] Any reply that Smith may have written is now lost, but in the event Hume moved back to his apartment in Jack's Land later that summer.

Alexander Carlyle reports that in September Hume and Smith both attended a dinner at William Robertson's house in Edinburgh that included Benjamin Franklin, among others.[6] Franklin was in the middle of a jaunt through Scotland with his son, a trip that he deemed "Six Weeks of the *densest* Happiness I have met with in any Part of my Life." Indeed, Franklin avowed that "the agreeable and instructive Society we found there in such Plenty, has left so pleasing an Impression on my Memory, that did not strong Connections draw me elsewhere, I believe Scotland would be the Country I should chuse to spend the Remainder of my Days in."[7] Hume had met Franklin earlier that year while in London, and when Franklin passed through Glasgow after leaving Edinburgh he met up with Smith again, and perhaps even stayed at his house.[8] Nor did the connections among them end there. Hume and Franklin exchanged letters sporadically for a number of years, and though Smith, true to form, does not seem to have ever corresponded with Franklin himself, he did ask to be "remembered" to him several times.[9] Franklin stayed at Hume's house for nearly a month during his second trip to Scotland, in 1771, and he also spent some time with Smith while the latter was in London in the mid-1770s. When Franklin returned to America for a couple of years in the early 1760s Hume wrote to say that he was "very sorry, that you intend soon to leave our Hemisphere. America has sent us many good things, Gold, Silver, Sugar, Tobacco, Indigo & c: But you are the first Philosopher, and indeed the first Great Man of Letters for whom we are beholden to her: It is our own Fault, that we have not kept him: Whence it appears, that we do not agree with Solomon, that Wisdom is above Gold: For we take care never to send back an Ounce of the latter, which we once lay our Fingers upon."[10] Franklin good-naturedly responded that the "Value of every thing . . . arises you know from the various Proportions of the Quantity to the Demand," and given that there was "such a Plenty of Wisdom" in Britain "your people are therefore not to be censur'd for desiring no more among them than they have; and if I have *any*, I should certainly carry it where from its Scarcity it may probably come to a better Market."[11]

Hume returned to London once again in June 1761 to do a bit more research on the last two volumes of his *History*, make some revisions, and publish the final version. As it happens, Smith planned to be in the city for a couple of months that autumn—his first trip there—to conduct some university business. Hume clearly knew of these plans, for he wrote to Smith from the road to let him know where he would be lodging and to express delight at the prospect of their reunion. "I beg it of you to let me hear from you the Moment of your Arrival," he implores.[12] Although there are no more surviving letters between them for nearly the next two years, we have indirect evidence that they did spend some time together in the city: a manuscript by Adam Ferguson that consists of a dialogue between Hume, Smith, and Robert Clerk, a rising soldier (later a general) who had served alongside Hume during the expedition to Brittany in 1746.[13] The conversation took place in London in the autumn of 1761, if it took place at all; we have no way of knowing how historically accurate the dialogue is, especially given that it was composed many decades after the fact. Nor, alas, do Hume and Smith speak more than a few words to one another in this work; instead, they take turns conversing with Clerk.[14]

The dialogue consists mostly of Clerk, who was known for his combativeness in conversation, drawing loosely on Ferguson's own ideas to castigate Hume's and Smith's moral theories.[15] While the work's philosophical value is questionable, it does have its humorous moments. Clerk opens the dialogue by provoking Hume with the now timeworn allegation that "you rather try to pull down other peoples Doctrines than Establish any of your own," to which Hume retorts: "Pardon me, did I not sett out with a complete Theory of Human Nature which was so ill received that I determined to refrain from System making[?]" A bit later, in response to Hume's supposed reduction of morality to utility, Clerk shoots back: "is there anything more Useful than a good Cornfield[?] People say there is a plentiful Crop but no one says there is a Virtuous Field." After some more discussion Smith enters the room, in typical form, "with a smile on his Countenance and Muttering Somewhat to himself." He fishes for a compliment from Clerk on *The Theory of Moral Sentiments*, opining that he had "removed all the difficulties & made [the] Theory Compleat," at which point the good soldier stuns him with his verdict: "Your Book is to me a Heap of absolute Nonsense."[16]

While in London Smith also managed to get into a spat with Samuel Johnson on their first meeting, perhaps because Johnson spoke ill of Hume in front of him. This was the Great Moralist's wont with respect to the Great Infidel; as the historian Peter Gay notes, Johnson's recorded comments about Hume display "an unphilosophical aversion that smacks almost of fear."[17] One version of the story has it that Johnson criticized Smith for praising Hume, calling him a liar, at which point Smith snapped back that Johnson was a son of a bitch.[18]

Around a month after Hume's volumes on the early history of England were published he hastened back to Edinburgh. From time to time over the next several years he contemplated expanding the already-massive work still further by writing on the period from the Glorious Revolution to the Hanoverian succession (1689–1714), or perhaps even pressing on still closer to his own time, but he never made any serious moves to do so. "The Truth is," he told one correspondent, "that I am entirely idle at present, so far as regards writing; and I am very happy in that indolent State. My Friends tell me, that I will not continue long so, and that I will tire of having nothing to do but read and converse; but I am resolvd to resist, as a Temptation of the Devil, any Impulse towards writing, and I am really so much ashamd of myself when I see my Bulk on a Shelf, as well as when I see it in a Glass, that I would fain prevent my growing more corpulent either way."[19]

In 1762 Hume moved back to the Lawnmarket, purchasing an apartment at James's Court, almost directly opposite his earlier residence at Riddle's Land. He kept this apartment for the rest of his life, renting it to Hugh Blair while he was in France and to James Boswell when he moved to the New Town. Positioned high on Castle Hill, the apartment commanded superb views of the city and across the Firth of Forth to the hills of Fife. Alas, the building burned down in the mid-nineteenth century and was rebuilt in the Victorian style, though the views remain splendid. Hume found his new home "somewhat dear," but he was pleased to know that he would be "exceedingly well lodged."[20] He was joined, as usual, by his sister Katherine and his housekeeper Peggy Irvine. At this point he had entered his fifties and assumed he was settled in Edinburgh for good, having "bought a very pretty little House, which I had repair'd and furnishd to my Fancy . . . and fix'd every thing about my Family, on such a Footing as to continue there the rest of my Days."[21]

The city's intellectual vitality continued apace. The Select Society had started to go into decline, but Adam Ferguson helped to form a sort of replacement in January 1762 in the Poker Club, so named because he hoped the group would "stir up" the question of instituting a Scottish militia, which had been banned by Parliament in the wake of the 1745 uprising.[22] Hume and Smith were both original members and joined the group often at its weekly tavern meetings to partake of a modest afternoon meal, sherry or claret, and lively debate on a wide variety of political topics. As with the Select Society, they enjoyed the convivial discussion that the group afforded even if they did not contribute frequently themselves. Hume did hold a sort of office in the club, however: when a criminal lawyer named Andrew Crosbie was jokingly named the group's "Assassin, in case any officer of that sort should be needed," the genial Hume was "added as his Assessor, without whose assent nothing should be done, so that between *plus* and *minus* there was likely to be no bloodshed."[23] Two years later, after Hume had been fêted in the very highest circles of French society, he admitted to Ferguson that "I really wish often for the plain roughness of the *Poker* . . . to correct and qualify so much lusciousness."[24] This "plain roughness" did not appeal to everyone, however. James Boswell, who was not a member, complained to his journal about "the *Poker Club*, as they are called. . . . They are doing all that they can to destroy politeness. They would abolish all respect due to rank and external circumstances, and they would live like a kind of literary barbarians."[25]

In February 1763 we finally arrive at Smith's earliest surviving letter to Hume, nearly a decade and a half after they first met, but in terms of the light it sheds on their friendship it comes as a major disappointment. It is little more than a brief letter of introduction to one Henry Herbert, a student at Glasgow who was planning to spend some time in Edinburgh and "who is very well acquainted with your works, and upon that account extremely desirous of being introduced to the Author." (This does, at least, lend further support to the idea that Smith encouraged his students to read Hume's writings, their reputation for impiety notwithstanding.) It appears, from this letter, that Smith was in the habit of returning Hume's recurrent pleas for a visit: "You have been long promising us a visit at Glasgow and I have made Mr Herbert promise to endeavour to bring you along with him [on his return]," Smith writes. "Tho you have resisted all my Sollicitations, I hope you will not resist this. I hope, I need not tell you that it will give me the greatest pleasure to see you."[26]

Hume responded a few weeks later to thank Smith for introducing Herbert, whom he found "a very promising young man"—he went on to become a prominent independent Member of Parliament—and to promise that he would take up Smith's request: "I set up a Chaise in May next, which will give me the Liberty of travelling about; and you may be sure a Journey to Glasgow will be one of the first I shall undertake." (We know that Hume traveled to North Yorkshire around this time, but we do not know whether he ended up including Glasgow on his itinerary.) "I intend to require with great Strictness," he warns Smith, "an Account [of] how you have been employing your Leizure; and I desire you to be ready for that purpose. Wo be to you, if the Ballance be against you." Even in the midst of pledging to visit Glasgow, Hume urges Smith toward Edinburgh: "Your Friends here will also expect, that I should bring you with me. It seems to me very long since I saw you."[27]

Hume wrote to Smith again that August with unexpected news: he had been invited by Lord Hertford, Britain's newly appointed ambassador to France, to accompany him to Paris as his private secretary.[28] The invitation was surprising not just because Hume had little experience in this line of work and was a Scot in a period of anti-Scottish sentiment, but also because he had never met Hertford, who, moreover, was noted for his religiosity. "I hesitated much on the Acceptance of this Offer, tho' in appearance very inviting; and I thought it ridiculous, at my Years"—he was fifty-two—"to be entering on a new Scene, and to put myself in the Lists as a Candidate of Fortune," Hume told Smith. "But I reflected, that I had in a manner abjur'd all literary Occupations, that I resolvd to give up my future Life entirely to Amusements, [and] that there coud not be a better Pastime than such a Journey." None of this is even to mention, of course, the presence of Hume's many professed admirers in Paris; earlier that year

Lord Elibank had informed him that "no author ever yet attained to that degree of Reputation in his own lifetime that you are now in possession of at Paris."[29] With the end of the Seven Years' War in February Hume no longer had a pretext for resisting their siren song. He told Smith that he had decided to take the plunge: he was to leave the next day. "I am a little hurry'd in my Preparations," his letter continues, "But I coud not depart without bidding you Adieu, my good Friend, and without acquainting you with the Reasons of so sudden a Movement. I have not great Expectations of revisiting this Country [i.e., Scotland] soon; but I hope it will not be impossible but we may meet abroad, which will be a great Satisfaction to me."[30] Little did he know that this hoped-for meeting would come to pass in a matter of months.

Hume traveled to Paris by way of London, where he wrote to Smith to pass along the latest political news—it was generally expected that Scots who journeyed to London would update their friends back home on current events—and to dilate a little more on his own situation. While he had been reluctant to leave Edinburgh, he reports, on arriving in London he found his position even more favorable than he could have hoped. His living arrangements promised to be comfortable, his financial situation would be improved still further, and Lord Hertford was of unimpeachable character in spite of his "great Piety." Indeed, Hume notes that he will "draw the more Honour" from serving as Hertford's secretary given that Hertford "overlookd so many seeming Objections which lay against me on that head." Yet all of these auspicious circumstances had not entirely convinced Hume that he had chosen wisely: "shall I tell you the Truth? I repine at my Loss of Ease and Leizure and Retirement and Independance, and it is not without a Sigh I look backwards nor without Reluctance that I cast my Eye forwards." Whether these feelings were a sign that he should have remained in Scotland or only "a momentary Disgust, the Effect of low Spirits, which Company and Amusement and a better State of Health will soon dissipate and remove," is, he says, a question for whose answer he "must wait with Patience."[31]

As Hume was making his way to the City of Light the wheels that would reunite him with Smith were, unbeknownst to him, set in motion. Charles Townshend wrote to Smith in late October to renew the invitation to serve as a traveling tutor to Townshend's step-son, the now seventeen-year-old Duke of Buccleuch.[32] It seems that Smith was unable to resist the promise of a generous salary, a lifelong pension, and the chance to spend some time on the Continent, as he wasted no time in accepting the proposal. The fact that Hume was due to arrive in France that very week must have served as a further inducement. By mid-February the two would rendezvous in Paris.

The welcome that Hume received in Paris almost beggars belief, even today. Royalty, aristocrats, public officials, salon hostesses, men of letters—everyone who was anyone tripped over themselves to meet Hume, to extol him, and above all to be seen with him. A few months into his stay he informed William Robertson, "I eat nothing but Ambrosia, drink nothing but Nectar, breathe nothing but Incense, and tread on nothing but Flowers. Every Man I meet, and still more every Lady, wou'd think they were wanting in the most indispensable Duty, if they did not make to me a long & elaborate Harangue in my Praise."[33] What is more, as Ernest Campbell Mossner notes, "the most amazing feature of Hume's vogue in Paris is that it was not a passing fad but lasted throughout the entire twenty-six months of his stay."[34] The contrast with Scotland, where Hume had endured decades of reproach and disdain on account of his irreligion, could hardly have been starker. It seems nothing short of remarkable that a somewhat awkward, rather corpulent, fifty-two-year-old philosopher who spoke halting French with a thick Scottish brogue became the toast of polite Parisian society. In fact, all of these quirks—and the contrast they presented with his polished, urbane writings—made Hume all the more loved. His experience in Paris was not unlike the later experience of Benjamin Franklin, with his fur cap and his homespun wisdom: the more rustic their manners, the more they were adored.

Hume's first message home, upon arriving in France in October, was to Smith. It is in this letter, accordingly, that we have Hume's first description of his astonishing reception there. He had been in the country less than a week, he tells Smith, but he had already "every where met with the most extraordinary Honours which the most exorbitant Vanity cou'd wish or desire." By this point, he says, "the

L'historien hume.

FIGURE 6.1 This watercolor painting by Louis Carrogis Carmontelle (1764) depicts Hume relaxing at his desk during his time in Paris. Photograph courtesy of the Scottish National Portrait Gallery (PG 2238).

Compliments of Dukes and Marischals of France and foreign Am-
bassadors go for nothing with me. . . . I retain a Relish for no kind
of flattery but that which comes from the Ladies." Hume notes that
he had not yet met any of the leading *philosophes*, "but every body is
forward to tell me the high Panegyrics I receive from [them]." Yet
he insists that he had not let any of this hero worship go to his head:
"I know you are ready to ask me, my dear Friend, if all this does not
make me very happy." His answer? "No, I feel little or no Difference.
As this is the first Letter I write to my Friends at home, I have amus'd
myself (and hope I have amus'd you) by giving you a very abridg'd
Account of these Transactions: But . . . I assure you I reap more internal Satisfaction from the very amiable Manners and Character of the
Family in which I live"—the Hertfords—"than from all these external Vanities." He was writing from Fontainebleau, the site of the royal
court, and he claims that during his two days there "I have sufferd
(the Expression is not improper) as much Flattery as almost any man
has ever done in the same time: But there are few days in my Life,
when I have been in good Health, that I would not rather pass over
again." Perhaps realizing that he is protesting too much, Hume brings
his narrative to a halt: "But enough of all these Follies. You see I trust
to your Friendship, that you will forgive me"—presumably meaning
for his vanity—"and to your Discretion, that you will keep my Secret."
Having recovered himself, Hume turns to "the Subject which first put
my Pen in my hand," namely informing Smith that the baron d'Holbach was supervising a French translation of *The Theory of Moral Sentiments* and inquiring whether Smith wished to make any alterations
for the translated version.[35]

Smith responded in December, pleased to report that he would be
joining Hume in France in the near future, although he was not sure
exactly how near: Smith hoped to postpone the trip until the end of
his classes in April, but he did not know if Buccleuch would be able
to put off his travels for that long. (As it turned out he was obliged to
leave the university mid-semester.) He also passes along his gratitude
to d'Holbach and his respects to the other "men of Genius in France
who do me the honour to know anything about me." Smith then turns
to Hume's reception in Paris, which he says, with the partiality of a
close friend, "is not in the least beyond what I expected." However,

he also reveals that he had amused himself somewhat at Hume's expense: "I took the liberty to show part of your letter to some of our female friends notwithstanding your injunction of secresy; We all laughed heartily at your pretending not to be pleased with the flattery you have met with. You see how modesty is rewarded in this world."[36] In fact, Hume himself admitted to Lord Elibank, just a little over a week later, that "my Modesty suffers much & will at last, I believe, be quite murderd among these People."[37]

One of the prime offenders in this regard was the Comtesse de Boufflers, mistress of the Prince de Conti, who hosted one of the leading salons of Paris. At thirty-eight she was fourteen years Hume's junior. In addition to her elite connections, her social charm, and her physical attractiveness, Boufflers was deeply interested in literature, philosophy, and the arts. Prior to Hume's arrival in France she had wooed him for several years with some of the most flattering letters ever written to a philosopher. When reading Hume's *History*, she effused, "I thought I had before my eyes the work of a celestial being, free of passions, who for the sake of mankind deigned to write the history of these recent times . . . in everything that comes from your pen you show yourself to be a perfect philosopher, a statesman, a historian full of genius, an enlightened political thinker, a true patriot."[38] When they finally met in person—after the comtesse had recovered from the measles—Hume fell under her spell, spawning rumors that he was madly in love with her. In light of her marriage and her liaison with the Prince de Conti, however, Hume ultimately concluded that he was unwilling to proceed beyond the bounds of affectionate friendship. Adding to his hesitance was the great value that he placed on his own independence, which would be fatally compromised if he were to become a paramour of a great lady. The two remained devoted to one another, nonetheless, and one of Hume's deathbed letters was addressed to the comtesse.[39]

Hume also found congenial companions in some of France's leading men of letters, counting among "those whose Persons & Conversation I like best" figures such as Jean le Rond d'Alembert, the Comte de Buffon, Denis Diderot, and Claude-Adrien Helvétius.[40] (He never met Voltaire, who had long ago decamped to Ferney on the Swiss border, and Montesquieu had died in 1755.) Hume's skepticism in religious matters, as deep as it was, was dwarfed by the militant atheism of the more radical *philosophes*. Indeed, he later recalled that some of them "used to laugh at me for my narrow way of thinking in these particulars."[41] It must have been startling indeed for Hume to suddenly find himself being teased for his failure to throw off the yoke of religion fully enough. A fellow freethinker, Edward Gibbon, lamented the "intolerant zeal" of the *philosophes* who "laughed at the scepticism of Hume, preached the tenets of Atheism with the bigotry of dogmatists, and damned all believers with ridicule and contempt."[42] The difference between Hume's brand of irreligion and that of the more radical French thinkers is illustrated by a now-famous story about a dinner at d'Holbach's house in Paris. When Hume commented that he did not believe in out-and-out atheists, having never actually met one, d'Holbach told him to count the number of people around him at the table—there were eighteen—and quipped, "not bad, to be able to show you fifteen at one stroke. The other three haven't yet made up their minds."[43] One imagines that Hume would have deemed these three the most sensible of the lot.

Meanwhile, Smith left his position at Glasgow in January 1764 in order to begin his tutorship. He was succeeded in the Chair of Moral Philosophy, perhaps against his own wishes, by Thomas Reid, the eminent "common sense" philosopher and one of Hume's greatest philosophical critics.[44] Between Hutcheson, Smith, and Reid, this chair enjoyed illustrious occupants indeed in the eighteenth century.[45] Smith and his new pupil met in London in January and then made their way across the Channel in February, arriving in Paris on the 13th. In all they would spend a little more than two and a half years traveling on the Continent. Buccleuch later recalled that the time they spent together passed "without the slightest disagreement or coolness," and Smith too "always spoke of it with pleasure and gratitude."[46] The two were to maintain a close connection for the remainder of Smith's life.

Smith's initial stay in Paris was quite brief—around ten days. He and Buccleuch naturally stayed with Hume, who was lodging in the ultra-fashionable Faubourg Saint-Germain, on the Left Bank near where the Eiffel Tower now stands. Hume surely would have introduced

Smith and the young duke to some of his Parisian friends and ad-mirers, though there is little record to go by. Smith and Buccleuch then proceeded on to Toulouse, where they spent the next eighteen months. At the time Toulouse was France's "second city" and a favorite destination of British visitors. With a university, a *parlement* (judicial court), and academies of science and art but without the myriad dis-tractions of Paris, it seemed an ideal locale for a young aristocrat's ed-ucation. Even after Smith left Paris he stayed connected with Hume in a sense, as one of his principal friends and guides in Toulouse was the Abbé Colbert, a cousin of Hume's. (Colbert had Gallicized his family name, Cuthbert, upon entering the Church.) Upon their meeting Colbert wrote to Hume to sing Smith's praises, avowing that he was everything Hume had promised.[47] Smith also discussed Hume's writings with Buccleuch during their time there, leading him to tease Hume that the duke "has read almost all your works several times over, and was it not for the more wholesome doctrine which I take care to instill into him, I am afraid he might be in dan-ger of adopting some of your wicked Principles. You will find him very much improved."[48]

Smith wrote to Hume fairly often from Toulouse, at least by his standards: we have three letters between July and November 1764, and then two more in 1765. Most of these notes are, however, fairly brief, and they consist largely of requests for Hume to use his influence to obtain introductions for Smith and Buccleuch to the local dignitaries in the south of France. In the first of these letters Smith laments that they had thus far been obliged to make their way "as well as we could by the help of the Abbé [Colbert] who is a Stranger here almost as much as we. The Progress, indeed, we have made is not very great. The Duke is acquainted with no french man whatever." Smith also tells Hume that this lack of local connections was rendering it difficult for him to fill his own time: "The Life which I led at Glasgow was a plea-surable, dissipated life in comparison of that which I lead here at Pres-ent. I have begun to write a book in order to pass away the time. You may believe I have very little to do."[49] Although we cannot be certain, odds are that the book here alluded to is *The Wealth of Nations*—the first mention of this work in Smith's extant correspondence.[50]

In response to Smith's plea Hume helped to procure him a letter of introduction to the duc de Richelieu, the governor of Bordeaux, for their visit to that city later in the month. As a result, Smith's next letter gratefully reports, they were treated "with the utmost Politeness and attention." He happily notes that Buccleuch had begun "to familiarize himself to French company and I flatter myself I shall spend the rest of the Time we are to live together, not only in Peace and contentment but in gayety and amusement."[51] They were accompanied on their trip to Bordeaux by Colbert as well as Isaac Barré, a member of the British Parliament. We have a glimpse of a somewhat critical comment from Smith in a letter from Barré to Hume, which mentions that "Smith agrees with me in thinking that you are turned soft by the *délices* [delights] of a French court, and that you don't write in that nervous manner you was remarkable for in the more northern climates."[52] Presumably this was a reference to Hume's letters rather than to his philosophical or historical writings, as he was not composing any of the latter at the time.

In the autumn of 1765 Smith left Toulouse with Buccleuch and the duke's younger brother, who had joined them earlier that year. Their first stop was Geneva, where they spent another two months. Smith had the opportunity to meet the most famous resident of the area, Voltaire, on five or six occasions, and they seem to have gotten on quite well. Smith and his charges then headed back to Paris, this time for a much longer stay of ten months. Smith was anxious to rejoin Hume in the city, but it is unclear whether he was able to do so, as Hume was obliged to depart just as Smith was arriving.[53]

In August 1765 Hume's employer, Lord Hertford, was named Lord Lieutenant of Ireland. While he hoped to keep Hume on as his secretary, the customary clamor against Hume's irreligion and Scottishness was too much this time. Hume was not entirely disappointed; he did not relish the idea of moving to Dublin and, as he told his brother, "I never had much Ambition . . . for Power & Dignities; and I am heartily cur'd of the little I had. I believe a Fireside & a Book, the best things in the World for my Age & Disposition."[54] Hume apprised

Smith of his changing situation in a letter of September 5. "I have been whirled about lately in a strange Manner," he writes, "but besides that none of the Revolutions have ever threatened me much, or been able to give me a Moment's Anxiety, all has ended very happily and to my wish." He relates the details of Hertford's move and his own reluctance to accompany him to Ireland, and reports that Hertford had secured him a lifelong pension of four hundred pounds a year in lieu of a new post. "Nothing coud be more to my Mind: I have now Opulence and Liberty: The last formerly renderd me content: Both together must do so, so far as the Encrease of Years will permit," he reckons. He promises to turn down all further job offers: "I woud not run into the Ways of the World and catch at Profit from all hands. I am sure you approve of my Philosophy."[55]

The real question vexing Hume, at this point, was where to settle down after his secretarial duties were at an end. He now had the freedom and the financial security to choose whatever locale suited him best, but he had formed no settled preference. When he had thought that he might be obliged to leave Paris a year earlier he had considered Toulouse as a possibility, but that option clearly had less appeal now that Smith was longer there.[56] His letter to Smith lays out the advantages and drawbacks of the most obvious choices, namely Paris, London, and Edinburgh: "Paris is the most agreeable Town in Europe, and suits me best; but it is a foreign Country. London is the Capital of my own Country; but it never pleasd me much. Letters are there held in no honour: Scotsmen are hated: Superstition and Ignorance gain Ground daily. Edinburgh has many Objections and many Allurements."[57] As Hume had already told Smith back in July 1759, his chief objection to Edinburgh was its religious "narrowness," and the chief allurement was the presence of his many friends there. Clearly, though, at this point he was still feeling the pull of Paris. As he put it to Hugh Blair, whereas the English were "relapsing fast into the deepest Stupidity, Christianity & Ignorance . . . in Paris, a man that distinguishes himself in Letters, meets immediatly with Regard & Attention."[58] Hume was "much in Perplexity," he tells Smith, about which of these cities to choose, but "my present Mind, this Forenoon the fifth of September is to return to France" after wrapping up his secretarial obligations in London. "I am much pressd here to accept of Offers, which would contribute to my agreeable Living, but might encroach on my Independence, by making me enter into Engagements with Princes and great Lords and Ladies. Pray give me your Judgement." He closes the letter by expressing his great regret that he is now unlikely to see Smith before leaving for London, remarking that "I have been looking for you every day these three Months."[59]

Smith too would soon face the question of where to fix his future abode, as his tutorship would be coming to an end within a year or two, and he too would have the financial wherewithal to settle almost anywhere he liked. Hume's intimation that he might remain in France on a permanent basis brought an uncharacteristically speedy and pointed reply from Smith: "It gives me the Greatest pleasure to find that you are so well contented with your present situation. I think however you are wrong in thinking of settling at Paris." Smith's underlying distrust of high French society is palpable in the list of reasons he offers: "A man is always displaced in a foreign Country, and notwithstanding the boasted humanity and politeness of this Nation . . . the cordiality of their friendship is much less to be depended on than that of our own countrymen. They live in such large societies and their affections are dissipated among so great a variety of objects, that they can bestow but a very small share of them upon any individual." What is more, he observes, Hume's offers from the nobility are not what they seem: "Do not imagine that the great Princes and Ladies who want you to live with them make this proposal from real and sincere affection to you. They mean nothing but to gratify their own vanity by having an illustrious man in their house."

Smith makes a pitch, instead, for London, seeking to alleviate Hume's worries about anti-Scottish prejudice and religious intolerance. As for the former, "the hatred of Scotch men can subsist, even at present, among nobody but the stupidest of the People, and is such a piece of nonsense that it must fall even among them in a twelvemonth." While Smith admits that there may be a certain degree of "Clamour against you on account of Deism," he is confident that this too would be dissipated in short order by Hume's genial presence there, much as it had been in Edinburgh in the wake of the failed attempt to excommunicate him from the Kirk. The reason Smith had such a "very great interest" in Hume settling in London, of course, is that he thought it likely that he would end up there himself. Thus, Smith's wistful proposal for the two of them to live out their days together: "Let us make short excursions together sometimes to see our friends in France and sometimes to see our friends in Scotland, but let London be the place of our ordinary residence."[60] As with all of the other schemes to bring the two together on a permanent basis, however, it was not to be.

It is unclear whether Smith returned to Paris in time to see Hume before Hume had to leave in order to shepherd Jean-Jacques Rousseau across the Channel—the subject of the next chapter—and wrap up his business as Hertford's secretary in London. We know that Hume departed Paris on January 4, 1766, but the timing of Smith's arrival is uncertain: it is likely that he reached the city sometime that December or January, but the evidence points in multiple directions.[61] In any event, Smith and his pupils quickly settled into the Hôtel du Parc Royal, on the rue Colombier, where Hume had spent the last few months of his stay. Smith even took on Hume's servant, whom he deemed "without exception the best I ever had in my life."[62]

Whether or not Hume introduced Smith to the elite circles of Paris either during Smith's first stop in the city in February 1764 or in December 1765–January 1766, during the next ten months Smith got to know many of the *philosophes* whom Hume had befriended over the past couple of years, including Diderot, d'Alembert, Helvétius, and d'Holbach. He also sought out a number of leading *économistes* such as François Quesnay, Anne Robert Jacques Turgot, and the Marquis de Mirabeau, indicating his growing interest in political economy. While Smith could not have hoped to duplicate the extraordinary splash that Hume had made in Paris, these men of letters welcomed him with enthusiasm. Despite his absent air and his poor spoken French, Smith was almost universally liked and respected thanks to his reputation as the author of *The Theory of Moral Sentiments*, his breadth of knowledge, and of course his friendship with Hume. Smith returned their esteem and, according to Dugald Stewart, "some of them he continued ever afterwards to reckon among his friends."[63] What Smith made of the ostentatious irreligion of the *phi-*

losophes has not come down to us. John Ramsay of Ochtertyre writes that during his time on the Continent Smith "became acquainted with Voltaire and the other French philosophers who were then labouring with unhallowed industry in the vineyard of infidelity. He was not the less welcome to them that he was the intimate friend of Mr David Hume, who was then in high vogue at home and abroad." Ramsay laments, however, that "what impression their arguments and enthusiastic eloquence made upon the mind of Dr Smith cannot be precisely known, because neither before nor after this period was his religious creed ever properly ascertained."[64]

The Comtesse de Boufflers, knowing how close Smith was to Hume, also gave him a warm welcome. Perhaps inspired by their meeting she began reading *The Theory of Moral Sentiments*, and she informed Hume in May that what she had read thus far pleased her greatly.[65] The rest of the book must have pleased her as well, as she is reported to have considered translating the work into French herself a few years later.[66] Hume, however, showed a less attractive side of himself in this instance, feeling the need to apologize for his closest friend's lack of social grace. In a letter to the comtesse, he thanks her for having "taken my friend Smith under your protection" and assures her that he is "a man of true merit," but he qualifies his approbation by owning that "perhaps his sedentary recluse life may have hurt his air and appearance, as a man of the world."[67] That said, Hume had made the same apology on his own behalf in his very first letter to the comtesse, warning that "I have rusted amid books and study; have been little engaged in the active, and not much in the pleasurable scenes of life; and am more accustomed to a select society than to general companies." Perhaps Hume's feelings of insecurity were aroused less by the demeanor of his friend, in particular, than by the thought of any provincial Scot in the company of a "lady of ... distinction" like Boufflers who had been "educated at the Court of France, and familiarized with every thing elegant and polite."[68] There are indications that Smith too may have had an amorous interlude while in Paris, though certainly not one as involved as Hume's with Boufflers.[69] There are occasional rumors, throughout Smith's life, of potential romantic connections, but none of them amounted to much. As his biographer Ian Simpson Ross writes, "It is to be feared that the biographer can do little more with the topic of Smith's sex life than contribute a footnote to the history of sublimation."[70]

While Smith's time in Paris was one of the most socially active periods of his life, he clearly regretted not being able to spend more of it in Hume's company. He wrote in March to assure Hume that he was "much wanted in Paris" and that "everybody I see enquires after the time of your return," though he is quick to admonish: "Do not, however, for gods sake, think of settling in this country but let both of us spend the remainder of our days on the same side of the Water. Come, however, to Paris in the mean time and we shall settle the plan of our future life together."[71] Evidently worried that Hume would ultimately choose to settle in Paris, he repeated the admonition six months later in a letter to Andrew Millar, their bookseller: "Tho I am very happy here, I long passionately to rejoin my old friends, and if I had once got fairly to your side of the water, I think I should never cross it again. Recommend the same sober way of thinking to Hume. He is light-headed, tell him, when he talks of coming to spend the remainder of his days here."[72] Smith's hopes were to be only partially fulfilled: Hume never did return to France, so the pair did spend the rest of their days on the same side of the Channel, but they ended up enjoying only relatively brief interludes in one other's company.

That autumn Smith's own time in Paris came to a rather abrupt and tragic end. The Duke of Buccleuch's younger brother, who had joined them in Toulouse, died of a fever in October, and soon thereafter Smith hastened back to London with the duke. At this point, however, we must return to Hume's departure from France at the beginning of the year, because during Smith's stay in Paris Hume was at the center of a maelstrom back in England.

CHAPTER 7

QUARREL WITH A
WILD PHILOSOPHER
(1766-1767)

O ne of the few philosophers—indeed, one of the few *people*—
who rivaled Hume's claim on the French public's attention
in the 1760s was Jean-Jacques Rousseau; rare is the writer
of any age who has had so many fanatical admirers. The dramatic
falling out between these two luminaries was one of the most talked-
about events of the entire century within Europe's republic of letters.
The Hume-Rousseau *affaire* is by now an oft-told tale, but it will be
worth recounting its basic outlines one more time, not just for the
irresistible combination of celebrity, genius, and betrayal, but also for
the light it sheds on Hume's friendship with Smith.[1]

The self-styled "citizen of Geneva" first came to public notice with
his contrarian *Discourse on the Sciences and Arts*, a work that took the
European world by storm upon publication in 1751; Denis Diderot's
report on its reception gushed, "it is succeeding beyond the skies;
there is no precedent for such a success."[2] Rousseau followed this up
with the *Discourse on Inequality* (1755), a sweeping attack on modern
civilization and the entire notion of "progress"; *Julie, or the New He-
loise* (1761), a runaway best-selling romantic novel; *The Social Contract*
(1762), a political treatise that called the legitimacy of all existing
states into question; and *Emile* (1762), a masterpiece on education or
child-rearing. The latter two works, in particular, put into motion the
wheels that would eventually drive Rousseau into the arms of Hume.
Because of their heterodox religious ideas the books were banned
and burned in both Paris and Geneva, and a warrant was issued for
Rousseau's arrest. Nor were the political and ecclesiastical authorities
the only influential individuals whose enmity Rousseau had earned.

While Rousseau was friends with many of the Parisian *philosophes* early in his career, by the late 1750s he had become estranged from almost all of them, both because his ideas ran so counter to theirs and because his extreme sensitivity, which bordered on paranoia, made it difficult for him to stay on good terms with anyone for long.

After the arrest warrant was issued Rousseau fled to northern Switzerland, at which point the Comtesse de Boufflers told Hume of Rousseau's plight and prompted him to offer the Genevan a refuge in Britain from his persecutions, both real and imagined, on the Continent. Hume was happy to oblige, but Rousseau, who disliked the English and did not speak their language, politely turned the offer down.[3] A few years later the hostility toward Rousseau bubbled up again, culminating in his house in Môtiers being stoned by an angry mob. Hearing of this new predicament, Hume renewed his offer of assistance; knowing a thing or two about being abused for one's ideas, he was determined to come to the aid of a persecuted philosopher, whatever he had heard of Rousseau from the Parisian *philosophes*. This time, after much pressure from mutual friends, Rousseau accepted, pronouncing himself "pleased to be indebted to the most illustrious of my contemporaries, whose goodness surpasses his glory."[4]

The two certainly presented a study in contrasts. Start with physical appearance. Where Hume was tall and portly, Rousseau was small and thin; Hume had a broad, fleshy face and on occasion a vacant stare, Rousseau delicate features and piercing eyes. Their temperaments were, if anything, even less alike. Hume was generally calm and serene, Rousseau passionate and irritable. Where Hume by and large felt at home in the world, Rousseau saw it as a hostile place, full of plots and conspiracies against him. Hume enjoyed moving in Parisian high society, while Rousseau regarded it with undisguised horror; Hume preferred city life, Rousseau the country, the woods, or the mountains. Where Hume remained best friends with Smith for more than a quarter of a century, Rousseau seems to have been almost incapable of sustained friendship. (Few statements in the history of philosophy are more dubious than his claim in *The Confessions* that "I was born for friendship.")[5]

So too their philosophies. Hume's thoroughgoing defense of the modern, liberal, commercial order was matched by Rousseau's blis-

FIGURE 7.1 This famous portrait by Allan Ramsay (1766), painted in London, depicts Hume wearing the official dress of an Embassy Secretary. Hume would later hang it alongside the parallel portrait of Rousseau (Figure 7.2) in his house in Edinburgh, their quarrel notwithstanding. Photograph courtesy of the Scottish National Portrait Gallery (PG 1057).

tering attack on that order.[6] Hume believed, more strongly than even Smith, that civilization, refinement, and commerce brought in their wake an indissoluble chain of industry, knowledge, and humanity, while Rousseau insisted that they led to little more than inequality, dependence, and corruption.[7] Where Hume was moderate and pragmatic,

FIGURE 7.2 Allan Ramsay's portrait of Jean-Jacques Rousseau (1766) in a tall fur cap and fur-lined robe nicely captures the stark contrast with Hume in terms of physique, physiognomy, and countenance. Notice that whereas Hume's arm rests casually on a pair of books, Rousseau's hand emerges from the shadows to point toward his heart. Photograph courtesy of the Scottish National Portrait Gallery (NG 820).

Rousseau was radical—radical in both his critique of the existing order and in the various prescriptions he offered to fix it. They were both critics of reason in the so-called Age of Reason, but even here their concerns were widely divergent: whereas Hume "merely" emphasized the inability of reason to tell us almost anything about ourselves or the world around us with certainty, Rousseau saw it as a major contributor to the moral, social, and political ills that he saw all around him. Hume's critique of reason culminated in a kind of skeptical empiricism, Rousseau's in a new "religion of sincerity."[8] Rousseau's innermost religious beliefs are difficult to discern, but his regular professions of his adoration of God's goodness and of his firm faith in an immortal soul had earned the scorn of the *philosophes*.

Rousseau had not read any of Hume's writings other than his history of the Stuarts (in translation), as he later admitted, but he was somehow able to form a reasonably accurate sense of how they differed from his own.[9] Hume, he declared, "has not loved truth more than I have, I dare to believe, but I have sometimes put passion into my researches, and he has put into his only his wisdom and genius."[10] These differences were not lost on Hume, either, who observed that Rousseau's writings "appear to me admirable, particularly on the head of eloquence; and if I be not much mistaken, he gives to the French tongue an energy, which it scarce seems to have reached in any other hands. But as his enemies have objected, that with this domineering force of genius there is always intermingled some degree of extravagance, it is impossible for his friends altogether to deny the charge."[11] Given the vast intellectual gulf that separated the two it is perhaps not surprising that in the twenty-five letters between them they refrained entirely from discussing substantive philosophical matters—a stark contrast, of course, with Hume's correspondence with Smith. In the end, though, it was not their intellectual differences so much as their contrasting personalities that made the break between them all but inevitable.

In mid-December 1765 Rousseau joined Hume in Paris, where curious crowds fought for a chance to glimpse the famous refugee. Hume, himself a celebrity of the first order in the city, wrote that "it is impossible to express or imagine the Enthusiasm of this Nation in his favour. . . . People may talk of antient Greece as they please; but no Nation was ever so fond of Genius as this; and no Person ever so much engag'd their Attention as Rousseau. Voltaire and every body else, are quite eclipsed by him. . . . His very Dog, who is no better than a Coly, has a Name and Reputation in the World." His incredulity at Rousseau's popularity aside, Hume was immediately charmed by his modest, gentle demeanor, and wondered how all of his own Parisian friends could possibly think so ill of him. Barely a week after meeting Rousseau in person, Hume was already daring to call him "my Friend."[12] On the eve of their departure, though, the baron d'Holbach warned Hume that he had misread Rousseau entirely: "My dear Mr. Hume, I am sorry to dispel the hopes and illusions that flatter you, but I tell you that it will not be long before you are painfully undeceived. You do not know your man. I tell you frankly that you are warming a viper in your bosom."[13] While Hume dismissed d'Holbach's warning at the time, it was not long before he ruefully saw the truth in it.

Hume and his "pupil," as he sometimes called Rousseau, left Paris on January 4. When the two philosophers were forced to share a room at a crowded inn en route to London, Rousseau heard—or thought he heard—Hume call out again and again, in a loud French voice, in the middle of the night, "Je tiens Jean-Jacques Rousseau" ("I have/ hold Jean-Jacques Rousseau").[14] The third member of their traveling party, Jean-Jacques de Luze, who was in the same room, slept soundly through the night. Rousseau's mistrustful mind had already begun to detect signs of Hume's supposedly sinister intentions toward him. Upon landfall in Dover, however, Rousseau was sufficiently overcome with gratitude that he cast his suspicions aside, embracing Hume in an emotional outburst that was typical of Rousseau but must have dumbfounded the placid Scot: "I threw myself around his neck," Rousseau later recalled, "I embraced him tightly without saying anything, but covered his face with kisses and tears that spoke for themselves."[15]

On January 13 Hume and Rousseau reached London, where Rousseau once again became a public spectacle, not least due to the tall fur cap and outlandish purple caftan that he wore, the latter on account of a physical condition that made it difficult for him to urinate. Almost in an instant Hume had gone from being the toast of his adored Paris to being the chaperone of a still more famous philosopher in a city that he despised. Having now spent a few weeks with Rousseau, he was more convinced than ever that their outlooks were widely divergent. He told one acquaintance that Rousseau "is indeed a very sensible, and wonderfully ingenious Man, but our Opinions are by no means the Same. He has a hankering after the Bible, and is indeed little better than a Christian in a Way of his own."[16] While Hume tried to remain firm in his positive opinion of Rousseau, he had started to waver somewhat. In a letter written around this time he told Smith that Rousseau was "very agreeable," but also "a little variable and fanciful."[17] A few weeks later Hume still deemed him "mild, gentle, modest, affectionate, disinterested," but, presciently, he also noted that Rousseau seemed "apt to entertain groundless suspicions of his best friends; and his lively imagination, working upon them, feigns chimeras, and pushes him to great extremes. I have seen no instance of this disposition; but I cannot otherwise account for the violent animosities which have arisen between him and several men of merit, with whom he was once intimately connected." Less presciently, Hume insists nonetheless that "for my part, I think I could pass all my life in his company, without any danger of our quarrelling."[18]

Rousseau was eager to avoid the crowds and commotion of the city, so Hume set about finding him a refuge in the country. After a frustrating search, with Rousseau spurning option after option, Hume finally secured him a residence at Wootton, among the remote, idyllic hills of Staffordshire. By this point Hume had begun to weary of his guest and was relieved to see him off. He had now spent enough time with Rousseau to realize that he was more than a little thin-skinned, describing him as being "like a Man . . . stript not only of his Cloaths but of his Skin, and turn'd out in that Situation to combat with the rude and boisterous Elements"—an assessment that one of Rousseau's biographers acknowledges was "all too accurate."[19] On March 19, almost three months to the day after they first met, Rousseau departed, never to see Hume again.

———————

In the relative seclusion of Wootton, and egged on by his longtime companion and common law wife, Thérèse le Vasseur, Rousseau continued to nurse his paranoid suspicions until he had detected an intricate international conspiracy to defame him, one headed by none other than David Hume. Rousseau leveled the accusation in a letter of June 23 and then, at Hume's demand, laid out the full, elaborate plot in an interminably long letter of July 10. In a carefully crafted epistle of thirty-eight tightly spaced manuscript pages, he contended that all of Hume's kindnesses—taking Rousseau under his wing, accompanying him to England, searching far and wide for a suitable place for him to live, securing him a pension from George III—were merely ways of gaining control over Rousseau, and placing him in his debt; that Hume had consorted with Rousseau's enemies in France; that Hume had encouraged a mild joke against him that made the rounds in Paris and London and was eventually leaked to the newspapers (the "King of Prussia letter" penned by Horace Walpole); that Hume had compelled the British press to depict him in an unflattering light; that Hume had opened his mail in order to spy on him; and, most damningly of all, that Hume had stared at him in an unsettling manner. Hume's ultimate goal in all of these machinations, it seems, was to arrange things so that Rousseau—one of his few real literary and philosophical rivals—would be buried in obscurity in England while his own image was enhanced in the process. To substantiate these charges Rousseau produced no evidence beyond his own gut feelings, which, typically, he was sure *must* be right. The viper in Hume's bosom had struck.

Predictably, the letter elicited a combination of bafflement and indignation in the normally unruffled Hume, who deemed it a "perfect Frenzy."[20] Despite the groundless nature of Rousseau's allegations, Hume was apprehensive that this celebrated author who wielded the most powerful pen in Europe—and who was currently using that pen to compose his memoirs—might succeed in ruining the reputation for honesty and good nature that he had spent a lifetime earning. From the beginning of his literary career Hume had made, and generally kept, a resolution to refrain from replying to criticisms of his works, but he considered this a different matter altogether. "It is nothing to dispute my Style or my Abilities as an Historian or a Philosopher; My Books ought to answer for themselves, or they are not worth the defending," he maintained, and thus "to fifty Writers, who have attacked me on this head, I never made the least Reply: But this is a different Case: Imputations are here thrown on my Morals and my

Conduct."[21] Wary of Rousseau's next move, Hume began to gather together their correspondence as potential evidence to bring before the court of public opinion.

Looking for sympathy and advice, Hume told a handful of people about "this foolish Affair," as he called it.[22] He turned to his Parisian friends first, presumably because of their all-too-acute awareness of Rousseau's mercurial nature. The *philosophes*—and, through them, Smith—first learned of Rousseau's accusations through letters (now lost) that Hume sent to d'Holbach on June 27 and July 1, before Hume had received Rousseau's second, more prolonged diatribe.[23] These letters were, to Hume's rather naïve surprise, enough to provoke a torrent of gossip and debate on both sides of the Channel. "I needed but to have told it to one person," he observed, for "the Account flew like Wild-fire all over London in a Moment."[24] As he later put it, "if the King of England had declared war against the King of France, it could not have been more suddenly the subject of conversation."[25]

Hume's friends quickly rallied to his side, with Smith being one of the first to provide much-needed support and counsel. Smith sympathized with Hume's predicament, of course, but he also urged him not to publish anything relating to the quarrel. "I am thoroughly convinced that Rousseau is as great a Rascal as you, and as every man here believes him to be," he wrote from Paris on July 6. "Yet let me beg of you not to think of publishing anything to the world upon the very great impertinence which he has been guilty of to you. . . . By endeavouring to unmask before the Public this hypocritical Pedant, you run the risk, of disturbing the tranquillity of your whole life. By letting him alone he cannot give you a fortnights uneasiness. To write against him, is, you may depend upon it, the very thing he wishes you to do. He is in danger of falling into obscurity in England and he hopes to make himself considerable by provoking an illustrious adversary." Smith reminds Hume that having the facts on his side was not enough, not when "the church, the Whigs, the Jacobites, [and] the whole wise English nation, who . . . love to mortify a Scotchman" will be so quick to put the blame squarely on his shoulders.[26] This sober advice was, as one of Hume's early biographers notes, "a model of good sense."[27] It would be unseemly for Hume to publicize the details of a petty personal squabble, however in the right he may have been, and Smith's deep, enduring antipathy to public controversy gave him the right instincts in this instance.

As Hume's Parisian friends became acquainted with the details of the quarrel they debated with one another about what Hume should do. At first, as Smith's letter reports, they were all agreed that he should refrain from publishing anything about it, but a dispatch that Hume sent to Jean le Rond d'Alembert on July 15 laying out the train of his correspondence with Rousseau served to change their minds.[28] Hume's letter happened to arrive just as a large group of his friends had congregated at the salon of Julie de Lespinasse on July 21, and d'Alembert read it aloud to the gathering. After a lively discussion they concluded—unanimously, d'Alembert reported—that the quarrel had reached a point where it would not die down on its own, so Hume should put the facts before the public.[29] D'Alembert's letter to Hume also notes that he and Smith had "spoken much of you and your affair" and that he had shown Smith Hume's letter of July 15, as Hume had requested.[30] Given this mention of Smith, along with d'Alembert's claim that the recommendation to publish was unanimous, it has been supposed that Smith ended up agreeing with the *philosophes* that Hume should publish an account of the quarrel, but this supposition seems unfounded.[31] After all, d'Alembert does not say explicitly that Smith agreed with the decision reached at Lespinasse's, only that he had seen Smith recently and talked with him about the affair. Moreover, the Comtesse de Boufflers saw Smith a few days later and immediately informed Hume that he (Smith) agreed with her that in contemplating publishing Hume was "mistaken in the heat of so just a resentment."[32] Similarly, Andrew Millar commented to Hume in November that Smith "thinks it was not worth yr while to Publish."[33]

Setting Smith's and Boufflers's continued objections aside, Hume completed his pamphlet, consisting of his correspondence with Rousseau linked by a brief narrative of their feud, and sent it to d'Alembert along with permission for d'Alembert to publish at his own discretion. He then wrote to Smith to express both his hope that there would be no need to go public and his fear that it would prove unavoidable. "My Conduct, in this affair, woud do me a great deal of Honor," he is unabashed in pointing out, while Rousseau's "woud blast him for ever;

and blast his Writings at the same time: For as these have been exalted much above their Merit, when his personal Character falls, they woud of Course fall below their Merit." As for his assessment of Rousseau's character, Hume had understandably turned quite sour: "Pray is it not a nice Problem, whether he be not an arrant Villain or an arrant Madman or both: The last is my Opinion; but the Villain seems to me to predominate most in his Character." Hume also asks Smith for his opinion on the pamphlet that he had sent to d'Alembert—"Pray, tell me your Judgement of my Work, if it deserves the name"—and asks him to inform d'Alembert that he should consider himself "absolute Master to retrench or alter what he thinks proper, in order to suit it to the Latitude of Paris."[34]

Convinced that the public was already too involved and that the facts would vindicate Hume beyond all doubt, d'Alembert published an *Exposé succinct de la contestation qui s'est élévée entre M. Hume et M. Rousseau* in October, and an English translation was brought out in London in November as *A Concise and Genuine Account of the Dispute between Mr. Hume and Mr. Rousseau.*[35] Hume claimed that he "never consented to anything with greater reluctance in my life," lamely adding, "I hope it will be considered that that publication is not, properly speaking, my deed, but that of my friends, in consequence of a discretionary power which I gave them, and which it was natural for me to give them, as I was at too great a distance to form a judgment in this case." Conveniently overlooking the advice of Smith, Boufflers, and others, he insisted that "had I found one man of my opinion, I should have persevered in my refusal."[36]

Rousseau ended up fleeing Wootton after a little more than a year there, leaving behind most of his baggage (other than Thérèse, Hume unkindly quipped) and no forwarding address.[37] Convinced that his very life was in danger, Rousseau made his way to Dover, where he anxiously requested a guard to escort him across the Channel, promising that he would burn his memoirs and refrain from ever speaking ill of Hume again if only he were allowed to escape his "captivity" in England. After finally arriving in Calais he stayed in Normandy for some time, discarding his purple caftan and adopting the name

"Renou" by way of disguise. By this point, Hume was sure that Rousseau was "plainly mad, after having been long maddish."[38]

Smith, like the rest of the literary world in Europe, remained interested in the outcome of the quarrel, and he wrote to Hume in June 1767 to ask sarcastically, "What has become of Rousseau? Has he gone abroad, because he cannot continue to get himself sufficiently persecuted in Great Britain?"[39] Hume's next message contained no mention of Rousseau, so Smith persisted in another letter in September: "I should be glad to know the true history of Rousseau before and since he left England. You may perfectly depend upon my never quoting you to any living soul upon that Subject."[40] Hume replied with a lengthy account of the "late heteroclite Exploits" of this "wild Philosopher" on October 8, assuring Smith that "there is no Need of any Secrecy: They are most of them pretty public, and are well known to every body that had Curiosity to observe the Actions of that strange, undefineable Existence," and then added some corrections in a letter dated October 17.[41] To his discredit, Hume seems to relish the indifference and contempt that Rousseau had met with on his return to France: "he has some Reason to be mortify'd with his Reception . . . no body enquired after him, no body visits him, no body talks of him, every one has agreed to neglect and disregard him: A more sudden Revolution of Fortune than almost ever happend to any man, at least to any man of Letters." Even after publishing his side of the story Hume evidently had not overcome his wariness regarding Rousseau's memoirs, as he mentions them several times. He continues to maintain that the very existence of the memoirs "is some Justification of me for publishing his Letters, and may apologize for a Step, which you, and even myself, have been inclind sometimes to blame and always to regreat."[42]

In the event Rousseau's *Confessions* remained unpublished until after both he and Hume had died, and even then it contained the narrative of Rousseau's life just up to the time when he first met Hume, and did not discuss their quarrel at all.[43] As Robert Zaretsky and John Scott write in their excellent account of the quarrel, Hume remained "almost unnamed in a book that is consumed with naming names."[44] All of Hume's fears had been for naught. Hume also omits any reference to Rousseau in *My Own Life*. Both, it seems, would have preferred to forget the entire episode.

While Rousseau has always had his fervent partisans, most observers of the quarrel from the eighteenth century onward have rightly concluded that the lion's share of the blame rests squarely on his shoulders. Hume went out of his way to assist Rousseau in a time of need, and he had done little or nothing to merit the wild accusations that Rousseau hurled at him. Yet the aftermath of the rupture did not show Hume at his best. His paranoia about Rousseau's memoirs and the glee that he seemed to take in Rousseau's plight after his flight from Wootton jar with our usual image of *le bon David*. Above all, his publication of their correspondence seems, at least in retrospect, gratuitous and perhaps a bit spiteful. Smith, who abhorred the tendency of intellectuals to "publish all their little gossiping stories in Newspapers," was almost certainly right to try to dissuade Hume from broadcasting details of the feud.[45] This would not be the last time that he would caution Hume against publishing something that he had written. The next one, however, would not be an airing of dirty laundry, but a philosophical masterpiece.

CHAPTER 8

MORTALLY SICK
AT SEA

(1767-1775)

I N SEPTEMBER 1766, after the commotion over the Rousseau *affaire* had started to die down, Hume returned to Edinburgh with a view to "burying myself in a philosophical retreat."[1] While the Comtesse de Boufflers and others urged him toward Paris, Hume was resistant: "finding myself at my own fire-side, amid my books, conversing with company who are both estimable and agreeable, my former passion for study . . . has seized me with greater violence, by reason of so long an interruption, and I am so occupied with present things, that I form no distant resolution."[2] It was not long, however, before he was called back to London for another stint of public service. Lord Hertford had recently returned from Dublin and been appointed Lord Chamberlain, and Hertford's brother, General Seymour Conway, had become the Secretary of State for the Northern Department—the body that handled diplomacy with Scotland, the northern European countries, and Russia. The two of them nominated Hume as the Under-Secretary of State for that department, and Hume felt obliged to accept, given all that Hertford had done for him. He thus set out for London once more in February 1767, "a Philosopher, degenerated into a petty Statesmen," as he lamented.[3] The work was not arduous, however, and left him plenty of leisure to pursue his preferred pastimes. As he told Hugh Blair, "reading and sauntering and lownging and dozing, which I call thinking, is my supreme Happiness."[4]

Smith, for his part, spent six months in London on his return to Britain, from November 1766 to May 1767, in order to finish up the duties of his tutorship and see the third edition of *The Theory of Moral*

Sentiments through the press. Hume arrived in London on February 20, so their stays in the city overlapped by around three months. We can be sure that they spent some of this time together, though there is virtually no record of it. (We do know that they did not meet until at least four days after Hume's arrival, as in a letter to Adam Ferguson on February 24 he noted, "I have not seen Smith: judge of my Hurry.")[5] A high society hostess who entertained both Hume and Smith during this period, Lady Mary Coke, recorded a classic Smith incident in her diary. Commenting that Smith "was the most Absent Man that ever was," she relates that one morning "as he was going to breakfast, & falling into discourse, Mr Smith took a piece of bread & butter, which, after he had rolled round & round, he put into the teapot & pour'd the water upon it; some time after he poured it into a cup, & when he had tasted it he said it was the worst tea he had ever met with."[6]

Smith returned to Kirkcaldy in May 1767 to live with his now-elderly mother and his cousin, Janet Douglas. He remained there for the next six years "in great tranquillity, and almost in complete retirement," as he later described it.[7] He had been thinking about the subjects that were to be the focus of *The Wealth of Nations* at least since his days as a professor at Glasgow, but it was only now that he began to delve into the book in earnest. Aside from advising Buccleuch on the management of his estates, Smith tried as much as possible to avoid interruptions to his research and writing during these years in Kirkcaldy. His letters during this period are filled with references to the difficulties he faced and the slowness of the progress he was making. In a letter to Lord Hailes thanking him for sending some papers on corn prices, for example, Smith writes that "tho' in my present situation I have properly speaking nothing to do, my own schemes of Study leave me very little leisure, which go forward too like the web of penelope, so that I scarce see any Probability of their ending."[8] Similarly, in a letter to his old friend William Pulteney he complains of "interruptions occasioned . . . by bad health arising from want of amusement and from thinking too much upon one thing."[9] Smith sought to ward off such ill health by going on long walks and taking dips in the Firth of Forth. According to legend, one morning, still in his dressing gown and lost in reverie, he walked fifteen miles to

Dunfermline before some ringing church bells brought him back to reality.[10]

Around a month after Smith's arrival in Kirkcaldy he informed Hume how he was employing his time: "My Business here is Study in which I have been very deeply engaged for about a Month past." When he needed a break from his researches, he says, "my Amusements are long, solitary walks by the Sea side. You may judge how I spend my time. I feel myself, however, extremely happy, comfortable and contented. I never was, perhaps, more so in all my life." However, Smith's love of solitude did not prevent him from asking after news from the city: "You will give me great comfort by writing to me now and then, and by letting me know what is passing among my friends at London."[11]

Hume responded a few days later to relate "the strangest Story you ever heard of." A while back he had dined with some friends in London, and among the company was John Oswald, an Anglican bishop. As the group was making merry after dinner Hume joked that he had been "very ill us'd" by his patron, Lord Hertford, as "I always expected to be made a Bishop by him during his Lieutenancy, but he had given away two Sees from me, to my great Vexation and Disappointment." Not taking the joke well, Oswald "without any farther Provocation, burst out into the most furious, and indecent, and orthodox Rage, that ever was seen: Told me that I was most impertinent; that if he did not wear a Gown I durst not, no, I durst not have us'd him so; that none but a Coward woud treat a Clergyman in that manner." Keeping his usual cool, Hume asked Oswald's pardon and assured him that "the Joke was not in the least against him, but entirely against myself, as if I were capable of such an Expectation as that of being a Bishop." Oswald was not to be appeased, though, and Hume was forced to take his leave of the group. The thing that most saddened him was that the clergyman's brother, James Oswald of Dunnikier, who was one of Hume's oldest and closest friends in London, had not spoken to him since. Hume closes the letter, however, playfully: "If I were sure Dear Smith that you and I shoud not one day quarrel in some such manner, I shoud tell you, that I am Yours very affectionately and sincerely, D. H."[12]

Writing from Dalkeith House—the residence of the recently married Duke of Buccleuch in Midlothian, where Smith stayed for around two months that autumn—Smith responded to Hume's story with appropriate sympathy: "I cannot easily express to you the indignation with which your last letter filled me. The Bishop [i.e., John Oswald] is a brute and a beast and unmerited preferment has rendered him, it seems, still more so. . . . He was at Kirkaldy since I received your letter and I was obliged to see him, but I did not behave to him as I otherwise would have done."[13] Hume in turn dashed off a quick note to thank Smith for his "friendly Resentment against the Right Reverend."[14]

Hume finally returned to Edinburgh, more or less for good, in August 1769. Soon after his arrival he wrote to Smith to beckon him to the city. Hume's house at James's Court faced north, and in clear weather he could see across the Firth of Forth to Kirkcaldy. "I am glad to have come within sight of you," Hume told his friend, "and to have a View of Kirkaldy from my Windows: But as I wish also to be within speaking terms of you, I wish we coud concert measures for that purpose. I am mortally sick at Sea, and regard with horror, and a kind of hydrophobia the great Gulph that lies between us." With no bridge yet connecting the two sides of the firth, the trip between Kirkcaldy and Edinburgh was a relatively short sail in good weather, but Hume proposed that Smith should make the trip rather than himself: "I am . . . tir'd of travelling, as much as you ought naturally to be, of staying at home: I therefore propose to you to come hither, and pass some days with me in this Solitude." (Hume also preferred not to make the trip himself because he tended to get seasick whenever he crossed the firth.)[15] Hume looked forward to being caught up on the state of Smith's research and writing: "I want to know what you have been doing, and propose to exact a rigorous Account of the method, in which you have employed yourself during your Retreat. I am positive you are in the wrong in many of your Speculations, especially where you have the Misfortune to differ from me." Unfortunately, he jokes, there was no middle ground to be found for their meeting, as there was little but water separating them: "There is no Habitation on the Island of Inch-keith"—a small island in the middle of the firth—"otherwise I shoud challenge you to meet me on that Spot, and neither [of] us ever to leave the Place, till we were fully agreed on all points of Controversy." Hume was to be away from town for a few days, but he tells Smith that on his return "I expect to find a Letter from you, containing a bold Acceptance of this Defiance."[16] As usual, we have no record of Smith taking Hume up on his offer at this time; indeed, for much of the next four years Smith remained in Kirkcaldy, buried in his studies.

Smith's reluctance to stir himself certainly did not prevent Hume from pressing him on that front. His letters from this period are full of pleas for Smith to join him in Edinburgh, along with reproofs for failing to do so as often, or for as long, as Hume would like: "What is the meaning of this, Dear Smith, which we hear, that you are not to be here above a day or two . . . ?" (February 1770). "Pray when do you come over to us?" (February 1770). "Mr Hume is very unhappy in never meeting with Mr Smith. He desires to remind him of his Engagement to dine with him tomorrow" (June 1772). "Shall we see you again this summer?" (June 1772). "Pray, come over this winter, and join us" (November 1772). "Surge et inhumanae senium depone Camenae"—a quotation from Horace's *Epistles* that translates, "Rise up and abandon the peevishness of the unsociable muse" (February 1773). "I expect to see you soon" (April 1773).[17]

Hume always kept a room ready for Smith, however, and Smith sometimes spent the winter holidays with him in the city—whether every year or only occasionally we do not know. Hume was unable to extend such an invitation in 1771 due to the illness of his sister, Katherine, but that did not prevent him from admonishing Smith about his own tendency to make excuses of this nature: "I shoud certainly, before this time, have challenged the Performance of your Promise, of being with me about Christmas, had it not been for the Misfortunes of my Family. . . . However, I expect, that time will re-instate [Katherine] in her former Health, in which case, I shall look for your Company. I shall not take any Excuse from your own State of Health, which I suppose only a Subterfuge invented by Indolence and Love of Solitude. Indeed, my Dear Smith, if you continue to hearken to Complaints of this nature, you will cut Yourself out entirely from human Society, to the great Loss of both Parties."[18]

Hume was equally reluctant to leave Edinburgh. Within a couple of months of his arrival he reported that he had settled in "Body & Soul," that he no longer gave the least thought to Paris or London, and that he deemed it improbable he would ever cross the Tweed again "except perhaps a Jaunt to the North of England, for Health or Amusement."[19] His letters during these years show him in great spirits, notwithstanding his growing pessimism regarding British politics. No longer having any pressing obligations, he spent his time as he pleased, mostly reading and socializing with friends. The novelist Henry Mackenzie recalled that Hume "liked to eat, and still more to give his friends a good dinner, and took a very sensible way of securing one. He had an old cook or *gouvernante* who had been with him ever since he took up house; when in France . . . he got most particular recipes for a few dishes which he liked. . . . Those few dishes he made the old woman completely mistress of, and satisfied himself with this knowledge in her, following his friend A. Smith's principle of the division of labour, limiting her excellence to those few articles."[20] More and more as time went on, though, Hume diverted himself by doing the cooking himself. In addition to his crowd-pleasing recipes for soup à la Reine and sheep's head broth, he boasted that "for Beef and Cabbage (a charming Dish), and old Mutton and old Claret, no body excels me."[21] While his friends appreciated the meals on offer, they cherished the company even more. Alexander Carlyle writes that "as Mr Hume's circumstances improved he enlarged his mode of living, and instead of the roasted hen and minced collops, and a bottle of punch, he gave both elegant dinners and suppers, and the best claret, and, which was best of all, he furnished the entertainment with the most instructive and pleasing conversation, for he assembled whosoever were most knowing and agreeable among either the laity or clergy."[22]

Upon his return to Scotland Hume found his house at James's Court still "very chearful, and even elegant, but too small to display my great Talent for Cookery, the Science to which I intend to addict the remaining Years of my Life."[23] The development of Edinburgh's New Town had begun a few years earlier, and in the autumn of 1770 he purchased a plot on the southwest corner of St. Andrew Square and began overseeing the construction of a new house.[24] The eighteenth-century equivalent of a suburb, the New Town provided a clean, spacious residential haven from the cramped squalor of what became the Old Town. Hume urged a well-traveled colonel "not to think of settling in London, till you have first seen our New Town, which exceeds anything you have seen in any part of the world."[25]

There are two delightful stories connected with Hume's move to the New Town. As his house was being built the North Bridge connecting the New Town with the Old had not yet opened, so Hume was forced to make his way across a bog that then separated the two. One day, so the story goes, he slipped from the narrow path, fell into the bog, and was unable to extract himself. Eventually he was able to draw the attention of a group of fishwives. The women, however, recognized him as "the wicked unbeliever David Hume" and refused to help him until he solemnly repeated the Lord's Prayer. He quickly complied and, true to their word, they proceeded to rescue the philosopher. According to the source for this story Hume "used to tell [it] himself with great glee, declaring that the Edinburgh fishwives were the most acute theologians he had ever encountered."[26] The second story too relates to Hume's reputation for impiety. In May 1771 he moved into the new house, which stood so far on the outskirts of town that its street had not yet even been given a name. According to legend, one day Nancy Ord, a young woman who was very close to Hume—he may have even considered proposing marriage to her— mischievously chalked "St. David Street" on the wall. Hume's housekeeper, Peggy Irvine, took offense, but Hume reassured her, "many a better man has been made a saint of before."[27] The street retains the name to this day.

The autumn after moving into the new house Hume hosted Benjamin Franklin for nearly a month. Franklin wrote to William Strahan that upon arriving in Edinburgh he was "lodg'd miserably at an Inn: But that excellent Christian David Hume, agreable to the Precepts of the Gospel, has *received the Stranger*, and I now live with him at his House in the new Town most happily."[28] The pair spent several weeks having dinner after dinner among the literati, though we have no record of Smith making the voyage from Kirkcaldy to join them.

A few months after Franklin departed Hume wrote to assure him that "the good Wishes of all your Brother Philosophers in this place [i.e., Edinburgh] attend you heartily and sincerely." He also muses on the factiousness of the age and its effects on his own reputation: "I expected, in entering on my literary Course, that all the Christians, all the Whigs, and all the Tories shoud be my Enemies: But it is hard, that all the English, Irish, and Welsh shoud be also against me. The Scotch, likewise, cannot be much my Friends, as no man is a Prophet in his own Country. . . . I fancy that I must have recourse to America for Justice."[29]

Hume's reputation would have to rest on the works that he had already completed, as he decided once and for all that he was done writing books. He had long been pressed by his publishers to extend his *History of England* beyond 1689. Though he sometimes flirted with the idea, the flirtation never lasted for long. Soon after leaving France, while still in the company of Rousseau, he had paused to consult Smith about the matter. While Hume was sure to have access to whatever papers he wanted and Andrew Millar was offering him "any Price," he found the prospect less than enticing: "Cui bono? Why shoud I forgo Idleness and Sauntering and Society; and expose myself again to the Clamours of a stupid, factious Public? I am not yet tir'd of doing nothing. . . . By and bye I shall be too old to undergo so much Labour."[30] We do not have a reply from Smith, but we do know his opinion on the subject. Later that year Millar sought to persuade Hume to add to his *History* by reporting that Smith "is of opinion . . . that the History of this country from the Revolution is not to be met with in books yet printed" but that it could easily be written based on manuscripts in London "to which he is sure you will have ready access . . . and therefor you should lay the ground Work here [in London] after the Perusal of the MSS you may have access to [in Edinburgh]. . . . I think it my duty to inform you the opinion of your most judicious friends and I think he . . . may be reckoned among that number."[31] In the end, however, Hume gave William Strahan four good reasons why he had determined to resist such entreaties: "Because I'm too old, too fat, too lazy, and too rich."[32]

Still, Hume was not one to remain intellectually idle for long. In addition to keeping up to date on the latest works of philosophy and history, he continued to tinker with his own writings; throughout his later years there are scores of letters to Strahan giving him instructions on that front. Although Hume claimed that these corrections were little more than a pleasant distraction, it is clear that he also had an eye on his future reputation: "I am sensible, it is an idle Amusement; but still it is an Amusement to think that Posterity will do me more Justice than the present Age, whose Suffrage indeed coud not have given me great Vanity."[33] He found that his philosophical works were selling better, and his historical works worse, than he expected, and he owned that "this proves only, that factious prejudices are more prevalent in England than religious ones" at the moment.[34]

In lieu of writing a new book of his own Hume sought to encourage Smith's work on *The Wealth of Nations* by gently prodding his friend, passing along relevant news, and occasionally obtaining books that Smith needed. In June 1772 he wrote to forward some information on the recent economic crisis precipitated by the collapse of the Ayr Bank—the first of three letters that would touch on that topic—and to inquire, "Do these Events any-wise affect your Theory? Or will it occasion the Revisal of any Chapters?" Hume offers his own opinion on the fall of the bank and its liberal lending policies: "On the whole, I believe, that the Check given to our exorbitant and ill grounded Credit will prove of Advantage in the long run, as it will reduce people to more solid and less sanguine Projects, and at the same time introduce Frugality among the Merchants and Manufacturers: What say you? Here is Food for your Speculation."[35] As it happens, the history, causes, and lessons of this crisis did make their way into Smith's book, and he too concluded that the Ayr Bank's failure might actually prove beneficial in the long run since if it had succeeded it "would only have transferred a great part of [Britain's capital] from prudent and profitable, to imprudent and unprofitable undertakings."[36]

Not content to confine their discussions to the mail, that November Hume tried yet again to persuade Smith to move to Edinburgh. This time the enticement on offer was not the promise of a university post but rather an available apartment in the New Town, not far from Hume's residence on St. David Street, with "five chearful Rooms, three of good Size" and a prospect of the surrounding hills, the firth, "and even, I believe Kirkaldy to the East." "Shall I bespeak it for you?" Hume asks. "Have you Resolution enough to determine Yourself for your good?"[37] Smith seems to have begged off once more in a now-lost letter—perhaps on the grounds that moving to the city would interrupt his work on *The Wealth of Nations*, or perhaps because he was soon to travel to London to publish the work—for Hume's next letter, written about a week later, begins by chiding: "I shou'd agree to your Reasoning, if I coud trust your Resolution. Come hither for some weeks about Christmas; dissipate yourself a little; return to Kirkaldy; finish your Work before Autumn; go to London; print it; return and settle in this Town, which suits your studious, independant turn even better than London: Execute this plan faithfully; and I forgive you."[38] Regrettably, Smith's deliberate work habits frustrated Hume's plans yet again. By the time Smith finally finished his work and had it printed in London Hume's terminal illness had set in, and Smith would not settle in Edinburgh for good until Hume had been in his grave for more than a year.

Evidently growing somewhat anxious about Smith's progress—or lack thereof—on *The Wealth of Nations*, Hume wrote in April 1773 to inquire, "Have you been busy, and whether in pulling down or building up?"[39] In fact, in less than a week Smith would at last be on his way to London to complete his book and have it published. At the time of his departure Smith was sufficiently concerned about his health that he stopped in Edinburgh to make arrangements for the event of his death, naming Hume his literary executor. Smith advises Hume that other than the papers related to *The Wealth of Nations*, which he would bring with him to London, "there are none worth the publishing, but a fragment of a great work which contains a history of the Astronomical Systems that were successively in fashion down to the time of Des Cartes." This is, obviously, a reference to the first part of *The Principles Which Lead and Direct Philosophical Enquiries*, discussed in chapter 2. "Whether that might not be published as a fragment of an intended juvenile work," Smith says, "I leave entirely to your judgement." He requests that all of his other papers—"eighteen thin paper folio books" along with some other loose papers—"may be destroyed without any examination." If Smith's health were to fail to the point that he could no longer publish *The Wealth of Nations* himself, he would have the manuscript sent to Hume to see through the press.[40] With these arrangements in place and his anxiety over his literary reputation assuaged, Smith headed for London, where he would remain for the next three years.

While in London Smith resumed the more socially active lifestyle that he had enjoyed during his time in Paris. He was elected a member of the Literary Club, better known as Samuel Johnson's Club, though he continued to clash with Johnson and his protégé. Johnson opined that Smith was "as dull a dog as he had ever met with," and James Boswell found it "strange . . . to find my old professor in London, a professed infidel with a bag-wig."[41] Smith, for his part, found some of Johnson's affectations baffling: "I have seen that creature bolt up in the midst of a mixed company; and, without any previous notice, fall upon his knees behind a chair, repeat the Lord's Prayer, and then resume his seat at the table. He has played this freak over and over, perhaps fix or six times in the course of an evening. It is not hypocrisy, but madness."[42] Smith got on much better with his longtime admirer Edmund Burke, as well as another new member of the Literary Club, Edward Gibbon—Smith's "brother infidel," as Boswell scoffed.[43] He also resumed his connection with Benjamin Franklin, who was in London until March 1775, and may have even discussed various chapters of *The Wealth of Nations* with him.[44]

Unhappily, Hume and Smith seem to have lost touch with one another during this period, comparatively speaking. Between Smith's departure for London in April 1773 and the winter of 1776 we have just one letter from Hume to Smith and another from Smith to Hume, and both refer to a lack of communication between the two. Hume's message of February 1774 begins, "You are in the wrong for never informing me of your Intentions and Resolutions, if you have fix'd any."[45] Smith apologizes, or rather does not apologize, in his note of May 1775: "I should be ashamed to write to you, if I had not long ago conquered all modesty of that sort. Taking it for granted, therefore, that you hate apologies as much as I do, I meant both making them and receiving them, I shall not pretend to make any for having so long neglected to write to you. I hope I need not tell you that my long silence did not arise from any want of the most affectionate and most grateful remembrance of you."[46] On the other hand, the two continued to show interest in each other's activities and concern about each other's welfare, and they were kept up to date on these scores through mutual friends in their respective cities.[47]

Now that it was Smith rather than Hume who lived in London, Hume hoped that he would pass along news from the city, as Hume had done while serving as Under-Secretary of State in the Northern Department. Smith was well placed to perform such a function, given that he met regularly with a number of prominent men of letters and politicians, but clearly it was not to his taste. In his letter of February 1774 Hume presses for a report on Benjamin Franklin's examination before the Privy Council in January of that year. Franklin stood accused of having surreptitiously sent back to Boston some letters from Thomas Hutchinson, the royal governor of Massachusetts, in which Hutchinson advocated the use of force against the people of the colony. "Pray, what strange Accounts are these we hear of Franklyn's Conduct?" Hume inquires. "I am very slow in believing that he has been guilty in the extreme Degree that is pretended; tho' I always knew him to be a very factious man, and Faction, next to Fanaticism, is, of all passions, the most destructive of Morality."[48] (Consciously or unconsciously, Smith would echo this claim in the sixth edition of *The Theory of Moral Sentiments*, writing that "of all the corrupters of moral sentiments . . . faction and fanaticism have always been by far the greatest.")[49]

While Hume must have expected that such queries would remain unanswered, he had not entirely given up hope that Smith would return to live with him in Edinburgh. Adam Ferguson, then Professor of Moral Philosophy at Edinburgh University, planned to be away from the university for a time to take on a traveling tutorship, but he hoped to return to his position when his travels came to an end. The town council objected to this idea, and Hume proposed to Smith that "the chief Difficulty wou'd be remov'd" if he (Smith) would agree to "supply [Ferguson's] Class, either as his Substitute or his Successor, with a Purpose of resigning upon his return."[50] To have Smith teaching nearby, even if on a temporary basis, would clearly be a step in the right direction, from Hume's point of view, but yet again nothing came of his efforts.

Smith was finally roused to take up his pen in May 1775 in order to perform a favor for a friend, namely recommending to Hume one Charles Bonnet, a natural historian, whom he describes as "one of the worthiest, and best hearted men in Geneva or indeed in the world; notwithstanding he is one of the most religious." He also reports that "your friends here [in London] have been all much diverted with Priestly's answer to Beatie"—that is, Joseph Priestley's recently published critique of James Beattie and the "common sense" school that included some of Hume's chief philosophical critics, titled *An Examination of Reid's Inquiry, Beattie's Essay, and Oswald's Appeal to Common Sense.*[51] Smith and his London friends hoped that Beattie would publish a reply and thereby keep the entertaining controversy alive, but Beattie was advised against doing so.

Smith's letter also includes a seemingly offhand statement that must have pleased Hume immensely: "I shall send my own book to the Press in the end of this month or the beginning of the next."[52] By the following February Hume still had not received word of the work's publication, leading him to write to Smith in a state of some alarm: "I am as lazy a Correspondent as you; yet my Anxiety about you makes me write. By all Accounts, your Book has been printed long ago; yet it has never yet been so much as advertised. What is the Reason?" Hume had heard through the Duke of Buccleuch that Smith was "very zealous in American Affairs"—meaning, of course, the recent struggles between Britain and its colonies—but he warns, "if you wait till the Fate of America be decided, you may wait long." Hume offers his own opinion that "the Matter is not so important as is commonly imagind," but he cheerfully accepts that "if I be mistaken, I shall probably correct my Error, when I see you or read you."[53] As we will see, the conflict did end up playing a key role in *The Wealth of Nations.*

Hume's other query, predictably, has to do with Smith's plans for after the book's publication: "By all accounts, you intend to settle with us this Spring: Yet we hear no more of it: What is the Reason? Your Chamber in my House is always unoccupied: I am always at home: I expect you to land here." This time, though, Hume's pleas took on a special urgency: "I have been, am, and shall be probably in an indifferent State of Health. I weighed myself t'other day, and I find I have fallen five compleat Stones [i.e., seventy pounds]. If you delay much longer, I shall probably disappear altogether."[54] Hume need not have worried, however: within two months he would be writing again to congratulate Smith on the publication of his second great work, and within another month they would finally reunite in the flesh.

CHAPTER 9

INQUIRING INTO THE WEALTH OF NATIONS

(1776)

THE FINAL YEAR of Hume and Smith's friendship was an eventful one. During the course of 1776 Smith published the book on which his reputation would come to rest; he and Hume clashed over the fate of the latter's *Dialogues Concerning Natural Religion*; Hume's health declined rapidly, culminating in his much-scrutinized death; and Smith composed a controversial account of Hume's end that would provoke the abiding ire of the devout. Each of these events will require a chapter of its own.

Whatever Smith himself may have thought about the relative merits of his two books, it was the second that had the greater impact. Hyperbolic tributes to the importance and influence of *The Wealth of Nations* could be multiplied almost without limit, but a few representative examples will suffice. Immediately after Smith's death his biographer Dugald Stewart called it "unquestionably . . . the most comprehensive and perfect work that has yet appeared, on the general principles of any branch of legislation."[1] The nineteenth-century historian Henry Thomas Buckle proclaimed that "looking at its ultimate results, [it] is probably the most important book that has ever been written."[2] More recently leading scholars have called it "the greatest and most enduring monument to the intellectual culture of the Scottish Enlightenment," "the most influential of all Enlightenment contributions to human science," "the greatest book ever written about economic life," and "one of the most remarkable books in the history of thought."[3] One best-selling author asserts that "Smith's *Wealth of Nations* may be the one book between Newton's *Principia* and Darwin's *Origin of Species* that actually, substantially, and almost immediately started improving the quality of human life and thought."[4]

While the book's power and fame are hardly in question, one unintended effect of such extraordinary encomiums is that they serve to minimize the contributions of Smith's predecessors in the field of political economy—including, of course, Hume.[5]

———

It is harder to gauge the level of Smith's engagement with Hume in his second book than in his first.[6] While Hume is never mentioned by name in *The Theory of Moral Sentiments*, his influence is palpable throughout; indeed, there is little question that Hume was Smith's primary—though certainly not sole—interlocutor in the construction and presentation of his moral theory. There is much to suggest that Hume also played a key role in the development of Smith's views on political economy. In *The Wealth of Nations* Smith cites Hume by name five times, and at another point he transcribes four full paragraphs from *The History of England*, calling its author "by far the most illustrious philosopher and historian of the present age."[7] One of the five explicit citations, to be discussed in the next section, appears in what may be the key paragraph of the entire book. In another Smith notes that while it had long been thought that interest rates depend principally on the quantity of gold and silver in circulation, "this notion, which at first sight seems so plausible, has been so fully exposed by Mr. Hume, that it is, perhaps, unnecessary to say any thing more about it."[8] (True to the book's prolix form, however, Smith proceeds to elaborate the point for several more pages.)

Dugald Stewart acknowledges that Smith's views on political economy were deeply shaped by others, including his teacher Francis Hutcheson and his childhood friend James Oswald of Dunnikier, but he nevertheless judges that "the Political Discourses of Mr Hume were evidently of greater use to Mr Smith, than any other book that had appeared prior to his lectures"—that is, Smith's lectures on political economy at Glasgow, on which *The Wealth of Nations* was partly based.[9] A contemporary scholar concurs that Hume's *Political Discourses* "exercised a profound influence on Smith" and that "without them, *The*

Wealth of Nations is almost unimaginable."¹⁰ Nor was it only the *Political Discourses* that influenced Smith's thinking on these matters. Hume also discusses commerce and commercial policy extensively in *The History of England*—Ernest Campbell Mossner calls it "the first popular history explaining and defending capitalistic society"—and in fact several of Smith's citations of Hume are to this work rather than to his essays.¹¹

Yet compared to *The Theory of Moral Sentiments* there are actually *fewer* passages in *The Wealth of Nations* in which Smith is clearly developing or contesting his friend's views. Moreover, some of the key themes of the book were scarcely even broached in Hume's writings, most notably Smith's claim regarding the centrality of the division of labor to productivity.¹² For these reasons, the distinguished economist Jacob Viner goes so far as to suggest that "in *The Wealth of Nations* there is little sign that Smith had profited from Hume's contribution."¹³ This seems much too strong. It is impossible to name a single key interlocutor or source of influence for a book as sprawling and detail-oriented as *The Wealth of Nations*, but Hume's impact was surely significant, even if it issued more from Hume's general attitude toward commerce and political economy than from specific passages in his writings. Regardless, if we leave the always-tricky question of intellectual influence aside, it is undeniable that some of the central arguments of Smith's book are also present in works that Hume published decades earlier.

If asked to nominate the single most important passage in *The Wealth of Nations*, a reasonable candidate would be the climactic claim of Book 3: "commerce and manufactures gradually introduced order and good government, and with them, the liberty and security of individuals, among the inhabitants of the country, who had before lived almost in a continual state of war with their neighbours, and of servile dependency on their superiors. This, though it has been the least observed, is by far the most important of all their effects."¹⁴ The significance of the passage should be obvious: it is Smith's most explicit and categorical statement in his entire corpus regarding what he sees as the most important benefit of commerce. Again, he contends that the promotion of personal liberty and security is *by far* the most important of *all* of commerce's effects. And on this pivotal point Smith fulsomely acknowledges his debt to Hume. Immediately after noting that the promotion of liberty and security has been "the least observed" effect of commerce, Smith writes: "Mr. Hume is the only writer who, so far as I know, has hitherto taken notice of it."[15]

Before assessing this claim it will be helpful to step back and look at the context in which Smith makes it. Much of Book 3 is dedicated to a historical narrative describing how and why the feudal order that prevailed throughout Europe for many centuries eventually gave way to a liberal, commercial order—that is, how a world dominated by hierarchy, dependence, and intrastate conflict was superseded by one in which the rule of law reigned and the people enjoyed comparative freedom and security. Smith's account of how the feudal lords squandered their immense power for the sake of frivolous luxuries has become a famous one. After the fall of the Roman Empire, he recounts, the great landowners throughout Europe possessed huge estates over which they exercised almost complete control, because the kings' authority was rarely strong enough to challenge them on a local level. Given the relative absence of luxuries and manufactured goods in these societies, the lords had little use for their wealth other than to "maintain" thousands of serfs, who in turn became utterly dependent on their patrons for sustenance, accommodation, and protection: "Every great landlord was a sort of petty prince. His tenants were his subjects. He was their judge, and in some respects their legislator in peace, and their leader in war. He made war at his own discretion, frequently against his neighbours, and sometimes against his sovereign."[16] Smith forcefully draws the reader's attention to the serfs' almost total lack of personal freedom: they could have no private property that was free from encroachment by their lord, they were bought and sold with the land and so were unable to move freely, they typically could not choose their own occupations, and they often had to obtain their lord's consent to get married. In all, they were little better than slaves.[17]

The kings struggled for centuries to limit the power of the lords without success, Smith writes, "but what all the violence of the feudal institutions could never have effected, the silent and insensible operation of foreign commerce and manufactures gradually brought about." Once commerce expanded and luxuries were introduced, the lords finally had something on which to spend their wealth other than maintaining their serfs; these goods gave them a way to spend their money on themselves alone, one that they immediately adopted out of greed and vanity. Thus, "for a pair of diamond buckles perhaps, or for something as frivolous and useless, they exchanged the maintenance, or what is the same thing, the price of the maintenance of a thousand men for a year, and with it the whole weight and authority which it could give them."[18] Once the lords began to spend the bulk of their wealth on luxuries, in other words, they could no longer afford to keep their dependents. And after the serfs were dismissed, Smith writes, "the great proprietors were no longer capable of interrupting the regular execution of justice, or of disturbing the peace of the country. Having sold their birth-right, not like Esau for a mess of pottage in a time of hunger and necessity, but in the wantonness of plenty, for trinkets and baubles, fitter to be the play-things of children than the serious pursuits of men, they became as insignificant as any substantial burgher or tradesman in a city."

According to Smith the fall of the feudal lords resulted in an enormous increase in the power of the kings—as happened in Britain under the Tudors—who were then able to establish a what he calls a "regular government," meaning one that was strong enough to effectively enforce order and administer justice throughout the country.[19] This in turn led to a great increase in personal freedom among the populace. In commercial societies governed by the rule of law, Smith holds, the rich may have a great deal of purchasing power, but their wealth does not lead to direct authority over others since everyone stands in a market relationship with everyone else and there are generally a multitude of potential buyers, sellers, and employers.[20] Of course, wealthy individuals frequently support many others *indirectly* by employing them or by buying goods that they produce, but Smith argues that this indirect support is not enough to place these people at their command. Even if employees are likely to try to please their employers in order to keep their jobs, for example, it is highly unlikely that they would surrender their rights to them or accompany them into battle. Hence the upshot of Smith's story is, to repeat, that commerce helped to introduce "order and good government, and with them, the liberty and security of individuals . . . who had before lived almost in a continual state of war with their neighbours, and of servile dependency on their superiors."

While the story is a dramatic and powerful one, it is striking, and a bit amusing, that it has become one of the most famous sections of Smith's most famous book, as its basic outlines are lifted straight from Hume: a similar narrative is present in both the *Political Discourses* (very briefly) and several volumes of *The History of England* (at greater length).[21] Hume too paints the feudal lords, even more than the clergy, as the chief enemies of liberty and security throughout much of European history, and he too suggests that after "the habits of luxury dissipated the immense fortunes of the ancient barons" they "retained only that moderate influence, which customers have over tradesmen, and which can never be dangerous to civil government."[22] Hume calls the downfall of the lords a "secret revolution of government"; Smith calls it "a revolution of the greatest importance to the publick happiness."[23] Of course, Smith told the story in much greater detail, and made its lessons far more central to his broader argument, than Hume had. He also adapted the story to other contexts, giving a nearly identical explanation of the decline of the temporal power of the clergy in medieval Europe, the decline of the nobility in ancient Athens and Rome, and the rise in public debt among commercial nations.[24] Still, the core of this all-important argument seems to have been borrowed directly from Hume—which explains, presumably, the fulsome acknowledgment quoted above.

Smith's claim that Hume was the "only writer" to have "taken notice of" the way in which commerce promoted "order and good government, and with them, the liberty and security of individuals" is perhaps not an entirely fair one. Several other prominent philosophers, from John Locke to Montesquieu, had also connected increased commerce with increased liberty and security. On the specific mechanism that Smith points to—the way in which luxury caused the fall of the feudal lords—Hume has a greater claim to priority, but even here a similar point had been made by others before the publication of *The Wealth of Nations*, including their friends William Robertson and John Millar.[25] On the other hand, Smith had told the same tale in similar terms to his students at least by 1763—several years ahead of Robertson's and Millar's books—and perhaps much earlier.[26] Smith's claim regarding Hume's uniqueness on this score may thus be a sign of the early provenance of this part of the book.[27] In any case, this passage suggests that Smith's central argument regarding the social and political benefits of commerce was inspired by Hume.

The most celebrated aspect of *The Wealth of Nations*, namely Smith's case in favor of free trade, too was at least anticipated by Hume, if not inspired by him. Smith's main polemical foe in the book was the same as Hume's had been in the *Political Discourses*: the reigning economic perspective of the day—it would be too much to call it a theory—which we now call mercantilism.[28] Most politicians, most merchants, and most of those who wrote on commercial matters in the eighteenth century assumed that gold and silver were the key sources of national power and thus that nations should do everything they could to skew the balance of trade so as to accumulate as much of these precious metals as possible. As Smith explains, based on these assumptions "nations have been taught that their interest consisted in beggaring all their neighbours. Each nation has been made to look with an invidious eye upon the prosperity of all the nations with which it trades, and to consider their gain as its own loss."[29] Commerce was seen as a form of war by other means, and the key weapons in this war came from governmental intervention in the economy: duties on imports, bounties on exports, and legal monopolies and trade prohibitions designed to protect or stimulate domestic industries.

One of Smith's primary aims in *The Wealth of Nations* was to combat this perspective and the errors and prejudices on which it was founded. The very fact that he set out to investigate the source of the wealth of *nations* (in the plural) shows just how deeply his entire mind-set diverged from that of the mercantilists. For Smith, trade is not a zero-sum game: France's gain need not be Britain's loss. On the contrary, both nations can benefit by trading with one another. In his view, the notion that trade is always a zero-sum contest stems principally from childish "national prejudice and animosity," though it is reinforced by the private interests of merchants.[30] Hume had taken a similarly cosmopolitan view in his *Political Discourses*, and he underlined the point in an essay added in 1758, titled "Of the Jealousy of Trade." In opposition to the "narrow and malignant opinion" that leads nations "to look on the progress of their neighbours with a suspicious eye, [and] to consider all trading states as their rivals," Hume argues, just as Smith later would, that nations are helped rather than hurt by having flourishing trading partners. When your trading partners flourish, after all, they have the means to buy your goods, and you can benefit from their inventions and improvements. Hence, Hume pointedly ends the essay by proclaiming that not only as a man, but also as a British subject, he prays (!) for the prosperity of Germany, Spain, Italy, and, yes, "even FRANCE itself."[31]

As its full title indicates, *An Inquiry into the Nature and Causes of the Wealth of Nations* is concerned with the *nature* as well as the *causes* of wealth, and Smith seeks to show that the mercantilists were mistaken on both fronts—just as Hume had in his essays. With respect to the nature of wealth, the mercantilists often confused gold and silver, the *markers* of wealth, with wealth itself. Yet Smith regards it as obvious that real wealth consists not in precious metals but rather in an abundance of affordable goods and services: "It would be too ridiculous to go about seriously to prove," he writes, "that wealth does not consist in money, or in gold and silver; but in what money purchases."[32] Hume too had insisted that money is nothing more than a medium of exchange: "It is none of the wheels of trade: It is the oil which renders the motion of the wheels more smooth and easy. If we consider any one kingdom by itself, it is evident, that the greater or less plenty of money is of no consequence; since the prices of commodities are always proportioned to the plenty of money, and a crown in HARRY VII.'s time served the same purpose as a pound does at present."[33] Though the point seems obvious to many today, and though Hume was not the first to make it, one historian of economic thought observes that "no one before him had stated the idea as clearly or as succinctly."[34]

As for the causes of wealth, Smith contends that the primary source of prosperity is not a favorable balance of trade, as the mercantilists held, but rather the division of labor. And given that the division of labor is limited by the extent of the market, free trade both within and among nations helps to promote the prosperity of all. Here too Hume had made a broadly similar argument. While Hume took virtually no notice of the division of labor, he too maintained that prosperity derives principally from a productive citizenry and that a general policy of free trade is the surest means to that end. This view is evident not only in his *Political Discourses*—especially "Of the Balance of Trade" and "Of the Jealousy of Trade"—but also throughout *The History of England*, particularly the Tudor volumes.[35] Similarly, in a recently discovered manuscript from 1758 Hume defends free trade in corn (i.e., grain) and makes a pitch for the usefulness of corn dealers, the widely despised "middlemen" of the grain trade—anticipating Smith's much more detailed case against the corn laws by almost two decades.[36]

Neither Hume nor Smith was a free market absolutist, of course: both recognized the need for government action for the sake of national defense, the administration of justice, the provision of certain public works, at the very least.[37] Indeed, both emphasized the need for the government to be *strong* enough to enforce order and rules of fair play; the absence of such a government was precisely what had made the feudal era such a sad spectacle. Yet Hume and Smith insisted that when politicians intervene in the economy for the sake of promoting national prosperity their actions are usually either futile or positively counterproductive.

As one of the earliest high-profile works to argue against mercantilism and in favor of free trade, the *Political Discourses* surely helped to pave the way for *The Wealth of Nations*. That said, Hume was probably *not* the direct inspiration for Smith's belief in the value of free trade. Indeed, Dugald Stewart suggests that Smith was eager to assert his originality on that score and that he had argued against unnecessary governmental interference in the economy as early as his public lectures in Edinburgh in the winter of 1751—around a year before Hume's *Political Discourses* were released.[38] It is also unquestionable that Smith's case on behalf of free trade was far more detailed and systematic than Hume's; indeed, even today it remains one of the most comprehensive such cases ever made. Still, it is striking that both the most important argument of *The Wealth of Nations* (regarding the way commerce helped to promote liberty and security) and the most celebrated argument of the book (regarding the benefits of free trade) are also found in earlier works by Hume.

As usual, though, Smith also diverged from his friend's views in important respects. One of their contemporaries, a natural scientist named John Playfair, commented that in *The Wealth of Nations* Smith "corrects David Hume on innumerable occasions, which his own delicacy, & respect for his Friend have not suffered him to mention."[39] While Playfair does not specify what these "innumerable occasions" were, one area in which Smith deviated notably from Hume was his much greater readiness to acknowledge the potential drawbacks of commerce and commercial society. As we have seen, Hume maintained, in stark opposition to many religious thinkers and civic republicans, that commerce helps to promote not just prosperity but also virtue, liberty, civility, knowledge, and happiness, and that these crucial advantages are not "attended with disadvantages, that bear any proportion to them."[40] A leading scholar of the Scottish Enlightenment writes that "this is Hume at his least sceptical: he had none of the doubts and misgivings which Adam Smith and all the other leading thinkers of the Scottish Enlightenment had about the all-round benefits of commercial civilization. The progress of civilization is an improvement on all fronts."[41]

To say that Hume had *no* doubts or misgivings is a slight overstatement, however. Hume did sound an alarm regarding two key features of the commercial societies of his day, namely their imperialistic tendencies and their rapidly mounting public debts. These problems were closely linked, in his eyes, insofar as much of the public debt of Britain and other European nations had been racked up to pay for their colonial adventures. In the last paragraph of the *Political Discourses* Hume ominously pronounces that "extensive conquests, when pursued, must be the ruin of every free government," and the essay "Of Public Credit" is easily the darkest of the group: Hume writes that the practice of amassing public debt "appears ruinous, beyond all controversy," that it will lead to "poverty, impotence, and subjection to foreign powers," and that ultimately "either the nation must destroy public credit, or public credit will destroy the nation."[42] Smith echoed Hume, though in far more detail, on both counts. The devastating chapter on colonies is one of the longest of *The Wealth of Nations*, and Smith too concludes his book with a warning about the costs of imperial conquest.[43] He also paints an equally dire picture of the accumulation of public debt, writing that "the progress of the enormous public debts which at present oppress, and will in the long-run probably ruin, all the great nations of Europe, has been pretty uniform."[44] Indeed, Smith's discussion of this topic reads like a lengthy elaboration on Hume's.[45]

Yet for Smith these problems represented only the tip of a veritable iceberg. As Smith scholars—the present author included—are forever fond of pointing out, he stressed the drawbacks of commercial society far more than might be expected from the figure who is now widely hailed as "the founding father of capitalism."[46] One of the deepest such drawbacks had already come to the fore in *The Theory of Moral Sentiments*, where Smith notes that in commercial societies people often undergo nearly endless toil and anxiety in the pursuit of frivolous material goods that provide only fleeting satisfaction.[47] (One of his most forceful statements to this effect, recall, came in Part 4, which is directed largely at Hume.) Hume maintained that action is a key ingredient of happiness and hence that in commercial societies, where people are "kept in perpetual occupation," they "enjoy, as their reward" not just the fruits of their labor but also "the occupation itself."[48] Smith maintains, in stark contrast, that "happiness consists in tranquillity and enjoyment," and he insists—even in *The Wealth of Nations*—that labor is "toil and trouble" and that it requires an individual to "lay down [a] portion of his ease, his liberty, and his happiness."[49] He speaks of "all that toil, all that anxiety, all those mortifications which must be undergone in the pursuit of [wealth and greatness]; and what is of yet more consequence, all that leisure, all that ease, all that careless security, which are forfeited for ever by the acquisition."[50] And the continual pursuit of wealth is, in Smith's view, not just a minor component of commercial society but rather the very engine that drives it: "The uniform, constant, and uninterrupted effort of every man to better his condition [is] the principle from which publick and national, as well as private opulence is originally derived."[51] For Smith, then, very much unlike for Hume, the wealth of nations is made possible only by a massive self-deception about the true nature and source of happiness.[52]

Smith also highlights a number of drawbacks of commercial society in *The Wealth of Nations*. One of them, which is closely linked with his critique of mercantilism, concerns the tendency of merchants to collude against the public interest. Smith's comments on the malicious activities of rich and powerful merchants could hardly be more disparaging; his attitude toward them has been called "hypercritical and almost pathologically suspicious."[53] He speaks, for instance, of their "impertinent jealousy," "mean rapacity," and "interested sophistry," and he declares that the laws that they have "extorted from the legislature, for the support of their own absurd and oppressive monopolies" may "like the laws of Draco . . . be said to be all written in blood."[54] Hume, while also critical of mercantilism, was generally effusive in his praise of merchants. He describes them, for example, as "one of the most useful races of men" because they help to link together distant regions and thereby enable the "intercourse of good offices [to] be carried on to the greatest extent and intricacy."[55] Indeed, Hume's applause for the merchant class was sufficiently enthusiastic that one scholar has wondered "why it was not Hume rather than Smith who became the poster boy for free-market capitalism."[56]

Another of Smith's foremost worries concerns the deleterious effects of the division of labor on workers. While Smith regards the division of labor as the prime driver of economic growth, he also suggests that when an individual spends the bulk of his life working at a single task, such as fashioning the eighteenth part of a pin, he has no occasion to utilize his mind and hence stands in danger of growing "as stupid and ignorant as it is possible for a human creature to become." His description of such a worker is as blunt and harsh as any passage in his works: "The torpor of his mind renders him, not only incapable of relishing or bearing a part in any rational conversation, but of conceiving any generous, noble, or tender sentiment. . . . The uniformity of his stationary life . . . corrupts even the activity of his body, and renders him incapable of exerting his strength with vigour and perseverance, in any other employment than that to which he has been bred. His dexterity at his own particular trade seems, in this manner, to be acquired at the expense of his intellectual, social, and martial virtues."[57] While Hume places almost no emphasis on the division of labor, he holds that commercial society more generally has virtually the opposite effects. Greater "knowledge" and "humanity" are, after all, two of the key links in the "indissoluble chain" to which he claims commerce and refinement give rise, and he also insists that luxury will not undermine people's martial spirit because the third link in the chain, "industry," renders them physically and mentally tougher.[58] While Smith's outlook was far less rose-colored than Hume's on this front, it was not quite as bleak as the above-quoted passage might suggest. He ends his harsh account of the division of labor's effects by observing that "in every improved and civilized society this is the state into which the labouring poor, that is, the great body of the people, must necessarily fall, unless government takes some pains to prevent it."[59] This last phrase is key: Smith holds that government can help to prevent this problem through compulsory, state-supported education aimed especially at the children of the poor.[60] Thus, while the mental mutilation caused by the division of labor is one of Smith's great worries, as his harsh language demonstrates, this is a danger that he believes can be largely avoided.

Still another important drawback of commercial society, one much less easily avoided, is its tendency to produce massive economic inequalities.[61] Indeed, Smith holds that "wherever there is great property, there is great inequality. For one very rich man, there must be at least five hundred poor, and the affluence of the few supposes the indigence of the many."[62] An early manuscript version of part of *The Wealth of Nations* is even more pointed. There Smith declares that "with regard to the produce of the labour of a great society there is never any such thing as a fair and equal division" since "those who labour most get least" and "the poor labourer . . . bears, as it were, upon his shoulders the whole fabric of society."[63] While commercial inequality may not lead to the kind of utter personal dependence that the serfs faced under feudalism, in Smith's view, in *The Theory of Moral Sentiments* he argues that it does serve to distort people's sympathies, leading them to admire and emulate the very rich and to neglect and even scorn the poor.[64] As a result, the latter suffer not just the material deprivations of poverty but also the feelings of invisibility and even shame that often accompany it. Moreover, Smith suggests that our admiration for the wealthy is especially problematic because the wealthy do not in fact tend to be terribly admirable people. On the contrary, he portrays the "superior stations" of society as suffused with "vice and folly," "presumption and vanity," "flattery and falsehood," "proud ambition and ostentatious avidity."[65] Hence Smith's striking claim, added in the sixth edition of *The Theory of Moral Sentiments*, that the "disposition to admire, and almost to worship, the rich and the powerful, and to despise, or, at least, to neglect persons of poor and mean condition" is "the great and most universal cause of the corruption of our moral sentiments."[66] While Hume occasionally touches on the potential drawbacks of economic inequality, in general he was far more complacent on this score than Smith was.[67]

None of this is to suggest that Smith's embrace of commercial society was in any way partial or halfhearted. On the contrary, he joined Hume in regarding commercial society as unequivocally preferable to the alternatives. More primitive ways of life struck him too as wholly disagreeable. Yet even as Smith agreed with Hume that the benefits of commercial society—liberty, security, prosperity, and the rest—vastly outweigh the costs, he was far more willing to acknowledge that there *are* costs involved, and to seek ways to ameliorate them.

* * *

The one issue on which Smith challenges Hume directly in *The Wealth of Nations* concerns the relationship between church and state. On the whole the book's language and outlook are notably secular. To begin with, the very fact that Smith so openly praises and promotes commerce struck some as sacrilegious; the Victorian critic John Ruskin called him a "half-bred and half-witted Scotchman" who propagated the "deliberate blasphemy . . . 'Thou shalt hate the Lord thy God, damn His laws, and covet thy neighbour's goods.'"[68] Beyond this, *The Wealth of Nations* contains none of the invocations of a providential order that pervade *The Theory of Moral Sentiments* (especially the early editions). Smith never so much as refers to "God," "providence," or "the author of nature" anywhere in the lengthy book, and his only mentions of "the Deity" come in the context of describing the subjects of study in the classical world and the medieval universities.[69] In the one section of the work dedicated to the subject of religion, or rather the question of religious establishment, the only authorities whom Smith cites are Machiavelli, Hume, and Voltaire—authors not exactly noted for their piety.[70]

Moreover, Smith's scattered comments on the moral, social, and political effects of Christianity are generally quite critical. For instance, in a passage reminiscent of Hume's derision of the "monkish virtues" in the *Second Enquiry*, Smith contrasts "the liberal, generous, and spirited conduct of a man" with "penance and mortification" and "the austerities and abasement of a monk."[71] Elsewhere he writes that religious prejudices are among "the most odious of all distinctions" since they, "more than any other, animate both the insolence of the oppressors and the hatred and indignation of the oppressed."[72] At one point he goes so far as to proclaim that during the Middle Ages the Catholic Church constituted "the most formidable combination that ever was formed against the authority and security of civil government, as well as against the liberty, reason, and happiness of mankind, which can flourish only where civil government is able to protect them."[73] That said, Smith's stance is not always or wholly anticlerical. Indeed, a few pages later he proclaims that "there is scarce perhaps to be found any where in Europe a more learned, decent, independent, and respectable set of men, than the greater part of the presbyterian clergy of Holland, Geneva, Switzerland, and Scotland."[74]

It is on the question of religious establishment that Smith takes an explicit stand against Hume. Despite Hume's broadly skeptical worldview and his frequent warnings about the baleful influence of religion on morality and politics, he also—startlingly, to many readers—mounts a vigorous case in favor of an established church. Hume is adamant about the need for religious toleration and so certainly does not suggest that church membership should be compulsory, but he maintains that the government should support a particular religious sect, both financially and through its official imprimatur. Indeed, he proclaims that "the union of the civil and ecclesiastical power serves extremely, in every civilized government, to the maintenance of peace and order," and he refers to the notion of a complete separation of church and state as "dangerous."[75] As might be expected, however, the rationale that he gives for this view is unconventional, if not unique.

Hume's most detailed case in favor of an established church appears in the third volume of *The History of England*. Before discussing the spread of the Protestant Reformation to Britain he proposes "to take the matter a little higher, and reflect a moment on the reasons, why there must be an ecclesiastical order, and a public establishment of religion in every civilized community." While Hume was generally a firm defender of the free market—allowing people to make their own economic choices, without undue interference from the state—he regarded this idea as pernicious when applied to religion. The market encourages competition, after all, and competition among religious sects is precisely what troubled him. The problem, as Hume depicts it, is that competition among the clergy to attract followers would have the effect of inspiring intolerance and fanaticism: "Each ghostly practitioner, in order to render himself more precious and sacred in the eyes of his retainers, will inspire them with the most violent abhorrence of all other sects, and continually endeavour, by some novelty, to excite the languid devotion of his audience. No regard will be paid to truth, morals, or decency in the doctrines inculcated. . . . Customers will be drawn to each conventicle by new industry and address in practising on the passions and credulity of the populace."

The best way to avoid this situation, Hume maintains, is for the government to privilege a particular sect and pay the salaries of its clergy in order to "bribe their indolence" and render it "superfluous for them to be farther active, than merely to prevent their flock from straying in quest of new pastures."[76] In other words, the beast can be tamed by feeding it: a church establishment unobtrusively dissuades the clergy from being overly diligent in their duties. Such a policy has the added advantages of giving the clergy a vested interest in maintaining social and political stability and of rendering them dependent on, and hence subservient to, the civil authorities. Needless to say, this was not an argument that the devout of Hume's day found particularly amenable. Indeed, as one prominent Hume scholar notes, "a less religious justification for establishing religion could scarcely be imagined. . . . The best we can do, it seems, is find the least objectionable form of religion, as a sort of inoculation against its more dangerous forms, and contrive things so that it will have the least unpleasing clerics attached to it."[77]

Smith approached the issue with the same objective as Hume, namely minimizing religious intolerance and fanaticism, but he came to the opposite conclusion regarding the surest means to this end.[78] In fact, Smith argues, in direct opposition to Hume, that a free market and competition would prove beneficial in the realm of religion, just as in the realm of commerce. He opens by acknowledging the truth of Hume's main claim regarding the incentives of the clergy, namely that "their exertion, their zeal and industry, are likely to be much greater" in the absence of any support from the government.[79] He then goes on to quote almost Hume's entire case to this effect—four full paragraphs from *The History of England*.[80] Smith responds by suggesting that, in effect, Hume has not thought through the implications of his position carefully enough. The clergy of an established church may be rendered moderate by putting them on the public dole, but if there are other, nonestablished churches—as there surely would be in any society with any degree of religious toleration and pluralism—then the clergy of those churches would *not* receive government support and so would *not* have their indolence bribed. In fact, the dissenting clergy may need to be doubly zealous in their efforts to attract followers due to the disadvantages they would face vis-à-vis the established church. As a result, Smith suggests, these more enthusiastic sects would start to win converts among the people, and the clergy of the established church would feel compelled to call in the political authorities to "persecute, destroy, or drive out their adversaries, as disturbers of the public peace."[81] Yet such attacks would naturally intensify the dissenters' zeal even further, leading to an endless cycle of persecution and conflict. Essentially, Smith contends that privileging a particular sect would just replicate the situation that led to Europe's devastating wars of religion in the first place. Religious establishment, rather than dampening intolerance and fanaticism, only fans the flames.

Smith goes on to speculate about what would happen if the government instead "dealt equally and impartially with all the different sects, and . . . allowed every man to chuse his own priest and his own religion as he thought proper." The likely result, he says, would be the proliferation of "a great multitude of religious sects," which would then naturally vie with one another for followers and influence, thereby checking one another's power. "The interested and active zeal of religious teachers . . . must be altogether innocent," Smith maintains, "where the society is divided into two or three hundred, or perhaps into as many thousand small sects, of which no one could be considerable enough to disturb the publick tranquillity."[82] Rather than seeking to tame the beast by feeding it, then, Smith advocates a divide and conquer strategy. He further suggests that any "disagreeably rigorous and unsocial" elements of these small religious sects could be ameliorated by means of the arts and sciences. He holds that "science is the great antidote to the poison of enthusiasm and superstition" and so proposes that the government should encourage its study, perhaps by requiring people to pass some sort of exam before they are admitted to "any liberal profession." He also recommends that the government give "entire liberty" to those who seek "to amuse and divert the people by painting, poetry, musick, dancing; by all sorts of dramatic representations and exhibitions," since these things help to inspire "gaiety and good humour" and thereby to "dissipate . . . that melancholy and gloomy humour which is almost always the nurse of popular superstition and enthusiasm."[83]

Smith's advocacy of a complete separation of church and state will seem unexceptionable, even predictable, to many today, but at the time it was quite a leap. In 1776 no government in the world abided by this principle outside of a few American colonies, and in Britain the idea of complete disestablishment was most closely linked with the Independents of the seventeenth-century civil wars, a group that Smith himself describes as "a sect . . . of very wild enthusiasts."[84] On the question of religious establishment, then, it was Smith who was the unapologetic radical and Hume the more cautious of the two.

On another topic that played a prominent role in *The Wealth of Nations*, the conflict between Britain and its American colonies, Hume and Smith were both firmly in the radical camp. This conflict was, of course, among the most pressing issues of British politics in the 1770s. Colonial policy had long been dictated by mercantilist demands: the mother country sought to ensure that it retained a favorable balance of trade with respect to the colonies through a complex scheme of regulations and tariffs. When the costs to the British started to mount—above all due to what was known in America as the French and Indian War (1756–63)—Parliament sought to pass along some of these costs to the colonies. The taxes that it imposed were widely resented by the colonists, and tensions between the two sides escalated until war finally broke out in 1775. Most of Hume's and Smith's friends among the Scottish literati were staunch supporters of Lord North's administration and advocated forceful measures to keep the colonies within the British fold.[85] Almost the lone dissenters on this score, Hume and Smith both denounced the war as well as the policies that had provoked it.

While Hume never published anything on the topic, his correspondence reveals that he was among the earliest and most consistent advocates of American independence in all of Britain. As early as March 1771—long before almost any American had seriously contemplated severing ties with the mother country—he had concluded that "our Union with America . . . in the Nature of things, cannot long subsist."[86] Once the war broke out he immediately advocated "that both Fleet and Army be withdrawn from America, and these Colonists be left entirely to themselves." Britain and America should, in his view, "lay aside all Anger; shake hands, and part Friends."[87] (His correspondent, William Strahan, was unconvinced, replying that "I am entirely for coercive Methods with these obstinate madmen . . . I am really surprised you are of a different opinion.")[88] At one point Hume went so far as to declare, "I am an American in my Principles, and wish we woud let them alone to govern or misgovern themselves as they think proper."[89] The notion that Hume was an American in his *principles* is a bit misleading, however. His advocacy of independence rested less on the kind of abstract principles that the American revolutionaries tended to appeal to—the self-evident truths and inalienable rights that would soon feature in the Declaration of Independence, for instance—than on pragmatic considerations. Whereas most Britons were sure that the colonies were a prime source of national wealth and power, Hume believed that they were an economic, political, and military burden and that all sides would benefit from ending the colonial relationship and setting up a system of free trade. Indeed, in a recently discovered letter from August 1775 he mutters that "we shoud do full as well without any Connections with these factious Colonists."[90]

The Wealth of Nations appeared in March 1776, around a year after the commencement of the war, and Smith devoted a number of passages in it to what he calls "the present disturbances." As might be expected, Smith too opposed Britain's colonial policy and the mercantilist assumptions on which it was based. Contrary to the view of almost everyone at the time except Hume, he insists that "under the present system . . . Great Britain derives nothing but loss from the dominion which she assumes over her colonies" and that a system of free trade would be far more advantageous for all.[91] Yet Smith points in two different directions regarding what such a system might look like. In the lengthy chapter on colonies in Book 4 he judges Hume's preferred outcome, the voluntary granting of American independence, to be a wild pipe dream: "To propose that Great Britain should voluntarily give up all authority over her colonies . . . would be to propose such a measure as never was, and never will be adopted, by any nation in the world. . . . The most visionary enthusiast would scarce be capable of proposing such a measure, with any serious hopes at least of its ever being adopted."[92] As an alternative—also rather visionary, it must be said—Smith proposes a constitutional union between Britain and America on the model of the union of 1707 between England and Scotland. Contrary to the wishes of almost all British politicians of the time, such a union would have allowed for full American representation in the British Parliament and granted Americans the same rights (and burdens) as all other British subjects. Smith even envisages the seat of the empire moving from London to the other side of the Atlantic "in the course of little more than a century," as America's population and economy surpassed that of the mother country.[93]

In the last paragraph of the book, though, Smith appears to reverse course and advocate voluntarily granting the colonies independence, after all. He writes that "the rulers of Great Britain have, for more than a century past, amused the people with the imagination that they possessed a great empire on the west side of the Atlantic." Given that maintaining the colonies entailed far more costs than benefits, however, he contends that "this empire . . . has hitherto existed in imagination only. It has hitherto been, not an empire, but the project of an empire; not a gold mine, but the project of a gold mine." Smith maintains that "if the project cannot be compleated, it ought to be given up," and he concludes the book by advising Britain to "accommodate her future views and designs to the real mediocrity of her circumstances."[94]

It is striking that Hume and Smith not only developed views on the American conflict that were so similar, and so far removed from the political and literary mainstream in Britain, but also did so in almost complete isolation from one another. Recall that their correspondence was quite limited between Smith's departure for London in April 1773 and the publication of his book.[95] Unfortunately, Hume would not live to see his pipe dream realized: word of the Declaration of Independence did not reach Scotland until just days before his death, and the Treaty of Paris was still seven war-filled years distant.

———————

The Wealth of Nations was finally published on March 9, 1776, and Smith naturally sent a presentation copy to Hume. A nineteenth-century editor of the book, James Thorold Rogers, claims in his preface to have seen this copy, and he tantalizingly informs us that it contained "a characteristic note by the author on the fly-leaf," but unfortunately he says nothing more about the note's contents, and the book's current whereabouts are unknown.[96] As might be expected, Hume sat down to read the work immediately despite his failing health, and his congratulatory letter of April 1 was the first one written to Smith, at least among those that survive. This one has little of the humor of Hume's congratulatory letter on *The Theory of Moral Sentiments*, but it exhibits a similar affection for Smith and similar satisfaction in his success. Hume opens: "Euge! Belle! Dear Mr Smith: I am much pleas'd with your Performance, and the Perusal of it has taken me from a State of great Anxiety." (*Euge* is Greek and *belle* Latin for "bravo" or "well done.") Hume admits that "it was a Work of so much Expectation, by yourself, by your Friends, and by the Public, that I trembled for its Appearance," but he is happy to report that he is "now much relieved." Which is not to say that he expects the work to be an instant best seller: "the Reading of it necessarily requires so much Attention, and the Public is disposed to give so little, that I shall still doubt for some time of its being at first very popular: But it has Depth and Solidity and Acuteness, and is so much illustrated by curious Facts, that it must at last take the public Attention."[97] Little did Hume know that the book would not only take the public's attention but hold it for several centuries.

Of course, Hume's friendship with Smith and his appreciation of Smith's ideas never prevented him from voicing his disagreements. "If you were here at my Fireside," he tells his friend, "I shoud dispute some of your Principles." In this case, however, the differences that he identifies are quite minor. Indeed, the biggest one that he mentions is that "I cannot think, that the Rent of Farms makes any part of the Price of the Produce, but that the Price is determined altogether by the Quantity and the Demand."[98] This is a reference to Smith's claim that the prices of many goods—particularly food and lumber—are determined not just by supply and demand but also by the rents charged by the owners of the property on which they are grown; Hume's doubts regarding this claim anticipate the later arguments of David Ricardo.[99] The other issue that Hume raises, concerning the degree of markup the French monarchy was able to make on its coinage, is even smaller.[100] It is interesting that Hume does not bring up their differences regarding commercial society's drawbacks or even Smith's detailed response to him on the question of church establishments, but perhaps, given how many of Smith's central ideas were prefigured by Hume's own writings, we should not be surprised that he found so little to dispute in the book.

This letter is not the only evidence that we have of Hume's high opinion of *The Wealth of Nations*. In James Boswell's account of his final interview with Hume, for instance, he reports that Hume raised the subject of Smith's book, "which he recommended much."[101] Some of Hume's other recorded commendations of the work, however, also include touches of criticism. In a note that he wrote to Smith from London around a month after his initial congratulatory letter, Hume observes that "by the little Company I have seen, I find the Town [i.e., London] very full of your Book, which meets with general Approbation. Many People think particular Points disputable; but this you certainly expected." Indeed, Hume says, "I am glad, that I am one of the Number; as these points will be the Subject of future Conversation between us."[102] Similarly, a few weeks later he wrote to his nephew to recommend a course of summer reading, and after mentioning a number of ancient authors he remarks: "I believe I recommended to you already the Perusal of Mr Smith's new Book if it falls in (as I believe it does) with Mr Millar's Course of Lectures"—that is, John Millar's course on civil law, which the nephew was then taking at Glasgow University. Hume continues: "It is a book of Science and deep Thought and as some of its Positions and Reasoning may seem to admit of Doubt, it will, on that account prove a better Exercise to your Thoughts & Researches."[103] As usual, then, Hume thought very highly of Smith's views but found something to question in them, as well.

In any case, after congratulating Smith, Hume turned, in his initial letter on *The Wealth of Nations*, to the first volume of Edward Gibbon's *History of the Decline and Fall of the Roman Empire*, which had been published less than a month earlier. He reports that he liked the book a great deal and that he had ventured to tell Gibbon that "had I not been personally acquainted with him, I shoud never have expected such an excellent Work from the Pen of an Englishman. It is lamentable to consider how much that Nation has declined in Literature during our time."[104] Hume hoped that Gibbon would not take this reflection amiss, but he need not have worried: Gibbon later proclaimed that Hume's letter to him had "over paid the labour of ten years."[105] Hume was, however, averse to go on at much length about Gibbon's book, or Smith's: "these and a hundred other Points are," he says, "fit only to be discussed in Conversation; which, till you tell me the contrary, I shall still flatter myself with soon. I hope it will be soon: For I am in a very bad State of Health and cannot afford a long Delay." He observes that he never received a response from Smith to his previous missive, but he assures him that "our Friendship does not depend on these Ceremonials."[106] We have no further letters from Smith to Hume for another two and a half months, but that very day Gibbon wrote to Adam Ferguson to inform him that Smith "proposes visiting you [in Edinburgh] very soon, and I find that he means to exert his most strenuous endeavours to persuade

Mr Hume to return with him to town [i.e., London]."[107] In fact their paths would cross within the month.

Despite the fact that Smith took on a number of vested interests in *The Wealth of Nations*—Adam Ferguson noted that Smith had "provoked" not only the merchants but also the churches, the universities, and the militias, among others—the book sold reasonably well and received generally positive reviews.[108] As Smith later commented, "I have . . . upon the whole been much less abused than I had reason to expect; so that in this respect I think myself rather lucky than otherwise."[109] By the end of his life the book would be a best seller and would exercise substantial influence over Britain's economic and trade policy.[110]

Hume's letter of April 1 was the first of many: further congratulatory messages continued to roll in from the other Scottish literati throughout the remainder of the month. While these messages sang Smith's praises in effusive terms, they were also tinged with sadness regarding Hume's ill health. On April 3, Hugh Blair told Smith that "your work ought to be, and I am perswaded will in some degree become, the Commercial Code of Nations. I did not read one Chapter of it without Acquiring much Light and instruction. I am Convinced that since Montesquieu's *Esprit des Loix*, Europe has not received any Publication which tends so much to Enlarge and Rectify the ideas of mankind." He also notes, however, that "your Friends here [in Edinburgh] are well; except (how miserable it is that we must make that exception!) poor D. Hume. He is declining Sadly. I dread, I dread— and I shudder at the prospect . . . such a blow as that would be utterly overwhelming."[111] Similarly, a few days later William Robertson proclaimed, "You have formed into a regular and consistent system one of the most intricate and important parts of political science . . . your Book must necessarily become a Political or Commercial Code to all Europe, which must be often consulted both by men of Practice and Speculation." Yet his missive too concludes on a somber note: "Mr Hume declines so fast, that I am under the greatest sollicitude about him. If he does not recruit with the return of good weather, I

The Author of the Wealth of Nations

FIGURE 9.1 This etching by the caricaturist John Kay was drawn soon after Smith's death (1790). By the end of Smith's life it was as the author of *The Wealth of Nations*, rather than *The Theory of Moral Sentiments*, that he was best known. Image courtesy of the United States Library of Congress's Prints & Photographs Division.

shall become very apprehensive about his fate. I need not say to you what a loss we shall all suffer."[112] Adam Ferguson agreed that "you are surely to reign alone on these subjects, to form the opinions, and I hope to govern at least the coming generations," but he likewise laments the state of Hume's health, noting however that "if anything in such a case could be agreeable, the easy and pleasant state of his mind and spirits would be really so."[113] Hume's physician, the eminent chemist Joseph Black, congratulated Smith on having developed "such a comprehensive System composed with such just and liberal Sentiments," but he quickly moved on to inform him that "your Freind David Humes' Health . . . is so bad that I am quite melancholy upon it and as I hear that you intend a Visit to this country [i.e., Scotland], soon, I wish if possible to hasten your coming that he may have the Comfort of your Company so much the sooner."[114]

Later that month Hume set out for London to seek further advice about his illness, just as Smith headed north to Edinburgh to see him. Happily, they ran into each other on the road. While they were surely thrilled to see one another for the first time in three years, this meeting also marked the commencement of a running disagreement between them about the fate of Hume's last great philosophical work.

CHAPTER 10

DIALOGUING ABOUT
NATURAL RELIGION

(1776)

W HEN HUME DREW up his will in January 1776 he naturally named Smith his literary executor, just as Smith
had asked Hume to serve in that capacity for him three
years earlier. One of the duties that Hume sought to bestow upon
his friend was that of overseeing the posthumous publication of his
Dialogues Concerning Natural Religion, but Smith resolutely refused
to carry out this request. It is often claimed that this episode significantly tarnished their friendship and caused Hume great pain during
his final months, and Smith's behavior is generally seen as unnec-
essarily cautious, utterly inexplicable, or even an act of betrayal—a
denial of his best friend's dying wish. Such views are common even
among scholars who are ordinarily highly sympathetic to Smith.
Nicholas Phillipson comments that "Smith's behaviour in the last
weeks of his closest friend's life is not easy to fathom" and that his
refusal to agree to publish the *Dialogues* "cast a shadow over their
relationship in the last weeks of Hume's life."[1] Ian Simpson Ross
agrees that Smith's actions "must have troubled Hume on his deathbed" and that Smith "erred on the side of prudence . . . at the expense of benevolence towards Hume."[2] Ryan Hanley too maintains
that Hume and Smith's "otherwise unblemished friendship . . . was
marred by [this] incident."[3] Gavin Kennedy, for his part, insists that
"Smith behaved less than loyally to Hume" and that the whole episode "leaves a bad taste."[4]

Let us review the evidence before assessing these claims.

Hume wrote the first draft of the *Dialogues Concerning Natural Religion* in the early 1750s, in the midst of an extraordinarily productive couple of years in which he also composed the *Second Enquiry*, the *Political Discourses*, and perhaps *The Natural History of Religion*. He returned to the work several times in subsequent years, revising it just after *The Natural History of Religion* appeared in print in 1757, making some more changes in the early 1760s, and finally adding a few polishing touches in 1776.[5] We do not know when Smith first read the work. It is possible that Hume shared it with him in the early 1750s, when he sent the first few sections to Gilbert Elliot, though it seems more likely that Smith did not see it until the early 1760s, when Hume discussed the revised manuscript with Elliot again and with Hugh Blair.[6] At all events, Smith was familiar with the *Dialogues* well before 1776—long enough before to have potentially "forgotten" it by that point.[7]

The *Dialogues* resists easy summary, but roughly speaking the interlocutors address four main topics. The first is the argument from design, or the idea that the order of the world implies a supremely wise, powerful, and benevolent designer—namely, God. This is in fact the primary subject of the work: after some introductory discussion in Part 1, Parts 2 to 8 all focus on this argument. In Part 9 the interlocutors turn to the first cause argument, according to which everything in the world has a cause and if we trace the string of causes back to the very beginning we will necessarily arrive at an initial cause, a creator of the world—namely, God. Parts 10 and 11 then delve into the problem of evil, or the question of how the presence of evil in the world can be reconciled with the idea of a supremely wise, powerful, and benevolent God. Finally, Part 12 considers the effects of religious belief and devotion on morality and politics. Though the book's conclusion is highly ambiguous, over the course of the dialogue Hume makes the weaknesses of the argument from design and the first cause argument—the two leading philosophical cases for God's existence in his day, and probably ours as well—readily apparent. Likewise, he shows the problem of evil to be extraordinarily difficult to resolve satisfactorily, and he casts grave doubt on religion's moral and political benefits.

All of this was exceedingly controversial, of course, but in fact none of the broad arguments or inquiries of the *Dialogues* were wholly new. As we have seen, Hume had already intimated that the argument from design is a dubious and useless hypothesis in section 11 of the *First Enquiry*. The shortcomings of the first cause argument were implicit in the discussion of causation in the *Treatise* and were made more explicit in Hume's recasting of that discussion in the *First Enquiry*.[8] While the problem of evil is addressed at greater length in the *Dialogues* than in any of Hume's other writings, it too had been taken up in the *First Enquiry*.[9] And the moral and political ills of religion were, of course, a prominent theme throughout Hume's *Essays*, the *Second Enquiry*, *The History of England*, and especially *The Natural History of Religion*. What *is* new in the *Dialogues* is the combination of all of these issues into a single devastating—and entertaining— package. While nearly everything Hume wrote bears on religion in one way or another, usually to its detriment, in his published writings he had always refrained from marshalling all of his skeptical challenges at once, thereby appearing to leave some kind of refuge for the devout. In his most trenchant examination of the leading arguments for God's existence, the *First Enquiry*, he avoided any detailed discussion of religion's moral and political effects. Conversely, in his most unsparing discussion of religion's moral and political effects, *The Natural History of Religion*, he appeared to leave the door open to something like the argument from design.[10] The uniqueness of the *Dialogues* lies in its comprehensiveness, which leaves the pious reader no way out, no safe haven.

The stage was set for the exchange between Hume and Smith regarding the fate of the *Dialogues* when Hume, realizing that he would not recover from his illness, drew up a new will on January 4, 1776. He bequeathed most of his possessions to his brother and sister, though he also included his servants and a few other friends and relatives. To Smith he left "all my manuscripts without exception, desiring him to publish my Dialogues concerning Natural Religion . . . but to publish no other papers which he suspects not to have been written within these five years, but to destroy them all at his leisure." For Smith to carry out this duty, Hume continues, "though I can trust to that intimate and sincere friendship, which has ever subsisted between us . . . yet, as a small recompense of his pains in correcting and publishing this work, I leave him two hundred pounds, to be paid immediately after the publication of it."[11]

Smith was still in London at the time, and it is unclear when exactly he became aware of this combination of bequest and request. Hume's letters of February 8 and April 1 did not mention the matter at all, focused as they were on *The Wealth of Nations*. As we will see in the next chapter, the two fortuitously met up at Morpeth, on the road between London and Edinburgh, on April 23, and this meeting was probably the first Smith heard of Hume's will. In any event, at Morpeth Smith seems to have expressed reservations about overseeing the publication of the *Dialogues*, for soon after arriving in London Hume wrote him two letters on the matter. The first of these letters (addressed to "My dear Friend") contains updates on Hume's health and other matters in his usual, casual tone, while the second is a more formal message (addressed "My dear Sir") absolving Smith of any obligation with regard to the *Dialogues*. In the latter message Hume declares that "after reflecting more maturely" on his request that Smith publish the *Dialogues* he had "become sensible, that, both on account of the Nature of the Work, and of your Situation, it may be improper to hurry on that Publication." Exactly what Hume meant by Smith's "situation" is not entirely clear; it may be a reference to the fact that Smith had published *The Wealth of Nations* less than two months earlier and did not want the book's reception to be impaired by involvement with a controversial work. In any case, Hume amends his "friendly Request" that Smith publish the *Dialogues*, now resting content to "leave it entirely to your Discretion at what time you will publish that Piece, or whether you will publish it at all."[12]

Hume's more informal letter, however, reveals that he had not given up hope of convincing Smith to publish the *Dialogues*, his formal promise of "entire discretion" notwithstanding. Hume opens by noting that he was enclosing the letter of absolution "conformably to your Desire," but he immediately continues: "I think, however, your Scruples groundless." Hume compares Smith's situation to that of David Mallet, who had published some controversial works of Lord

Bolingbroke back in 1752, immediately after Bolingbroke's death, and who seemed to suffer no ill consequences as a result. Indeed, Hume notes that Mallet later received an office from King George III and Lord Bute, "the most prudish Man in the World," and that Mallet "always justify'd himself by his sacred Regard to the Will of a dead Friend" (as, presumably, Smith would be able to do for the *Dialogues*).[13] Hume may have underestimated the damage done to Mallet's reputation in this instance, however. Witness Samuel Johnson's indictment of Bolingbroke, and of Mallet as his accomplice: "he [i.e., Bolingbroke] was a scoundrel, and a coward: a scoundrel, for charging a blunderbuss against religion and morality; a coward, because he had not resolution to fire it off himself, but left half a crown to a beggarly Scotchman [i.e., Mallet], to draw the trigger after his death!"[14] If Smith was aware of this comment he may have been dissuaded rather than encouraged by Hume's analogy.

Hume goes on, in his more informal letter, to tell Smith that if he were to live a few more years he would publish the *Dialogues* himself, but at all events he wanted to ensure that the work would be preserved for posterity. He therefore requests that "if, upon my Death, you determine never to publish these papers, you shoud leave them, seal'd up with my Brother and Family, with some Inscription, that you reserve to Yourself the Power of reclaiming them, whenever you think proper." Hume's concluding remark, however, hints that he knew what a potential burden he was seeking to place on Smith's shoulders: "I consider an Observation of Rochefoucault, that a Wind, though it extinguishes a Candle, blows up a fire."[15] Precisely what kind of a fire, and how big, Smith surely wanted to know, would he be facing if he carried out Hume's request? Smith's response—which may or may not have ever reached Hume—thanks Hume for "the unlimited confidence which you repose in me" and assures him that "if I should have the misfortune to survive you, you may depend on my taking every possible measure which may prevent anything from being lost which you wish to be preserved."[16] Smith pointedly does not, however, show any sign of changing his mind on the question of publication.

Apparently this arrangement did not sit well with Hume, as a month later he wrote to William Strahan to tell him about the *Dia-*

logues—this was, it seems, the first his longtime publisher had heard of the work—and to ask him to take on the responsibility of seeing it through the press. Hume instructs him that "it is not necessary you shoud prefix your Name to the Title Page," but he insists that since Strahan had publicly acknowledged publishing the *First Enquiry* "I know no Reason why you shoud have the least Scruple with regard to these Dialogues. They will be much less obnoxious to the Law, and not more exposed to popular Clamour."[17] Strahan agreed, so Hume changed his will to leave the property of the *Dialogues* to him rather than Smith. He further stipulated that if, for whatever reason, Strahan did not publish the work within two and a half years of Hume's death then "the Property shall return to my Nephew, David, whose Duty, in publishing them as the last Request of his Uncle, must be approved of by all the World."[18] In a note thanking Strahan for taking on this charge, Hume remarks that "it is an idle thing in us to be concerned about any thing that shall happen after our Death; yet this is natural to all Men, and I often regretted that a Piece, for which I had a particular Partiality, should run any hazard of being suppressed after my Decease."[19]

Even after amending his will Hume remained anxious about the fate of the *Dialogues*, so in mid-August he wrote to Smith to ask if he would accept a copy for safe keeping. "It will bind you to nothing, but will serve as a Security," Hume assures him. Yet he could not resist intimating once again that Smith's reservations were overblown: "On revising them (which I have not done these 15 Years) I find that nothing can be more cautiously and more artfully written. You had certainly forgotten them." Then, almost immediately after assuring Smith that he was not seeking to bind him to anything, he backtracks and suggests yet another change to his will: "Will you permit me to leave you the Property of the Copy, in case they shoud not be published in five Years after my Decease?"[20] Smith responded with his assurances that he would be "very happy" to receive a copy of the *Dialogues* and that "if I should happen to die before they are published, I shall take care that my copy shall be as carefully preserved as if I was to live a hundred years." He also tells Hume that "you may do as you think proper" with regard to leaving him the property of the work after five years, though he does not promise to see the work through

the press himself. In addition, he warns Hume not to "menace Strahan with the loss of anything in case he does not publish your work
within a certain time. There is no probability of his delaying it, and if
anything could make him delay it, it would be a clause of this kind,
which would give him an honourable pretence for doing so."[21] Hume's
final response to Smith on the matter, in the last letter he ever wrote,
expresses his confidence in Strahan and informs Smith that he had
decided to leave the current version of his will intact.[22] Their dispute,
such as it was, was finally at an end, and Smith was excluded altogether
from the publishing arrangements, suitable to his desires. Yet the matter had not been settled entirely.

A couple of weeks after Hume's death, Smith wrote to Strahan to con-
fer about the *Dialogues*. The work, he says, "tho' finely written I could
have wished had remained in Manuscript to be communicated only to
a few people. When you read the work you will see my reasons without my giving you the trouble of reading them in a letter. But he [i.e.,
Hume] has ordered it otherwise." If it were entirely up to him, Smith
continues, "the manuscript should have been most carefully preserved
and upon my decease restored to [Hume's] family; but it should never
have been published in my lifetime." Smith instructs Strahan that,
whatever he may decide on the matter, under no circumstances should
the *Dialogues* be published together with his own account of Hume's
final illness—what became the *Letter to Strahan*—"as I am resolved,
for many reasons, to have no concern in the publication of those dialogues."[23] Though Smith does not spell out these "many reasons" here,
in a pair of draft letters that he wrote a few weeks later (but never actually sent to Strahan) he remarks that he is "still uneasy about the clamour which I foresee [the *Dialogues*] will excite," a clamor that could be
expected to affect both his own "quiet" and the sales of the new edition
of Hume's collected writings.[24]

Strahan responded to promise that "I shall do nothing precipitately, and without the Advice of my Friends, to whose Opinion, and
particularly to yours, I shall pay great Regard." He looks forward to
giving the *Dialogues* "a very attentive Perusal" in order to form his own
opinion, but he expresses surprise at the depth of Smith's reservations:

"I own I did not expect to hear they were so very exceptionable, as in one of his [i.e., Hume's] late Letters to me he tells me *there is nothing in them worse than what I have already published*, or Words to that Effect." Especially given Hume's "extreme Solicitude" that the work be published, Strahan says, "if it is at all judged proper to let them see the Light, I should wish to execute his Intentions."[25] In the end, however, Strahan seems to have judged it improper to let the *Dialogues* see the light, at least under his auspices: after wavering for around six months he decided that the work "might be published with more propriety" by Hume's nephew *"in obedience to the last request of his Uncle*, as . . . Hume himself expressed it."[26]

Hume's nephew duly saw the *Dialogues* through the press in 1779, three years after Hume's death. Recent scholarship has been almost unanimous in maintaining that the work's publication brought none of the expected outcry, but an inspection of the periodicals of the time suggests otherwise.[27] In the first major review of the work, in September 1779, the *Critical Review* commented that if Hume's "pernicious" principles were allowed to prevail they "would throw a gloom over the whole creation, and really terminate in the blind amazement, the diffidence and melancholy of mankind."[28] That same month the *London Magazine* declared baldly that Hume's outlook "terminates in Atheism" and lamented that "he left no sincere friend behind him, who had so much regard for his character as to bury [the *Dialogues*] with him." The anonymous reviewer went on to advise those readers "who do not wish to disturb their reason and endanger their peace of mind" to forego reading the work.[29] The *Monthly Review*, for its part, insisted that Hume had done little more than "throw the most exceptionable parts of his philosophical works into a new form." According to this reviewer, Hume sought to establish principles whereby "the wicked are set free from every restraint but that of the laws; the virtuous are robbed of their most substantial comforts; every generous ardor of the human mind is damped; the world we live in is a fatherless world; we are chained down to a life full of wretchedness and misery; and we have no hope beyond the grave." The work must "shock the sense and virtue" of all good citizens.[30] The *London Review*, the sole periodical to issue a reasonably favorable review, came under attack from its readers for doing so.[31] As far afield as Germany, the *Göttingischen gelehrten Anzeigen* regretted that Hume had "flung such stains on the otherwise so beautiful canvas of his character" and warned "young men not yet practiced in thinking against a precipitate reading of this book."[32] Ultimately, then, it seems that James Boswell's reaction to the *Dialogues* was more the rule than the exception: while he liked Hume's nephew personally, he said, he was "offended by his publishing his uncles posthumous poison."[33]

What are we to make of this episode? To begin with, there is little evidence to support the common claim that the disagreement between Hume and Smith over the *Dialogues* was particularly acrimonious. Hume was clearly partial to the work and anxious to see it published, but the idea that Smith's refusal to take on this responsibility caused Hume great pain and significantly tarnished their friendship seems decidedly exaggerated. Indeed, Hume's feelings of affection toward Smith do not seem to have diminished in the slightest. The first letter that we have from Hume on the subject—the one in which he tells Smith that his scruples are "groundless"—concludes with a characteristic plea for Smith to write more often, along with an equally characteristic expression of regret at not being together in person: "If you write to me, hem! hem! I say, if you write to me, send your Letters under Cover to Mr Strahan, who will have my Direction. I regret much, in leaving Edinburgh, that I shall lose much of your Company, which I shoud have enjoy'd this Summer."[34] As we will see in the next chapter, Hume then invited Smith to stay at his house for over a month, from the time of his return to Edinburgh on July 3 through mid-August, just a couple of weeks before his death. We will also see that Hume readily gave him "entire liberty to make what Additions you please" to his autobiography, *My Own Life*—the piece that would serve as the preface to future editions of his collected works. His last letter to Smith both opens and closes by calling him "My Dearest Friend."[35] None of this suggests a serious falling out or deep-seated feelings of resentment.

The main question confounding most scholars, though, is *why* Smith was so adamant in his refusal to publish the *Dialogues*. The difficulty of comprehending Smith's behavior has been heightened by two factors. First, Smith himself emphasizes the sanctity of deathbed wishes in his jurisprudence lectures, remarking that "we naturally find a pleasure in remembering the last words of a friend and in executing his last injunctions," in part because we realize "how much we would be distressed to see our last injunctions not performed."[36] Why, then, many have wondered, would Smith refuse a request that his best friend made, if not on his deathbed then at least in his will, during his final illness? Adding to the mystery is the extremely high esteem in which Hume's *Dialogues* is now held. Leading scholars have called it "one of the glories of the Scottish, and indeed the European, Enlightenment"; "beyond any question the greatest work on philosophy of religion in the English language"; "perhaps the most remarkable treatise upon this subject ever composed"; Hume's "philosophical testament"; and "the epitome of his life's work."[37] How could Smith have refused to publish a work of such obvious greatness?

One surprisingly common answer to these questions has been that Smith objected to the contents of the *Dialogues*—that he was disturbed or even scandalized by the work, or saw it as deeply incompatible with his own philosophy, or was personally unable to come to grips with Hume's barrage of skepticism.[38] If Smith's religious views were as close to Hume's as the present book has suggested, however, this explanation seems unlikely. Smith's keen interest in Hume's thought, starting from his Oxford days; the skepticism of his early *Principles Which Lead and Direct Philosophical Enquiries*; the ambiguities and revisions of *The Theory of Moral Sentiments*; the resolutely secular worldview of *The Wealth of Nations*; the numerous jokes and asides about religion in his correspondence with Hume—all of this seems difficult to square with the idea that Smith was overly troubled by Hume's skepticism. And none of this is even to mention the *Letter to Strahan*: only a few months after their exchange over the *Dialogues* Smith went on to publicly describe Hume as a paragon of wisdom and virtue.

These general indications regarding Smith's stance are corroborated by some more specific ones related to the *Dialogues* itself. Recall that Smith promised time and again that he would be "very happy" to take "every possible measure" to ensure that the work would be "most carefully preserved," and he also deemed it "finely written"—he just wished that it "had remained in Manuscript to be communicated only to a few people."³⁹ In other words, while Smith seems to have thought that such bold criticisms of religion are best kept away from the public eye, he had no problem with the idea of circulating the work among friends. In fact, Smith appears to have actively disseminated the work himself—how widely we do not know—as we have a letter from the duc de La Rochefoucauld (the moralist's great-great-great-grandson) thanking Smith for sending a copy of the *Dialogues* to him in France almost immediately after it was released.⁴⁰

The likeliest explanation for Smith's refusal to publish the *Dialogues* is also the simplest: as he himself indicated in his draft letters to Strahan, he was wary of the public "clamor" that the book would provoke and the effects that this clamor would have on his own "quiet" and Hume's posthumous reputation. Smith may have also had the interests of the public in mind. Recall that in *The Theory of Moral Sentiments* he had suggested that religion often helps to buttress morality by reinforcing people's adherence to moral norms; perhaps he worried that a work like the *Dialogues* might weaken this buttress. We have a letter from Anne Keith, whose family was close to Hume, reporting that Smith "remonstrated against publishing" the *Dialogues* on the grounds that the work was "of a nature prejudicial to Society."⁴¹ (She also notes that Hume "is in general condemned for rejecting Mr Smith's advice.") Indeed, Smith's refusal to publish the *Dialogues* may have been, at least in part, a matter of simple politeness: his mother, the majority of his friends, and indeed almost everyone he knew would have been offended by the work, and by his involvement with it. At any rate, the bottom line is that Smith was always far more wary of public controversy than Hume was—think of the Rousseau quarrel—and it is thoroughly unsurprising that he would exercise greater caution with respect to a work like the *Dialogues*.

Was this, then, an instance of excessive caution, or even cowardice, as is often suggested? If it was, then it was a failing that was not unique to Smith: every one of Hume's friends who knew about the *Dialogues* urged him not to publish it, at least if the surviving record is anything to go by. We know that Gilbert Elliot opposed publication, as we have a letter from Hume to Elliot in which he complains: "Is it not hard & tyrannical in you, more tyrannical than any Act of the Stuarts, not to allow me to publish my Dialogues? Pray, do you not think that a proper Dedication may atone for what is exceptional in them?"[42] Hugh Blair likewise admonished Hume, "for Gods sake let that be a posthumous work, if ever it shall see the light: Tho' I really think it had better not."[43] (In reply Hume told Blair that "I have no present thoughts of publishing the work you mention," but then teasingly added: "when I do, I hope you have no objection of my dedicating it to you.")[44] We have a report that Adam Ferguson too "remonstrated" against publishing the work.[45] And of course Strahan, who was close to Hume personally as well as professionally, ultimately declined to publish the *Dialogues*—and this after he had, unlike Smith, promised Hume that he would do so.

If the unanimous counsel of some of Hume's closest friends is not enough to exonerate Smith from charges of cowardice, then Hume's own words and actions should be. Despite Hume's greater willingness to court controversy and despite his obvious fondness for the *Dialogues*, he himself had refrained from publishing the work for *two and a half decades*. Indeed, he did not even mention the manuscript's existence to his publisher until just a couple of months before his death. He did ponder the possibility of publication from time to time, as the letter to Elliot quoted above suggests, but he realized that it would be an audacious move, even for him—hence his acknowledgment, in that letter, that there is something "exceptionable" about the work that would require a proper dedication to "atone for." Even more striking is Hume's explanation, in his letter to Strahan of June 1776 asking him to take on responsibility for the *Dialogues*, of why he had not published long ago: "I have hitherto forborne to publish it, because I was of late desirous to live quietly, and keep remote from all Clamour: For though it be not more exceptionable than some things I had formerly published; yet you know some of these were thought very exceptionable; and in prudence, perhaps, I ought to have suppressed them. I there introduce a Sceptic [i.e., the character Philo], who is indeed refuted, and at last gives up the Argument . . . yet before he is silenced, he advances several Topics, which will give Umbrage, and will be deemed very bold and free."[46] In other words, up until his final illness Hume had refrained from publishing the *Dialogues* for the exact same reason that Smith refused to do so: because it would create a "clamor" that would prevent him from living "quietly." Even the wording of their explanations is nearly identical.

The more perplexing question, in a way, is not why Smith refused to publish the *Dialogues* but rather why Hume was suddenly so adamant about publication after holding the work back for twenty-five years, and even more why he sought to foist this obligation on Smith. Hume may have reckoned that he had little left to lose at that point, with one foot almost in the grave, but obviously Smith was not in the same position. Moreover, Hume knew full well that Smith was always anxious to preserve his privacy and tranquility—his "quiet." It would not have taken a great feat of sympathy to realize that Smith would be averse to the public "clamor" that Hume himself foresaw would be provoked by the *Dialogues*. Nor should it be forgotten that Hume asked Smith to bear this burden only a month and a half after *The Wealth of Nations* was published. Given the many years of painstaking effort that Smith had poured into the book, the great anticipation that surrounded its release, and Smith's high hopes that its arguments would prove influential in both thought and practice, this was among the worst possible times for him to become mired in public controversy. (As we will see, this context made the *Letter to Strahan* all the more daring.) All things considered, then, Hume's part in this exchange is more difficult to account for than Smith's.

CHAPTER II

A PHILOSOPHER'S
DEATH
(1776)

EVEN BEFORE THE *Dialogues Concerning Natural Religion* was published, Hume's reputation for impiety was such that his death was a highly anticipated event. As one contemporary put it, during his final months "his situation became the universal topick of conversation and enquiry; each individual expressing an anxious solicitude about his health, as if he had been his intimate and particular friend."[1] The reason for this widespread interest, of course, was that everyone wanted to know whether Hume would persist in his skepticism to the very end—and if so, whether he would experience the anguish and despair that was assumed to attend the death of the unrepentant. The *Monthly Review*'s introduction to its printing of Hume's *My Own Life* captures the fixation nicely: "When men of such PARTS, and such PRINCIPLES, as those which distinguished the character and writings of Mr. Hume, come to face the immediate terrors of death, the world is always curious to learn in what manner they support the trying conflict: whether the near approach of that awful change of situation which they are about to experience, (in an hour wherein one would think, the boldest mortal would not dare either to DISSEMBLE or to TRIFLE) has produced any change in their *minds*; whether they continue fixed, and steady to their past professions; or, whether '*new light*' is let into 'the soul's dark cottage,' as the poet [Edmund Waller] expresses it, 'through the chinks' of its ruins,—opening wider, at the moment when the batter'd fabric is tottering to its dissolution."[2]

Hume's health had been somewhat erratic since the early 1770s, but it began to deteriorate seriously in the spring of 1775. As we have seen, in January 1776 he deemed it advisable to draw up a new will, and in February he told Smith that he had "fallen five compleat Stones," or seventy pounds.[3] As his physician, Joseph Black, informed Smith, Hume suffered from night fevers, internal bleeding, and severe diarrhea—probably the result of colon cancer, and perhaps also ulcerative colitis.[4] By the spring Hume was certain that the end was near, particularly because his mother had experienced the same symptoms in the months leading up to her death. By all indications, however, he continued to live as he had since his return to Edinburgh. He visited with friends, hosted dinners, and played whist; he devoured books both old and new, including the just-released tours de force of Smith and Edward Gibbon; he polished his existing writings, preparing new editions of his collected philosophical works and *The History of England*. His sudden fretting about the future of the *Dialogues* was practically the lone sign that anything was amiss. As a much younger man Hume had expected to find old age a time of "Sorrow" and "certain Misery," but in fact his spirits remained so high, even in the midst of his fatal illness, that he claimed that "were I to name the period of my life, which I should most choose to pass over again, I might be tempted to point to this later period."[5]

While all of this seems to have been perfectly true, Hume was eager to let everyone *know* that it was true. He was well aware of the intense curiosity that surrounded his looming death, and he was determined to die as he thought a philosopher should—cheerfully and tranquilly, without undue hopes or fears—and to do it for a public audience. Hume and Smith had both argued that religion arises principally in order to fulfill a psychological need, to help people reconcile themselves to their natures and their fate. By living and dying, happily and virtuously, *without* religion, Hume was demonstrating himself to be above such needs. He was showing, through his example, that this world is enough, that this *life* is enough, if one approaches it in the right way.

As part of this effort Hume wrote an autobiography, *My Own Life*, in mid-April—a "funeral oration of myself," as he described it.[6] He opens the piece with the good-natured acknowledgment that "it is difficult for a man to speak long of himself without vanity; therefore, I shall be short." This pledge is certainly upheld, as the work is less than ten pages long. "It may be thought an instance of vanity that I pretend at all to write my life," he continues, "but this Narrative shall contain little more than a History of my Writings; as, indeed, almost all my life has been spent in literary pursuits and occupations. The first success of most of my writings was not such as to be an object of vanity."[7] It is not, strictly speaking, true that Hume limits *My Own Life* to the history of his writings. Throughout the narrative he highlights his steady rise in the world, from relative obscurity to worldwide renown and from a slender patrimony to unexpected affluence. We are also informed that the good and the great frequently sought him out, rather than the other way around: the invitations to serve as a tutor to Lord Annandale, on military and diplomatic missions with General St. Clair, at the French embassy with Lord Hertford, and in the Northern Department with General Conway all came unbidden. It is true, though, that the work contains little in the way of intimate personal details. Those hoping for revelations about Hume's liaison with the Comtesse de Boufflers or for further mud to be slung at Rousseau would be disappointed. While Hume alludes to his friends a few times, none of them are named: Smith gets no mention, nor do any of Hume's friends among the Edinburgh literati or the Parisian *philosophes*.[8]

Hume also says surprisingly little—almost nothing, in fact—about the *contents* of his writings. Instead, the narrative centers around the poor reception of his publications, along with the optimistic and resilient temperament that enabled him to recover quickly from the disappointment each time. The *Treatise*, he tells us, "fell *dead-born from the press*"; the *First Enquiry* was "entirely overlooked and neglected"; the *Second Enquiry* "came unnoticed and unobserved into the world"; the "public entry" of *The Natural History of Religion* "was rather obscure"; the first volume of *The History of England* was "assailed by one cry of reproach, disapprobation, and even detestation"; the "clamour against" the Tudor volumes "was almost equal to that against the History of the two first Stuarts"; and the volumes on the early history of England met "with tolerable, and but tolerable success."[9] On Hume's telling, only his essays and the second Stuart volume of his *History* were favorably received on their first release. Yet through it all he managed to maintain his "cheerful and sanguine temper" and to keep himself "clear of all literary squabbles," and he persisted in regarding "every object as contemptible, except the improvement of my talents in literature."[10]

Both parts of this story were clearly exaggerated for effect. If almost all of Hume's writings were utterly ignored or universally condemned, the reader cannot help but wonder, then how did he become so rich and famous? He received salaries and pensions from the handful of years that he spent in government service, of course, but his writings were the chief source of his celebrity and his fortune. Hume wanted to underscore the poor reception of his publications, presumably, in order to forestall the charges of vanity that he anticipated in the opening paragraph, but he may have overshot his mark a bit. As for cheerfully keeping clear of literary squabbles and quietly devoting himself to his studies, Hume's account ignores almost entirely just how irreverent and contentious his writings were. A reader coming to *My Own Life* with no prior knowledge of Hume or his books would scarcely realize that she was reading the autobiography of a notorious infidel. The only hints in the narrative to this effect are his lament that the *Treatise* did not even manage to reach "such distinction, as even to excite a murmur among the zealots," his acknowledgment that he had "wantonly exposed" himself "to the rage of both civil and religious factions," and a pair of references to the aspersions cast on him by William Warburton and Richard Hurd.[11] Even these hints are in a way counterbalanced by Hume's remark that the Archbishop of Canterbury and the Primate of All Ireland "separately sent me messages not to be discouraged" after the first volume of *The History of England* fared so poorly with the public.[12] Hume also refrains from discussing the various ways in which his controversial views affected his career, such as his two failed candidacies for university posts and the attempts to excommunicate him from the Kirk.

Of course, there was little need for Hume to dilate on his lack of piety: every reader of *My Own Life* would have been keenly aware of it. Indeed, Hume knew that many would scour the work for incriminating evidence—for some kind of sign that deep down he was depraved or despondent, fearful or remorseful. He was determined to frustrate these efforts, and indeed to demonstrate that the contrary was true. The last two paragraphs drive the point home. In the penultimate paragraph Hume describes his state of mind in the face of a disease that he knew was "mortal and incurable." He observes that he now expects "a speedy dissolution" but that he has "never suffered a moment's abatement of my spirits. . . . I possess the same ardour as ever in study, and the same gaiety in company." The approach of death, in other words, did nothing to change his attitude, his views, or his lifestyle. Instead he serenely accepts the inevitable, commenting that "a man of sixty-five, by dying, cuts off only a few years of infirmities."[13] All of this must have seemed exasperatingly flippant to most eighteenth-century readers. Should not the end of this life be spent preparing for the all-important life to come? As one scholar notes, "one might think Hume were speaking of taking a stroll."[14]

Hume concludes the essay with an assessment of his own character, not unlike the character sketches of monarchs that cap off each reign in *The History of England*. This final paragraph is written in the past tense, almost as if from beyond the grave, and it does not avoid entirely the vanity that Hume had disavowed in the introductory paragraph. "I am, or rather was," he writes, "a man of mild dispositions, of command of temper, of an open, social, and cheerful humour, capable of attachment, but little susceptible of enmity, and of great moderation in all my passions. Even my love of literary fame, my ruling passion, never soured my temper, notwithstanding my frequent disappointments." This description, though a bit rose-colored—think once again of the Rousseau quarrel—is on the whole reasonably accurate: Hume *was* famously affable. He overreaches considerably, however, when he declares that "I was never touched . . . by [the] baleful tooth [of calumny]: and though I wantonly exposed myself to the rage of both civil and religious factions, they seemed to be disarmed in my behalf of their wonted fury. My friends never had occasion to vindicate any one circumstance of my character and conduct."[15] These claims can have been motivated only by heavy irony or astonishing forgetfulness: Hume had in fact experienced a great deal of calumny, and his friends had in fact leapt to his defense often. His best friend would soon find the need to do so again, and the resulting work, the *Letter to Strahan*, would complete the story of Hume's life, thereby confirming what *My Own Life* was meant to suggest: that a skeptic could die with composure and grace.

A few days after completing *My Own Life*, Hume set out for London in order to consult the doctors there about his health. Around the same time, Smith and their mutual friend John Home (the playwright), not knowing of Hume's plans, headed north toward Edinburgh in order to see him. A lucky stroke prevented them from passing each other by: while Hume was resting at an inn in Morpeth, on the road between the two capitals, his valet happened to be standing at the gate when the carriage bearing Smith and Home drew up.[16] This meeting marked the first time in three years that Hume and Smith were together in person. Hume was in good form: Home commented that "he talks of his illness, of his death, as matters of no moment. . . . I never saw him more cheerful, or in more perfect possession of all his faculties, his memory, his understanding, his wit."[17] As we have seen, it was probably here that Hume first broached the issue of the *Dialogues* with Smith. The two soon parted ways once again, however: while Home turned back to keep Hume company on the road to London, Smith was obliged to proceed on to Scotland to care for his mother, who was also ill and expected her son to arrive any day.[18] As Hume slowly made his way to London he kept his brother up to date on his health via the post, asking that he forward the reports on to Smith as well.[19]

Soon after arriving in London on May 1, Hume wrote to Smith to let him know that his health had improved somewhat: "though I cannot come up entirely to the sanguine Notions of our Friend, John [i.e., Home], I find myself very much recovered on the Road." In addition to amending the instructions of his will with respect to the *Dialogues*, Hume apprised Smith of another important item that he had apparently forgotten to mention in Morpeth: "You will find among my Papers a very inoffensive Piece, called *My Own Life*," he writes, and "there can be no Objection, that this small piece shoud be sent to Messrs. Strahan and Cadell and the Proprietors of my other Works to be prefixed to any future Edition of them."[20] Hume's description of *My Own Life* as "very inoffensive" was clearly meant to distance it from the *Dialogues*. In fact some readers *were* offended by *My Own Life*, though as we will see it was Smith's addition to it that really provoked public outrage.

On the advice of the doctors Hume soon moved on to Bath to take the waters there. His health once again seemed to be improved by the journey, and his first trial of the waters was so successful that even he began to hope that he might recover sufficiently to live a few more years. He was, he claimed, "in good Spirits, and . . . never in a passion except at some perverse Strokes I meet with at Whist."[21] The news from Bath continued positive for some time; as late as June 6, Alexander Wedderburn wrote to Smith to say that he had seen "a very chearfull Letter from D. Hume" and that Hume "is not likely to leave you any Commissions [as his literary executor] for a considerable time."[22] The hopeful news, however, did not last. A few days later Hume wrote to William Strahan to "retract all the good Accounts, which I gave you of my Health," and Strahan in turn sent Smith a "melancholy Account of our most valuable Friend," reporting that "all the good Symptoms that attended his first Tryal of the Bath Water are now vanished."[23] On receiving Strahan's message, Smith wrote to Hume to express his sorrow that the waters no longer seemed to be working their restorative magic. Though Hume had already consulted several leading doctors about his case, Smith felt compelled to pass along his own advice: "You have found one Medicine which has agreed with you; travelling and change of air. I would continue, if I was you, during the continuance of the fine Season the constant application of that medicine without troubling myself with any other, and would spend the summer in Sauntering thro all the different corners of England without halting above two or three nights in any one place."[24]

Hume's health continued to deteriorate, and toward the end of June he headed back to Scotland. Smith was there to greet him when he finally arrived in Edinburgh on July 3. He found that Hume was "by no means in the state in which I could have wished to have seen him. His spirits, however, continue perfectly good."[25] Knowing that the end must be coming soon, Hume hosted a sort of homecoming-and-farewell dinner for his friends the day after his return; the dinner took place on July 4, 1776, a date better remembered for events on the other side of the Atlantic. Smith was, naturally, one of those present. Perhaps dispirited by the nearing demise of his closest friend, at one point Smith grumbled that the world was spiteful and ill-natured. "No, no," Hume responded, apparently in fine fettle. "Here am I, who have written on all sorts of subjects calculated to excite hostility, moral, political, and religious, and yet I have no enemies; except, indeed, all the Whigs, all the Tories, and all the Christians."[26]

James Boswell managed to contrive a visit with Hume the following Sunday, July 7. As his famous account of their conversation makes plain, the purpose of Boswell's visit was less to pay his respects to a dying man, or even to gratify a sense of morbid curiosity, than to try to fortify his own religious convictions by confirming that even Hume could not remain a sincere infidel to the end. In this, he failed utterly. "Being too late for church," Boswell made his way to St. David Street, where he was surprised to find Hume "placid and even cheerful . . . talking of different matters with a tranquillity of mind and a clearness of head which few men possess at any time." Ever tactful, Boswell immediately brought up the subject of the afterlife, asking if there might not be a future state. Hume replied that "it was possible that a piece of coal put upon the fire would not burn; and he added that it was a most unreasonable fancy that we should exist for ever." Boswell persisted, asking if he was not made uneasy by the thought of annihilation, to which Hume responded that he was no more perturbed by the idea of ceasing to exist than by the idea that he had not existed before he was born. What was more, Hume "said flatly that the morality of every religion was bad, and, I really thought, was not jocular when he said that when he heard a man was religious, he concluded he was a rascal, though he had known some instances of very good men being religious."[27] Clearly disturbed by what he had heard, Boswell tried to call on Hume again on two future occasions to press him further, but was turned away.[28]

Boswell's longtime friend William Johnson Temple, as curious as everyone else about Hume's frame of mind, wrote to ask Boswell: "How did he bear himself in the near approach of dissolution? Had he no apprehensions, no misgivings? Did he neither fear nor desire a futurity?"[29] When Boswell reported that Hume's views and attitude had not changed at all, Temple was contemptuously dismissive: "As to your desperate infidel David Hume . . . His persisting in his impiety & irreligion makes no impression upon me. The opposite sentiments are much [more] pleasing, reasonable & consoling & have been & still are entertained by much better, wiser & greater men. If he continue obstinate [he] will die the death of a Dog. . . . Let him die then & be thrown into the ditch."[30] This reaction is all the more remarkable given that Temple had long been an *admirer* of Hume's, and indeed considered him "one of the greatest historians in the world."[31]

Nor was it only meddling acquaintances and religious enthusiasts who were unsettled by Hume's steadfast skepticism. Just before Hume's death William Strahan wrote to ask, somewhat incredulously, whether he still doubted the existence of an afterlife. "Do you *now* believe, or suspect," Strahan inquires, "that all the Powers and Faculties of your own mind, which you have cultivated with so much care and success, will cease and be extinguished with your Vital Breath? Our Soul . . . some say, is able, when on the Brink of Dissolution, to take a Glimpse of Futurity; and for that Reason I earnestly wish to have your *last Thoughts* on this important subject."[32] Hume received the letter but was in no condition to respond by that point. Hume's pious brother later replied on Hume's behalf, and even he had to admit that "so far as I can judge, his sentiments with regard to futurity" during his final days "were the same, as when he was in perfect health."[33]

Though Hume and Smith had seen each other very little in the previous three years, they did their best to make up for lost time: Smith stayed at Hume's house on St. David Street for most of the period from Hume's return to Edinburgh on July 3 through mid-August.[34] Unfortunately, there is little surviving evidence of what they did or said during this time. We do have one fleeting reference in a letter from Hume to John Home on July 16. The weather was magnificent, but Hume was unable to venture out of the house to enjoy it, and he writes that "instead of grudging that I cannot partake, directly, of this Pleasure; Mr Smith tells me, that I ought to enjoy it by Sympathy, which I endeavour to do."[35]

The only conversation between the two for which we have a detailed record took place on August 8. Smith first recounted this exchange in a letter to Alexander Wedderburn a few days afterward and then immortalized a slightly toned-down version in the *Letter to Strahan*. According to these reports, Smith stopped by Hume's room and found him reading a letter from an old friend, James Edmonstoune, bidding him a final good-bye. When Hume showed him the touching letter, Smith suggested that Hume's spirits were so good that perhaps his health might take a favorable turn. Hume, however, would have none of it: "Smith, your hopes are groundless; an habitual diarrhea, which has now continued for several years, is a dangerous disease to a man of any age. At my age it is a mortal one. When I rise in the morning I find myself weaker than when I went to bed at night, and when I go to bed at night weaker than when I rose in the morning, so that in a few days I trust the business will be over."[36] Despite this gloomy forecast, the exchange that followed showed that Hume had not lost his sense of humor.

Even if Hume were to die soon, Smith supposed, he must be comforted by the fact that his family would be left in prosperity. Hume agreed, acknowledging that he had few regrets and little left to do. He illustrated the point by comparing his situation to that of the characters in a dialogue by Lucian that he had recently reread. (Lucian was a scourge of superstition and a favorite of both Hume and Smith.[37] Smith later claimed that Hume's reference was to Lucian's *Dialogues of the Dead*, but in fact the work in question was more likely *The Downward Journey*.)[38] The characters that Hume had in mind were pleading with Charon, the boatman who carries the souls of the recently deceased across the River Styx into Hades, in hopes of procuring a stay of execution. One hoped to first marry off a daughter, another to finish building his house, and a third to make some provisions for his young children. Hume tried to conjure up a similar excuse for himself, but he found that, having done everything that he had ever intended to do, he was unable to come up with any plausible candidates. "At last I thought I might say," he continued, "Good Charon, I have been endeavouring to open the eyes of the people; have a little patience only till I have the pleasure of seeing the churches shut up, and the Clergy sent about their business." But he was well aware that such an excuse would not fly: "Charon would reply, O you loitering rogue; that wont happen these two hundred years; do you fancy I will give you a lease for so long a time? Get into the boat this instant."[39]

This is where Smith's account of the conversation ends in his private letter to Wedderburn, but in the *Letter to Strahan* he both expands on the anecdote and softens its antireligious character somewhat. In the published version Hume invents a couple of different "jocular excuses" to make to Charon, along with "very surly answers" from the boatman. Hume begins by reasoning, "Good Charon, I have been correcting my works for a new edition. Allow me a little time, that I may see how the Public receives the alterations." But Charon, apparently knowing Hume well, replies: "When you have seen the effect of these, you will be for making other alterations. There will be no end of such excuses; so, honest friend, please step into the boat." Hume persists: "Have a little patience, good Charon, I have been endeavouring to open the eyes of the Public. If I live a few years longer, I may have the satisfaction of seeing the downfal of some of the prevailing systems of superstition." While in this version Hume no longer goes so far as to hope to see "the churches shut up, and the Clergy sent about their business," Charon is no more charitable than in the harsher version related to Wedderburn: "You loitering rogue, that will not happen these many hundred years. Do you fancy I will grant you a lease for so long a term? Get into the boat this instant, you lazy loitering rogue."[40]

In addition to the good fun that Hume was clearly having here, it is perhaps worth noting that even where he playfully indulges in the fantasy of an afterlife he imagines meeting not the Christian God at the pearly gates, but a figure from pagan mythology. It is also worth noting that the following week he did manage to identify one regret regarding his imminent death, namely the "good Friends . . . whom one must leave behind."[41]

A day or two after this conversation—it is unclear exactly when—Smith departed for Kirkcaldy, finding that Hume was so weak that "even my company fatigues him, especially as his spirits are so good that he cannot help talking incessantly when anybody is with him. When alone he diverts himself with correcting his own works, and with all [the] ordinary amusements."[42] Smith agreed to leave on the condition that Hume's physician, Joseph Black, would keep him updated on Hume's health and that Hume would send for him any time he wished to see him, at which point Smith would hasten back to the city.[43] In his letter to Wedderburn, written from Kirkcaldy on August 14, Smith passed along the bad news regarding Hume's health and the good news regarding his spirits, employing as caustic a tone toward Christianity as Hume himself had ever used: "Poor David Hume is dying very fast, but with great chearfulness and good humour and with more real resignation to the necessary course of things, than any Whining Christian ever dyed with pretended resignation to the will of God."[44] Smith was well aware of the importance that many were attaching to the manner of Hume's death, and he too wanted him to prove the critics wrong: "Since we must lose our friend," he writes, "the most agreable thing that can happen is that he dyes as a man of sense ought to do."[45] Hume was, happily, doing his part: that same day Black wrote to Smith to let him know that Hume had been "remarkably Easy and chearfull, these three last days."[46]

The next day Hume opened his last exchange of letters with Smith. After requesting that Smith preserve a copy of the *Dialogues*, as quoted in the previous chapter, he concludes by pleading, "Be so good as to write me an answer soon. My State of Health does not permit me to wait Months for it."[47] Despite Hume's anxiety for a response, the letter was sent to Kirkcaldy via the carrier rather than the post, which saved Smith a grand total of one penny sterling but caused the letter to sit at the carrier's house for a week before being delivered—"a strange blunder," as Hume later admitted.[48] Smith finally received the letter on August 22 and sat down immediately to pen a reply. In addition to assuring Hume that he would carefully preserve a copy of the *Dialogues*, Smith also presents him with a proposition: "If you

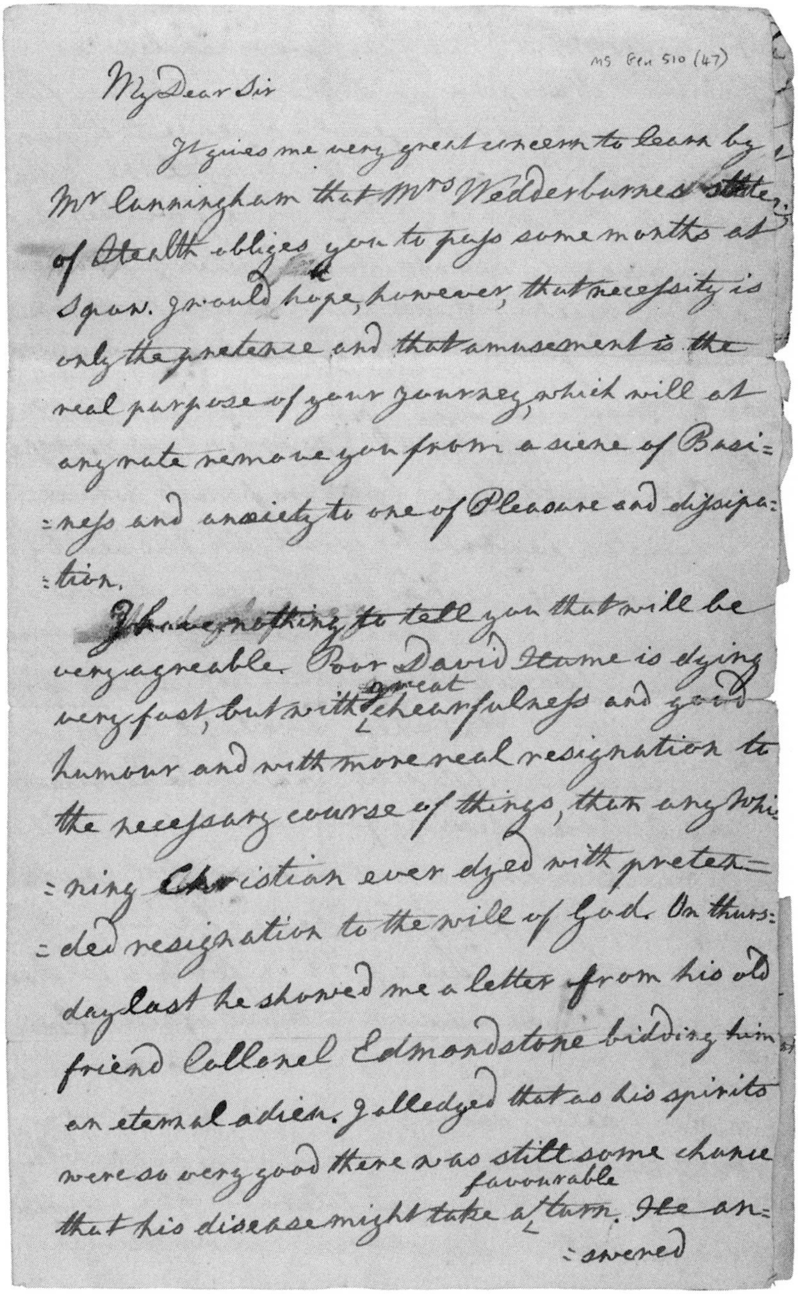

MS Gen 510 (47)

My Dear Sir

It gives me very great concern to learn by Mr Cunningham that Mrs Wedderburnes state of Health obliges you to pass some months at Spaw. I would hope, however, that necessity is only the pretence and that amusement is the real purpose of your journey, which will at any rate remove you from a scene of Business and anxiety to one of Pleasure and dissipation.

I have nothing to tell you that will be very agreeable. Poor David Hume is dying very fast, but with great chearfulness and good humour and with more real resignation to the necessary course of things, than any Whining Christian ever dyed with pretended resignation to the will of God. On thursday last he showed me a letter from his old friend Collonel Edmonstone bidding him an eternal adieu. I alledged that as his spirits were so very good there was still some favourable chance that his disease might take a turn. He answered

FIGURE 11.1 Smith's letter to Alexander Wedderburn includes his caustic comment that "Poor David Hume is dying very fast, but with great chearfulness and good humour and with more real resignation to the necessary course of things, than any Whining Christian ever dyed with pretended resignation to the will of God." Photograph courtesy of the University of Glasgow Library, Special Collections (MS Gen 510/47).

will give me leave I will add a few lines to your account of your own life; giving some account, in my own name, of your behaviour in this illness, if, contrary to my own hopes, it should prove your last."[49] In other words, Smith was requesting permission to complete his friend's autobiography, in a sense, bringing the narrative of *My Own Life* from April 18, where the work leaves off, up to Hume's death. Knowing the keen public interest in how Hume approached his end, Smith wanted to write the "authorized" version of the story, and to demonstrate to the world that Hume had died as a philosopher should.

Smith provides Hume a hint of what the work would look like: "Some conversations we had lately together," he writes, "particularly that concerning your want of an excuse to make to Charon, the excuse you at last thought of, and the very bad reception which Charon was likely to give it, would, I imagine, make no disagreeable part of the history." While Smith would later express surprise that the *Letter to Strahan* provoked so much outrage, then, in fact he knew—or should have known—from the beginning that it would do so: this conversation was hardly calculated to soothe the sensibilities of the pious. Smith also planned to emphasize Hume's continual good spirits in the face of a protracted and obviously fatal illness: "You have in a declining state of health, under an exhausting disease, for more than two years together, now looked at the approach, or what you at least believed to be the approach of Death with a steady chearfulness such as very few men have been able to maintain for a few hours, tho' otherwise in the most perfect Health."[50] This, clearly, was a story that the public needed to hear.

Smith also offers, in this letter, to revise the forthcoming edition of Hume's collected works in accordance with Hume's final corrections, though it is unclear whether he did end up carrying out this task.[51] Smith then catches himself, realizing that he was writing as if Hume was already dead. "All this, I have written upon the supposition that the event of your disease should prove different from what I still hope it may do," he continues. "For your spirits are so good, the Spirit of Life is still so very strong in you, and the progress of your disorder is as slow and gradual that I still hope it may take a turn." Smith concludes, in the final words he would write to his friend, by reminding Hume that "I hope I need not repeat to you that I am ready to wait on you whenever you wish to see me. Whenever you do so, I hope you will not scruple to call on me."[52] Smith's hopes regarding Hume's health, such as they were, were not to be realized. That same day Black wrote to inform him that while Hume's morale continued strong, his physical condition was deteriorating steadily: "he sits up, goes down [the] Stairs once a day and amuses himself with reading, but hardly sees any Body. He finds that the conversation of even his most intimate freinds fatigues and oppresses him for the most part." Happily, however, "he is quite free from Anxiety impatience or low Spirits and passes his time very well with the assistance of amuseing Books." Hume, not realizing that his previous letter had been delayed so long, and not having yet received Smith's response to it (written that day), seems to have grown impatient with Smith's apparent negligence. Black concludes his report to Smith, "He [i.e., Hume] says he wrote you lately and expects an answer."[53]

Hume finally received Smith's letter the next day, August 23. His response was the last letter that he ever wrote. By this point he was so weak that he was forced to dictate the note to his nephew, rather than penning it himself. "I go very fast to decline," Hume tells Smith, although not quite fast enough for his tastes: "last night [I] had a small fever, which I hoped might put a quicker period to this tedious Illness, but unluckily it has in a great measure gone off." While he appreciated Smith's eagerness to come to Edinburgh to see him, Hume felt obliged to turn down the offer: "I cannot submit to your coming over here on my account as it is possible for me to see you so small a Part of the day." He also gives Smith complete discretion to complete his autobiography in whatever way he deems suitable: "You are too good in thinking any trifles that concern me are so much worth your attention, but I give you entire liberty to make what Additions you please to the account of my Life." While Hume's tone here is cheerfully complaisant, this was no small proposition that he was accepting. *My Own Life* was, after all, Hume's final message to his readers, the one that would serve as the preface to future editions of his collected works. His immediate willingness to grant Smith "entire liberty" regarding such a central ingredient of his posthumous legacy reveals the ultimate degree of trust and confidence. He signs off his final letter, "Adieu My dearest Friend."[54]

Two days later, August 25, Hume died in his house on St. David Street at the age of sixty-five. Black had the sad duty of informing Smith of the news, which he did in a letter written the next day: "Yesterday about 4 o'clock afternoon Mr Hume expired. . . . He continued to the last perfectly sensible and free from much pain or feelings of distress." While it was obvious by the evening of the 24th that the end would come soon, Black had deemed it improper to ask Smith to come to Edinburgh, especially given Hume's own directions to the contrary. He assures Smith, however, that Hume "died in such a happy composure of mind that nothing could have made it better."[55]

CHAPTER 12

TEN TIMES
MORE ABUSE
(1776-1777)

T HE FUNERAL TOOK place on August 29 in a driving rain in
what is now the Old Calton Burial Ground in Edinburgh.
A large crowd gathered for the event despite the weather, "as
if," a bemused contemporary wrote, "they had expected the hearse to
have been consumed in livid flames, or encircled with a ray of glory."[1]
We have no positive evidence that Smith was in attendance, though it
is hard to imagine him missing it. It seems that even in death Hume
continued to provoke the animosity of some, as Hume's family was
forced to station guards around the grave in the days after the funeral
to prevent it from being desecrated.[2] Hume arranged to have Robert
Adam—a friend and one of the foremost architects of the age—design his tomb, a plain but large neoclassical mausoleum, instructing
him that he wanted nothing more than his name and dates inscribed
on it, "leaving it to posterity to add the rest."[3] At the time the tomb
stood alone on the prospect of Calton Hill, dramatically overlooking
both the Old and New Towns. Smith later commented to a companion, while walking over the North Bridge connecting the two parts of
the city, "I don't like that monument; it is the greatest piece of vanity
I ever saw in my friend Hume."[4]

Two days after the funeral Smith wrote to Hume's brother, John
Home, to release Hume's family from the obligation to pay the two
hundred pounds that had been allotted to him in Hume's will as
recompense for serving as his literary executor. Especially given that
he had refused to publish the *Dialogues Concerning Natural Religion*,
Smith felt that it would be improper for him to accept the bequest.[5]
Home assured Smith that Hume intended the money to be given to

FIGURE 12.1 Hume's tomb in the Old Calton Burial Ground, designed by Robert Adam, once dramatically overlooked Edinburgh's Old and New Towns, before it was surrounded by subsequent development. Photograph by the author.

him not as payment for services rendered but rather "as a testimony of his friendship," but Smith persisted in declining it.[6]

In the meantime, Smith composed his supplement to Hume's *My Own Life* in the form of an ostensible letter to William Strahan describing Hume's final months. The letter was addressed to Strahan because he was, in accordance with Hume's will, responsible for publishing *My Own Life* and thus also Smith's addition to it. Smith seems to have begun writing the *Letter to Strahan* in late September.[7] He dated the work November 9, but he had finished a draft by October 7, at which point he sent copies to Joseph Black and to John Home (Hume's brother) for their comments. Black, in turn, also solicited the thoughts of John Home (the playwright) and other friends.[8] After making a few revisions, Smith sent the final version to Strahan on November 13.[9]

Hume had instructed both Smith and Strahan that his autobiography should be "prefixed to any future Edition" of his works, and that is how Smith assumed *My Own Life* and the *Letter to Strahan* would be issued.[10] From the outset, however—even before he had seen either of the pieces—Strahan wanted to publish them separately, as well.[11] When Strahan received Smith's letter he liked it "exceedingly," but he found that it was too short, even when paired with *My Own Life*, to "make a Volume even of the *smallest Size*." He proposed to combine them with some letters on political subjects that Hume had written to him over the years and asked for Smith's opinion on the matter, promising to "do nothing without your Advice and Approbation."[12] Smith quickly thwarted this idea. While "sensible that many of Mr Humes letters would do him great honour and that [Strahan] would publish none but such as would," Smith insisted that they ought to respect Hume's wishes above all else, and he had made it clear that he did not want any of his papers published beyond *My Own Life* and the *Dialogues*. "I know he always disliked the thought of his letters ever being published," Smith noted—ignoring for the moment the fact that he himself included Hume's last letter in his soon-to-be-published account of his friend's dying days.[13]

Smith did implicitly consent to the separate publication of *My Own Life* and the *Letter to Strahan*, however, commenting that they "will not make a volume; but [they] will make a small pamphlet."[14]

That is accordingly how Strahan issued the two works in March 1777, in order, he said, "to gratify the impatience of the public curiosity."[15] Somewhat mysteriously, however, they had already appeared in full in the January 1777 issue of the *Scots Magazine*. It is unclear how this pre-publication came about, or under whose auspices; the correspondence of the relevant parties is entirely silent on the matter, as if it never happened.[16] In any case, the separate publication of *My Own Life* and the *Letter to Strahan* so soon after Hume's death—much earlier than they would have appeared had Strahan waited to include them in the next edition of Hume's collected works, per Hume's instructions—conferred on these pieces a prominence that they would not otherwise have had.

Smith opens the *Letter to Strahan* by declaring, "it is with a real, though a very melancholy pleasure, that I sit down to give you some account of the behaviour of our late excellent friend, Mr. Hume, during his last illness." He begins the narrative where *My Own Life* leaves off, in late April 1776. While Hume believed that his condition was "mortal and incurable," Smith reports, he was prevailed on by his friends "to try what might be the effects of a long journey." He then recounts the details of Hume's trip—his fortuitous encounter with Smith and John Home at Morpeth; the advice of the London doctors to visit Bath to take the waters; the temporary abeyance of Hume's illness at Bath, followed by the return of the symptoms "with their usual violence"; and his return to his home and friends in Edinburgh. Back in Scotland, Smith notes, Hume's growing weakness did not prevent him from living as he always had: "he continued to divert himself, as usual, with correcting his own works for a new edition, with reading books of amusement, with the conversation of his friends; and, sometimes in the evening, with a party at his favourite game of whist." At this point some of Hume's friends refused to believe that he was actually dying, given that "his cheerfulness was so great, and his conversations and amusements run so much in their usual strain." But Hume knew that this was wishful thinking; Smith quotes him as declaring, "I am dying as fast as my enemies, if I have any, could wish, and as easily and cheerfully as my best friends could desire."[17]

Hume's manner toward his friends, as he took his leave of them, comes in for special praise from Smith: "Mr. Hume's magnanimity and firmness were such, that his most affectionate friends knew, that they hazarded nothing in talking or writing to him as to a dying man, and that so far from being hurt by this frankness, he was rather pleased and flattered by it." As an illustration of Hume's composure and tranquility in the face of death he recounts their playful conversation about Charon, toning down, as we have seen, one of Hume's more stridently antireligious remarks in the process. Smith also notes that "though Mr. Hume always talked of his approaching dissolution with great cheerfulness, he never affected to make any parade of his magnanimity. He never mentioned the subject but when the conversation naturally led to it, and never dwelt longer upon it than the course of the conversation happened to require."[18]

Smith was no longer in Hume's company during his friend's last two weeks, having returned to Kirkcaldy in mid-August, so he carries the narrative forward through extracts from three letters, leaving aside for the moment his general aversion to publishing private correspondence. The extracts are taken from the August 22 report from Joseph Black on Hume's declining health and good spirits; Hume's last letter to Smith, written in his nephew's hand; and Black's announcement of Hume's death and account of his "happy composure of mind" in the moments leading up to it.[19] Presumably Smith wanted to include these letters as hard evidence of Hume's cheerful mood in his final days, so that the reader would not have to simply accept his word for it.[20]

In the concluding paragraph Smith attempts to sum up Hume's character, confirming—even amplifying—Hume's self-presentation in *My Own Life*. As his biographer Ian Simpson Ross rightly notes, this passage is "a beautifully flighted piece of prose, perhaps the best Smith ever wrote."[21] Smith opens with a preamble that must have been at least partly disingenuous: "Thus died our most excellent, and never to be forgotten friend; concerning whose philosophical opinions men will, no doubt, judge variously, every one approving or condemning them, according as they happen to coincide or disagree with his own; but concerning whose character and conduct there can scarce be a difference of opinion."[22] While Hume's affable demeanor did disarm a number of critics whom he met in person, Smith must have

known that some—likely many—of his readers would disagree vocif-
erously with the idea that a skeptic like Hume could have been of unimpeachable character. Even so, he proceeds to make his case.

Smith starts by describing Hume's temper, which he proclaims
was "more happily balanced . . . than that perhaps of any other man
I have ever known." As an example of such balance, he points to
Hume's "charity and generosity" even while "in the lowest state of
his fortune," along with his "great and necessary frugality" which was
"founded, not upon avarice, but upon the love of independency." In
another instance of Hume achieving a kind of Aristotelian golden
mean, Smith notes that "the extreme gentleness of his nature never
weakened either the firmness of his mind, or the steadiness of his
resolutions." Perhaps most of all, he emphasizes Hume's ready sense
of humor, his talent for enjoyable conversation, and his exceptional
capacity for friendship, all of which were thoroughly familiar to the
Edinburgh literati and to the many French admirers of *le bon David*.
"It never was the meaning of his raillery to mortify," Smith observes,
"and therefore, far from offending, it seldom failed to please and delight, even those who were the objects of it. To his friends, who were
frequently the objects of it, there was not perhaps any one of all his
great and amiable qualities, which contributed more to endear his
conversation." Finally, he comments that Hume's "gaiety of temper"
was combined with "the most severe application, the most extensive
learning, the greatest depth of thought, and a capacity in every respect
the most comprehensive"—all traits to which any reader of Hume's
works can attest.[23]

Smith concludes the *Letter* with one of the most fateful sentences
that he ever wrote: "Upon the whole, I have always considered him,
both in his lifetime and since his death, as approaching as nearly to
the idea of a perfectly wise and virtuous man, as perhaps the nature
of human frailty will permit."[24] There is a clear echo here of Plato's
epitaph for Socrates in the concluding sentence of the *Phaedo*, in
which the narrator, Phaedo, pronounces Socrates to be "of all those
whom we knew in our time, the bravest and also the wisest and most
upright."[25] This association of his friend's end with one of the most
iconic deaths in the Western tradition, while audacious, was not the
aspect of the sentence that proved most controversial. The real scan-

dal, rather, was Smith's assertion that Hume, an avowed skeptic, was a model of wisdom and virtue.

———————————

As short as it is, the *Letter to Strahan* adroitly serves a number of different roles. First, and most obviously, it is a moving eulogy. As J. Y. T. Greig writes, "No man could ask, and few have ever had, a finer tribute from a friend."[26] Even leaving aside the contents of the *Letter*, the very fact that Smith chose, of his own accord, to complete Hume's account of his life constitutes a remarkable compliment. If a friend is truly "another self," as Aristotle claimed, then Smith was undoubtedly the single best-placed person to round out Hume's autobiographical sketch.[27] And Smith's description of Hume's character and conduct is about as laudatory as it could be within the bounds of plausibility, not to say veracity. Hume's irrepressible good spirits, unbroken equanimity, prodigious intellect, and engaging sense of humor are chronicled with an assurance and affection that only a close friend could bring to the narrative. It is evident that Smith considered himself lucky to have known someone of Hume's goodness and greatness so well, and for so long.

Somewhat less obviously, the *Letter to Strahan* also represents a kind of paean to friendship.[28] Smith opens the work by announcing his intention to give an "account of the behaviour of our late excellent friend," and he concludes with a character sketch of "our most excellent, and never to be forgotten friend."[29] In fact, he uses the word "friend" a remarkable seventeen times within the work's half dozen pages. Hume's comportment toward his friends and his great capacity for friendship were, according to Smith's depiction, among the principal proofs of the goodness of his character, and the friendships themselves were in turn among the chief rewards that he derived from this good character. The *Letter* thus illustrates and reinforces the claims of both Hume and Smith, in their philosophical works, that friendship is a central and indeed indispensable component of a good and happy life. The work also, by its very nature, calls attention to Hume and Smith's own friendship, and unobtrusively proposes it as a model of what a friendship should look like. This seems to be the essence of Dugald Stewart's somewhat cryptic claim that theirs "was a friendship on both sides founded on the admiration of genius, and the love of simplicity; and, which forms an interesting circumstance in the history of each of these eminent men, from the ambition which both have shewn to record it to posterity."[30]

Above all, the *Letter* was an attempt to vindicate Hume's reputation and secure his legacy in a world that was frequently hostile to him and almost always hostile to his ideas. In the context in which Smith wrote the work this meant affirming, in the face of nearly universal sentiment to the contrary, that a skeptic could both live and die well. Smith's description of Hume as a paragon of wisdom and virtue and his constant references to Hume's cheerfulness in his final months and days are difficult to read as anything other than a deliberate challenge to the devout. To be sure, Smith softened the antireligious barb in their badinage about Charon—replacing Hume's desire to see "the churches shut up, and the Clergy sent about their business" with the desire to see "the downfal of some of the prevailing systems of superstition"—but he still chose to make this story, which was certain to cause offense, the centerpiece of the work. In discussing Hume's death Smith does not even allude to God, the soul, or the afterlife, any more than Hume himself had in *My Own Life*.

At least implicitly, then, the *Letter* is also a defense of the possibility and morality of a life without religion. In *The Theory of Moral Sentiments* Smith had indicated that religious faith offers comfort in the face of death as well as consolation for those who are wronged or wrongly judged here on earth. Hume knew that his death was imminent and was frequently misjudged, but the *Letter* makes clear that he had no need for otherworldly comforts and consolations. Smith had also argued in his first book that belief in God and an afterlife often helps to buttress morality. Even there he never went so far as to suggest that religion is an *indispensable* component of a virtuous life, but the *Letter* establishes just how dispensable it is: the individual whom Smith regarded as "approaching as nearly to the idea of a perfectly wise and virtuous man, as perhaps the nature of human frailty will permit" was a religious skeptic. His model of wisdom and virtue was not a Christian saint, but rather the former resident of St. David Street.

Publishing the *Letter to Strahan* was a brave act, especially given Smith's perennial aversion to public controversy. For the pious it was obnoxious enough that Hume remained a skeptic to the end, but they had long since written him off as an incorrigible infidel in any case. The greater outrage was that Smith, a widely respected former professor of moral philosophy, proceeded to rub their noses in it. He paid for it in spades. Smith later claimed that "a single, and as, I thought a very harmless Sheet of paper, which I happened to Write concerning the death of our late friend Mr Hume, brought upon me ten times more abuse than the very violent attack I had made upon the whole commercial system of Great Britain."[31] Virtually all Smith scholars are familiar with this line because of the colorful reference to *The Wealth of Nations*—a book that, it is important to remember, was published just a year before the *Letter*—but far fewer know the precise nature and extent of the abuse that Smith faced as a consequence of his tribute to his friend.

Not everyone was offended, of course. Hume's other friends, who were in the best position to corroborate Smith's character sketch, were entirely persuaded by it. Hugh Blair—who was a minister, recall—wrote to Strahan: "Poor David! What an irreparable blank does he make amongst us here [in Edinburgh]. Taking him all in all, we shall never see the like. Indeed I cannot but agree with what Adam Smith says of him in the last sentence of his printed letter to you."[32] Hume and Smith also had one overeager defender named Samuel Jackson Pratt who opened his effusive *Apology for the Life and Writings of David Hume* with the exceedingly inflated pronouncement: "David Hume is dead! Never were the pillars of Orthodoxy so desperately shaken, as they are now, by that event."[33] (Pratt too came under immediate fire.) In most circles, however, the reaction was very different. As John Ramsay of Ochtertyre writes, the *Letter to Strahan* "gave very great offence, and made [Smith] henceforth be regarded as an avowed sceptic, to the no small regret of many who revered his character and admired his writings. That his friend was an amiable philosopher of great parts and greater eloquence was not disputed. But when Dr Smith declared without any qualification that 'he had always considered Mr Hume, both in his lifetime and since his death, as approaching as nearly to the idea of a perfectly wise and virtuous man as perhaps the nature of human frailty would permit,' everybody was astonished that a man who had once been a professor should have expressed himself in these terms. It went so far as to affirm that it mattered not what speculative opinions men might entertain—a proposition which shocked every sober Christian."[34]

The attack was led by George Horne, who was at the time the Vice-Chancellor of Oxford University, the President of Oxford's Magdalen College, and a chaplain in ordinary to King George III. Horne was a staunch defender of "high church" Anglicanism, and would later become Dean of Canterbury and then Bishop of Norwich. Horne's open (but anonymous) letter to Smith, derisively titled *A Letter to Adam Smith LL.D. on the Life, Death, and Philosophy of His Friend David Hume Esq. by One of the People Called Christians*, appeared in April 1777, and it was sufficiently popular that two more editions were printed that year, followed by a half dozen more over the next few decades. Horne's basic point was one that would recur time and again in the course of the controversy: Hume could not have been truly virtuous because he was an atheist, and sought to spread his atheism to others through his writings. (As John Rae notes, this line of argument begs the entire question at issue.)[35] Horne opens his indictment in the sarcastic tone that pervades the whole: "You have been lately employed in embalming a philosopher; his *body*, I believe I must say; for concerning the other part of him, neither you nor he seem to have entertained an idea, sleeping or waking. Else, it surely might have claimed a little of your care and attention; and one would think, the belief of the soul's existence and immortality could do no harm, if it did no good, in a *Theory of Moral Sentiments*. But every gentleman understands his own business best."[36]

Turning to Smith's declaration that everyone will approve or condemn Hume's philosophical views "according as they happen to coincide or disagree with his own," Horne pronounces himself sorry that this would be the case: "since the design of them is to banish out of the world every idea of truth and comfort, salvation and immortality, a future state, and the providence, and even existence of GOD, it seems a pity, that we cannot be all of a mind about them"—even if, he snidely adds, "we might have formerly liked to hear the author crack a joke, over a bottle." Horne accepts that Hume may have been "a so-cial agreeable person, of a convivial turn, told a good story, and played well at 'his favourite game of whist,'" but he insists that Hume could not have been—as Smith claimed—genuinely gentle mannered, good natured, compassionate, generous, and charitable "when he so often sate down calmly and deliberately to obliterate from the hearts of the human species every trace of the knowledge of GOD and his dispen-sations; all faith in his kind providence, and fatherly protection; all hope of enjoying his grace and favour, here, or hereafter; all love of him, and of their brethren for his sake; all the patience under tribu-lation, all the comforts, in time of sorrow, derived from these fruitful and perennial sources."[37]

Above all Horne upbraids Smith for reporting, and apparently en-dorsing, Hume's nonchalant attitude toward death and the afterlife. Smith seems to want to persuade his readers, Horne says, "that athe-ism is the only cordial for low spirits, and the proper antidote against the fear of death. But, surely, he who can reflect, with complacency, on a friend . . . amusing himself with LUCIAN, WHIST, and CHARON, at his death, may smile over BABYLON in ruins; esteem the earthquake, which destroyed LISBON, an agreeable occurrence; and congratulate the hardened PHARAOH, on his overthrow in the Red sea." If Smith had been a true friend, or even a decent person, in other words, he would have pleaded with Hume to seek eternal salvation, rather than playing cards or joking about Lucian, and he certainly would not have advertised—indeed paraded—Hume's impious attitude to all the world. Horne concludes that their joint conduct in this instance is a sure sign of the "baneful and pestilential influences of false philosophy on the human heart."[38]

Horne was soon joined by an author who signed himself only "E. M." and who wondered aloud, in the *Weekly Magazine*, whether the *Letter to Strahan* could have been anything other than satirical. While Smith doubtless meant to produce "a panegyric upon his friend," this author claims, in fact his portrait of "a man of distin-guished intellectual powers acting the fool at his end" can only "ex-pose Mr H–'s memory to the pity, if not to the contempt, of the truly wise and virtuous part of mankind." Like Horne, this commentator suggests that nothing could be "more frivolous, more childish, more indecently wanton and presumptuous in a dying man, perceiving himself on the verge of time, than Mr H–'s sportful dialogue with *Charon*" and that Hume's example cannot come close to comparing "for true greatness, with the meanest Christian *dying in faith*."[39] Shorter but similarly critical appraisals appeared in the *London Review*, the *Gentleman's Magazine*, and the *Weekly Magazine* (again), among others.[40]

True to form, Samuel Johnson and James Boswell concurred with these judgments. Johnson simply refused to believe that Hume died as Smith and Boswell claimed he did. When Boswell remarked that "the thought of annihilation gave Hume no pain," Johnson retorted: "It was not so, Sir. He had a vanity in being thought easy." Turning Hume's own argument regarding miracles against him, Johnson continued: "It is more probable that he should assume an appearance of ease, than that so very improbable a thing should be, as a man not afraid of going . . . into an unknown state, and not being uneasy at leaving all he knew. And you are to consider, that upon his own principle of annihilation he had no motive to speak the truth."[41] Boswell, we have seen, did believe that Hume remained a skeptic even in the face of death, and this disturbed him to no end. Accordingly, he considered the *Letter to Strahan* a piece of "daring effrontery" and an example of the "poisonous productions with which this age is infested," and he beseeched Johnson to "step forth" and "knock Hume's and Smith's heads together, and make vain and ostentatious infidelity exceedingly ridiculous. Would it not," he pleaded, "be worth your while to crush such noxious weeds in the moral garden?"[42] Boswell remarks elsewhere that when he read the *Letter*'s concluding sentence, "delivered by my old Professor of Moral Philosophy, I could not help exclaiming with the Psalmist, 'Surely I have now more understanding than my teachers!'"[43] Nor were these comments confined to private conversation; on the contrary, they all appeared in print, and all but the last were included in Boswell's wildly popular *Life of Samuel Johnson*. (Thankfully for Smith's sake, this work was not published until the year after his death.) More than two years after the *Letter to Strahan* Boswell still felt aggrieved enough to express his indignation to Smith: "I fairly told him that I did not like his having praised

David Hume so much. He went off to the board huffed"—they were at the customs house—"yet affecting to treat my censure as foolish. I did not care how he took it. Since his absurd eulogium on Hume . . . I have had no desire to be much with him."[44]

Boswell's friend William Johnson Temple, for his part, thought Smith should be ashamed of himself: "A professor (once) of Moral Philosophy, an instructor of youth, ought to be ashamed to own so intimate a connection & so blamable an admiration of a man who gloried & died in the disbelief of a Providence & a Futurity. I should think he must have hurt his character greatly & essentially by his publick avowal of this man. It is equal to adopting all his worst opinions both in Religion & Government."[45] If Boswell is to be believed, even Edmund Burke, a great admirer of Smith's, deemed the *Letter to Strahan* a laughable attempt to spread the gospel of infidelity: "Talking of David Hume, Mr. Burke laughed at his life [i.e., *My Own Life*] and at Smith's appendix 'most virtuous,' etc. 'This,' said he, 'is said for the credit of their church, and the members of no church use more art for its credit. . . . Here was a man at a great age, who had been preparing all along to die without showing fear, does it, and rout is made about it. Men in general die easily.'"[46]

Nor did the controversy die down quickly. Well over a decade later, in a sermon delivered just months before Smith's death, John Wesley, the founder of the Methodist movement, thundered (apparently to Hume's ghost): "What think you now of Charon? Has he ferried you over [the] Styx? . . . At length you know it is a fearful thing to fall into the hands of the living God!"[47] Still later, in the early nineteenth century, stories began to circulate that, despite the accounts given by Smith, Black, Home, Boswell, and others of Hume's cheerfulness and serenity during his final weeks, he was in fact filled with anguish, fear, and remorse during much of this period, and only put on a good face while visitors were present.[48] Not to put too fine a point on it, Smith was loudly called a liar—or, at best, the dupe of Hume's ploy to portray himself as more tranquil than he really was in the face of death. All of the sources of this rumor were, predictably, fervently religious, and they all attribute Hume's alleged anguish to his irreligion rather than to his physical ailments. One of the accounts even extended the torments to include Smith.

According to a thirdhand report published in 1852, Smith extracted a promise from Hume during his final days that after his death, "if it were in his power, to meet [him] in the shady avenue of 'the Meadows,' behind George-square"—south of the Old Town, adjacent to the university—in order to "tell the secrets of the world unknown." Such was the effect of this pledge on Smith, the report has it, that "no persuasion would induce him to walk in the meadows after sunset."[49] How far to credit such stories can safely be left to the reader to determine, but they do testify to the continuing impact that Hume's death, and Smith's account of it, had on religious sensibilities, even many decades after the fact. Indeed, nearly a century after the *Letter to Strahan* was published one prolific author of religious tomes was still sufficiently incensed by it to proclaim that he knew "no more lamentable evidence of the weakness and folly of irreligion and infidelity" in "all the range of English literature."[50]

While Smith himself regarded (or affected to regard) the *Letter to Strahan* as "a very harmless Sheet of paper," then, clearly many others did not see it that way.[51] And it is important to remember that all of this invective ensued even after he omitted some of his and Hume's more offensive remarks. There is no telling how much obloquy he would have endured had the critics known that Hume hoped for "the pleasure of seeing the churches shut up, and the Clergy sent about their business" and that Smith proclaimed that Hume died "with more real resignation to the necessary course of things, than any Whining Christian ever dyed with pretended resignation to the will of God."[52]

Though Smith later commented that the *Letter* brought on him ten times more abuse than *The Wealth of Nations*, he never retracted the claims he made in it, never expressed regret for having published it, and never responded to the critics. As Greig writes, "he had delivered his opinion of 'le bon David,' and he stood by it, without another word. Adam Smith knew his man."[53]

SMITH'S FINAL YEARS IN EDINBURGH

(1777-1790)

I N THE WAKE of the publication of *The Wealth of Nations* and Hume's death in 1776, Smith emerged as the unquestioned leader among the Scottish literati in terms of international renown and intellectual influence. Ironically, not long after Hume died Smith made the move to Edinburgh that Hume had advocated for so many decades. Now that he had finally finished his second great work he was at last willing to leave the relative solitude of Kirkcaldy. Smith took up residence in the city early in 1778 and lived there for the remaining dozen years of his life, with the exception of two jaunts to London of four months each, in 1782 and 1787.

The move was precipitated by a new job: to the great amusement and consternation of posterity, after publishing *The Wealth of Nations* Smith spent around a decade as a customs officer. History's most celebrated champion of free trade, that is to say, took a day job collecting tariffs for His Majesty's Government. Indeed, he actively sought out the position. The move was not as baffling as it might seem at first glance. First of all, it was something of a family tradition, as several of Smith's relatives, including his father, had worked as customs officers in Kirkcaldy, and he was obviously well versed and highly interested in the issues involved.[1] More to the point, Smith was not simply opposed to all tariffs. On the contrary, he realized that they were an important source of government revenue in the Britain of his day. While he opposed using them as an instrument of monopoly or a means of favoring domestic industries over imports, he had no objection to tariffs that were moderate, equitably levied, and used to pay for necessary expenditures such as defense, the administration of justice, and public works. The job was not simply a sinecure, or at least he did not treat it as such. He commented that the position "requires a good deal of attendance," but he also found it "both easy and honourable, and for my Way of living sufficiently beneficial." His only regret was "the interruptions to my literary pursuits, which the duties of my office necessarily occasion."[2]

During these years Smith lived in Panmure House, a plain L-shaped building in the Canongate, just off the east end of today's Royal Mile—the only one of Smith's residences that still stands. (The house is currently being converted into a visitor and events center.) As usual, he lived with his mother, at least until 1784 when she died at the ripe old age of ninety, and his cousin, Janet Douglas, who had served as a live-in housekeeper since Smith's Glasgow days. Soon after the move to Edinburgh they added another member to the household, David Douglas, the son of another cousin, who was nine years old at the time and who eventually became Smith's principal heir.

Up to this point Smith had never lived in Edinburgh for long or even particularly cared for the city, but he quickly became something of an institution there. Tourists frequently sought out his acquaintance, and his company was always in demand among the city's elite. With Hume no longer around to play host, Smith took up the baton: Dugald Stewart writes that he kept "a simple, though hospitable table, where, without the formality of an invitation, he was always happy to receive his friends."[3] Smith also helped to form a weekly dining group called the Oyster Club—also sometimes known as Adam Smith's Club—along with Joseph Black and James Hutton, who eventually became his literary executors. This was quite a triumvirate: as John Rae notes, Smith, Black, and Hutton have a credible claim to being the founders of modern economics, chemistry, and geology, respectively.[4] All of this conviviality must have helped to take the sting out of the loss of Hume, though not entirely: in 1784 Smith commented to William Strahan that "my friends grow very thin in the world, and I do not find that my new ones are likely to supply their place."[5] One can also detect a bit of wistfulness in a comment that Smith made to Strahan's partner, Thomas Cadell, a couple of years later. He was recommending a work on moral philosophy by one John Bruce, and he writes that "tho' he and I differ a little, as David Hume and I used to do; I expect [it] will do him very great honour."[6] It seems that Hume's name and ideas also sometimes came up within the Oyster Club, as one of its members for a time, an Austrian physician and freethinker named François Xavier Schwediauer, felt confident enough to tell Jeremy Bentham that Smith "was an intimate friend of the late David Hume and has the same principles."[7]

Though the customs position took up much of Smith's time, he did continue to write. Soon after Hume's death, while he was still in Kirkcaldy, he began working on a book on what he called "the imitative arts"—a category in which he included poetry, painting, sculpture, dancing, and even music.[8] He never finished this work, though he did read a couple of papers on the topic to the Literary Society of Glasgow in 1788, and some of what he drafted appeared in his posthumous *Essays on Philosophical Subjects*.[9] For a time, at least, his ambitions grew even larger, as he reported to a correspondent in 1785 that he had two "great works upon the anvil," the first being "a sort of Philosophical History of all the different branches of Literature, of Philosophy, Poetry and Eloquence" and the other "a sort of theory and History of Law and Government." He reported that "the materials of both are in a great measure collected, and some Part of both is put into tollerable good order," but he allowed that "the indolence of old age, tho' I struggle violently against it, I feel coming fast upon me, and whether I shall ever be able to finish either is extremely uncertain."[10] This worry was realized, as he never completed either of these works to his own satisfaction.

Smith also continued to revise his existing works, as Hume had in his later years. The second edition of *The Wealth of Nations*, published in 1778, contained some minor additions and corrections, but the revisions for the third edition were more substantial. This edition, published in 1784, was the last to receive any real attention from Smith himself. Much of the added material came in Book 4, Smith's devastating analysis of mercantilist ideas and policies. He described the additions to Strahan as containing "some new arguments against the corn bounty; against the Herring buss bounty; a new concluding Chapter upon the mercantile System; [and] A short History and,

I presume, a full exposition of the Absurdity and hurtfulness of almost all our chartered trading companies"—above all the East India
Company.[11]

In the meantime, the influence of the book continued to grow.
Smith was by no means the first to advocate free trade, as he would
have been the first to stress, but he helped to give the idea a prominence and dignity that it had previously lacked. Walter Bagehot observes that before the publication of *The Wealth of Nations* free trade
was "a tenet against which a respectable parent would probably caution
his son," though "it was known as a tempting heresy, and one against
which a warning was needed."[12] Within a decade of the book's publication this heresy had become official government policy. According
to a story that features right about here in nearly every account of
Smith's life, during his 1787 visit to London Smith entered a room
containing the Prime Minister, William Pitt, and several of his top
ministers, all of whom rose to greet him, and when he asked them to
be seated Pitt responded, "No, we will stand till you are first seated, for
we are all your scholars."[13] The story may be apocryphal, but it is true
that Pitt studied Smith's book carefully and was deeply influenced by
its arguments, and the policies, treaties, and budgets of his administration were in many respects quite Smithian in character, at least until
war broke out with revolutionary France.

Smith's greatest literary efforts during these years, however, were devoted to his earlier book. The sixth edition of *The Theory of Moral Sentiments*, which was published in 1790—more than three decades after
the first edition, and just months before Smith's death—incorporated
a great many revisions and additions, including an entirely new Part 6,
titled "Of the Character of Virtue."[14] Scholars differ as to the significance of these changes. Some maintain that the new material does not
add much of substance to the work, but instead clarifies and fleshes
out ideas that were already present in earlier editions.[15] Others con-
tend that the sixth edition contains important new arguments—for
instance, that it includes, for the first time, a systematic discussion
of what virtue actually consists of (as opposed to what leads people
to approve of it); that it emphasizes, to a much greater degree than

the earlier editions, the moral and political ills of commercial society; or, conversely, that it goes much further in proposing remedies for these ills.[16] Wading into these debates would lead this epilogue too far astray, but it may not be amiss to observe that a number of the revisions can be read in another way: as a tribute to the life and writings of David Hume.[17]

To begin with, several of the new passages echo arguments that were prominent in Hume's works. Smith's trenchant analysis of "the spirit of system," for instance, recalls Hume's long-standing opposition to ideological politics.[18] His critique of civil and ecclesiastical factions too is quite Humean in character, and his claim that "of all the corrupters of moral sentiments . . . faction and fanaticism have always been by far the greatest" could serve as a thesis statement for many of Hume's *Essays* and a great deal of *The History of England*.[19] Smith's praise of the virtues of "the middling and inferior stations of life" and the "prudent man" mirrors Hume's staunch insistence that commercial societies are the most virtuous.[20] Smith's objections to viewing the prosperity of neighboring nations with "malignant jealousy" follows not just his own standpoint in *The Wealth of Nations* but also Hume's earlier arguments in "Of the Jealousy of Trade."[21] Smith's discussion of suicide was likely occasioned by Hume's posthumous essay on the subject; though he does not go as far as Hume had in defending the morality of suicide, he does agree that "the unfortunate persons who perish in this miserable manner are the proper objects, not of censure, but of commiseration. To attempt to punish them, when they are beyond the reach of all human punishment, is not more absurd than it is unjust."[22]

Smith also tempered some of his claims on behalf of religion in this edition of the book. As one scholar writes, the revisions tend to "play down the notion of God, and make God's existence, where they do touch on it, more something we posit than something we know to be true."[23] Whether these moves were triggered by increased skepticism or reduced caution is difficult to say.[24] Any shift in this direction would bring Smith's views closer to Hume's, of course, but a couple of the changes appear to have been directly inspired by his friend. The first appears in a new chapter on the important distinction between the desire to be praised and the desire to be praiseworthy.

Smith concludes the chapter by criticizing, in quite mocking fashion, the idea that "the duties of devotion, the public and private worship of the Deity" are the most important of virtues. He suggests that God is not so weak and craven as to need constant adulation, and he ridicules "the futile mortifications of a monastery" as inconsequential compared to "the arts which contribute to the subsistence, to the conveniency, or to the ornament of human life"—surely an allusion to Hume's useless and disagreeable "monkish virtues" in the *Second Enquiry*.[25]

The other change that appears to have been inspired by Hume—one of the most conspicuous and commented-upon of all of the revisions—was Smith's replacement of the only overtly Christian passage in the entire work, a discussion of the doctrine of atonement, with the sardonic observation that "in every religion, and in every superstition that the world has ever beheld . . . there has been a Tartarus as well as an Elysium; a place provided for the punishment of the wicked, as well as one for the reward of the just."[26] A controversy later emerged over whether Smith had been induced to make the change due to "the infection of David Hume's society," as William Magee, the Archbishop of Dublin, put it. Magee regarded this revision as but "one proof more . . . of the danger, even to the most enlightened, from a familiar contact with infidelity."[27] He might not have been entirely wrong: given that this passage forms the conclusion of a chapter in which Smith challenges Hume's conception of justice, it seems likely that the change *was* motivated, at least to some degree, by their friendship. As D. D. Raphael remarks, when Smith turned to revise *The Theory of Moral Sentiments* after Hume's death "he must surely have felt some revulsion from concluding a criticism of Hume with a paragraph whose language echoed the sermons of those 'high-flying' preachers who had been the bitterest detractors of Hume. . . . So instead of Christian doctrine about expiation and atonement, Smith made his own atonement by substituting a sentence so Humean in tone that it might almost be called a libation to Hume's ghost."[28]

More broadly, much of the new Part 6, "Of the Character of Virtue," could be read as a tribute of sorts to Hume.[29] After all, Smith had already, by his own reckoning, described a character of supreme virtue in the *Letter to Strahan*. The crowning virtue of Part 6 is self-command: Smith writes that "self-command is not only itself a great virtue, but from it all the other virtues seem to derive their principal lustre."[30] Smith's emphasis on this virtue is typically thought to have been derived from the Stoics, but it is possible that it was also inspired by the self-command that Hume displayed during his final illness. Smith observes that people often find it difficult to control their passions as death nears, and thus that self-command is especially admirable in this situation: "The man who . . . upon the approach of death, preserves his tranquillity unaltered, and suffers no word, no gesture to escape him which does not perfectly accord with the feelings of the most indifferent spectator, necessarily commands a very high degree of admiration."[31] The idea that Smith may have had Hume in mind while writing this passage is supported by the fact that he had alluded to Hume's thought—specifically, to the connection that Hume drew between beauty and utility—just a few sentences earlier. He goes on, in this paragraph, to offer the example of the death of Socrates—which was, of course, the example to which he had implicitly compared Hume in the *Letter to Strahan*'s closing sentence. "Had the enemies of Socrates suffered him to die quietly in his bed," Smith writes, "the glory even of that great philosopher might possibly never have acquired that dazzling splendour in which it has been held in all succeeding ages."[32] While Hume was spared the hemlock, his death was not an altogether quiet one, either, given the outcry from the pious over his unrepentant skepticism.

Finally, Smith's discussion of friendship in Part 6 cannot fail to bring to mind his own friendship with Hume.[33] He contrasts true friendship with the "friendships" that often develop among blood relatives, neighbors, and even "colleagues in office" or "partners in trade." The latter, he notes, arise from "constrained sympathy," or "sympathy which has been assumed and rendered habitual for the sake of conveniency and accommodation." True friendships, by contrast, arise from "natural sympathy," or "an involuntary feeling that the persons to whom we attach ourselves are the natural and proper objects of esteem and approbation." Smith claims that the latter kind of friendship, especially when "confirmed by much experience and long acquaintance," is "of all attachments, the most virtuous; so it is likewise the happiest, as well as the most permanent and secure." It is inconceivable that he was not thinking of Hume here. He goes on to insist that such friendships depend on the friends' mutual recognition of each other's wisdom and virtue—the very characteristics that he had ascribed to Hume in the fateful concluding sentence of the *Letter to Strahan*. Smith ends the discussion by declaring that only friendships among the wise and virtuous "deserve the sacred and venerable name of friendship."[34]

Though Smith's constitution had never been particularly robust, by the time the sixth edition of *The Theory of Moral Sentiments* appeared in January 1790 his health had begun to deteriorate rapidly. He drew up a will on February 6, and virtually every letter written by, to, or about Smith from that point forward mentioned his ailments. Dugald Stewart later observed that "his last illness, which arose from a chronic obstruction in his bowels, was lingering and painful; but had every consolation to sooth it which he could derive from the tenderest sympathy of his friends, and from the complete resignation of his own mind. . . . The serenity and gaiety he enjoyed, under the pressure of his growing infirmities, and the warm interest he felt to the last, in every thing connected with the welfare of his friends, will be long remembered by a small circle, with whom, as long as his strength permitted, he regularly spent an evening in the week."[35]

By the summer it was clear to everyone, including Smith himself, that his demise was imminent. Not wanting to leave behind any writings that had not been completed to his satisfaction, on July 11 he arranged—much to the regret of later scholars—to have Joseph Black and James Hutton, his Oyster Club companions and literary executors, burn the great majority of his papers. Of the many volumes of manuscripts that he possessed at the time, the only pieces spared from the flames were the handful of essays that were later included in the posthumous collection of *Essays on Philosophical Subjects*.

Just under a week later, on July 17, Smith died at Panmure House at the age of sixty-seven. Though he seems to have endured more pain than Hume did during his final illness, by all accounts he died

FIGURE 13.1 Smith's modest grave in the Canongate kirkyard, designed by Robert Adam, lies just a short walk from his last home, Panmure House. Photograph by the author.

with similar equanimity. He was buried in the Canongate kirkyard on July 22. His monument, also designed by Robert Adam, is far more modest than the grand one Hume commissioned for himself. The tombstone, unobtrusively tucked away in a corner of the kirkyard, simply gives Smith's dates and notes that the remains of the author of *The Theory of Moral Sentiments* and *The Wealth of Nations* are deposited there.

Smith's death excited little of the fascination and commotion that Hume's had. One admirer in London was "surprised, and I own a little indignant, to observe how little impression his death has made here. Scarce any notice has been taken of it, while for above a year together, after the death of Dr. Johnson [in 1784], nothing was to be heard of but panegyrics of him."[36] The anonymous obituary that made the rounds in the London papers was in fact fairly mean-spirited, stressing Smith's awkward bearing, the dearth of originality to be found in his books, and the fact that he "had early become a disciple of Voltaire in matters of religion" and "admired David Hume as by far the greatest Philosopher that the world had ever produced."[37] The initial notice in the *Times* also included a snide remark about his having "published such a laboured eulogium on the stoical end of David Hume."[38] The Edinburgh press, for its part, paid astonishingly little attention to Smith's death. The *Scots Magazine*, for instance, allotted only nine bland lines to the event, mixed in with dozens of other local death notices.[39] Though it seems like a shame, from today's vantage point, for a thinker of Smith's importance to have departed with so little fanfare, one suspects that he would have wanted it that way.

APPENDIX

—————◆—————

T HIS APPENDIX CONTAINS the full text of two works that have featured prominently in the preceding narrative: David Hume's autobiography, *My Own Life*, and Adam Smith's supplement to it, *Letter from Adam Smith, LL.D. to William Strahan, Esq.* (For discussion of these works, see especially chapters 11 and 12.) The two were published together as *The Life of David Hume, Esq., Written by Himself* (London: Printed for W. Strahan; and T. Cadell, in the Strand, 1777), and I have used this version—the one authorized by Smith—as the copy text.

DAVID HUME: MY OWN LIFE

It is difficult for a man to speak long of himself without vanity; therefore, I shall be short. It may be thought an instance of vanity that I pretend at all to write my life; but this Narrative shall contain little more than the History of my Writings; as, indeed, almost all my life has been spent in literary pursuits and occupations. The first success of most of my writings was not such as to be an object of vanity.

I was born the 26th of April 1711, old style, at Edinburgh. I was of a good family, both by father and mother: my father's family is a branch of the Earl of Home's, or Hume's; and my ancestors had been proprietors of the estate, which my brother possesses, for several generations. My mother was daughter of Sir David Falconer, President of the College of Justice: the title of Lord Halkerton came by succession to her brother.

My family, however, was not rich, and being myself a younger brother, my patrimony, according to the mode of my country, was of course very slender. My father, who passed for a man of parts, died when I was an infant, leaving me, with an elder brother and sister, under the care of our mother, a woman of singular merit, who, though young and handsome, devoted herself entirely to the rearing and educating of her children. I passed through the ordinary course of education with success, and was seized very early with a passion for literature, which has been the ruling passion of my life, and the great source of my enjoyments. My studious disposition, my sobriety, and my industry, gave my family a notion that the law was a proper profession for me; but I found an unsurmountable aversion to every thing but the pursuits of philosophy and general learning; and while they fancied I was poring upon Voet and Vinnius, Cicero and Virgil were the authors which I was secretly devouring.

My very slender fortune, however, being unsuitable to this plan of life, and my health being a little broken by my ardent application, I was tempted, or rather forced, to make a very feeble trial for entering into a more active scene of life. In 1734, I went to Bristol, with some recommendations to eminent merchants, but in a few months found that scene totally unsuitable to me. I went over to France, with a view of prosecuting my studies in a country retreat; and I there laid that plan of life, which I have steadily and successfully pursued. I re-solved to make a very rigid frugality supply my deficiency of fortune, to maintain unimpaired my independency, and to regard every object as contemptible, except the improvement of my talents in literature.

During my retreat in France, first at Reims, but chiefly at La Fleche, in Anjou, I composed my *Treatise of Human Nature*. After passing three years very agreeably in that country, I came over to London in 1737. In the end of 1738, I published my Treatise, and immediately went down to my mother and my brother, who lived at his country-house, and was employing himself very judiciously and successfully in the improvement of his fortune.

Never literary attempt was more unfortunate than my Treatise of Human Nature. It fell *dead-born from the press*, without reaching such distinction, as even to excite a murmur among the zealots. But being naturally of a cheerful and sanguine temper, I very soon recovered the blow, and prosecuted with great ardour my studies in the country. In 1742, I printed at Edinburgh the first part of my Essays: the work was favourably received, and soon made me entirely forget my former dis-appointment. I continued with my mother and brother in the country, and in that time recovered the knowledge of the Greek language, which I had too much neglected in my early youth.

In 1745, I received a letter from the Marquis of Annandale, inviting me to come and live with him in England; I found also, that the friends and family of that young nobleman were desirous of putting him under my care and direction, for the state of his mind and health required it.—I lived with him a twelvemonth. My appointments during that time made a considerable accession to my small fortune. I then received an invitation from General St. Clair to attend him as a secretary to his expedition, which was at first meant against Canada, but ended in an incursion on the coast of France. Next year, to wit, 1747, I received an invitation from the General to attend him in the same station in his military embassy to the courts of Vienna and Turin. I then wore the uniform of an officer, and was introduced at these courts as aid-de-camp to the general, along with Sir Harry Erskine and Captain Grant, now General Grant. These two years were almost the only interruptions which my studies have received during the course of my life: I passed them agreeably, and in good company; and my appointments, with my frugality, had made me reach a fortune, which I called independent, though most of my friends were inclined to smile when I said so; in short, I was now master of near a thousand pounds.

I had always entertained a notion, that my want of success in publishing the Treatise of Human Nature, had proceeded more from the manner than the matter, and that I had been guilty of a very usual indiscretion, in going to the press too early. I, therefore, cast the first part of that work anew in the Enquiry concerning Human Understanding, which was published while I was at Turin. But this piece was at first little more successful than the Treatise of Human Nature. On my return from Italy, I had the mortification to find all England in a ferment, on account of Dr. Middleton's Free Enquiry, while my performance was entirely overlooked and neglected. A new edition, which had been published at London of my Essays, moral and political, met not with a much better reception.

Such is the force of natural temper, that these disappointments made little or no impression on me. I went down in 1749, and lived two years with my brother at his country-house, for my mother was now dead. I there composed the second part of my Essays, which I called Political Discourses, and also my Enquiry concerning the

APPENDIX

Principles of Morals, which is another part of my treatise that I cast anew. Meanwhile, my bookseller, A. Millar, informed me, that my former publications (all but the unfortunate Treatise) were beginning to be the subject of conversation; that the sale of them was gradually increasing, and that new editions were demanded. Answers by Reverends, and Right Reverends, came out two or three in a year; and I found, by Dr. Warburton's railing, that the books were beginning to be esteemed in good company. However, I had fixed a resolution, which I inflexibly maintained, never to reply to any body; and not being very irascible in my temper, I have easily kept myself clear of all literary squabbles. These symptoms of a rising reputation gave me encouragement, as I was ever more disposed to see the favourable than unfavourable side of things; a turn of mind which it is more happy to possess, than to be born to an estate of ten thousand a year.

In 1751, I removed from the country to the town, the true scene for a man of letters. In 1752, were published at Edinburgh, where I then lived, my Political Discourses, the only work of mine that was successful on the first publication. It was well received abroad and at home. In the same year was published at London, my Enquiry concerning the Principles of Morals; which, in my own opinion (who ought not to judge on that subject), is of all my writings, historical, philosophical, or literary, incomparably the best. It came unnoticed and unobserved into the world.

In 1752, the Faculty of Advocates chose me their Librarian, an office from which I received little or no emolument, but which gave me the command of a large library. I then formed the plan of writing the History of England; but being frightened with the notion of continuing a narrative through a period of 1700 years, I commenced with the accession of the House of Stuart, an epoch when, I thought, the misrepresentations of faction began chiefly to take place. I was, I own, sanguine in my expectations of the success of this work. I thought that I was the only historian, that had at once neglected present power, interest, and authority, and the cry of popular prejudices; and as the subject was suited to every capacity, I expected proportional applause. But miserable was my disappointment: I was assailed by one cry of reproach, disapprobation, and even detestation; English, Scotch, and Irish, Whig and Tory, churchman and sectary, freethinker and reli-

242

gionist, patriot and courtier, united in their rage against the man, who had presumed to shed a generous tear for the fate of Charles I. and the Earl of Strafford; and after the first ebullitions of their fury were over, what was still more mortifying, the book seemed to sink into oblivion. Mr. Millar told me, that in a twelvemonth he sold only forty-five copies of it. I scarcely, indeed, heard of one man in the three kingdoms, considerable for rank or letters, that could endure the book. I must only except the primate of England, Dr. Herring, and the primate of Ireland, Dr. Stone, which seem two odd exceptions. These dignified prelates separately sent me messages not to be discouraged.

I was, however, I confess, discouraged; and had not the war been at that time breaking out between France and England, I had certainly retired to some provincial town of the former kingdom, have changed my name, and never more have returned to my native country. But as this scheme was not now practicable, and the subsequent volume was considerably advanced, I resolved to pick up courage and to persevere.

In this interval, I published at London my Natural History of Religion, along with some other small pieces: its public entry was rather obscure, except only that Dr. Hurd wrote a pamphlet against it, with all the illiberal petulance, arrogance, and scurrility, which distinguish the Warburtonian school. This pamphlet gave me some consolation for the otherwise indifferent reception of my performance.

In 1756, two years after the fall of the first volume, was published the second volume of my History, containing the period from the death of Charles I. till the Revolution. This performance happened to give less displeasure to the Whigs, and was better received. It not only rose itself, but helped to buoy up its unfortunate brother.

But though I had been taught by experience, that the Whig party were in possession of bestowing all places, both in the state and in literature, I was so little inclined to yield to their senseless clamour, that in above a hundred alterations, which farther study, reading, or reflection engaged me to make in the reigns of the two first Stuarts, I have made all of them invariably to the Tory side. It is ridiculous to consider the English constitution before that period as a regular plan of liberty.

In 1759, I published my History of the House of Tudor. The clamour against this performance was almost equal to that against the

History of the two first Stuarts. The reign of Elizabeth was particularly obnoxious. But I was now callous against the impressions of public folly, and continued very peaceably and contentedly in my retreat at Edinburgh, to finish, in two volumes, the more early part of the English History, which I gave to the public in 1761, with tolerable, and but tolerable success.

But, notwithstanding this variety of winds and seasons, to which my writings had been exposed, they had still been making such advances, that the copy-money given me by the booksellers, much exceeded anything formerly known in England; I was become not only independent, but opulent. I retired to my native country of Scotland, determined never more to set my foot out of it; and retaining the satisfaction of never having preferred a request to one great man, or even making advances of friendship to any of them. As I was now turned of fifty, I thought of passing all the rest of my life in this philosophical manner, when I received, in 1763, an invitation from the Earl of Hertford, with whom I was not in the least acquainted, to attend him on his embassy to Paris, with a near prospect of being appointed secretary to the embassy; and, in the meanwhile, of performing the functions of that office. This offer, however inviting, I at first declined, both because I was reluctant to begin connexions with the great, and because I was afraid that the civilities and gay company of Paris, would prove disagreeable to a person of my age and humour: but on his lordship's repeating the invitation, I accepted of it. I have every reason, both of pleasure and interest, to think myself happy in my connexions with that nobleman, as well as afterwards with his brother, General Conway.

Those who have not seen the strange effects of modes, will never imagine the reception I met with at Paris, from men and women of all ranks and stations. The more I resiled from their excessive civilities, the more I was loaded with them. There is, however, a real satisfaction in living at Paris, from the great number of sensible, knowing, and polite company with which that city abounds above all places in the universe. I thought once of settling there for life.

I was appointed secretary to the embassy; and, in summer 1765, Lord Hertford left me, being appointed Lord Lieutenant of Ireland. I was *chargé d'affaires* till the arrival of the Duke of Richmond, towards the end of the year. In the beginning of 1766, I left Paris, and next summer went to Edinburgh, with the same view as formerly, of burying myself in a philosophical retreat. I returned to that place, not richer, but with much more money, and a much larger income, by means of Lord Hertford's friendship, than I left it; and I was desirous of trying what superfluity could produce, as I had formerly made an experiment of a competency. But, in 1767, I received from Mr. Conway an invitation to be Under-secretary; and this invitation, both the character of the person, and my connexions with Lord Hertford, prevented me from declining. I returned to Edinburgh in 1769, very opulent (for I possessed a revenue of 1000 l. a year), healthy, and though somewhat stricken in years, with the prospect of enjoying long my ease, and of seeing the increase of my reputation.

In spring 1775, I was struck with a disorder in my bowels, which at first gave me no alarm, but has since, as I apprehend it, become mortal and incurable. I now reckon upon a speedy dissolution. I have suffered very little pain from my disorder; and what is more strange, have, notwithstanding the great decline of my person, never suffered a moment's abatement of my spirits; insomuch, that were I to name the period of my life, which I should most choose to pass over again, I might be tempted to point to this later period. I possess the same ardour as ever in study, and the same gaiety in company. I consider, besides, that a man of sixty-five, by dying, cuts off only a few years of infirmities; and though I see many symptoms of my literary reputation's breaking out at last with additional lustre, I knew that I could have but few years to enjoy it. It is difficult to be more detached from life than I am at present.

To conclude historically with my own character. I am, or rather was (for that is the style I must now use in speaking of myself, which emboldens me the more to speak my sentiments); I was, I say, a man of mild dispositions, of command of temper, of an open, social, and cheerful humour, capable of attachment, but little susceptible of enmity, and of great moderation in all my passions. Even my love of literary fame, my ruling passion, never soured my temper, notwithstanding my frequent disappointments. My company was not unacceptable to the young and careless, as well as to the studious and literary; and as I took a particular pleasure in the company of modest women, I had no reason to be displeased with the reception I met with from them. In a word, though most men any wise eminent, have found reason to complain of calumny, I never was touched, or even attacked by her baleful tooth: and though I wantonly exposed myself to the rage of both civil and religious factions, they seemed to be disarmed in my behalf of their wonted fury. My friends never had occasion to vindicate any one circumstance of my character and conduct: not but that the zealots, we may well suppose, would have been glad to invent and propagate any story to my disadvantage, but they could never find any which they thought would wear the face of probability. I cannot say there is no vanity in making this funeral oration of myself, but I hope it is not a misplaced one; and this is a matter of fact which is easily cleared and ascertained.

APRIL 18, 1776.

LETTER FROM ADAM SMITH, LL.D.
TO WILLIAM STRAHAN, ESQ.

Kirkaldy, Fifeshire, Nov. 9, 1776.

DEAR SIR,

It is with a real, though a very melancholy pleasure, that I sit down to give you some account of the behaviour of our late excellent friend, Mr. Hume, during his last illness.

Though, in his own judgment, his disease was mortal and incurable, yet he allowed himself to be prevailed upon, by the entreaty of his friends, to try what might be the effects of a long journey. A few days before he set out, he wrote that account of his own life, which, together with his other papers, he has left to your care. My account, therefore, shall begin where his ends.

He set out for London towards the end of April, and at Morpeth met with Mr. John Home and myself, who had both come down from London on purpose to see him, expecting to have found him at Edinburgh. Mr. Home returned with him, and attended him during the whole of his stay in England, with that care and attention which might be expected from a temper so perfectly friendly and affectionate. As I had written to my mother that she might expect me in Scotland, I was under the necessity of continuing my journey. His disease seemed to yield to exercise and change of air, and when he arrived in London, he was apparently in much better health than when he left Edinburgh. He was advised to go to Bath to drink the waters, which appeared for some time to have so good an effect upon him, that even he himself began to entertain, what he was not apt to do, a better opinion of his own health. His symptoms, however, soon returned with their usual violence, and from that moment he gave up all thoughts of recovery, but submitted with the utmost cheerfulness, and the most perfect complacency and resignation. Upon his return to Edinburgh, though he found himself much weaker, yet his cheerfulness never abated, and he continued to divert himself, as usual, with correcting his own works for a new edition, with reading books of amusement, with the conversation of his friends; and, sometimes in the evening, with a party at his favourite game of whist. His cheerfulness was so great, and his conversation and amusements run so much in their usual strain, that, notwithstanding all bad symptoms, many people could not believe he was dying. "I shall tell your friend, Colonel Edmondstone," said Doctor Dundas to him one day, "that I left you much better, and in a fair way of recovery." "Doctor," said he, "as I believe you would not chuse to tell any thing but the truth, you had better tell him, that I am dying as fast as my enemies, if I have any, could wish, and as easily and cheerfully as my best friends could desire." Colonel Edmondstone soon afterwards came to see him, and take leave of him; and on his way home, he could not forbear writing him a letter bidding him once more an eternal adieu, and applying to him, as to a dying man, the beautiful French verses in which the Abbé Chaulieu, in expectation of his own death, laments his approaching separation from his friend, the Marquis de la Fare. Mr. Hume's magnanimity and firmness were such, that his most affectionate friends knew, that they hazarded nothing in talking or writing to him as to a dying man, and that so far from being hurt by this frankness, he was rather pleased and flattered by it. I happened to come into his room while he was reading this letter, which he had just received, and which he immediately showed me. I told him, that though I was sensible how very much he was weakened, and that appearances were in many respects very bad, yet his cheerfulness was still so great, the spirit of life seemed still to be so very strong in him, that I could not help entertaining some faint hopes. He answered, "Your hopes are groundless. An habitual diarrhœa of more than a year's standing, would be a very bad disease at any age: at my age it is a mortal one. When I lie down in the evening, I feel myself weaker than when I rose in the morning; and when I rise in the morning, weaker than when I lay down in the evening. I am sensible, besides, that some of my vital parts are affected, so that I must soon die." "Well," said I, "if it must be so, you have at least the satisfaction of leaving all your friends, your brother's family in particular, in great prosperity." He said that he felt that satisfaction so sensibly, that when he was reading a few days before, Lucian's Dialogues of the Dead, among all the excuses which are alleged to Charon for not entering readily into his boat, he could not find one that fitted him; he had no house to finish, he had no daughter to provide for, he had no enemies upon whom he wished to revenge himself. "I could not well imagine," said he, "what excuse I could make to Charon in order to obtain a little delay. I have done every thing of consequence which I ever meant to do, and I could at no time expect to leave my relations and friends in a better situation than that in which I am now likely to leave them; I, therefore, have all reason to die contented." He then diverted himself with inventing several jocular excuses, which he supposed he might make to Charon, and with imagining the very surly answers which it might suit the character of Charon to return to them. "Upon further consideration," said he, "I thought I might say to him, Good Charon, I have been correcting my works for a new edition. Allow me a little time, that I may see how the Public receives the alterations." But Charon would answer, "When you have seen the effect of these, you will be for making other alterations. There will be no end of such excuses; so, honest friend, please step into the boat." But I might still urge, "Have a little patience, good Charon, I have been endeavouring to open the eyes of the Public. If I live a few years longer, I may have the satisfaction of seeing the downfal of some of the prevailing systems of superstition." But Charon would then lose all temper and decency. "You loitering rogue, that will not happen these many hundred years. Do you fancy I will grant you a lease for so long a term? Get into the boat this instant, you lazy loitering rogue."

But, though Mr. Hume always talked of his approaching dissolution with great cheerfulness, he never affected to make any parade
of his magnanimity. He never mentioned the subject but when the
conversation naturally led to it, and never dwelt longer upon it than
the course of the conversation happened to require: it was a subject
indeed which occurred pretty frequently, in consequence of the inquiries which his friends, who came to see him, naturally made concerning the state of his health. The conversation which I mentioned above,
and which passed on Thursday the 8th of August, was the last, except
one, that I ever had with him. He had now become so very weak,
that the company of his most intimate friends fatigued him; for his
cheerfulness was still so great, his complaisance and social disposition
were still so entire, that when any friend was with him, he could not
help talking more, and with greater exertion, than suited the weakness of his body. At his own desire, therefore, I agreed to leave Edinburgh, where I was staying partly upon his account, and returned to
my mother's house here, at Kirkaldy, upon condition that he would
send for me whenever he wished to see me; the physician who saw
him most frequently, Doctor Black, undertaking, in the mean time, to
write me occasionally an account of the state of his health.

On the 22nd of August, the Doctor wrote me the following letter:
"Since my last, Mr. Hume has passed his time pretty easily, but
is much weaker. He sits up, goes down stairs once a day, and amuses
himself with reading, but seldom sees any body. He finds that even
the conversation of his most intimate friends fatigues and oppresses
him; and it is happy that he does not need it, for he is quite free from
anxiety, impatience, or low spirits, and passes his time very well with
the assistance of amusing books."

I received the day after a letter from Mr. Hume himself, of which
the following is an extract:

Edinburgh, 23d August, 1776.

"MY DEAREST FRIEND,

I am obliged to make use of my nephew's hand in writing to you,
as I do not rise today. . . .

I go very fast to decline, and last night had a small fever, which
I hoped might put a quicker period to this tedious illness, but

unluckily it has, in a great measure, gone off. I cannot submit to your coming over here on my account, as it is possible for me to see you so small a part of the day, but Doctor Black can better inform you concerning the degree of strength which may from time to time remain with me. Adieu, & c."

Three days after I received the following letter from Doctor Black:

Edinburgh, Monday, 26th August, 1776.

"DEAR SIR,

Yesterday about four o'clock afternoon, Mr. Hume expired. The near approach of his death became evident in the night between Thursday and Friday, when his disease became excessive, and soon weakened him so much, that he could no longer rise out of his bed. He continued to the last perfectly sensible, and free from much pain or feelings of distress. He never dropped the smallest expression of impatience; but when he had occasion to speak to the people about him, always did it with affection and tenderness. I thought it improper to write to bring you over, especially as I heard that he had dictated a letter to you desiring you not to come. When he became very weak, it cost him an effort to speak, and he died in such a happy composure of mind, that nothing could exceed it."

Thus died our most excellent, and never to be forgotten friend; concerning whose philosophical opinions men will, no doubt, judge variously, every one approving, or condemning them, according as they happen to coincide or disagree with his own; but concerning whose character and conduct there can scarce be a difference of opinion. His temper, indeed, seemed to be more happily balanced, if I may be allowed such an expression, than that perhaps of any other man I have ever known. Even in the lowest state of his fortune, his great and necessary frugality never hindered him from exercising, upon proper occasions, acts both of charity and generosity. It was a frugality founded, not upon avarice, but upon the love of independency. The extreme gentleness of his nature never weakened either the firmness of his mind, or the steadiness of his resolutions. His constant pleasantry was the genuine effusion of good-nature and good-humour, tempered with delicacy and modesty, and without even the slightest tincture of malignity, so frequently the disagreeable source of what is called wit in other men. It never was the meaning of his raillery to mortify; and therefore, far from offending, it seldom failed to please and delight, even those who were the objects of it. To his friends, who were frequently the objects of it, there was not perhaps any one of all his great and amiable qualities, which contributed more to endear his conversation. And that gaiety of temper, so agreeable in society, but which is so often accompanied with frivolous and superficial qualities, was in him certainly attended with the most severe application, the most extensive learning, the greatest depth of thought, and a capacity in every respect the most comprehensive. Upon the whole, I have always considered him, both in his lifetime and since his death, as approaching as nearly to the idea of a perfectly wise and virtuous man, as perhaps the nature human frailty will permit.

> I ever am, dear Sir,
> Most affectionately your's,
> ADAM SMITH.

NOTES ON WORKS CITED

I HAVE USED THE following abbreviations for some of the more frequently cited texts. Where appropriate I include references to the volume, book, part, chapter, and/or paragraph number in addition to the page number.

WORKS OF DAVID HUME

EHU   *An Enquiry Concerning Human Understanding*, ed. Tom L. Beauchamp (Oxford: Clarendon, [1748] 2000).

EMPL   *Essays, Moral, Political, and Literary*, ed. Eugene F. Miller (Indianapolis: Liberty Fund, [1741–77] 1987).

EPM   *An Enquiry Concerning the Principles of Morals*, ed. Tom L. Beauchamp (Oxford: Clarendon, [1751] 1998).

FHL   *Further Letters of David Hume*, ed. Felix Waldmann (Edinburgh: Edinburgh Bibliographical Society, 2014).

HE   *The History of England, from the Invasion of Julius Caesar to the Revolution in 1688*, 6 vols. (Indianapolis: Liberty Fund, [1754–62] 1983).

HL   *The Letters of David Hume*, ed. J. Y. T. Greig, 2 vols. (Oxford: Clarendon, 1932).

MOL   *My Own Life*, in *Essays, Moral, Political, and Literary*, ed. Eugene F. Miller (Indianapolis: Liberty Fund, [1777] 1987).

NHL   *New Letters of David Hume*, ed. Raymond Klibansky and Ernest C. Mossner (Oxford: Clarendon, 1954).

NHR   *The Natural History of Religion*, in *A Dissertation on the Passions and The Natural History of Religion*, ed. Tom L. Beauchamp (Oxford: Clarendon, [1757] 2007).

THN   *A Treatise of Human Nature*, ed. David Fate Norton and Mary J. Norton (Oxford: Clarendon, [1739–40] 2007).

WORKS OF ADAM SMITH

CAS   *Correspondence of Adam Smith*, ed. Ernest Campbell Mossner and Ian Simpson Ross (Indianapolis: Liberty Fund, 1987).

EPS   *Essays on Philosophical Subjects*, ed. W. P. D. Wightman and J. C. Bryce (Indianapolis: Liberty Fund, [1795] 1980).

LJ   *Lectures on Jurisprudence*, ed. R. L. Meek, D. D. Raphael, and P. G. Stein (Indianapolis: Liberty Fund, [1762–64] 1982).

LRBL   *Lectures on Rhetoric and Belles Lettres*, ed. J. C. Bryce (Indianapolis: Liberty Fund, [1762–63] 1985).

Strahan   *Letter from Adam Smith, LL.D. to William Strahan, Esq.*, in David Hume, *Essays, Moral, Political, and Literary*, ed. Eugene F. Miller (Indianapolis: Liberty Fund, [1777] 1987).

TMS   *The Theory of Moral Sentiments*, ed. D. D. Raphael and A. L. Macfie (Indianapolis: Liberty Fund, [1759–90] 1982).

WN   *An Inquiry into the Nature and Causes of the Wealth of Nations*, ed. R. H. Campbell, A. S. Skinner, and W. B. Todd, 2 vols. (Indianapolis: Liberty Fund [1776], 1981).

OTHER WORKS

Fieser   James Fieser, ed., *Early Responses to Hume*, 2nd ed., 10 vols. (Bristol: Thoemmes Continuum, 2005).

Harris   James A. Harris, *Hume: An Intellectual Biography* (Cambridge: Cambridge University Press, 2015).

Mossner   Ernest Campbell Mossner, *The Life of David Hume*, 2nd ed. (Oxford: Clarendon, 1980).

Phillipson   Nicholas Phillipson, *Adam Smith: An Enlightened Life* (New Haven, CT: Yale University Press, 2010).

Rae   John Rae, *Life of Adam Smith* (New York: Augustus M. Kelley, [1895] 1965).

Ross   Ian Simpson Ross, *The Life of Adam Smith*, 2nd ed. (Oxford: Oxford University Press, 2010).

Stewart   Dugald Stewart, *Account of the Life and Writings of Adam Smith, LL.D.*, ed. I. S. Ross, in Adam Smith, *Essays on Philosophical Subjects* (Indianapolis: Liberty Fund, [1794] 1980).

NOTES

NOTES TO INTRODUCTION

1. Adam Smith to Andreas Holt, 26 October 1780, in CAS, 251.
2. Strahan, xlix.
3. For Hume's statement, see David Hume to Andrew Millar, 21 July 1757, in HL I, 256; see also David Hume to Andrew Millar, 20 May 1757, in HL I, 249; and Adam Smith to William Strahan, 2 December 1776, in CAS, 223. For Smith's statement, see Adam Smith to Count Joseph Niclas Windisch-Grätz, 4 July 1785, in "Adam Smith and Count Windisch-Grätz: New Letters," ed. Ian Ross and David Raynor, *Studies on Voltaire and the Eighteenth Century* 358 (1997): 181.
4. Adam Smith to William Strahan, 2 December 1776, in CAS, 223–24.
5. On Hume, see his will of 4 January 1776, quoted in HL II, 317, and CAS, 195–96; and Adam Smith to William Strahan, 2 December 1776, in CAS, 223. On Smith, see Adam Smith to David Hume, 16 April 1773, in CAS, 168; and Stewart, 303, 327–28.
6. LRBL, 132.
7. James Boswell, *Journal of a Tour to the Hebrides with Samuel Johnson, LL.D.*, ed. Frederick A. Pottle and Charles H. Bennett (New York: McGraw-Hill, [1785] 1961), 9.
8. Knud Haakonssen's *Science of a Legislator* might seem to qualify here, but in fact this work contains only one chapter on Hume, which is included as a setup for Haakonssen's much more detailed study of Smith. Moreover, Haakonssen focuses entirely on Hume's and Smith's theories of justice and explicitly "renounce[s] the nearly inexhaustible fund of other points of comparison and contrast between the two thinkers—interesting and important though they are." Knud Haakonssen, *The Science of a Legislator: The Natural Jurisprudence of David Hume & Adam Smith* (Cambridge: Cambridge University Press, 1981), 2. There are a few dozen shorter studies of various aspects of Hume's and Smith's thought, some of which are cited in these pages. For two brief overviews of their friendship, see Karl Graf Ballestrem, "David Hume und Adam Smith: Zur philosophischen Dimension einer Freundschaft," in *Adam Smith als Moralphilosoph*, ed. Christel Fricke and Hans-Peter Schütt (Berlin: Walter de Gruyter, 2005), 331–46; and Ian Simpson Ross, "The Intellectual Friendship of David Hume and Adam Smith," in *New Essays on David Hume*, ed. Emilio Mazza and Emanuele Ronchetti (Milan: FrancoAngeli, 2007), 345–63.
9. See Adam Smith to William Strahan, October 1776, in CAS, 217.

10. David Hume to Adam Smith, ?end of January 1766, in HL II, 5, and CAS, 110; and David Hume to Adam Smith, 8 February 1776, in HL II, 308, and CAS, 185.

11. See Christopher J. Berry, "Introduction: Adam Smith: An Outline of Life, Times, and Legacy," in *The Oxford Handbook of Adam Smith*, ed. Christopher J. Berry, Maria Pia Paganelli, and Craig Smith (Oxford: Oxford University Press, 2013), 1.

12. Hume used this epithet with Henry Home in 1745, before he met Smith, and Smith used it with James Menteath in 1785, after Hume had long since passed away. See David Hume to Henry Home, 13 June 1745, in NHL, 16; and Adam Smith to James Menteath, 22 February 1785, in CAS, 281. The only piece of evidence that would cast doubt on the idea that Hume and Smith each considered the other his closest friend once they had gotten to know one another is Hume's statement to John Home, the playwright, soon after the death of William Mure of Caldwell, that Mure "was the oldest and best friend I had in the World." David Hume to John Home, 12 April 1776, in HL II, 314. Hume softened the claim when writing to Smith himself, stating that Mure "was among the oldest and best Friends I had in the World." David Hume to Adam Smith, 1 April 1776, in HL II, 312, and CAS, 187.

13. See David Edmonds and John Eidinow, *Wittgenstein's Poker: The Story of a Ten-Minute Argument between Two Great Philosophers* (New York: HarperCollins, 2001); David Edmonds and John Eidinow, *Rousseau's Dog: Two Great Thinkers at War in the Age of Enlightenment* (New York: HarperCollins, 2006); Yuval Levin, *The Great Debate: Edmund Burke, Thomas Paine, and the Birth of Left and Right* (New York: Basic Books, 2014); Steven Nadler, *The Best of All Possible Worlds: A Story of Philosophers, God, and Evil* (New York: Farrar, Straus and Giroux, 2008); Matthew Stewart, *The Courtier and the Heretic: Leibniz, Spinoza, and the Fate of God in the Modern World* (New York: Norton, 2006); and Robert Zaretsky and John T. Scott, *The Philosophers' Quarrel: Rousseau, Hume, and the Limits of Human Understanding* (New Haven, CT: Yale University Press, 2009).

14. For Aristotle's claim, see Aristotle, *Nicomachean Ethics*, trans. Robert C. Bartlett and Susan D. Collins (Chicago: University of Chicago Press, 2011), 1155a5–6, 163.

15. EHU 1.20, 105; and TMS I.ii.5.1, 41. Smith actually writes in this passage that "the chief part of human happiness arises from the consciousness of being beloved," but the context makes clear that by "being beloved" he is referring to the esteem and affection of one's friends more than to romantic love.

16. THN 2.2.5.15, 235. See also Hume's rhetorical question at EMPL, 185: "Destroy love and friendship; what remains in the world worth accepting?"

17. Annette C. Baier, *The Cautious Jealous Virtue: Hume on Justice* (Cambridge, MA: Harvard University Press, 2010), 14; see also 9.

18. TMS VI.ii.1.18, 225. For a comparison of Smith's view of friendship to Aristotle's, see Douglas J. Den Uyl and Charles L. Griswold, "Adam Smith on Friendship and Love," *Review of Metaphysics* 49.3 (March 1996): 609–37.

19. For a useful anthology of some of these philosophical reflections on friendship, see Michael Pakaluk, ed., *Other Selves: Philosophers on Friendship* (Indianapolis: Hackett, 1991). For a serious and thoughtful analysis of a number of these works—one whose scope is quite a bit wider than its title implies—see Lorraine Smith Pangle, *Aristotle and the Philosophy of Friendship* (Cambridge: Cambridge University Press, 2003). For a recent study with a somewhat lighter touch and an eye on the contemporary world, see A. C. Grayling, *Friendship* (New Haven, CT: Yale University Press, 2013).

20. For a study of Erasmus and More's friendship, see E. E. Reynolds, *Thomas More and Erasmus* (London: Burns & Oates, 1965).

21. David Hume to Edward Gibbon, 18 March 1776, in HL II, 310.

22. David Hume to Gilbert Elliot of Minto, 2 July 1757, in HL I, 255.

23. Dugald Stewart, *Dissertation, Exhibiting a General View of the Progress of Metaphysical, Ethical, and Political Philosophy, since the Revival of Letters in Europe*, in *The Collected Works of Dugald Stewart*, ed. Sir William Hamilton, vol. 1 (Edinburgh: Thomas Constable and Co., [1815] 1854), 551.

24. Walter Scott, *The Miscellaneous Prose Works of Sir Walter Scott*, vol. 1 (Edinburgh: Robert Cadell, [1824] 1847), 345.

25. Edward Gibbon to Adam Ferguson, 1 April 1776, in *The Letters of Edward Gibbon*, ed. Jane Elizabeth Norton, vol. 2 (London: Cassell & Co., 1956), 100–101.

26. Arthur Herman, *How the Scots Invented the Modern World: The True Story of How Western Europe's Poorest Nation Created Our World and Everything in It* (New York: Three Rivers, 2001). For more scholarly overviews of the Scottish Enlightenment, see Christopher J. Berry, *Social Theory of the Scottish Enlightenment* (Edinburgh: Edinburgh University Press, 1997); and Alexander Broadie, *The Scottish Enlightenment: The Historical Age of the Historical Nation* (Edinburgh: Birlinn, 2001).

27. See Richard B. Sher, *Church and University in the Scottish Enlightenment: The Moderate Literati of Edinburgh* (Edinburgh: Edinburgh University Press, 1985), 10–11.

28. On the parish schools, see T. C. Smout, *A History of the Scottish People, 1560–1830* (New York: Charles Scribner's Sons, 1969), chap. 18. On the universities, see Roger L. Emerson, *Academic Patronage in the Scottish Enlightenment: Glasgow, Edinburgh and St Andrews Universities* (Edinburgh: Edinburgh University Press, 2008); and Roger L. Emerson, *Professors, Patronage and Politics: The Aberdeen Universities in the Eighteenth Century* (Aberdeen: Aberdeen University Press, 1992). The fullest account of the various clubs and societies of eighteenth-century Scotland is D. D. McElroy, "The Literary Clubs and Societies of Eighteenth-Century Scotland, and Their Influence on the Literary Productions of the Period from 1700 to 1800" (PhD diss., Edinburgh University, 1952); for a somewhat less complete but published work by the same author, see Davis D. McElroy, *Scotland's Age of Improvement: A Survey*

of Eighteenth-Century Literary Clubs and Societies (Pullman: Washington State University Press, 1969). On the book industry, see Richard B. Sher, *The Enlightenment and the Book: Scottish Authors & Their Publishers in Eighteenth-Century Britain, Ireland, & America* (Chicago: University of Chicago Press, 2006). On the Moderates and the Kirk, see Sher, *Church and University in the Scottish Enlightenment.*

29. For a short, excellent general history of eighteenth-century Scotland, see Richard B. Sher, "Scotland Transformed: The Eighteenth Century," in *Scotland: A History*, ed. Jenny Wormald (Oxford: Oxford University Press, 2005), 177–208. For a longer and older but still very readable account, a classic that deserves its status, see Smout, *History of the Scottish People*, pt. 2. For a more recent work focusing on Enlightenment Edinburgh, see James Buchan, *Crowded with Genius: The Scottish Enlightenment, Edinburgh's Moment of the Mind* (New York: HarperCollins, 2003).

30. Sher, *Church and University in the Scottish Enlightenment*, 152.

31. Voltaire, *Letters Concerning the English Nation*, ed. Nicholas Cronk (Oxford: Oxford University Press, [1733] 1994), 29–30.

32. On this case, see Michael Hunter, "'Aikenhead the Atheist': The Context and Consequences of Articulate Irreligion in the Late Seventeenth Century," in *Atheism from the Reformation to the Enlightenment*, ed. Michael Hunter and David Wootton (Oxford: Clarendon, 1992), 221–54; and Michael F. Graham, *The Blasphemies of Thomas Aikenhead: Boundaries of Belief on the Eve of the Enlightenment* (Edinburgh: Edinburgh University Press, 2008).

33. See Smout, *History of the Scottish People*, 204, 207.

34. The best study of the Moderates is Sher, *Church and University in the Scottish Enlightenment.*

35. See John R. McIntosh, *Church and Theology in Enlightenment Scotland: The Popular Party, 1740–1800* (East Linton: Tuckwell, 1998).

36. The claim regarding Smith's eclecticism is found in a classic article: Jacob Viner, "Adam Smith and Laissez Faire," *Journal of Political Economy* 35.2 (April 1927): 199. I say that *almost* all Smith scholars recognize Hume's influence on Smith because at least one, Athol Fitzgibbons, has gone to some lengths to take issue with "the general assumption that Smith's philosophy reflected that of his friend David Hume," even going so far as to say that Smith "differed from Hume in both morals and methods as chalk does from cheese. Smith rejected every one of Hume's major philosophic propositions, including utility, scepticism, the relativity of values, radical individualism, and the rigorous distinction between positive and normative ideas." Athol Fitzgibbons, *Adam Smith's System of Liberty, Wealth, and Virtue: The Moral and Political Foundations of The Wealth of Nations* (Oxford: Oxford University Press, 1995), v, 28–29. As the latter part of the quotation suggests and as Stephen Darwall points out, however, Fitzgibbons comes to his conclusion only by wildly misreading Hume as essentially a caricature of Bernard Mandeville: "an egoistic moral skeptic who holds that a the-

oretical concern with virtue is incompatible with a properly positive economics and, as well, that a practical concern with virtue is incompatible with a flourishing economy." Stephen Darwall, "Sympathetic Liberalism: Recent Work on Adam Smith," *Philosophy & Public Affairs* 28.2 (April 1999): 147–48.

37. Phillipson, 65, 71, 67.

38. Samuel Fleischacker, "Adam Smith," in *A Companion to Early Modern Philosophy*, ed. Steven Nadler (Oxford: Blackwell, 2002), 508.

39. Samuel Fleischacker, "Sympathy in Hume and Smith: A Contrast, Critique, and Reconstruction," in *Intersubjectivity and Objectivity in Adam Smith and Edmund Husserl: A Collection of Essays*, ed. Christel Fricke and Dagfinn Føllesdal (Frankfurt: Ontos Verlag, 2012), 282.

40. See Duncan Forbes, *Hume's Philosophical Politics* (Cambridge: Cambridge University Press, 1975), esp. chap. 5; and Duncan Forbes, "Sceptical Whiggism, Commerce, and Liberty," in *Essays on Adam Smith*, ed. Andrew S. Skinner and Thomas Wilson (Oxford: Clarendon, 1975), 179–201. For Hume's self-characterization as "a Whig, but a very sceptical one," see David Hume to Henry Home, 9 February 1748, in HL I, 111.

41. I have made a case for this reading at some length in Dennis C. Rasmussen, *The Pragmatic Enlightenment: Recovering the Liberalism of Hume, Smith, Montesquieu, and Voltaire* (Cambridge: Cambridge University Press, 2014), esp. chaps. 2 and 4.

42. For some of the debate at the margins, compare J. C. A. Gaskin, *Hume's Philosophy of Religion*, second edition (Atlantic Highlands, NJ: Humanities Press, 1988), esp. 219–23; and Paul Russell, *The Riddle of Hume's Treatise: Skepticism, Naturalism, and Irreligion* (Oxford: Oxford University Press, 2008), esp. 284–85.

43. J. C. A. Gaskin, "Hume on Religion," in *The Cambridge Companion to Hume*, 2nd ed., ed. David Fate Norton and Jacqueline Taylor (Cambridge: Cambridge University Press, 2009), 480.

44. MOL, xxxiv.

45. John Ramsay of Ochtertyre, *Scotland and Scotsmen in the Eighteenth Century*, ed. Alexander Allardyce, vol. 1 (Edinburgh: William Blackwood, 1888), 463; see also 467.

46. James Wodrow to Samuel Kenrick, 10 July 1759, Dr. Williams's Library, London, MSS 24.157(33).

47. Among the works that go furthest in reading Smith as a *Christian* believer (as opposed to a deist) are Brendan Long, "Adam Smith's Theism," in *The Elgar Companion to Adam Smith*, ed. Jeffrey T. Young (Cheltenham: Edward Elgar, 2009), 73–99; and several of the essays collected in Paul Oslington, ed., *Adam Smith as Theologian* (New York: Routledge, 2011). The most detailed reading of Smith as a closet atheist, at least later in his life, can be found in Peter Minowitz, *Profits, Priests, and Princes: Adam Smith's Emancipation of Economics from Politics and Religion* (Stanford, CA: Stanford University Press, 1993), esp. chaps. 6–10.

48. Emma Rothschild, *Economic Sentiments: Adam Smith, Condorcet, and the Enlightenment* (Cambridge, MA: Harvard University Press, 2001), 301n84; see

also 130. For an exchange between Rothschild and Samuel Fleischacker on this point, see Samuel Fleischacker, "Smith's Ambiguities: A Response to Emma Rothschild's *Economic Sentiments*," *Adam Smith Review* 1 (2004): 143–44; and Emma Rothschild, "Dignity or Meanness," *Adam Smith Review* 1 (2004): 160–61.

49. The idea that Smith's reticence was inspired primarily by a desire to avoid offending his mother has been suggested by Gavin Kennedy. See Gavin Kennedy, *Adam Smith's Lost Legacy* (New York: Palgrave Macmillan, 2005), 40; and Gavin Kennedy, "Adam Smith on Religion," in Berry, Paganelli, and Smith, *Oxford Handbook of Adam Smith*, 467.

50. I have also put forward this view in Rasmussen, *Pragmatic Enlightenment*, 178–79. For similarly skeptical readings, see Rothschild, *Economic Sentiments*, 129–34; Gavin Kennedy, "The Hidden Adam Smith in His Alleged Theology," *Journal of the History of Economic Thought* 33.3 (September 2011): 385–402; and Colin Heydt, "The Problem of Natural Religion in Smith's Moral Thought," *Journal of the History of Ideas* 78.1 (January 2017): 73–94.

CHAPTER 1: THE CHEERFUL SKEPTIC

1. See David Bourget and David J. Chalmers, "What Do Philosophers Believe?" *Philosophical Studies* 170.3 (September 2014): 476.

2. David Hume to Gilbert Elliot of Minto, 22 September 1764, in HL I, 470.

3. Isaiah Berlin, *The Age of Enlightenment: The 18th Century Philosophers* (New York: George Braziller, 1956), 163.

4. The basic facts of Hume's life are drawn from Hume's letters, *My Own Life*, and the indispensable biographies by Ernest Campbell Mossner and James Harris (cited above).

5. It is often stated that Hume entered the university at age eleven, but this is when he formally signed the matriculation register, not when he first began attending classes. For the most complete account of Hume's time at the university and his early intellectual development more generally, see M. A. Stewart, "Hume's Intellectual Development, 1711–1752," in *Impressions of Hume*, ed. M. Frasca-Spada and P. J. E. Kail (Oxford: Clarendon, 2005), 11–58. For a supplement to Stewart's essay that focuses on the intellectual development of Hume as a historian, see Roger L. Emerson, "Hume's Intellectual Development: Part II," in *Essays on David Hume, Medical Men and the Scottish Enlightenment: "Industry, Knowledge and Humanity"* (Farnham: Ashgate, 2009), 103–25. Also useful is Harris, chap. 1.

6. David Hume to James Birch, 18 May 1735, in E. C. Mossner, "Hume at La Flèche, 1735: An Unpublished Letter," *University of Texas Studies in English* 37 (1958): 32. On Hume and natural philosophy, see Michael Barfoot, "Hume and the Culture of Science in the Early Eighteenth Century," in *Studies in the*

Philosophy of the Scottish Enlightenment, ed. M. A. Stewart (Oxford: Clarendon, 1990), 151–90.

7. MOL, xxxii–xxxiii; see also David Hume to George Cheyne, March/April 1734, in HL I, 13. On Hume's attendance of law lectures, see William Zachs, *David Hume: Man of Letters, Scientist of Man* (Edinburgh: Writers' Museum, 2011), 59.

8. David Hume to Michael Ramsay, 4 July 1727, in HL I, 9.

9. Richard Allestree, *The Whole Duty of Man, Laid Down in a Plain and Familiar Way, for the Use of All, but Especially the Meanest Reader* (Dublin: A. Reilly, [1658] 1756), 358–59. For Hume's claim that he used this work to test his character, see James Boswell, *Boswell in Extremes, 1776–1778*, ed. Charles McC. Weis and Frederick A. Pottle (New York: McGraw-Hill, 1970), 11.

10. David Hume to Gilbert Elliot of Minto, 10 March 1751, in HL I, 154.

11. Boswell, *Boswell in Extremes*, 11.

12. See Peter Gay, *The Enlightenment: An Interpretation*, vol. 1: *The Rise of Modern Paganism* (New York: Norton, 1966), 326.

13. David Hume to George Cheyne, March/April 1734, in HL I, 13–15.

14. MOL, xxxiii.

15. MOL, xxxiv.

16. Alexander Pope, *Epilogue to the Satires*, in *The Major Works*, ed. Pat Rogers (Oxford: Oxford University Press, [1738] 2006), 407.

17. Thomas H. Huxley, *Hume: With Helps to the Study of Berkeley* (London: Macmillan, [1887] 1908), 12.

18. THN intro.1, 3; and intro.6, 4.

19. THN intro.7, 4.

20. See THN intro.7, 5.

21. On the widespread recognition of the irreligious nature of the *Treatise* among Hume's contemporaries, see Paul Russell, *The Riddle of Hume's Treatise: Skepticism, Naturalism, and Irreligion* (Oxford: Oxford University Press, 2008), chap. 2.

22. On the section on miracles, see David Hume to Henry Home, 2 December 1737, in NHL, 2. For a conjecture that the posthumously published essay "Of the Immortality of the Soul" was originally composed as part of the *Treatise*, perhaps fitting just after (or within) the section "Of the Immateriality of the Soul," see J. C. A. Gaskin, *Hume's Philosophy of Religion*, second edition (Atlantic Highlands, NJ: Humanities Press, 1988), 102.

23. David Hume to Henry Home, 2 December 1737, in NHL, 2–3.

24. David Hume to Francis Hutcheson, 17 September 1739, in HL I, 34.

25. David Hume to Gilbert Elliot of Minto, March/April 1751, in HL I, 158.

26. David Hume to John Stewart, February 1754, in HL I, 187; see also David Hume, "A Letter from a Gentleman to His Friend in *Edinburgh*," in *A Treatise of Human Nature*, ed. David Fate Norton and Mary J. Norton (Oxford: Clarendon, [1745] 2007), 431.

27. See the advertisement in EHU, 1, which was written in the autumn of 1775 and printed in January 1776.
28. T. H. Grose, "History of the Editions," in *The Philosophical Works of David Hume*, ed. T. H. Green and T. H. Grose, vol. 3 (London: Longmans, Green, 1875), 39n.
29. See the advertisement in EHU, 1.
30. EMPL, 535.
31. EMPL, 534–35.
32. EMPL, 55, 53.
33. EMPL, 78, 77, 62.
34. Hume describes the life of the Platonist as a life of "*philosophical* devotion" rather than one of religious devotion, but the type of philosophy that he describes in this piece appears to be inextricably religious: see EMPL, 155.
35. EMPL, 170; see also 179n12.
36. EMPL, 5, 7.
37. On this episode, see Roger L. Emerson, "The 'Affair' at Edinburgh and the 'Project' at Glasgow: The Politics of Hume's Attempts to Become a Professor," in *Hume and Hume's Connexions*, ed. M. A. Stewart and John P. Wright (University Park: Pennsylvania State University Press, 1994), 1–22; Richard B. Sher, "Professors of Virtue: The Social History of the Edinburgh Moral Philosophy Chair in the Eighteenth Century," in Stewart, *Studies in the Philosophy of the Scottish Enlightenment*, esp. 103–8; and M. A. Stewart, "The Kirk and the Infidel," inaugural lecture delivered at Lancaster University on 9 November 1994 (Lancaster: Lancaster University Publications Office, 1995), 1–29.
38. David Hume to Matthew Sharpe of Hoddam, 25 April 1745, in HL I, 59; see also David Hume to William Mure of Caldwell, 4 August 1744, in HL I, 57–58.
39. See Sher, "Professors of Virtue," 99–100.
40. David Hume to Francis Hutcheson, 17 September 1739, in HL I, 34.
41. David Hume to James Edmonstoune, April 1764, in NHL, 83.
42. David Hume to Henry Home, end of June 1747, in NHL, 25–26.
43. David Hume to Gilbert Elliot of Minto, March/April 1751, in HL I, 158.
44. For a suggestion that Hume might have written the *Philosophical Essays* in part as a response to his failure to obtain the Edinburgh chair, see M. A. Stewart, "Two Species of Philosophy: The Historical Significance of the First *Enquiry*," in *Reading Hume on Human Understanding: Essays on the First Enquiry*, ed. Peter Millican (Oxford: Clarendon, 2002), 67–95.
45. The title page of the first edition of the *Philosophical Essays* did not include Hume's name, but it did note that the work was "By the author of the Essays moral and political"—a reference to the edition of the *Essays* that was released later that same year (1748) by the same publisher (Andrew Millar) and that includes "By David Hume, Esq." on the title page. Thus, Hume's identity was indicated at least indirectly.

46. David Hume to James Oswald of Dunnikier, 2 October 1747, in HL I, 106; see also David Hume to Henry Home, 9 February 1748, in HL I, 111.
47. For the earlier versions of the arguments of "Of the Original Contract" and "Of Passive Obedience" in the *Treatise*, see THN 3.2.8–9, 345–54.
48. David Hume to Lord Elibank, 8 January 1748, in Ernest Campbell Mossner, "New Hume Letters to Lord Elibank, 1748–1776," *Texas Studies in Literature and Language* 4.3 (Autumn 1962): 437.
49. David Hume to Henry Home, 9 February 1748, in HL I, 111; see also David Hume to Charles Erskine, Lord Tinwald, 13 February 1748, in HL I, 112.
50. EMPL, 208. This footnote was first included in the 1753 edition of Hume's *Essays* and was later revised. The version quoted in the text appeared in the first posthumous edition of his collected works (1777).
51. TMS V.2.9, 206.
52. David Hume to James Oswald of Dunnikier, 29 January 1748, in HL I, 109.
53. David Hume to John Home of Ninewells, 15 April 1748, in HL I, 127.
54. MOL, xxxv.

CHAPTER 2: ENCOUNTERING HUME

1. Robert L. Heilbroner, *The Worldly Philosophers: The Lives, Times, and Ideas of the Great Economic Thinkers*, 7th ed. (New York: Simon & Schuster, 1999), 41.
2. Smith was baptized on 5 June, but the date of his actual birth is unknown. For Smith, no fewer than four biographies are essential: those of Dugald Stewart, John Rae, Ian Simpson Ross, and Nicholas Phillipson (all cited above).
3. Smith did have a half-brother, Hugh, from his father's previous marriage, but he does not seem to have had much contact with him.
4. Friedrich Nietzsche, *On the Genealogy of Morals*, in *Basic Writings of Nietzsche*, trans. Walter Kaufmann (New York: Modern Library, [1887] 1992), 543.
5. Adam Smith to William Strahan, 10 June 1784, in CAS, 275.
6. Adam Smith to Archibald Davidson, 16 November 1787, in CAS, 309.
7. Strahan, xlviii; see also Adam Smith to John Home of Ninewells, 7 October 1776, in CAS, 214.
8. Stewart, 270.
9. TMS III.2.20, 124.
10. WN V.i.f.8, 761; V.i.f.34, 772.
11. Adam Smith to William Cullen, 20 September 1774, in CAS, 173.
12. See Roger L. Emerson, "Scottish Universities in the Eighteenth Century, 1690–1800," *Studies on Voltaire and the Eighteenth Century* 167 (1977): 453–74.
13. Adam Smith to William Smith, 24 August 1740, in CAS, 1.
14. See Adam Smith to his mother, 29 November 1743, in CAS, 3; and Adam Smith to his mother, 2 July 1744, in CAS, 3.
15. Stewart, 271.

16. To be clear, Balliol's sympathies tended to be pro-Jacobite, Smith's pro-Hanoverian. For the text that includes the claim about Smith departing from Oxford in disgust, written by the antiquarian George Chalmers and citing the authority of Smith's former student David Callander of Westertown, see D. D. Raphael, "Adam Smith 1790: The Man Recalled; the Philosopher Revived," in *Adam Smith Reviewed*, ed. Peter Jones and Andrew S. Skinner (Edinburgh: Edinburgh University Press, 1992), 93–94.

17. Recall, from the introduction, that in the eighteenth century the established church of Scotland was Presbyterian; the (nonestablished) Anglican Church was there dubbed Episcopalian.

18. See Stewart, 272. On Smith and the Snell Exhibition, see Iain McLean, *Adam Smith, Radical and Egalitarian: An Interpretation for the 21st Century* (Edinburgh: Edinburgh University Press, 2006), 6–7.

19. Review of Adam Smith's *Essays on Philosophical Subjects*, in *Monthly Review*, vol. 22 (January 1797): 60.

20. Ibid. On Leslie's identity as the author of this piece, see Ross, 71. On Smith's employment of and high regard for Leslie, see Adam Smith to Sir Joseph Banks, 18 December 1787, in CAS, 309–10.

21. See John Ramsay McCulloch, *Treatises and Essays on Subjects Connected with Economic Policy, with Biographical Sketches of Quesnay, Adam Smith, and Ricardo* (Edinburgh: Adam and Charles Black, 1853), 445–46; and John Strang, *Glasgow and Its Clubs, or Glimpses of the Condition, Manners, Characters, and Oddities of the City, during the Past and Present Centuries* (Glasgow: Richard Griffin, 1857), 27–28.

22. Strang, *Glasgow and Its Clubs*, 27–28. Gavin Kennedy writes that Smith "agreed with his tutors' assessment, but not their remedy: Hume's *Treatise* was not appropriate reading for a candidate for ordination, so he decided finally to cease to be a candidate." Gavin Kennedy, *Adam Smith's Lost Legacy* (New York: Palgrave Macmillan, 2005), 19.

23. It was long thought that Hutcheson *did* introduce the *Treatise* to Smith, his star pupil, and in fact asked him to write an abstract of it, which turned out to be so impressive that he forwarded it to Hume, who in turn sent Smith a copy of the work and sought to have the abstract published. This conjecture was based on a letter in which Hume informs Hutcheson that "My Bookseller has sent to Mr Smith a Copy of my Book" and inquires about "what he has done with the Abstract." David Hume to Francis Hutcheson, 4 March 1740, in HL I, 37. The conjecture seems to have originated in John Hill Burton, *Life and Correspondence of David Hume*, vol. 1 (Edinburgh: William Tait, 1846), 116–17, although it was repeated by many others for many decades. However, that the "Mr Smith" in question was not Adam Smith has been demonstrated time and again by more recent scholarship. Rather, Hume's reference was either to John Smith, Hutcheson's bookseller and publisher in Dublin, or (more likely) William Smith, one of the publishers of the *Bibliothèque raisonnée* in Amsterdam. The "Abstract" of the *Treatise* that Hume mentions was written by Hume himself. See the

editors' introduction in *An Abstract of a Treatise of Human Nature, 1740: A Pamphlet hitherto unknown by David Hume*, ed. J. M. Keynes and P. Sraffa (Cambridge: Cambridge University Press, 1938); R. W. Connon and M. Pollard, "On the Authorship of 'Hume's' *Abstract*," *Philosophical Quarterly* 27.106 (January 1977): 60–66; Jeff Broome, "On the Authorship of the *Abstract*: A Reply to John O. Nelson," *Hume Studies* 18.1 (April 1992): 95–104; David Raynor, "The Author of the *Abstract* Revisited," *Hume Studies* 19.1 (April 1993): 213–15; and David Fate Norton, "More Evidence That Hume Wrote the *Abstract*," *Hume Studies* 19.1 (April 1993): 217–22. For a dissenting view, see John O. Nelson, "Has the Authorship of *An Abstract of a Treatise of Human Nature* Really Been Decided?," *Philosophical Quarterly* 26.102 (January 1976): 82–91; and John O. Nelson, "The Authorship of the *Abstract* Revisited," *Hume Studies* 17.1 (April 1991): 83–86.

24. This plausible chain of events is suggested in Phillipson, 65.

25. Phillipson, 71. Given his stress on Smith's intellectual affinities with Hume, it is striking that Phillipson bestows only a few passing glances on his *Principles Which Lead and Direct Philosophical Enquiries*.

26. On the timing of this work's composition, see W. P. D. Wightman's introduction in EPS, 6–7. This work—or rather the first part of it—is generally referred to as *The History of Astronomy*; both the original editors, Joseph Black and James Hutton, and the editors of the modern Glasgow edition of Smith's works give it that title. Yet the full title that Smith gave the work was *The Principles Which Lead and Direct Philosophical Enquiries; Illustrated by the History of Astronomy*. He also left two more fragmentary pieces that seem to have been envisioned as part of the same work, as evidenced by the fact that they bear the identical title and parallel subtitles: *Illustrated by the History of the Ancient Physics* and *Illustrated by the History of the Ancient Logics and Metaphysics*. There is also a reference, within the astronomy essay, to a passage in the *Ancient Logics* as "appear[ing] hereafter" (EPS, 53). Accordingly, I will refer to these three pieces collectively by the main title, or by the abbreviation *Principles*.

27. Adam Smith to David Hume, 16 April 1773, in CAS, 168. For Hume's designation of the *Treatise* as a "juvenile work," see the advertisement in EHU, 1.

28. On the addition of the section on Newton, which is found at EPS, 97–105, see Wightman's introduction in EPS, 7. For the claim that Smith revised the astronomy essay toward the end of his life, see Lord Loughborough to David Douglas, 14 August 1790, in William Robert Scott, *Adam Smith as Student and Professor* (New York: Augustus M. Kelley, [1937] 1965), 313.

29. EPS, 45–46.

30. EPS, 105.

31. EPS, 104.

32. EPS, 40–41. For Hume's chapter title, see THN 1.1.4, 12. For other allusions to the *Treatise*, see EPS, 34 and 42, both of which are noted by the editor, as well as EPS, 37, where Smith employs the Humean language of "ideas" and "impressions," and EPS, 45, where he continues his discussion of constant conjunction.

33. John Millar to David Douglas, 10 August 1790, in Scott, *Adam Smith as Student and Professor*, 313. For some of the modern scholarship on this connection, see D. D. Raphael and A. S. Skinner's general introduction in EPS, 16–19; D. D. Raphael, "'The True Old Humean Philosophy' and Its Influence on Adam Smith," in *David Hume: Bicentenary Papers*, ed. G. P. Morice (Austin: University of Texas Press, 1977), 23–38; and Eric Schliesser, "Wonder in the Face of Scientific Revolutions: Adam Smith on Newton's 'Proof' of Copernicanism," *British Journal for the History of Philosophy* 13.4 (2005): 697–732. Ryan Hanley claims that Smith's astronomy essay is essentially *anti*-Humean, insofar as his conception of philosophical inquiry in that work depends on the sort of speculation beyond experience that Hume opposed. See Ryan Patrick Hanley, "Skepticism and Imagination: Smith's Response to Hume's *Dialogues*," in *New Essays on Adam Smith's Moral Philosophy*, ed. Wade L. Robison and David B. Suits (Rochester, NY: Rochester Institute of Technology Press, 2012), esp. 174–75, 183–84, 190. Although I cannot pursue the point here, in my view Hanley both understates the skepticism implicit in Smith's *Principles* and overstates Hume's hostility toward pushing inquiry beyond experience.
34. EPS, 48–49.
35. EPS, 50; see also EPS, 112–13.
36. EPS, 113; see also EPS, 50–51, 114.
37. EPS, 113.
38. See Eric Schliesser, "Toland and Adam Smith's Posthumous Work," *Diametros* 40 (2014): 123.
39. On the composition of *The Natural History of Religion*, see the editor's introduction in NHR, xx–xxi. For a thought-provoking essay comparing this work to Smith's *Principles*, see Spencer J. Pack, "Theological (and Hence Economic) Implications of Adam Smith's 'Principles Which Lead and Direct Philosophical Enquiries,'" *History of Political Economy* 27.2 (Summer 1995): 289–307.
40. Pack lays out these parallels nicely: see Pack, "Theological (and Hence Economic) Implications."
41. See Adam Smith to David Hume, 16 April 1773, in CAS, 168, where Smith describes the work in terms suggesting that Hume is not familiar with it.
42. See David Hume to Adam Smith, March 1757, in HL I, 245, and CAS, 20.
43. See Ross, chap. 7.
44. Chalmers cites Smith's former student David Callander of Westertown as the source of his information. See Raphael, "Adam Smith 1790," 94. Dugald Stewart admits that "at what particular period [Smith's] acquaintance with Mr David Hume commenced, does not appear from any information that I have received." Stewart, 273.
45. See Scott, *Adam Smith as Student and Professor*, 49–50. Hume was elected secretary of the Philosophical Society in December 1751, a role that he likely retained until his departure for France in 1763: see Mossner, 257–58.
46. See David Hume to Adam Smith, 8 June 1758, in HL I, 280, and CAS, 24.

47. James Caulfeild, *Memoirs of the Political and Private Life of James Caulfeild, Earl of Chestermont*, ed. Francis Hardy (1810), in Fieser X, 210.
48. David Hume to John Wilkes, 16 October 1754, in HL I, 205.
49. Alexander Carlyle, *Autobiography of the Rev. Dr Alexander Carlyle, Minister of Inveresk, Containing Memorials of the Men and Events of His Time*, 2nd ed. (Edinburgh: William Blackwood, 1860), 273, 276.
50. Smith had, however, written a very short preface for a collection of poems by William Hamilton around a year earlier: see EPS, 261.
51. John Ramsay of Ochtertyre, *Scotland and Scotsmen in the Eighteenth Century*, ed. Alexander Allardyce, vol. 1 (Edinburgh: William Blackwood, 1888), 461; see also Rae, 28.
52. On the fact that Smith "sometimes offended serious people by laughing or smiling in the time of divine worship," see Ramsay of Ochtertyre, *Scotland and Scotsmen in the Eighteenth Century*, 461.
53. James Boswell, *London Journal, 1762–1763*, ed. Frederick A. Pottle (New York: McGraw-Hill, 1950), 248; Stewart, 329.
54. Carlyle, *Autobiography of the Rev. Dr Alexander Carlyle*, 279.
55. Ibid., 280; see also Ramsay of Ochtertyre, *Scotland and Scotsmen in the Eighteenth Century*, 464.
56. J. Y. T. Greig, *David Hume* (New York: Garland, [1931] 1983), 252.
57. On Hume's preference for "a few select companions," see EMPL, 7, 626; and David Hume to the Comtesse de Boufflers, 15 May 1761, in HL I, 345.
58. Rae, 27.
59. Walter Bagehot, "Adam Smith as a Person," in *Biographical Studies* (London: Longmans, Green, [1895] 1907), 285.

CHAPTER 3: A BUDDING FRIENDSHIP

1. Smith's acceptance letter was sent from Edinburgh the day after he was elected in Glasgow—an impressive feat given the speed at which mail then traveled!
2. On the increasingly enlightened nature of Glasgow University at this time, see Roger L. Emerson, "Politics and the Glasgow Professors, 1690–1800," in *The Glasgow Enlightenment*, ed. Andrew Hook and Richard B. Sher (East Linton: Tuckwell Press, 1995), 21–39.
3. See the editors' introduction in *Scottish Philosophy in the Eighteenth Century*, vol. 1: *Morals, Politics, Art, Religion*, ed. Aaron Garrett and James A. Harris (Oxford: Oxford University Press, 2015), 6.
4. See Stewart, 274–75.
5. For two sets of student notes from Smith's jurisprudence lectures—one from the 1762–63 academic year and the other likely from the following year, Smith's last at Glasgow—see LJ. The potential third set of notes, which are usually referred to as the "Anderson Notes," were found in the commonplace book

of one of Smith's professorial colleagues at Glasgow, John Anderson. These notes are far less complete than either of the sets printed in LJ; they read like selected extracts from a fuller set of student notes. If they are indeed from Smith's course, they are from an earlier session than the two in LJ, likely sometime in the early or mid-1750s. See Ronald L. Meek, "New Light on Adam Smith's Glasgow Lectures on Jurisprudence," *History of Political Economy* 8.4 (Winter 1976): 439–77.

6. Stewart, 274.

7. John Ramsay of Ochtertyre, *Scotland and Scotsmen in the Eighteenth Century*, ed. Alexander Allardyce, vol. 1 (Edinburgh: William Blackwood, 1888), 462.

8. Ibid., 463; see also Henry Grey Graham, *Scottish Men of Letters in the Eighteenth Century* (London: Adam and Charles Black, 1908), 153. For a letter revealing Smith's obvious irritation at having to perform Easter exercises at the university, see Adam Smith to William Johnstone, March/April 1752–63, in CAS, 326.

9. Ramsay of Ochtertyre, *Scotland and Scotsmen in the Eighteenth Century*, 462–63.

10. See Théodore Tronchin to Louis François Tronchin, 17 July 1762, in *Correspondance complète de Jean-Jacques Rousseau*, ed. R. A. Leigh et al., vol. 12 (Geneva: Institut et Musée Voltaire, 1967), 125–26.

11. Stewart, 275.

12. See James Boswell to John Johnston of Grange, 11 January 1760, in *The Correspondence of James Boswell and John Johnston of Grange*, ed. Ralph S. Walker (New York: McGraw-Hill, 1966), 7.

13. See also Gordon Turnbull, "Boswell in Glasgow: Adam Smith, Moral Sentiments and the Sympathy of Biography," in Hook and Sher, *Glasgow Enlightenment*, esp. 164–65, 167.

14. Adam Smith to William Strahan, winter 1766–67, in CAS, 122; see also Stewart, 350–51.

15. Adam Smith to Archibald Davidson, 16 November 1787, in CAS, 309.

16. David Hume to John Clephane, 4 February 1752, in HL I, 164. James Harris suggests that Hume probably did not really want either of the university posts for which he was a candidate: see Harris, viii, 17–18, 209, 306–7.

17. Adam Smith to William Cullen, November 1751, in CAS, 5–6.

18. J. Y. T. Greig, *David Hume* (New York: Garland, [1931] 1983), 188–89.

19. Rae, 47–48. For Hume's letter thanking Cullen for his efforts on his behalf, see David Hume to William Cullen, 21 January 1752, in HL I, 163.

20. Mossner, 249.

21. On the number of faculty at the university, see the editors' introduction in Hook and Sher, *Glasgow Enlightenment*, 10–11.

22. See Gerhard Streminger, *David Hume: Der Philosoph und sein Zeitalter* (Munich: Verlag C. H. Beck, [1994] 2011), 324. Watt was not a professor at the university, but worked there as an instrument maker. On Smith's friendship with Watt, see Rae, 74.

23. David Hume to John Clephane, 4 February 1752, in HL I, 164–65.

24. MOL, xxxvi. For eighteenth-century population figures for Edinburgh and Glasgow, see T. C. Smout, *A History of the Scottish People, 1560–1830* (New York: Charles Scribner's Sons, 1969), 261.

25. Tobias Smollett, *The Expedition of Humphry Clinker*, ed. Lewis M. Knapp and Paul-Gabriel Boucé (Oxford: Oxford University Press, [1771] 2009), 233.

26. Adam Smith to Lord Shelburne, 29 October 1759, in CAS, 59. As late as 1788, at which point he had lived in Edinburgh for over a decade, Smith still preferred Glasgow: see Adam Smith to Henry Herbert, Lord Porchester, 23 September 1788, in CAS, 432. See also LJ, 333, 486.

27. For an attempt to redress the imbalance, see Hook and Sher, *Glasgow Enlightenment*.

28. See the editors' introduction in ibid., 13–14. For Smith's dissatisfaction with this aspect of Glasgow, see, for example, Adam Smith to William Johnstone, March/April 1752–63, in CAS, 326.

29. For an excellent overview of the *Second Enquiry* and discussion of how it differs from Book 3 of the *Treatise*, see Annette C. Baier, "*Enquiry concerning the Principles of Morals*: Incomparably the Best?," in *A Companion to Hume*, ed. Elizabeth S. Radcliffe (Oxford: Blackwell, 2008), 293–320.

30. David Hume to Francis Hutcheson, 17 September 1739, in HL I, 32; see also THN 3.3.6.6, 395.

31. For a helpful discussion of this point, see Kate Abramson, "Sympathy and the Project of Hume's Second Enquiry," *Archiv für Geschichte der Philosophie* 83.1 (May 2000): esp. 66–71.

32. EPM 9.3, 73.

33. David Hume to the abbé le Blanc, 5 November 1755, in HL I, 227; see also David Hume to David Dalrymple, 3 May 1753, in HL I, 175.

34. MOL, xxxvi.

35. EMPL, 255.

36. EMPL, 324.

37. EMPL, 269, 271, 277.

38. MOL, xxxvi.

39. J. H. Hollander, "Adam Smith 1776–1926," *Journal of Political Economy* 35.2 (April 1927): 164.

40. For an account of the Literary Society, see D. D. McElroy, "The Literary Clubs and Societies of Eighteenth-Century Scotland, and Their Influence on the Literary Productions of the Period from 1700 to 1800" (PhD diss., Edinburgh University, 1952), 118–27.

41. See William James Duncan, *Notes and Documents Illustrative of the Literary History of Glasgow, During the Greater Part of the Last Century* (Glasgow: Maitland Club, 1831), 132; and James Coutts, *A History of the University of Glasgow, from Its Foundation in 1451 to 1909* (Glasgow: James MacLehose and Sons, 1909), 316.

42. The precise timing of the work's publication is uncertain; for a discussion, see Jacob Viner, "Guide to John Rae's *Life of Adam Smith*," in Rae, 55–56.

43. Stewart, 300; see also 320–21.

44. See Meek, "New Light," 470.

45. LJ, 507. The notes from the previous year's jurisprudence course discuss the specie-flow mechanism at greater length, but without mentioning Hume by name: see LJ, 386–89. See also the brief reference to Hume in the same context in the manuscript generally referred to as the "Early Draft of Part of *The Wealth of Nations*," at LJ, 576. For Hume's criticisms of paper money, see esp. EMPL, 284–85, 316–18. Hume later softened his position on paper money—see the passage added to the 1764 edition of his essays at EMPL, 318–20—and in *The Wealth of Nations* Smith ended up taking a position fairly close to Hume's revised view. For discussion of this point, see Carl C. Wennerlind, "The Humean Paternity to Adam Smith's Theory of Money," *History of Economic Ideas* 8.1 (Spring 2000): esp. 89–92. Wennerlind's essay also contains a helpful discussion of the long-standing debate about whether, or to what extent, Smith incorporated Hume's specie-flow mechanism into the economic theory of *The Wealth of Nations*.

46. LJ, 514.

47. For Smith's rehearsal of Hume's arguments, see LJ, 316–25, 402–4. For his reference to Hume as "a very ingenious gentleman," see LJ, 317. For Hume's analogy, see EMPL, 475.

48. Duncan Forbes, "Sceptical Whiggism, Commerce, and Liberty," in *Essays on Adam Smith*, ed. Andrew S. Skinner and Thomas Wilson (Oxford: Clarendon, 1975), 181.

49. The only mention of Hume by name other than the one cited above is at LJ, 332, but the Glasgow editors note additional allusions to his various works at LJ, 25, 31, 51, 87, 93, 153, 180, 181, 182, 193, 194, 239, 240, 245, 248, 249, 255, 257, 261, 262, 266, 270, 275, 276, 279, 307, 320, 334, 390, 393, 519, 548, and 550, and there are doubtless many more scattered throughout the reports.

50. For echoes of the "four stages" theory in Hume, see EMPL, 256, 260–61. A more likely source for Smith here is Montesquieu: see esp. Charles de Secondat, baron de Montesquieu, *The Spirit of the Laws*, trans. Anne M. Cohler, Basia C. Miller, and Harold S. Stone (Cambridge: Cambridge University Press, [1748] 1989), XVII.8–17, 289–93. Many of Smith's contemporaries employed a version of the "four stages" theory; the fullest analysis of the precursors and exponents of this theory is still Ronald L. Meek, *Social Science and the Ignoble Savage* (Cambridge: Cambridge University Press, 1976).

51. On the transition from the feudal era to commercial society, compare EMPL, 277; HE II, 108–9, 522–24; HE III, 76–77, 80; and HE IV, 383–85; with LJ, 50–51, 202–3, 261–64, 420. On crime during Elizabeth's reign, compare HE IV, 414; with LJ, 332.

52. See LRBL, 116.

53. David Hume to Adam Smith, 24 September 1752, in HL I, 167–69, and CAS, 8–9. Hume echoes this last claim in *My Own Life*, where he writes that he began his *History* with the Stuarts because he saw this as the "epoch when, I thought, the misrepresentations of faction began chiefly to take place." MOL, xxxvi.

54. David Hume to Andrew Millar, 20 May 1757, in HL I, 249. Hume admitted the mistake to a number of other correspondents, as well: see David Hume to Lord Elibank, 8 June 1756, in Ernest Campbell Mossner, "New Hume Letters to Lord Elibank, 1748–1776," *Texas Studies in Literature and Language* 4.3 (Autumn 1962): 440; David Hume to William Strahan, 25 May 1757, in HL I, 251; David Hume to John Clephane, 3 September 1757, in HL I, 264; and David Hume to William Robertson, 25 January 1759, in HL I, 294.

55. See the editor's introduction in David Hume, *The History of Great Britain: The Reigns of James I and Charles I*, ed. Duncan Forbes (Middlesex: Penguin, 1970), 24.

56. David Hume to Adam Smith, 24 September 1752, in HL I, 168, and CAS, 8.

57. David Hume to Adam Smith, 26 May 1753, in HL I, 176, and CAS, 9–10. On Hume making the resources of the Advocates' Library available to Smith, see William Robert Scott, *Adam Smith as Student and Professor* (New York: Augustus M. Kelley, [1937] 1965), 116.

58. David Hume to Adam Smith, 24 September 1752, in HL I, 168, and CAS, 9.

59. David Hume to Adam Smith, 27 February 1754, in NHL, 35–37, and CAS, 10–11.

60. See David Hume to the Dean and Faculty of Advocates, November 1754; and David Hume to Robert Dundas of Arniston the Younger, 20 November 1754, both of which are found in J. C. Hilson, "More Unpublished Letters of David Hume," *Forum for Modern Language Studies* 6.4 (1970): 323–24.

61. David Hume to Adam Smith, 17 December 1754, in HL I, 212, and CAS, 16–17.

62. Mossner, 253.

63. David Hume to Adam Smith, 17 December 1754, in HL I, 212, and CAS, 17.

64. See Fieser IX, 198–230.

65. John Rae explains that *The Criterion* "is often stated to have been written for the express purpose of converting Adam Smith to a belief in the miraculous evidences of Christianity. . . . It is written in the form of a letter to an anonymous correspondent, who . . . is said in [Alexander] Chalmers's *Biographical Dictionary* to have been 'since known to be Adam Smith.' From Chalmers's *Dictionary* the same statement has been repeated in the same words in subsequent biographical dictionaries and elsewhere, but neither Chalmers nor his successors reveal who it was to whom this was known, or how he came to know it; and on the other hand, [William] Macdonald, the son-in-law and biographer of Douglas, makes no mention of Smith's name in connection with this work at all, and explicitly states that the book was written for the satisfaction of more than one of the author's friends, who had been influenced by

the objections of Hume and others to the reality of the Gospel miracles. This leaves the point somewhat undetermined." Rae, 129.

66. John Douglas, *The Criterion; or, Miracles Examined, with a View to Expose the Pretensions of Pagans and Papists* (London: A. Millar, 1754), 1–2.

67. On Smith remaining on friendly terms with Douglas, see Adam Smith to John Douglas, 6 March 1787, in CAS, 301.

68. See David Hume to William Strahan, 30 January 1773, in HL II, 269; but see also David Hume to William Strahan, 22 February 1773, in HL II, 276.

69. Rae, 101.

70. Alexander Carlyle, *Autobiography of the Rev. Dr Alexander Carlyle, Minister of Inveresk, Containing Memorials of the Men and Events of His Time*, 2nd ed. (Edinburgh: William Blackwood, 1860), 275.

71. For accounts of the Select Society, see Roger L. Emerson, "The Social Composition of Enlightened Scotland: The Select Society of Edinburgh, 1754–1764," *Studies on Voltaire and the Eighteenth Century* 114 (1973): 291–329; and McElroy, "Literary Clubs and Societies of Eighteenth-Century Scotland," 138–97.

72. Wedderburn in fact had the great good luck of having a reading list drawn up for him by Hume and Smith: see Streminger, *David Hume*, 363.

73. See Carlyle, *Autobiography of the Rev. Dr Alexander Carlyle*, 279.

74. See Mossner, 281.

75. See Dugald Stewart, *Biographical Memoirs of Adam Smith, LL.D., of William Robertson, D.D., and of Thomas Reid, D.D.* (Edinburgh: George Ramsay, 1811), 316.

76. See Mossner, 281–83.

77. David Hume to Allan Ramsay, April/May 1755, in HL I, 219–20.

78. Carlyle, *Autobiography of the Rev. Dr Alexander Carlyle*, 298.

CHAPTER 4: THE HISTORIAN AND THE KIRK

1. See Richard Hurd, *Moral and Political Dialogues* (London: A. Millar, 1759), 304.

2. Hume titled these two volumes *The History of Great Britain*, and switched to *The History of England* only with the Tudor volumes.

3. George Berkeley Mitchell, *Hume's History of England, Revised for Family Use; With Such Omissions and Alterations as May Render It Salutary to the Young, and Unexceptionable to the Christian*, 8 vols. (London: J. Hatchard, 1816).

4. MOL, xxxviii.

5. Voltaire, review of David Hume, *L'Histoire complète de l'Angleterre depuis Jules César jusqu'à sa révolution*, from *La Gazette Littéraire*, 2 May 1764, in *Oeuvres complètes de Voltaire*, ed. Louis Moland, vol. 25 (Paris: Garnier, 1879), 169; and Edward Gibbon to Georges Deyverdun, 7 May 1776, in *The Letters of Edward Gibbon*, ed. Jane Elizabeth Norton, vol. 2 (London: Cassell & Co., 1956), 107.

6. David Hume to John Clephane, 5 January 1753, in HL I, 170; see also James Oswald of Dunnikier, 28 June 1753, in HL I, 179.
7. THN intro.10, 6.
8. EMPL, 566.
9. David Hume to William Mure of Caldwell, October 1754, in HL I, 210.
10. David Hume to the abbé le Blanc, 12 September 1754, in HL I, 193.
11. Andrew Sabl, "David Hume: Skepticism in Politics?," in *Skepticism and Political Thought in the Seventeenth and Eighteenth Centuries*, ed. John Christian Laursen and Gianni Paganini (Toronto: University of Toronto Press, 2015), 151.
12. David Hume to James Oswald of Dunnikier, 28 June 1753, in HL I, 179; see also David Hume to John Clephane, 28 October 1753, in HL I, 180; David Hume to Matthew Sharp of Hoddam, 25 February 1754, in HL I, 185; David Hume to William Strahan, 3 May 1755, in HL I, 221–22; David Hume to William Mure of Waldwell, February 1757, in HL I, 242; and MOL, xxxvii.
13. David Hume to Andrew Millar, 18 December 1759, in HL I, 317; see also David Hume to the Comtesse de Boufflers, 15 May 1761, in HL I, 344. For a classic essay on this issue, see Ernest Campbell Mossner, "Was Hume a Tory Historian? Facts and Reconsiderations," *Journal of the History of Ideas* 2.2 (April 1941): 225–36.
14. HE III, 329; see also HE V, 142; and EMPL, 278, 464.
15. David Hume to Thomas Percy, 16 January 1773, in NHL, 198.
16. HE II, 525. For fuller discussion of these points, see Dennis C. Rasmussen, *The Pragmatic Enlightenment: Recovering the Liberalism of Hume, Smith, Montesquieu, and Voltaire* (Cambridge: Cambridge University Press, 2014), 221–23.
17. See Frederick G. Whelan, "'Contrary Effects' and the Reverse Invisible Hand in Hume and Smith," in *The Political Thought of Hume and His Contemporaries: Enlightenment Projects*, vol. 2 (New York: Routledge, 2015), 84–147.
18. David Hume to John Clephane, 18 February 1755, in J. C. A. Gaskin, "Hume's Attenuated Deism," *Archiv für Geschichte der Philosophie* 65 (1983): 172; see also David Hume to William Strahan, 22 March 1755, in Heiner Klemme, "'And Time Does Justice to All the World': Ein unveröffentlichter Brief von David Hume an William Strahan," *Journal of the History of Philosophy* 29.4 (October 1991): 659.
19. HE II, 14.
20. HE II, 518; see also 520.
21. HE V, 558.
22. HE IV, 145–46.
23. Don Herzog, *Without Foundations: Justification in Political Theory* (Ithaca, NY: Cornell University Press, 1985), 199. As Duncan Forbes notes, Hume frequently adopts a kind of "bifocal" approach in the *History*, arguing that certain ideas and actions were simultaneously blameworthy at the time and justified in retrospect because of their salutary effects. See Duncan Forbes, *Hume's Philosophical Politics* (Cambridge: Cambridge University Press, 1975), chap. 8, sec. 2.
24. David Hume to Adam Smith, 17 December 1754, in HL I, 213, and CAS, 17.

25. David Hume to Adam Smith, 9 January 1755, in HL I, 216–17, and CAS, 18. For the quotation about the Irish massacre, see HE V, 341.

26. David Hume to Adam Smith, 9 January 1755, in HL I, 216, and CAS, 17–18.

27. Richard B. Sher, *The Enlightenment and the Book: Scottish Authors & Their Publishers in Eighteenth-Century Britain, Ireland, & America* (Chicago: University of Chicago Press, 2006), 66.

28. They were the *Review*'s only two issues in its eighteenth-century manifestation, at least: in 1802 Francis Jeffrey began publishing a magazine by the same name, which went on to have a long and distinguished career.

29. For an analysis of the second letter, couching it as an attempt to promote a Humean "science of man" while carefully avoiding mentioning Hume by name, see Jeffrey Lomonaco, "Adam Smith's 'Letter to the Authors of the *Edinburgh Review*,'" *Journal of the History of Ideas* 63.4 (October 2002): 659–76.

30. I have analyzed this portion of the letter in Dennis C. Rasmussen, *The Problems and Promise of Commercial Society: Adam Smith's Response to Rousseau* (University Park: Pennsylvania State University Press, 2008), esp. 59–70.

31. David Raynor has suggested that Hume may have in fact had a hand in Smith's second letter to the *Review*, but M. A. Stewart, Ian Simpson Ross, and (according to Stewart) David Fate Norton are all doubtful. See David Raynor, "Adam Smith, David Hume, and the 'Extravagances' of Rousseau" (lecture, Scotland, Europe, and Empire in the Age of Adam Smith and Beyond conference, Université Paris-Sorbonne, 4 July 2013); the editor's introduction in *Studies in the Philosophy of the Scottish Enlightenment*, ed. M. A. Stewart (Oxford: Clarendon, 1990), 6–8; and Ross, 150–51.

32. For the claim that the *Review* was ended due to theological backlash, see Alexander Fraser Tytler, *Memoirs of the Life and Writings of Henry Home of Kames* (Edinburgh: William Creech, 1807), 1:169.

33. Quoted in Mossner, 545. For a similar complaint, see David Hume to Hugh Blair, autumn 1761?, in HL I, 351.

34. David Hume to John Clephane, 18 February 1755, in Gaskin, "Hume's Attenuated Deism," 172; see also David Hume to William Strahan, 22 March 1755, in Klemme, "'And Time Does Justice to All the World,'" 659.

35. David Hume to Allan Ramsay, June 1755, in HL I, 224.

36. James Bonar, *An Analysis of the Moral and Religious Sentiments Contained in the Writings of Sopho, and David Hume, Esq.* (1755), in Fieser IX, 38–48.

37. See, for example, EPM D.19, 114; D.32, 117; and D.47–48, 120–21.

38. David Hume to James Edmonstoune, 29 September 1757, in NHL, 43.

39. Bonar, *Analysis of the Moral and Religious Sentiments*, 48. See also Harris, 356–57.

40. David Hume to Hugh Blair, autumn 1761?, in HL I, 351.

41. *Annals of the General Assembly of the Church of Scotland, from the Origin of the Relief in 1752, to the Rejection of the Overture on Schism in 1766* (Edinburgh: John Johnstone, 1840), 58.

42. David Hume to Adam Smith, March 1757, in HL I, 246, and CAS, 20.
43. For the supposition that Smith helped to persuade Hume not to publish these essays, see Mossner, 323.
44. David Hume to William Strahan, 25 January 1772, in HL II, 253.
45. NHR 15.6, 86.
46. NHR 14.1, 81.
47. NHR 14.7–8, 83–84.
48. For a summary of what we know about Hume's changes to the work prior to publication, see the editor's introduction in NHR, xxiv–xxvi.
49. David Hume to Adam Smith, March 1757, in HL I, 245, and CAS, 19–20.
50. See William Warburton and Richard Hurd, *Remarks on Mr. David Hume's Essay on the Natural History of Religion* (1757), in Fieser V, 301–48.
51. MOL, xxxvii.
52. David Hume to Adam Smith, March 1757, in HL I, 246, and CAS, 20–21.
53. David Hume to Gilbert Elliot of Minto, 9 August 1757, in HL I, 262.
54. David Hume to Adam Smith, March 1757, in HL I, 246, and CAS, 21.
55. David Hume to Adam Smith, 8 June 1758, in HL I, 279–80, and CAS, 24–25.

CHAPTER 5: THEORIZING THE MORAL SENTIMENTS

1. Adam Smith to Thomas Cadell, 15 March 1788, in CAS, 311.
2. Stewart, 326.
3. For a detailed account of the careers of Millar, Strahan, and Cadell, see Richard B. Sher, *The Enlightenment and the Book: Scottish Authors & Their Publishers in Eighteenth-Century Britain, Ireland, & America* (Chicago: University of Chicago Press, 2006), 275–306, 327–72.
4. Quoted in James Boswell, *The Life of Samuel Johnson*, ed. David Womersley (New York: Penguin, [1791] 2008), 157.
5. Samuel Romilly to Madame G, 20 August 1790, in *Memoirs of the Life of Sir Samuel Romilly, Written by Himself*, vol. 1 (London: John Murray, 1840), 404.
6. TMS VII.i.2, 265.
7. See Richard F. Teichgraeber III, *"Free Trade" and Moral Philosophy: Rethinking the Sources of Adam Smith's Wealth of Nations* (Durham, NC: Duke University Press, 1986), 132.
8. See D. D. Raphael, *The Impartial Spectator: Adam Smith's Moral Philosophy* (Oxford: Clarendon, 2007), 96.
9. TMS IV.1.2, 179; see also IV.2.3, 188. For more or less open engagements with Hume in the first edition of the work, see TMS I.i.1.2–13, 9–13; I.i.3.8, 18; I.i.4.4, 20; II.ii.3.6–12, 87–91; IV.1.2, 179; IV.2.2–12, 187–93; V.1.2, 194; VII.ii.3.21, 305–6; VII.iii.1.2, 316; VII.iii.3.3, 321; and VII.iii.3.17, 327. For a response to Hume that was added in the second edition (and that is discussed later in this chapter), see TMS I.iii.1.9, 46n. Finally, for some passages that may allude

more subtly to Hume, see TMS I.i.5.1, 23; I.iii.2.1, 50; I.iii.2.3, 52; II.i.2.5, 71; III.1.3, 110; III.2.35, 134 (added in the sixth edition); III.3.2, 135 (added in the second edition); III.3.4, 136–37 (added in the second edition); VI.iii.4, 238 (added in the sixth edition); VI.conlc.6, 264 (added in the sixth edition); VII. ii.1.34, 287 (added in the sixth edition); and VII.iii.2.7, 320.

10. The obvious exception is the last part of the work, whose purpose is to examine a number of previous "Systems of Moral Philosophy." On why Smith avoided explicit engagement with other philosophers in the rest of the book, see Charles L. Griswold, *Adam Smith and the Virtues of Enlightenment* (Cambridge: Cambridge University Press, 1999), 47.

11. See TMS VII.i.1, 265.

12. See TMS VII.ii.3.21, 306; and VII.iii3.17, 327.

13. An entire book could be—and, frankly, should be—written on the relationship between Hume's and Smith's moral theories. The most extensive discussion of this relationship to date is a still-unpublished doctoral dissertation: John William McHugh, "Sympathy, Self, and Society: Adam Smith's Response to David Hume's Moral Theory" (PhD diss., Boston University, 2011). For a shorter but very useful overview, see Ryan Hanley, "Hume and Smith on Moral Philosophy," in *The Oxford Handbook of Hume*, ed. Paul Russell (Oxford: Oxford University Press, 2016), 708–28.

14. TMS III.5.5, 165.

15. TMS VII.iii.2.7, 320.

16. See TMS III.4.5, 158; and VII.iii.3, 321–27.

17. See THN 3.3.1.15, 371–72; 3.3.1.18, 373; 3.3.1.30, 377; and EPM 9.6, 75.

18. TMS III.3.3, 135. This passage was added in the second edition, but the idea is clearly present in the first edition as well.

19. See THN 3.3.1.14, 371; 3.3.1.30, 377; and EPM 5.1, 33.

20. See Raphael, *Impartial Spectator*, 30–31.

21. See EPM 5.41, 43; and TMS III.3.2–3, 134–35. Here too the passage from TMS was added in the second edition, but the idea is clearly present in the first edition as well.

22. The relationship between Hume's and Smith's conceptions of sympathy has been the subject of much scholarly commentary. For two particularly helpful studies, see Samuel Fleischacker, "Sympathy in Hume and Smith: A Contrast, Critique, and Reconstruction," in *Intersubjectivity and Objectivity in Adam Smith and Edmund Husserl: A Collection of Essays*, ed. Christel Fricke and Dagfinn Føllesdal (Frankfurt: Ontos Verlag, 2012), 273–311; and Geoffrey Sayre-McCord, "Hume and Smith on Sympathy, Approbation, and Moral Judgment," *Social Philosophy and Policy* 30.1–2 (December 2013): 208–36.

23. THN 2.2.5.15, 234–35.

24. THN 2.1.11.2, 206.

25. See THN 3.3.1.7, 368.

26. See THN 3.3.3.5, 386; and EPM 7.2, 59; 7.21, 64. Admittedly, Hume does not always describe sympathy as taking place in such a simple and direct manner. He discusses this faculty on at least five separate occasions in the *Treatise*—in sections 2.1.11, 2.2.7, 2.2.9, 3.3.1, and 3.3.6—and in the later discussions he sometimes speaks of an "extensive" sympathy that takes into account the future feelings of an individual and/or the feelings of many individuals at once. For discussion of this point, see Jennifer A. Herdt, *Religion and Faction in Hume's Moral Philosophy* (Cambridge: Cambridge University Press, 1997), chap. 2; and Kate Abramson, "Sympathy and the Project of Hume's Second Enquiry," *Archiv für Geschichte der Philosophie* 83.1 (May 2000): 45–80. Yet Hume makes clear that he regards the "extensive" form(s) of sympathy as rather exceptional, not the way this faculty standardly "works": see Andrew S. Cunningham, "The Strength of Hume's 'Weak' Sympathy," *Hume Studies* 30.2 (November 2004): 237–56.
27. See TMS I.i.1.6, 11.
28. TMS I.i.1.7, 11. On our disinclination to sympathize with the unsocial passions, see also TMS I.ii.3.1, 34; and I.ii.3.5, 36–37.
29. TMS I.i.1.10, 12.
30. See Fleischacker, "Sympathy in Hume and Smith," 276. Hume too believes that the imagination plays a central role in the sympathetic process, to be sure, but according to his account the role of the imagination is not to project ourselves into the situation of another person but rather to convert our "idea" of that person's feelings into a livelier "impression."
31. See esp. ibid., 279–82. For an alternative view, according to which Smith is *not* engaging with Hume in the first chapter of *The Theory of Moral Sentiments*, see David Raynor, "Adam Smith and the Virtues," *Adam Smith Review* 2 (2006): 240.
32. TMS I.i.1.2, 9.
33. TMS I.i.1.10, 12; THN 2.2.7.5, 239. The similarity between these passages is noted in Fleischacker, "Sympathy in Hume and Smith," 281.
34. TMS I.i.3.7, 18; see also II.i.intro.2, 67.
35. TMS II.i.intro.2, 67; see also I.i.3.5, 18.
36. TMS II.i.5.1, 74.
37. TMS IV.1.2, 179.
38. THN 3.3.1.8, 368; see also 2.2.5.16, 235; and EPM 5.19, 38.
39. TMS IV.1.3, 179–80.
40. TMS IV.1.4–5, 180.
41. TMS IV.1.7, 181.
42. Hume too argues that we tend to sympathize with the rich and powerful more easily than with others because it is easier for us to "enter into" (what we imagine to be) their agreeable situation: see THN 2.2.5, 231–36.
43. TMS IV.1.8, 182–83.

44. I have examined this aspect of Smith's thought in more detail in Dennis C. Rasmussen, "Does 'Bettering Our Condition' Really Make Us Better Off? Adam Smith on Progress and Happiness," *American Political Science Review* 100.3 (August 2006): 309–18; and Dennis C. Rasmussen, *The Problems and Promise of Commercial Society: Adam Smith's Response to Rousseau* (University Park: Pennsylvania State University Press, 2008), 82–89, 131–50.

45. TMS IV.2.3, 188; see also VII.iii.1.2, 316.

46. TMS IV.2.4, 188; see also VII.iii.3.17, 327.

47. See TMS IV.2.12, 192–93.

48. See THN 3.1.2.4, 303; 3.3.5.6, 393; and EPM 5.1, 33n17.

49. THN 3.3.5.6, 393.

50. See TMS IV.2.5, 188.

51. TMS IV.2.2, 187–88; IV.2.11, 192; see also VII.iii.1.2, 316.

52. See TMS I.i.4.4, 20; and IV.2.11, 192.

53. See Marie A. Martin, "Utility and Morality: Adam Smith's Critique of Hume," *Hume Studies* 16.2 (November 1990): 110.

54. Smith does mention Hume's "agreeable" virtues at a couple of points—see TMS IV.2.3, 188; and VII.ii.3.21, 306—but they do not appear to play much of a role in his overall interpretation of Hume: see esp. TMS VII.iii.3.17, 327.

55. EPM 5.44, 45.

56. As David Raynor points out, Hume silently corrects Smith's one-sided interpretation in his anonymous review of the book. See David R. Raynor, "Hume's Abstract of Adam Smith's Theory of Moral Sentiments," *Journal of the History of Philosophy* 22.1 (January 1984): 59–60.

57. This topic too has received a good deal of scholarly commentary. See, for instance, Knud Haakonssen, *The Science of a Legislator: The Natural Jurisprudence of David Hume & Adam Smith* (Cambridge: Cambridge University Press, 1981), esp. chap. 4; Samuel Fleischacker, *On Adam Smith's Wealth of Nations: A Philosophical Companion* (Princeton, NJ: Princeton University Press, 2004), 151–52, 154; Spencer J. Pack and Eric Schliesser, "Smith's Humean Criticism of Hume's Account of the Origin of Justice," *Journal of the History of Philosophy* 44.1 (January 2006): esp. 61–63; and Michael Frazer, *The Enlightenment of Sympathy: Justice and the Moral Sentiments in the Eighteenth Century and Today* (Oxford: Oxford University Press, 2010), chap. 4.

58. Hume's discussions of justice tend to focus almost entirely on the protection of property, but some of his comments make clear that he also means to include the protection of life and liberty in this category: see, for instance, THN 3.2.2.7, 313; and EPM 3.10–11, 16. For Smith's understanding of justice, see TMS II.ii.1.5, 79; and II.ii.1.9, 82.

59. EPM App. 3.5, 97.

60. TMS II.ii.3.4, 86.

61. See THN 3.2.2.22, 319; 3.2.3.1, 322; EPM App. 3.6, 97; and TMS III.6.10, 175.

62. TMS II.i.3.1, 71.

63. TMS II.ii.3.10, 90. Smith does concede that there are certain cases in which we punish on the grounds of the general interests of society. He argues, for instance, that a sentinel who falls asleep at his watch ought to be executed, in accordance with common laws of war, even though to most observers this punishment would seem to far exceed the crime, because this kind of carelessness can endanger an entire army: see TMS II.ii.3.11, 90; see also II.ii.3.7, 88–89. I have discussed this passage in Dennis C. Rasmussen, "Whose Impartiality? Which Self-Interest? Adam Smith on Utility, Happiness, and Cultural Relativism," *Adam Smith Review* 4 (2008): 248.
64. TMS II.ii.3.6, 87.
65. TMS II.ii.3.9, 89.
66. Pack and Schliesser, "Smith's Humean Criticism," 47.
67. Emma Rothschild, *Economic Sentiments: Adam Smith, Condorcet, and the Enlightenment* (Cambridge, MA: Harvard University Press, 2001), 129; see also 129–33 more generally.
68. See, for example, A. L. Macfie, *The Individual in Society: Papers on Adam Smith* (London: George Allen & Unwin, 1967), 102; Haakonssen, *Science of a Legislator*, 77; and Fleischacker, *On Adam Smith's Wealth of Nations*, 44–45.
69. Haakonssen, *Science of a Legislator*, 75.
70. TMS III.5.10, 169.
71. See, for instance, TMS III.2.12, 120–21; and III.2.33, 131–32.
72. TMS III.5.3, 163.
73. Henry, Lord Brougham, *Lives of Philosophers of the Time of George III*, 3rd ed. (London: Richard Griffin, 1855), 195.
74. TMS III.5.13, 170.
75. NHR 14.1, 81.
76. TMS III.6.12, 176.
77. See David Hume to Adam Smith, 12 April 1759, in NHL, 51–55, and CAS, 33–36. All quotations in this section of the text are drawn from this letter unless otherwise noted.
78. David Hume to Adam Smith, 28 July 1759, in HL I, 312, and CAS, 42. Burke wrote to Smith, "I am not only pleased with the ingenuity of your Theory; I am convinced of its solidity and Truth; and I do not know that it ever cost me less trouble to admit so many things to which I had been a stranger before." Edmund Burke to Adam Smith, 10 September 1759, in CAS, 46. In the *Annual Register* he pronounced that Smith's theory "is in all its essential parts just, and founded on truth and nature," and that it is "one of the most beautiful fabrics of moral theory, that has perhaps ever appeared." See *Adam Smith: Critical Responses*, ed. Hiroshi Mizuta, vol. 1 (New York: Routledge, 2000), 77–78.
79. It is also interesting to note that Dugald Stewart discreetly omitted this sentence from his transcription of Hume's letter, along with a sentence (quoted in the next paragraph in the text) that refers to bishops as "Retainers to Superstition." See Stewart, 297–98.

80. David Hume to Adam Smith, 28 July 1759, in HL I, 314, and CAS, 44.
81. See Raynor, "Hume's Abstract." For further confirmation that the anonymous work was indeed by Hume, see D. D. Raphael and Tatsuya Sakamoto, "Anonymous Writings of David Hume," *Journal of the History of Philosophy* 28.2 (April 1990): 271–81.
82. Raynor, "Hume's Abstract," 65–66.
83. Ibid., 78–79.
84. Ibid., 66–67, italics added.
85. Ibid., 74.
86. As David Raynor points out, in his review Hume says that only "a great part" of his own moral theory is founded on utility. See ibid., 59–60, 74.
87. Ibid., 61.
88. Ibid., 79.
89. THN 2.3.2.3, 263. Hume makes the same point, using almost identical language, at EHU 8.26, 73.
90. David Hume to Adam Smith, 28 July 1759, in HL I, 312–13, and CAS, 43. In his anonymous review Hume had passed over this claim of Smith's without passing judgment on it either way: see Raynor, "Hume's Abstract," 56, 67–68.
91. TMS I.iii.1.9, 46n.
92. TMS I.i.2.2–4, 14–15.
93. TMS I.i.2.6, 15–16. David Raynor, Eugene Heath, and Alexander Broadie all generally side with Hume on this point, while Samuel Fleischacker generally sides with Smith. See Raynor, "Hume's Abstract," 57–58; Eugene Heath, "The Commerce of Sympathy: Adam Smith on the Emergence of Morals," *Journal of the History of Philosophy* 33.3 (July 1995): esp. 453, 455–57; Alexander Broadie, "Sympathy and the Impartial Spectator," in *The Cambridge Companion to Adam Smith*, ed. Knud Haakonssen (Cambridge: Cambridge University Press, 2006), 173–74; and Fleischacker, "Sympathy in Hume and Smith," 300–301.
94. Adam Smith to Gilbert Elliot, 10 October 1759, in CAS, 49.

CHAPTER 6: FÊTED IN FRANCE

1. Iain McLean suggests that Smith may in fact have advised Townshend to tax the American colonists in order to pay for their own defense, but he also notes that Smith would have disapproved of the specific form that the Townshend duties took given that there were inefficient, served Townshend's own vested interests, helped to protect the East India Company's monopoly on tea exportation to the colonies, and bypassed colonial legislatures—all contrary to Smith's maxims on taxation in *The Wealth of Nations*. See Iain McLean, *Adam Smith, Radical and Egalitarian: An Interpretation for the 21st Century* (Edinburgh: Edinburgh University Press, 2006), 16–17.
2. David Hume to Adam Smith, 12 April 1759, in NHL, 54, and CAS, 36.

3. See Adam Smith to Charles Townshend, 17 September 1759, in CAS, 48; and Charles Townshend to Adam Smith, 25 October 1763, in CAS, 95.
4. David Hume to Adam Smith, 28 July 1759, in HL I, 313–14, and CAS, 43–44.
5. David Hume to Adam Smith, 28 July 1759, in HL I, 314, and CAS, 44.
6. See Alexander Carlyle, *Autobiography of the Rev. Dr Alexander Carlyle, Minister of Inveresk, Containing Memorials of the Men and Events of His Time*, 2nd ed. (Edinburgh: William Blackwood, 1860), 394–95.
7. Benjamin Franklin to Lord Kames, 3 January 1760, in *The Papers of Benjamin Franklin*, ed. Leonard W. Larabee (New Haven, CT: Yale University Press, 1966), 9:9–10.
8. See Rae, 151.
9. See Benjamin Franklin to David Hume, 27 September 1760, in *Papers of Benjamin Franklin*, 9:227–30; Benjamin Franklin to David Hume, 21 January 1762, in *Papers of Benjamin Franklin*, 10:17–23; David Hume to Benjamin Franklin, 10 May 1762, in NHL, 66–68; Benjamin Franklin to David Hume, 19 May 1762, in *Papers of Benjamin Franklin*, 10:82–84; David Hume to Benjamin Franklin, 7 February 1772, in NHL, 193–95; Adam Smith to William Strahan, 4 April 1760, in CAS, 68; and Adam Smith to William Strahan, 30 December 1760, in CAS, 73.
10. David Hume to Benjamin Franklin, 10 May 1762, in NHL, 67–68.
11. Benjamin Franklin to David Hume, 19 May 1762, in *Papers of Benjamin Franklin*, 10:83–84.
12. David Hume to Adam Smith, 29 June 1761, in HL I, 346, and CAS, 77.
13. This dialogue was first published in Ernest Campbell Mossner, " 'Of the Principle of Moral Estimation: A Discourse between David Hume, Robert Clerk, and Adam Smith': An Unpublished MS by Adam Ferguson," *Journal of the History of Ideas* 21.2 (April–June 1960): 222–32. For a more recent version with more up-to-date editorial apparatus, see Adam Ferguson, "Of the Principle of Moral Estimation. A Discourse between David Hume, Robert Clerk and Adam Smith," in *The Manuscripts of Adam Ferguson*, ed. Vincenzo Merolle (London: Pickering & Chatto, 2006), 207–15.
14. The only words between the two come in a transitional interlude in which Hume tells Smith that he (Hume) and Clerk had been discussing "a Subject in which you are well versed," namely "the Theory of Moral Sentiment[s]," "& should have been glad of your assistance," at which point Smith pronounces himself sorry to have been absent, as he would "willingly profit by your remarks," and turns his attention to Clerk. Ferguson, "Of the Principle of Moral Estimation," 209–10. In the view of one scholar the absence of any real discussion between the two suggests that the dialogue must have been fictional: "This is not believable behaviour from two best friends under attack." Jack Russell Weinstein, "The Two Adams: Ferguson and Smith on Sympathy and Sentiment," in *Adam Ferguson: Philosophy, Politics and Society*, ed. Eugene Heath and Vincenzo Merolle (London: Pickering & Chatto, 2009), 93.

15. For discussion, see Richard B. Sher, *Church and University in the Scottish Enlightenment: The Moderate Literati of Edinburgh* (Edinburgh: Edinburgh University Press, 1985), 168; Eugene Heath, "Ferguson's Moral Philosophy," in Merolle, *Manuscripts of Adam Ferguson*, lxiv–lxviii; Weinstein, "Two Adams," 92–95, 98, 105; and Ross, 200–203.

16. Ferguson, "Of the Principle of Moral Estimation," 207–10. Smith had in fact asked Gilbert Elliot to solicit Clerk's opinion of his book: see Adam Smith to Gilbert Elliot, 10 October 1759, in CAS, 49.

17. Peter Gay, *The Enlightenment: An Interpretation*, vol. 1: *The Rise of Modern Paganism* (New York: Norton, 1966), 402.

18. See John H. Middendorf, "Dr. Johnson and Adam Smith," *Philological Quarterly* 40.2 (April 1961): esp. 287; and Ross, 203–4.

19. David Hume to David Mallet, 8 November 1762, in HL I, 369.

20. David Hume to Gilbert Elliot of Minto, 5 July 1762, in HL I, 367.

21. David Hume to James Edmonstoune, 9 January 1764, in NHL, 77.

22. See Adam Ferguson to Lord Shelburne, 3 February 1762, in *The Correspondence of Adam Ferguson*, ed. Vincenzo Merolle, vol. 2 (London: Pickering & Chatto, 1995), 533–34; and Carlyle, *Autobiography of the Rev. Dr Alexander Carlyle*, 419–20. For an account of the Poker Club, see D. D. McElroy, "The Literary Clubs and Societies of Eighteenth-Century Scotland, and Their Influence on the Literary Productions of the Period from 1700 to 1800" (PhD diss., Edinburgh University, 1952), 516–30.

23. Carlyle, *Autobiography*, 420.

24. David Hume to Adam Ferguson, 9 November 1763, in HL I, 410–11.

25. James Boswell, *London Journal, 1762–1763*, ed. Frederick A. Pottle (New York: McGraw-Hill, 1950), 300.

26. Adam Smith to David Hume, 22 February 1763, in CAS, 89.

27. David Hume to Adam Smith, 28 March 1763, in HL I, 381, and CAS, 89–90.

28. Hume served as Hertford's de facto secretary from the autumn of 1763 until the summer of 1765, but he did not attain the official title (and full salary) until July 1765. Soon thereafter Hertford left Paris, and from his departure through mid-November Hume was *chargé d'affaires*—essentially, the acting ambassador.

29. Lord Elibank to David Hume, 11 May 1763, in HL I, 388.

30. David Hume to Adam Smith, 9 August 1763, in HL I, 391–92, and CAS, 91.

31. David Hume to Adam Smith, 13 September 1763, in HL I, 394–95, and CAS, 93.

32. See Charles Townshend to Adam Smith, 25 October 1763, in CAS, 95–96.

33. David Hume to William Robertson, 1 December 1763, in NHL, 74.

34. Mossner, 445.

35. David Hume to Adam Smith, 26 October 1763, in HL I, 407–9, and CAS, 96–98. This letter is dated 28 October in both of these volumes, but the correct date is in fact 26 October: see FHL, 253.

36. Adam Smith to David Hume, 12 December 1763, in CAS, 413–14.

37. David Hume to Lord Elibank, 21 December 1763, in Ernest Campbell Mossner, "New Hume Letters to Lord Elibank, 1748–1776," *Texas Studies in Literature and Language* 4.3 (Autumn 1962): 452.

38. Comtesse de Boufflers to David Hume, 13 March 1761, in HL II, 367.

39. See David Hume to the Comtesse de Boufflers, 20 August 1776, in HL II, 335.

40. David Hume to Hugh Blair, December 1763, in HL I, 419.

41. David Hume to Sir John Pringle, 10 February 1773, in HL II, 274.

42. Edward Gibbon, *Memoirs of My Life*, ed. Georges A. Bonnard (London: Thomas Nelson and Sons, [1796] 1966), 127.

43. Denis Diderot, letter to Sophie Volland, 6 October 1765, in *Correspondance*, ed. Georges Roth, vol. 5 (Paris: Minuit, 1959), 134. It was with heavy irony, then, that Hume assured Hugh Blair and the other ministers back in Edinburgh that "the Men of Letters here are really very agreeable" and that "it woud give you . . . great Satisfaction to find that there is not a single Deist among them." David Hume to Hugh Blair, December 1763, in HL I, 419.

44. See John Millar to Adam Smith, 2 February 1764, in CAS, 99–100. Although none of his various comments on *The Theory of Moral Sentiments* were published during his lifetime, it seems that Reid was also critical of Smith: see David Fate Norton and J. C. Stewart-Robertson, "Thomas Reid on Adam Smith's Theory of Morals," *Journal of the History of Ideas* 41.3 (July–September 1980): 381–98.

45. For a history of the chair during the eighteenth century, see Paul Wood, "'The Fittest Man in the Kingdom': Thomas Reid and the Glasgow Chair of Moral Philosophy," *Hume Studies* 23.2 (November 1997): 277–314.

46. Stewart, 306, 301. On the other hand, in *The Wealth of Nations* Smith cast doubt on the value of such tours for young people: see WN V.i.f.36, 773–74.

47. See Ross, 214.

48. Adam Smith to David Hume, August 1765, in CAS, 105.

49. Adam Smith to David Hume, 5 July 1764, in CAS, 101–2.

50. For some of the difficulties in verifying the identity of the work, as well as some reasons to suppose that the reference *is to The Wealth of Nations*, see Ross, 215–17.

51. Adam Smith to David Hume, 21 October 1764, in CAS, 102–3.

52. Isaac Barré to David Hume, 4 September 1764, in *Letters of Eminent Persons Addressed to David Hume*, ed. John Hill Burton (Edinburgh: William Blackwood and Sons, 1849), 37–38.

53. On Smith's anxiety to reunite with Hume in Paris, see Adam Smith to David Hume, August 1765, in CAS, 105.

54. David Hume to John Home of Ninewells, 14 July 1765, in HL I, 512.

55. David Hume to Adam Smith, 5 September 1765, in HL I, 520–21, and CAS, 106.

56. See David Hume to Gilbert Elliot of Minto, 22 September 1764, in HL I, 470.

57. David Hume to Adam Smith, 5 September 1765, in HL I, 521, and CAS, 107.

58. David Hume to Hugh Blair, 6 April 1765, in HL I, 498.

59. David Hume to Adam Smith, 5 September 1765, in HL I, 521, and CAS, 107.

60. Adam Smith to David Hume, September 1765, in CAS, 107–8.

61. In a letter written from London, probably at the end of January 1766, Hume wrote Smith to say, "I am sorry I did not see you before I left Paris." David Hume to Adam Smith, ?end of January 1766, in HL II, 5, and CAS, 110. This would seem to suggest that the two did not meet, of course, though Hume could have meant that he was sorry not to have seen Smith *again* in Paris (i.e., they had already met, and at that meeting they promised one another to meet again before Hume left). Dugald Stewart reports that Smith returned to Paris "around Christmas 1765," and John Rae speculates, on the basis of a letter from Horace Walpole written on 5 December saying that the Duke of Buccleuch was expected to arrive in Paris the following week, that Smith "arrived in Paris about the middle of December, just in time to have a week or two with Hume before he finally left Paris for London with Rousseau." Stewart, 302; Rae, 194. As Ian Simpson Ross notes, however, the first conclusive news of Smith being in Paris did not come until 2 March 1766, when Walpole recorded that he went to see an Italian play with Smith, and a letter dated 5 February from George-Louis Le Sage, a Genevese physician, that implies that he had seen Smith recently in Geneva. See Ross, 222. Smith is said to have uncharacteristically kept a diary during his trip, but unfortunately no trace of it has been found since it was sold in the 1920s from a bookshop in Edinburgh. See W. R. Scott, "Studies Relating to Adam Smith during the Last Fifty Years," in *Proceedings of the British Academy*, ed. A. L. Macfie (London: British Academy, 1940), 273.

62. Adam Smith to David Hume, 13 March 1766, in CAS, 112.

63. Stewart, 303.

64. John Ramsay of Ochtertyre, *Scotland and Scotsmen in the Eighteenth Century*, ed. Alexander Allardyce, vol. 1 (Edinburgh: William Blackwood, 1888), 464.

65. See Mme de Boufflers to David Hume, 6 May 1766, in Burton, *Letters of Eminent Persons*, 237–38.

66. See Mary Margaret Stewart, "Adam Smith and the Comtesse de Boufflers," *Studies in Scottish Literature* 7.3 (January 1970): 185–86.

67. David Hume to the Comtesse de Boufflers, 25 July 1766, in HL II, 63.

68. David Hume to the Comtesse de Boufflers, 15 May 1761, in HL I, 345, 343.

69. See Rae, 212–13; and Ross, 227.

70. Ross, 228.

71. Adam Smith to David Hume, 13 March 1766, in CAS, 112.

72. Adam Smith to Andrew Millar, October 1766, in CAS, 121.

CHAPTER 7: QUARREL WITH A WILD PHILOSOPHER

1. The most popular work on the quarrel is an engaging read, but also a bit too generous to Rousseau and much too harsh on Hume: see David Edmonds and John Eidinow, *Rousseau's Dog: Two Great Thinkers at War in the Age of Enlightenment* (New York: HarperCollins, 2006). The best book-length account

can be found in Robert Zaretsky and John T. Scott, *The Philosophers' Quarrel: Rousseau, Hume, and the Limits of Human Understanding* (New Haven, CT: Yale University Press, 2009).

2. See Jean-Jacques Rousseau, *The Confessions*, in *The Collected Writings of Rousseau*, vol. 5, ed. Christopher Kelly, Roger D. Masters, and Peter G. Stillman (Hanover, NH: University Press of New England, 1995), 304.

3. See David Hume to the Comtesse de Boufflers, 1 July 1762, in HL I, 363–64; David Hume to Jean-Jacques Rousseau, 2 July 1762, in HL I, 364–65; and David Hume to the Comtesse de Boufflers, 3 July 1763, in HL I, 388–89.

4. Jean-Jacques Rousseau to David Hume, 4 December 1765, in *Correspondance complète de Jean-Jacques Rousseau*, ed. R. A. Leigh, vol. 28 (Oxford: Voltaire Foundation, 1977), 17, and HL II, 383; see also David Hume to Jean-Jacques Rousseau, 22 October 1765, in HL I, 525–27.

5. Rousseau, *Confessions*, 304.

6. I explore this contrast in depth in a forthcoming essay: Dennis C. Rasmussen, "Rousseau and Hume: The Philosophical Quarrel," in *The Rousseauian Mind*, ed. Eve Grace and Christopher Kelly (New York: Routledge, forthcoming).

7. I have argued elsewhere that the challenge presented by Rousseau's thought played an important and underappreciated role in shaping Smith's outlook. Hume's writings, most of which were composed before Rousseau's rise to prominence, show no such impact, which may be one reason why his view of commercial society is so much more categorically positive than Smith's. See Dennis C. Rasmussen, *The Problems and Promise of Commercial Society: Adam Smith's Response to Rousseau* (University Park: Pennsylvania State University Press, 2008).

8. See Arthur M. Melzer, "The Origin of the Counter-Enlightenment: Rousseau and the New Religion of Sincerity," *American Political Science Review* 90.2 (June 1996): 344–60.

9. See Rousseau, *Confessions*, 527.

10. Jean-Jacques Rousseau to the Comtesse de Boufflers, 20 August 1762, in *Correspondance complète de Jean-Jacques Rousseau*, ed. R. A. Leigh, vol. 12 (Geneva: Institut et Musée Voltaire, 1967), 217–18.

11. David Hume to the Comtesse de Boufflers, 22 January 1763, in HL I, 373.

12. David Hume to Hugh Blair, 28 December 1765, in HL I, 529–30.

13. This statement was related after the fact by André Morellet: see *Mémoires de l'abbé Morellet*, vol. 1 (Paris: Librarie Française de Ladvocat, 1821), 105.

14. Jean-Jacques Rousseau to David Hume, 10 July 1766, in *Correspondance complète de Jean-Jacques Rousseau*, ed. R. A. Leigh, vol. 30 (Oxford: Voltaire Foundation, 1977), 44, and HL II, 399.

15. Jean-Jacques Rousseau to David Hume, 10 July 1766, in *Correspondance complète de Jean-Jacques Rousseau*, 30:30–31, and HL II, 386.

16. Quoted in Mossner, 523.

17. David Hume to Adam Smith, ?end of January 1766, in HL II, 6, and CAS, 110.

18. David Hume to the Marquise de Barbentane, 16 February 1766, in HL II, 14; see also David Hume to Hugh Blair, 11 February 1766, in HL II, 13.

19. David Hume to Hugh Blair, 25 March 1766, in HL II, 29; Leo Damrosch, *Jean-Jacques Rousseau: Restless Genius* (Boston: Houghton Mifflin, 2005), 408.

20. Hume used this exact phrase in three different letters written on the same day: David Hume to Hugh Blair, 15 July 1766, in HL II, 63; David Hume to William Strahan, 15 July 1766, in HL II, 63; and David Hume to William Strahan, 15 July 1766, in NHL, 142.

21. David Hume to Jean-Charles Trudaine de Montigny, 12 August 1766, in HL II, 81.

22. David Hume to Richard Davenport, 8 July 1766, in NHL, 135.

23. See the editors' introduction in NHL, xv n. 2.

24. David Hume to Mme la Présidente de Meinières, 25 July 1766, in NHL, 150.

25. David Hume to the Comtesse de Boufflers, 12 August 1766, in HL II, 77.

26. Adam Smith to David Hume, 6 July 1766, in CAS, 112–13.

27. J. Y. T. Greig, *David Hume* (New York: Garland, [1931] 1983), 344.

28. For Hume's letter, see David Hume to Jean le Rond d'Alembert, 15 July 1766, in NHL, 136–41.

29. See Jean le Rond d'Alembert to David Hume, 21 July 1766, in HL II, 413.

30. Jean le Rond d'Alembert to David Hume, 21 July 1766, in HL II, 415.

31. See Rae, 209.

32. Comtesse de Boufflers to David Hume, 25 July 1766, in *Letters of Eminent Persons Addressed to David Hume*, ed. John Hill Burton (Edinburgh: William Blackwood and Sons, 1849), 245.

33. Andrew Millar to David Hume, 22 November 1766, in *Correspondance complète de Jean-Jacques Rousseau*, ed. R. A. Leigh et al., vol. 31 (Oxford: Voltaire Foundation, 1967), 199.

34. David Hume to Adam Smith, 9 September 1766, in HL II, 82–83, and CAS, 118. This letter is dated August 1766 in both of these volumes, but R. A. Leigh conjectures that the correct date is 9 September: see FHL, 259.

35. On the relationship between Hume's original manuscript and the published French and English versions of the pamphlet, see Paul H. Meyer, "The Manuscript of Hume's Account of His Dispute with Rousseau," *Comparative Literature* 4.4 (Autumn 1952): 341–50.

36. David Hume to Horace Walpole, 20 November 1766, in HL II, 108; see also David Hume to John Crawford, 20 December 1766, in NHL, 156.

37. See David Hume to Hugh Blair, 20 May 1767, in HL II, 135.

38. David Hume to Richard Davenport, 15 May 1767, in NHL, 164.

39. Adam Smith to David Hume, 7 June 1767, in CAS, 125.

40. Adam Smith to David Hume, 13 September 1767, in CAS, 132.

41. David Hume to Adam Smith, 8 October 1767, in NHL, 176, and CAS, 133; see also David Hume to Adam Smith, 17 October 1767, in HL II, 168–69, and CAS, 136–37. Hume frequently calls Rousseau a "wild philosopher" in his

correspondence, though he seems to have borrowed the label from Richard Davenport, the owner of the house at Wootton where Rousseau stayed.

42. David Hume to Adam Smith, 17 October 1767, in HL II, 168–69, and CAS, 136–37.

43. There are a few oblique references to the quarrel, however, in one of Rousseau's other posthumous autobiographical works: see Jean-Jacques Rousseau, *Rousseau, Judge of Jean-Jacques: Dialogues*, in *The Collected Writings of Rousseau*, vol. 1, ed. Roger D. Masters and Christopher Kelly (Hanover, NH: University Press of New England, 1990), 62, 91–95, 205, 232.

44. Zaretsky and Scott, *Philosophers' Quarrel*, 206.

45. Adam Smith to David Hume, 6 July 1766, in CAS, 113.

CHAPTER 8: MORTALLY SICK AT SEA

1. MOL, xxxix.

2. David Hume to the Comtesse de Boufflers, 2 February 1767, in HL II, 119.

3. David Hume to the Marquise de Barbentane, 13 March 1767, in HL II, 128.

4. David Hume to Hugh Blair, 1 April 1767, in HL II, 134.

5. David Hume to Adam Ferguson, 24 February 1767, in HL II, 121.

6. Lady Mary Coke, *The Letters and Journals of Lady Mary Coke*, vol. 1 (Bath: Kingsmead Bookshops, [1889] 1970), 141.

7. Adam Smith to Andreas Holt, 26 October 1780, in CAS, 252.

8. Adam Smith to Lord Hailes, 15 January 1769, in CAS, 140.

9. Adam Smith to William Pulteney, 3 September 1772, in CAS, 164.

10. See Charles Rogers, *Social Life in Scotland: From Early to Recent Times*, vol. 3 (Edinburgh: William Paterson, 1886), 180–81.

11. Adam Smith to David Hume, 7 June 1767, in CAS, 125.

12. David Hume to Adam Smith, 13 June 1767, in HL II, 142–43, and CAS, 126–27.

13. Adam Smith to David Hume, 13 September 1767, in CAS, 131. On the appropriateness of Smith's sympathy here, see TMS I.i.2.5, 15: "We are not half so anxious that our friends should adopt our friendships, as that they should enter into our resentments." This is the case, Smith explains, because "the bitter and painful" feeling of resentment can be alleviated by "the healing consolation of sympathy."

14. David Hume to Adam Smith, ?end of September 1767, in HL II, 163, and CAS, 133.

15. See David Hume to the Earl of Balcarres, 17 December 1754, in HL I, 214; and David Hume to James Oswald of Dunnikier, October 1766, in HL II, 95.

16. David Hume to Adam Smith, 20 August 1769, in HL II, 206–7, and CAS, 155–56.

17. David Hume to Adam Smith, 6 February 1770, in HL II, 214, and CAS, 156; David Hume to Adam Smith, February 1770, in HL II, 217, and CAS, 158; David Hume to Adam Smith, 3 June 1772, in HL II, 338, and CAS, 327;

David Hume to Adam Smith, 27 June 1772, in HL II, 264, and CAS, 163; David Hume to Adam Smith, 23 November 1772, in HL II, 267, and CAS, 166; David Hume to Adam Smith, 24 February 1773, in HL II, 277, and CAS, 167; and David Hume to Adam Smith, 10 April 1773, in HL II, 281, and CAS, 168.

18. David Hume to Adam Smith, 28 January 1772, in HL II, 256, and CAS, 160.

19. David Hume to Gilbert Elliot of Minto, 16 October 1769, in HL II, 208.

20. Henry Mackenzie, *Anecdotes and Egotisms, 1745–1831*, ed. Harold William Thompson (Oxford: Oxford University Press, 1927), 172.

21. David Hume to Gilbert Elliot of Minto, 16 October 1769, in HL II, 208.

22. Alexander Carlyle, *Autobiography of the Rev. Dr Alexander Carlyle, Minister of Inveresk, Containing Memorials of the Men and Events of His Time*, 2nd ed. (Edinburgh: William Blackwood, 1860), 275.

23. David Hume to Gilbert Elliot of Minto, 16 October 1769, in HL II, 208.

24. The classic work on the construction of the New Town is A. J. Youngson, *The Making of Classical Edinburgh, 1750–1840* (Edinburgh: Edinburgh University Press, 1969).

25. David Hume to Col. Alexander Dow, 1772, in HL II, 267.

26. William Mure, *Selections from the Family Papers Preserved at Caldwell*, pt. 2, vol. 2 (Glasgow: Maitland Club, 1854), 177–78.

27. John Hill Burton, *Life and Correspondence of David Hume*, vol. 2 (Edinburgh: William Tait, 1846), 436; see also Mossner, 566–67, 620.

28. Benjamin Franklin to William Strahan, 27 October 1771, in *The Papers of Benjamin Franklin*, ed. William B. Willcox, vol. 18 (New Haven, CT: Yale University Press, 1974), 236.

29. David Hume to Benjamin Franklin, 7 February 1772, in NHL, 193–94.

30. David Hume to Adam Smith, ?end of January 1766, in HL II, 6, and CAS, 110.

31. Andrew Millar to David Hume, 22 November 1766, in *Correspondance complète de Jean-Jacques Rousseau*, ed. R. A. Leigh et al., vol. 31 (Oxford: Voltaire Foundation, 1967), 199.

32. *New Evening Post*, 6 December 1776, quoted in Mossner, 556.

33. David Hume to William Strahan, 2 January 1772, in HL II, 252; see also David Hume to William Strahan, 8 June 1776, in HL II, 322.

34. David Hume to William Strahan, 21 January 1771, in HL II, 233.

35. David Hume to Adam Smith, 27 June 1772, in HL II, 263–64, and CAS, 162–63. For Hume's further comments to Smith on the Ayr Bank crisis, see David Hume to Adam Smith, October 1772, in HL II, 265–66, and CAS, 165; and David Hume to Adam Smith, 10 April 1773, in HL II, 280, and CAS, 167.

36. WN II.ii.77, 317; see also more generally II.ii.73–77, 313–17.

37. David Hume to Adam Smith, 17 November 1772, in CAS, 415. This letter does not appear in any of the collections of Hume's writings at present. For discussion of the letter's discovery and the reasons to believe it was addressed to Smith, see Toshihiro Tanaka, "Hume to Smith: An Unpublished Letter," *Hume Studies* 12.2 (November 1986): 201–9.

38. David Hume to Adam Smith, 23 November 1772, in HL II, 266, and CAS, 166.
39. David Hume to Adam Smith, 10 April 1773, in HL II, 281, and CAS, 168.
40. Adam Smith to David Hume, 16 April 1773, in CAS, 168.
41. James Boswell, *Boswell: The Ominous Years, 1774–1776*, ed. Charles Ryskamp and Frederick A. Pottle (New York: McGraw-Hill, 1963), 337.
42. Amicus, "Anecdotes Tending to Throw Light on the Character and Opinions of the Late Adam Smith, LLD," *The Bee, or Literary Weekly Intelligencer* (Edinburgh), 11 May 1791, 2–3.
43. James Boswell, *Boswell: Laird of Auchinleck, 1778–1782*, ed. Joseph W. Reed and Frederick A. Pottle (New York: McGraw-Hill, 1977), 298.
44. See Thomas D. Eliot, "The Relations between Adam Smith and Benjamin Franklin before 1776," *Political Science Quarterly* 39.1 (March 1924): 67–96; and Jacob Viner, "Guide to John Rae's *Life of Adam Smith*," in Rae, 44–47.
45. David Hume to Adam Smith, 13 February 1774, in HL II, 285, and CAS, 171.
46. Adam Smith to David Hume, 9 May 1775, in CAS, 181.
47. See, for example, Adam Ferguson to Adam Smith, 2 September 1773, in CAS, 169; and Adam Ferguson to Adam Smith, 11 March 1774, in CAS, 172.
48. David Hume to Adam Smith, 13 February 1774, in HL II, 286, and CAS, 171; see also David Hume to William Strahan, 1 March 1774, in HL II, 287.
49. TMS III.3.43, 156.
50. David Hume to Adam Smith, 13 February 1774, in HL II, 286, and CAS, 171.
51. Adam Smith to David Hume, 9 May 1775, in CAS, 181–82.
52. Adam Smith to David Hume, 9 May 1775, in CAS, 182.
53. David Hume to Adam Smith, 8 February 1776, in HL II, 308, and CAS, 185–86.
54. David Hume to Adam Smith, 8 February 1776, in HL II, 308, and CAS, 185–86.

CHAPTER 9: INQUIRING INTO THE WEALTH OF NATIONS

1. Stewart, 311.
2. Henry Thomas Buckle, *History of Civilization in England*, 2nd ed., vol. 1 (London: John W. Parker and Son, 1858), 194.
3. Phillipson, 237; Robert Wokler, "The Enlightenment Science of Politics," in *Inventing Human Science*, ed. Christopher Fox, Roy Porter, and Robert Wokler (Berkeley: University of California Press, 1995), 336; Emma Rothschild and Amartya Sen, "Adam Smith's Economics," in *The Cambridge Companion to Adam Smith*, ed. Knud Haakonssen (Cambridge: Cambridge University Press, 2006), 364; and Richard F. Teichgraeber III, *"Free Trade" and Moral Philosophy: Rethinking the Sources of Adam Smith's Wealth of Nations* (Durham, NC: Duke University Press, 1986), xi.
4. Timothy Ferris, *The Science of Liberty* (New York: HarperCollins, 2010), 174.
5. Economics did not yet exist as a separate discipline in the eighteenth century, but it is clear that Smith regarded *The Wealth of Nations* as a work in political

economy, as he equates the study of "the nature and causes of the wealth of nations" with "what is properly called Political Oeconomy": see WN IV.ix.38, 678–79.

6. As with the relationship between Hume's and Smith's moral theories, a comprehensive comparative study of their views of politics, commerce, and economics is much to be desired.

7. See WN I.xi.m.6, 247; II.ii.96, 325; II.iv.9, 354; III.iv.4, 412; IV.i.30, 445; and V.i.g.3–6, 790–91.

8. WN II.iv.9, 354. On the similarities between Hume's and Smith's views on interest rates, and the extent to which Hume influenced Smith on this score, see W. L. Taylor, *Francis Hutcheson and David Hume as Predecessors of Adam Smith* (Durham, NC: Duke University Press, 1965), 90–102; and Carl C. Wennerlind, "The Humean Paternity to Adam Smith's Theory of Money," *History of Economic Ideas* 8.1 (Spring 2000): 92–94.

9. Stewart, 320–21.

10. Stephen Buckle, "Hume and Smith on Justice," in *The Routledge Companion to Social and Political Philosophy*, ed. Gerald F. Gaus and Fred D'Agostino (New York: Routledge, 2013), 93.

11. Ernest Campbell Mossner, "An Apology for David Hume, Historian," *PMLA* 56.3 (September 1941): 679. For Smith's citations of *The History of England*, see WN I.xi.m.6, 247; III.iv.4, 412 (which may refer to the *Political Discourses*, as well); IV.i.30, 445; and V.i.g.3–6, 790–91.

12. Hume in fact never uses the term "the division of labor" anywhere in his corpus. For the closest he comes to addressing this idea, see his very brief discussions of "the partition of employments" at THN 3.2.2.3, 312; and 3.2.4.1, 330. On this topic, Smith's main inspirations seem to have been Francis Hutcheson and Bernard Mandeville: see Taylor, *Francis Hutcheson and David Hume*, 55–62.

13. Jacob Viner, "Guide to John Rae's *Life of Adam Smith*," in Rae, 54.

14. WN III.iv.4, 412. I have argued for the importance of this passage in Dennis C. Rasmussen, *The Problems and Promise of Commercial Society: Adam Smith's Response to Rousseau* (University Park: Pennsylvania State University Press, 2008), esp. 136–37, but also chap. 4 more generally; and Dennis C. Rasmussen, *The Pragmatic Enlightenment: Recovering the Liberalism of Hume, Smith, Montesquieu, and Voltaire* (Cambridge: Cambridge University Press, 2014), 120.

15. WN III.iv.4, 412.

16. WN III.ii.3, 383; see also III.iv.7, 415.

17. See WN III.ii.8, 386–87; see also LJ, 48, 53–55, and 255.

18. WN III.iv.10, 418–19.

19. WN III.iv.15, 421.

20. See WN I.v.3, 48; III.iv.11–12, 419–20; and V.i.b.7, 712.

21. See EMPL, 277; HE II, 108–9, 522–24; HE III, 76–77, 80; and esp. HE IV, 383–85.

22. HE IV, 384. A leading authority on Hume's *History* comments, "That the barons are the chief villains of Hume's *History* is no secret." Andrew Sabl, *Hume's*

Politics: Coordination and Crisis in the History of England (Princeton, NJ: Princeton University Press, 2012), 66.

23. HE IV, 385; WN III.iv.17, 422.

24. See WN V.i.g.22–25, 800–804; V.iii.1–3, 907–9; LJ, 227; and LRBL, 150.

25. See William Robertson, *The History of the Reign of the Emperor Charles V*, vol. 1 (London: W. Strahan and T. Cadell, 1769), 30–39; and John Millar, *The Origin of the Distinction of Ranks*, ed. Aaron Garrett (Indianapolis: Liberty Fund, [1771] 2006), 236–39.

26. The story about the fall of the feudal lords is recounted a number of times throughout both reports in LJ.

27. W. R. Scott suggests that Book 3 of *The Wealth of Nations* may have originated in Smith's public lectures in Edinburgh in 1748–50. See William Robert Scott, *Adam Smith as Student and Professor* (New York: Augustus M. Kelley, [1937] 1965), 56; and see also the note by the Glasgow editors of *The Wealth of Nations* regarding the passage quoted above: WN, 412n6. If this is indeed the case, then it is possible that it was Hume who drew on Smith here, in his *Political Discourses* (1752) and the relevant volumes of *The History of England* (1759–61), rather than vice versa, but this question seems impossible to resolve at this point. Smith's fulsome tribute to Hume in *The Wealth of Nations* (quoted in the text) leads me to assume that, as in so many cases, it was Hume who got there first. Note also that in illustrating the "hospitality" of the feudal lords Smith employs examples drawn from Hume: compare WN III.iv.5, 413 and LJ, 51, 261, 420 with HE I, 307 and HE II, 428.

28. As for the other "system of political economy" that Smith criticizes in Book 4, that of the Physiocrats, Hume was even harsher toward them than Smith was. In a letter to the abbé Morellet, whose *Dictionnaire du Commerce* was expected to appear soon, Hume expresses his hope that Morellet "will thunder them, and crush them, and pound them, and reduce them to dust and ashes," opining that "they are, indeed, the set of men the most chimerical and most arrogant that now exist, since the annihilation of the Sorbonne." He also promises to hand-deliver a copy of Morellet's book to Smith, although in the end the book was never even published. David Hume to the abbé Morellet, 10 July 1769, in HL II, 205.

29. WN IV.iii.c.9, 493.

30. WN IV.iii.a.1, 474.

31. EMPL, 328, 331.

32. WN IV.i.17, 438.

33. EMPL, 281.

34. Taylor, *Francis Hutcheson and David Hume*, 77.

35. See, for instance, HE II, 177; HE III, 77–79, 330, 462; HE IV, 48, 145, 344–45, 360–61; and HE V, 20, 114, 144, 231.

36. See David R. Raynor, "Who Invented the Invisible Hand? Hume's Praise of Laissez-Faire in a Newly Discovered Pamphlet," *Times Literary Supplement*,

14 August 1998, 22. For Smith's case against the corn laws, see esp. WN IV.v.b, 524–43.

37. See esp. WN IV.ix.51, 687–88; EMPL, 37; and THN 3.2.7.8, 345. The fact that Smith was not an absolutist about free trade is now widely appreciated among Smith scholars. The classic essay on his "departures" from a strict laissez-faire outlook is Jacob Viner, "Adam Smith and Laissez Faire," *Journal of Political Economy* 35.2 (April 1927): 198–232.

38. See Stewart, 321–22.

39. John Playfair to William Robertson, Jr., 12 December 1777, National Library of Scotland, Robertson Macdonald Papers, MS 3943, fol. 52.

40. EMPL, 271.

41. Duncan Forbes, *Hume's Philosophical Politics* (Cambridge: Cambridge University Press, 1975), 87–88.

42. EMPL, 529, 350–51, 360–61; see also 95–96; and HE II, 454.

43. See WN IV.vii, 556–641; and V.iii.92, 947.

44. WN V.iii.10, 911.

45. For a discussion of Smith's views on public debt that highlights a number of parallels with Hume, see Donald Winch, *Adam Smith's Politics: An Essay in Historiographic Revision* (Cambridge: Cambridge University Press, 1978), chap. 6.

46. The literature on this topic is vast, but for a few overviews see Lisa Hill, "Adam Smith and the Theme of Corruption," *Review of Politics* 68.4 (November 2006): 636–62; Ryan Patrick Hanley, *Adam Smith and the Character of Virtue* (Cambridge: Cambridge University Press, 2009), chap. 1; Rasmussen, *Problems and Promise of Commercial Society*, chap. 2; and Spiros Tegos, "Adam Smith: Theorist of Corruption," in *The Oxford Handbook of Adam Smith*, ed. Christopher J. Berry, Maria Pia Paganelli, and Craig Smith (Oxford: Oxford University Press, 2013), 353–71.

47. See, for instance, TMS I.iii.2.1, 50–51; III.3.30–31, 149–50; and IV.1.8–9, 181–83.

48. EMPL, 270.

49. TMS III.3.30, 149; WN I.v.2, 47; I.v.7, 50.

50. TMS I.iii.2.1, 51.

51. WN II.iii.31, 343.

52. Smith himself calls it a deception: see TMS IV.1.10, 183.

53. Nathan Rosenberg, "Adam Smith and Laissez-Faire Revisited," in *Adam Smith and Modern Political Economy: Bicentennial Essays on* The Wealth of Nations, ed. Gerald P. O'Driscoll, Jr. (Ames: Iowa State University Press, 1979), 21.

54. WN IV.iii.c.9–10, 493–94; IV.viii.17, 648.

55. EMPL, 300.

56. Margaret Schabas, "Hume on Economic Well-Being," in *The Continuum Companion to Hume*, ed. Alan Bailey and Dan O'Brien (London: Bloomsbury, 2012), 338.

57. WN V.i.f.50, 782.

58. See EMPL, 271, 274.

59. WN V.i.f.50, 782.

60. See WN V.i.f.52–57, 784–86.

61. I have explored this aspect of Smith's thought in Dennis C. Rasmussen, "Adam Smith on What Is Wrong with Economic Inequality," *American Political Science Review* 110.2 (May 2016): 342–52.

62. WN V.i.b.2, 709–10.

63. LJ, 563–64; see also 339–41, 489–90.

64. See esp. TMS I.iii.2, 50–61.

65. TMS I.iii.3.2–6, 62–63.

66. TMS I.iii.3.1, 61.

67. See, for instance, EMPL, 265–66; and EPM 3.25–28, 20–21.

68. John Ruskin, *Fors Clavigera*, in *The Complete Works of John Ruskin*, ed. E. T. Cook and Alexander Wedderburn, vol. 28 (London: George Allen, [1876] 1907), 516, 764.

69. See WN V.i.f.28, 770; and V.i.f.31, 772.

70. See WN V.i.g.2–6, 790–91; and V.i.g.39, 811. This point is noted by Peter Minowitz, *Profits, Priests, and Princes: Adam Smith's Emancipation of Economics from Politics and Religion* (Stanford, CA: Stanford University Press, 1993), 156. I would not, however, go so far as to say, as Minowitz does, that "*The Wealth of Nations* is an atheistic and anti-Christian work." Ibid., 139.

71. WN V.i.f.30, 771.

72. WN V.iii.89, 944.

73. WN V.i.g.24, 802–3.

74. WN V.i.g.37, 810. For whatever reason, in his jurisprudence lectures Smith was far more willing to credit the clergy with playing a beneficial role: see esp. LJ, 90, 146, 173, 175, 188–89, 191, 441, 449, and 454–55.

75. HE I, 311, 163; see also 208; and EMPL, 520.

76. HE III, 134–36.

77. Annette C. Baier, *Death and Character: Further Reflections on Hume* (Cambridge, MA: Harvard University Press, 2008), 92.

78. Smith's explicit response to Hume on this score has received surprisingly little scholarly attention. For one helpful discussion, see Frederick G. Whelan, "Church Establishments, Liberty & Competition in Religion," *Polity* 23.2 (Winter 1990): 155–85.

79. WN V.i.g.1, 788.

80. See WN V.i.g.3–6, 790–91.

81. WN V.i.g.1, 789.

82. WN V.i.g.8, 792–93.

83. WN V.i.g.12–15, 796.

84. WN V.i.g.8, 793.

85. See Richard B. Sher, *Church and University in the Scottish Enlightenment: The Moderate Literati of Edinburgh* (Edinburgh: Edinburgh University Press, 1985), 262–76.

86. David Hume to William Strahan, 11 March 1771, in HL II, 237. A few years earlier Hume had declared, "O! how I long to see America . . . revolted totally & finally," but this declaration seems to have been fairly tongue-in-cheek. See David Hume to Gilbert Elliot of Minto, 22 July 1768, in HL II, 184.

87. David Hume to William Strahan, 26 October 1775, in HL II, 300–301.

88. William Strahan to David Hume, 30 October 1775, in HL II, 301n1.

89. David Hume to William Mure of Caldwell, 27 October 1775, in HL II, 303.

90. David Hume to Andrew Stuart of Torrance, 1 August 1775, in Maurice Baum-stark, "The End of Empire and the Death of Religion: A Reconsideration of Hume's Later Political Thought," in *Philosophy and Religion in Enlightenment Britain*, ed. Ruth Savage (Oxford: Oxford University Press, 2012), 257.

91. WN IV.vii.c.65, 616.

92. WN IV.vii.c.66. 616–17.

93. WN IV.vii.c.79, 625–26. See also Adam Smith, "Thoughts on the State of the Contest with America, February 1778," in CAS, 381–82.

94. WN V.iii.92, 946–47.

95. One of these letters, we saw, did discuss the American conflict, but it was sent by Hume only a month before *The Wealth of Nations* was published and did not go into much detail. Hume writes, "The Duke of Bucleugh tells me, that you are very zealous in American Affairs. My Notion is, that the Matter is not so important as is commonly imagind. If I be mistaken, I shall probably correct my Error, when I see you or read you. Our Navigation and general Commerce may suffer more than our Manufactures." David Hume to Adam Smith, 8 February 1776, in HL II, 308, and CAS, 186.

96. See the editor's preface in Adam Smith, *An Inquiry into the Nature and Causes of the Wealth of Nations*, ed. James E. Thorold Rogers (Oxford: Clarendon, 1869), xix. The available evidence suggests that Hume's copy of *The Wealth of Nations* was bequeathed to his nephew of the same name (who apparently added "a vast of Manuscript Notes" to the book) and was then eventually sold, in the early 1850s, by an Edinburgh bookseller named Thomas G. Stevenson. Soon thereafter it was owned by Charles Babbage, whose library was sold off in 1872, but I have been unable to trace the book's whereabouts beyond this point. The Crawford Library of the Royal Observatory of Edinburgh, which houses much of Babbage's library, does not appear to have the book in its collection. See Rae, 286; David Fate Norton and Mary J. Norton, *The David Hume Library* (Edinburgh: Edinburgh Bibliographical Society, 1996), 51, 129; and James Bonar, *A Catalogue of the Library of Adam Smith*, 2nd ed. (New York: Augustus M. Kelley, 1966), 174.

97. David Hume to Adam Smith, 1 April 1776, in HL II, 311, and CAS, 186. In a letter to William Strahan written a week later, Hume declares that "Dr Smith's Performance is another excellent Work that has come from your Press this Winter; but I have ventured to tell him, that it requires too much thought to be as popular as Mr Gibbon's"—that is, the first volume of Edward Gibbon's

History of the Decline and Fall of the Roman Empire, which was published less than a month before *The Wealth of Nations*. David Hume to William Strahan, 8 April 1776, in HL II, 314.

98. David Hume to Adam Smith, 1 April 1776, in HL II, 311, and CAS, 186.

99. See WN I.vi.8, 67; and David Ricardo, *On the Principles of Political Economy and Taxation*, in *The Works and Correspondence of David Ricardo*, ed. Piero Sraffa and M. H. Dobb, vol. 1 (Indianapolis: Liberty Fund, [1812] 2005), chap. 24.

100. Hume writes, "it appears to me impossible, that the King of France can take a Seigniorage of 8 per cent upon the Coinage. No body would bring Bullion to the mint: It woud be all sent to Holland or England, where it might be coined and sent back to France for less than two per cent." David Hume to Adam Smith, 1 April 1776, in HL II, 311–12, and CAS, 186–87. For Smith's statements about the markup, see WN I.v.39, 62; IV.iii.a.10, 478; and IV.vi.19, 551.

101. James Boswell, *Boswell in Extremes, 1776–1778*, ed. Charles McC. Weis and Frederick A. Pottle (New York: McGraw-Hill, 1970), 13.

102. David Hume to Adam Smith, 3 May 1776, in HL II, 317, and CAS, 195.

103. David Hume to David Hume the Younger, 20 May 1776, in Tadeusz Kozanecki, "Dawida Hume's Nieznane Listy W Zbiorach Muzeum Czartoryskich (Polska)," *Archiwum Historii Filozofii I Mysli Spoleczhej* 9 (1963): 138.

104. David Hume to Adam Smith, 1 April 1776, in HL II, 312, and CAS, 187. For Hume's letter to Gibbon, see David Hume to Edward Gibbon, 18 March 1776, in HL II, 309–10.

105. Edward Gibbon, *Memoirs of My Life*, ed. Georges A. Bonnard (London: Thomas Nelson and Sons, [1796] 1966), 158.

106. David Hume to Adam Smith, 1 April 1776, in HL II, 312, and CAS, 187.

107. Edward Gibbon to Adam Ferguson, 1 April 1776, in *The Letters of Edward Gibbon*, ed. Jane Elizabeth Norton, vol. 2 (London: Cassell & Co., 1956), 100–101.

108. Adam Ferguson to Adam Smith, 18 April 1776, in CAS, 193–94.

109. Adam Smith to Andreas Holt, 26 October 1780, in CAS, 251.

110. See Richard B. Sher, "New Light on the Publication and Reception of the *Wealth of Nations*," *Adam Smith Review* 1 (2004): 3–29.

111. Hugh Blair to Adam Smith, 3 April 1776, in CAS, 188–90.

112. William Robertson to Adam Smith, 8 April 1776, in CAS, 192–93.

113. Adam Ferguson to Adam Smith, 18 April 1776, in CAS, 193–94.

114. Joseph Black to Adam Smith, April 1776, in CAS, 190.

CHAPTER 10: DIALOGUING ABOUT NATURAL RELIGION

1. Phillipson, 244, 242.

2. Ross, 319, 445; see also 359–60.

3. Ryan Patrick Hanley, "Skepticism and Imagination: Smith's Response to Hume's *Dialogues*," in *New Essays on Adam Smith's Moral Philosophy*, ed. Wade L. Robison

and David B. Suits (Rochester, NY: Rochester Institute of Technology Press, 2012), 173.

4. Gavin Kennedy, *Adam Smith's Lost Legacy* (New York: Palgrave Macmillan, 2005), 9–10.

5. See M. A. Stewart, "The Dating of Hume's Manuscripts," in *The Scottish Enlightenment: Essays in Reinterpretation*, ed. Paul Wood (Rochester, NY: University of Rochester Press, 2000), esp. 291, 300–303.

6. See David Hume to Gilbert Elliot of Minto, 10 March 1751, in HL I, 153–57; David Hume to Gilbert Elliot of Minto, 12 March 1763, in NHL, 71; and David Hume to Hugh Blair, 6 October 1763, in NHL, 72.

7. See David Hume to Adam Smith, 15 August 1776, in HL II, 334, and CAS, 205.

8. See esp. EHU 12.28–29, 122. For an argument that the shortcomings of the first cause argument were implicit in the *Treatise*, see Paul Russell, *The Riddle of Hume's Treatise: Skepticism, Naturalism, and Irreligion* (Oxford: Oxford University Press, 2008), chap. 10.

9. See esp. EHU 8.36, 77–78; and 11.17, 104–5.

10. See Hume's opening statement that "the whole frame of nature bespeaks an intelligent author; and no rational enquirer can, after serious reflection, suspend his belief a moment with regard to the primary principles of genuine Theism and Religion"—a statement that some scholars have, rather inexplicably, taken at face value: NHR intro.1, 34.

11. See HL II, 317n1.

12. David Hume to Adam Smith, 3 May 1776, in HL II, 317–18, and CAS, 195–96.

13. David Hume to Adam Smith, 3 May 1776, in HL II, 316, and CAS, 194–95.

14. James Boswell, *The Life of Samuel Johnson*, ed. David Womersley (New York: Penguin, [1791] 2008), 145.

15. David Hume to Adam Smith, 3 May 1776, in HL II, 316, and CAS, 195.

16. Adam Smith to David Hume, 16 June 1776, in CAS, 201–2. On whether this letter reached Hume, see Adam Smith to William Strahan, 6 July 1776, in CAS, 202.

17. See David Hume to William Strahan, 8 June 1776, in HL II, 323–24.

18. See HL II, 453.

19. David Hume to William Strahan, 12 June 1776, in HL II, 325–26.

20. David Hume to Adam Smith, 15 August 1776, in HL II, 334, and CAS, 205.

21. Adam Smith to David Hume, 22 August 1776, in CAS, 206.

22. See David Hume to Adam Smith, 23 August 1776, in HL II, 335–36, and CAS, 208.

23. Adam Smith to William Strahan, 5 September 1776, in CAS, 211.

24. Adam Smith to William Strahan, October 1776, in CAS, 216; and Adam Smith to William Strahan, October 1776, in CAS, 216–17.

25. William Strahan to Adam Smith, 16 September 1776, in CAS, 212.

26. William Strahan to John Home of Ninewells, 3 March 1777, in *Letters of David Hume to William Strahan*, ed. G. Birkbeck Hill (Oxford: Clarendon, 1888), 362.

27. See, for example, Ross, 423; Phillipson, 246; and Harris, 445. These scholars appear to base this claim almost entirely on a single letter from Hugh Blair, written just months after the book's release, in which he expresses surprise that the *Dialogues* had "made so little noise." See Hugh Blair to William Strahan, 3 August 1779, in HL II, 454.

28. *Critical Review*, vol. 48 (September 1779), in Fieser VI, 204.

29. *London Magazine*, vol. 48 (September 1779), in Fieser VI, 206.

30. *Monthly Review*, vol. 61 (November 1779), in Fieser VI, 209, 221.

31. See Fieser VI, 230.

32. *Zugabe zu den Göttingischen gelehrten Anzeigen*, vol. 48 (27 November 1779), in Fieser VI, 229.

33. James Boswell, *Boswell: Laird of Auchinleck, 1778–1782*, ed. Joseph W. Reed and Frederick A. Pottle (New York: McGraw-Hill, 1977), 173.

34. David Hume to Adam Smith, 3 May 1776, in HL II, 317, and CAS, 195.

35. David Hume to Adam Smith, 23 August 1776, in HL II, 335–36, and CAS, 208.

36. LJ, 466–67; see also 63–64.

37. Alexander Broadie, *The Scottish Enlightenment: The Historical Age of the Historical Nation* (Edinburgh: Birlinn, 2001), 128; Terence Penelhum, *Hume* (London: Macmillan, 1975), 171; Isaiah Berlin, *The Age of Enlightenment: The 18th Century Philosophers* (New York: George Braziller, 1956), 163; Ernest C. Mossner, "Hume and the Legacy of the *Dialogues*," in *David Hume: Bicentenary Papers*, ed. G. P. Morice (Austin: University of Texas Press, 1977), 3; and Peter Gay, *The Enlightenment: An Interpretation*, vol. 1: *The Rise of Modern Paganism* (New York: Norton, 1966), 414.

38. See, for instance, T. D. Campbell and Ian Ross, "The Theory and Practice of the Wise and Virtuous Man: Reflections on Adam Smith's Response to Hume's Deathbed Wish," *Studies in Eighteenth-Century Culture* 11 (1982): 70–72; Karl Graf Ballestrem, "David Hume und Adam Smith: Zur philosophischen Dimension einer Freundschaft," in *Adam Smith als Moralphilosoph*, ed. Christel Fricke and Hans-Peter Schütt (Berlin: Walter de Gruyter, 2005), 344–45; Brendan Long, "Adam Smith's Theism," in *The Elgar Companion to Adam Smith*, ed. Jeffrey T. Young (Cheltenham: Edward Elgar, 2009), 81–82; Annette C. Baier, *The Pursuits of Philosophy: An Introduction to the Life and Thought of David Hume* (Cambridge, MA: Harvard University Press, 2011), 121; and Hanley, "Skepticism and Imagination."

39. Adam Smith to David Hume, 16 June 1776, in CAS, 201–2; Adam Smith to David Hume, 22 August 1776, in CAS, 206; Adam Smith to William Strahan, 5 September 1776, in CAS, 211.

40. See the duc de La Rochefoucauld to Adam Smith, 6 August 1779, in CAS, 238.

41. Anne Keith to Sir Robert Murray Keith, 6 November 1776, Public Record Office of Northern Ireland, D2433/D/1/25.

42. David Hume to Gilbert Elliot of Minto, 12 March 1763, in NHL, 71.

43. Hugh Blair to David Hume, 29 September 1763, in NHL, 73n4.
44. David Hume to Hugh Blair, 6 October 1763, in NHL, 72.
45. See Anne Keith to Sir Robert Murray Keith, 6 November 1776, Public Record Office of Northern Ireland, D2433/D/1/25.
46. David Hume to William Strahan, 8 June 1776, in HL II, 323.

CHAPTER II: A PHILOSOPHER'S DEATH

1. Samuel Jackson Pratt, *Supplement to the Life of David Hume* (1777), in Fieser IX, 312.
2. *Monthly Review*, vol. 56 (March 1777), in Fieser IX, 266–67.
3. David Hume to Adam Smith, 8 February 1776, in HL II, 308, and CAS, 186.
4. See Joseph Black to Adam Smith, April 1776, in CAS, 191. For a modern diagnosis see J. Wilkinson, "The Last Illness of David Hume," *Proceedings of the Royal College of Physicians of Edinburgh* 18.1 (January 1988): 72–79.
5. David Hume to Cochrane Stewart, 8 August 1751, in FHL, 99; MOL, xl.
6. MOL, xli.
7. MOL, xxxi.
8. Annette Baier suggests that Hume may not have deemed his friendships relevant for what was effectively a curriculum vitae. She also proposes that "maybe there were too many to list? Maybe he feared invidious omissions, were he to attempt any such list? Which of us would not?" Annette C. Baier, *Death and Character: Further Reflections on Hume* (Cambridge, MA: Harvard University Press, 2008), 273–74.
9. MOL, xxxiv–xxxviii.
10. MOL, xxxiv, xxxvi.
11. MOL, xxxiv, xli, xxxvi, xxxvii.
12. MOL, xxxvii.
13. MOL, xl.
14. Donald T. Siebert, *The Moral Animus of David Hume* (Newark: University of Delaware Press, 1990), 209.
15. MOL, xl–xli.
16. See John Home, "Diary of a Journey with Hume from Morpeth to Bath," in Fieser IX, 279.
17. Ibid., 280.
18. See Strahan, xliv.
19. See David Hume to John Home of Ninewells, 27 April 1776, in Sadao Ikeda, *David Hume and the Eighteenth Century British Thought: An Annotated Catalogue* (Tokyo: Chuo University Library, 1986), 193.
20. David Hume to Adam Smith, 3 May 1776, in HL II, 316–18, and CAS, 195–96.
21. David Hume to Andrew Stuart of Torrance, 20 May 1776, in FHL, 93.
22. Alexander Wedderburn to Adam Smith, 6 June 1776, in CAS, 198.

23. David Hume to William Strahan, 8 June 1776, in HL II, 322; William Strahan to Adam Smith, 10 June 1776, in CAS, 199.

24. Adam Smith to David Hume, 16 June 1776, in CAS, 201.

25. Adam Smith to William Strahan, 6 July 1776, in CAS, 202.

26. See Henry, Lord Brougham, *Lives of Men of Letters and Science, Who Flourished in the Time of George III* (London: Charles Knight, 1845), 233.

27. James Boswell, *Boswell in Extremes, 1776–1778*, ed. Charles McC. Weis and Frederick A. Pottle (New York: McGraw-Hill, 1970), 11–13.

28. See ibid., 22, 25.

29. William Johnson Temple to James Boswell, 25 June 1776, in *The Correspondence of James Boswell and William Johnson Temple, 1756–1795, Volume 1: 1756–1777*, ed. Thomas Crawford (New Haven, CT: Yale University Press, 1997), 418.

30. William Johnson Temple to James Boswell, 25 August 1776, in *Correspondence of James Boswell and William Johnson Temple*, 422.

31. William Johnson Temple to James Boswell, 27 May 1768, in *Correspondence of James Boswell and William Johnson Temple*, 238.

32. William Strahan to David Hume, 19 August 1776, in HL II, 325–26n2.

33. See John Home of Ninewells to William Strahan, 17 February 1777, in *Letters of David Hume to William Strahan*, ed. G. Birkbeck Hill (Oxford: Clarendon, 1888), 359.

34. See David Hume to John Home of Ninewells, 25 July 1776, in Ikeda, *David Hume and the Eighteenth Century British Thought*, 219.

35. David Hume to John Home, 16 July 1776, in Gerhard Streminger, "David Hume and John Home: Two New Letters," *Hume Studies* 10.1 (April 1984):81.

36. Adam Smith to Alexander Wedderburn, 14 August 1776, in CAS, 203.

37. One of Hume's correspondents in fact suggests that Lucian was his "favorite author": see the abbé Morellet to David Hume, 8 September 1766, in HL II, 157–58n1. Smith, for his part, proclaimed to his students that "in a word there is no author from whom more reall instruction and good sense can be found than Lucian." Just over a week later he informed them that Lucian's "design" was "to overthrow the present fabric of Theology and Philosophy" without, however, having any "design of erecting an other in its place." LRBL, 51, 60; see also 49–50.

38. For Smith's claim, see Strahan, xlv. For evidence that Smith may have mistaken the work in question, see William Cullen to John Hunter, 17 September 1776, in Fieser IX, 294; and Annette C. Baier, *Death and Character: Further Reflections on Hume* (Cambridge, MA: Harvard University Press, 2008), 102–3.

39. Adam Smith to Alexander Wedderburn, 14 August 1776, in CAS, 204. There is a slight echo here of a recently discovered letter of the previous year in which Hume expresses his desire to see "all the Churches . . . converted into Riding Schools, Manufactories, Tennis Courts or Playhouses." In this letter, however, he says—surely jokingly—that he expects to see this objective "much advanced" within his own lifetime. David Hume to Andrew Stuart of Torrance,

NOTES TO CHAPTER 12

1 August 1775, in Maurice Baumstark, "The End of Empire and the Death of Religion: A Reconsideration of Hume's Later Political Thought," in *Philosophy and Religion in Enlightenment Britain*, ed. Ruth Savage (Oxford: Oxford University Press, 2012), 257.

40. Strahan, xlv–xlvi. In William Cullen's version of this conversation, apparently related secondhand from Smith, Hume claims that he is "busily employed in making his countrymen wiser, and particularly in delivering them from the Christian superstition."William Cullen to John Hunter, 17 September 1776, in Fieser IX, 294.

41. David Hume to Sir John Pringle, 13 August 1776, in HL II, 333.

42. Adam Smith to Alexander Wedderburn, 14 August 1776, in CAS, 204; see also Strahan, xlvi.

43. See Strahan, xlvi–xlvii.

44. Adam Smith to Alexander Wedderburn, 14 August 1776, in CAS, 203. Smith seems to have reserved the word "whining" for references to Christians and Christian-inspired ideas: see also TMS III.3.8, 139 and VII.ii.1.29, 283; in both cases, the term was added in the sixth edition of 1790.

45. Adam Smith to Alexander Wedderburn, 14 August 1776, in CAS, 204.

46. Joseph Black to Adam Smith, 14 August 1776, in CAS, 204.

47. David Hume to Adam Smith, 15 August 1776, in HL II, 334, and CAS, 205.

48. David Hume to Adam Smith, 23 August 1776, in HL II, 336, and CAS, 208; see also Adam Smith to David Hume, 22 August 1776, in CAS, 206.

49. Adam Smith to David Hume, 22 August 1776, in CAS, 206.

50. Adam Smith to David Hume, 22 August 1776, in CAS, 206.

51. Smith repeated the offer to William Strahan a couple of weeks later: see Adam Smith to William Strahan, 5 September 1776, in CAS, 211. Ian Simpson Ross writes that "it is to be presumed that [Smith] carried out his promise to correct Hume's works for the 'New Edition' of 1777." Ross, 321. However, there is no definitive evidence that he did so: see the editor's introduction in EPM, xxxv.

52. Adam Smith to David Hume, 22 August 1776, in CAS, 206–7.

53. Joseph Black to Adam Smith, 22 August 1776, in CAS, 207.

54. David Hume to Adam Smith, 23 August 1776, in HL II, 336, and CAS, 208.

55. Joseph Black to Adam Smith, 26 August 1776, in CAS, 208–9.

CHAPTER 12: TEN TIMES MORE ABUSE

1. Samuel Jackson Pratt, *Supplement to the Life of David Hume* (1777), in Fieser IX, 312.

2. See Mossner, 605–6.

3. For a detailed study of the tomb and its history, see Iain Gordon Brown, "David Hume's Tomb," *Proceedings of the Society of Antiquaries of Scotland* 121 (1991): 391–422.

4. See John Sinclair, *Memoirs of the Life and Works of Sir John Sinclair, Bart., by His Son*, vol. 1 (Edinburgh: William Blackwood and Sons, 1837), 38.

5. See Adam Smith to John Home of Ninewells, 31 August 1776, in CAS, 209.

6. John Home of Ninewells to Adam Smith, 2 September 1776, in CAS, 210; see also Adam Smith to John Home of Ninewells, 7 October 1776, in CAS, 214.

7. See Adam Smith to William Strahan, October 1776, in CAS, 216.

8. See Adam Smith to John Home of Ninewells, 7 October 1776, in CAS, 214; and Adam Smith to William Strahan, October 1776, in CAS, 216.

9. See Adam Smith to William Strahan, 13 November 1776, in CAS, 221.

10. David Hume to Adam Smith, 3 May 1776, in HL II, 318, and CAS, 196; see also David Hume to William Strahan, 8 June 1776, in HL II, 323; and Adam Smith to William Strahan, 5 September 1776, in CAS, 211.

11. See William Strahan to Adam Smith, 16 September 1776, in CAS, 212.

12. William Strahan to Adam Smith, 26 November 1776, in CAS, 222.

13. Adam Smith to William Strahan, 2 December 1776, in CAS, 223.

14. Adam Smith to William Strahan, 2 December 1776, in CAS, 224.

15. See the printer's note to *My Own Life* in Fieser IX, 267.

16. See Iain Gordon Brown, "Introduction: 'Embalming a Philosopher'—The Writing, Reception, and Resonance of David Hume's 'My Own Life,'" in *David Hume: My Own Life*, ed. Iain Gordon Brown (Edinburgh: Royal Society of Edinburgh, 2014), 23–24.

17. Strahan, xliii–xliv. The phrase "if I have any" in the last sentence quoted seems to have been inserted at the suggestion of Hume's brother: see John Home of Ninewells to Adam Smith, 14 October 1776, in CAS, 215.

18. Strahan, xlv–xlvi.

19. See Strahan, xlv–xlviii.

20. See Smith's comment to Strahan that he was striving to write "a very well authenticated account" of Hume's final illness: Adam Smith to William Strahan, 5 September 1776, in CAS, 211.

21. Ross, 323.

22. Strahan, xlviii.

23. Strahan, xlviii–xlix. Andrew Corsa has called attention to the many similarities between Smith's description of Hume here and Hume's own description of the "model of perfect virtue," Cleanthes, at EPM 9.2, 72–73: see Andrew Corsa, "Modern Greatness of Soul in Hume and Smith," *Ergo* 2.2 (2015): 48–49.

24. Strahan, xlix.

25. Plato, *Phaedo*, in *The Collected Dialogues of Plato*, ed. Edith Hamilton and Huntington Cairns (Princeton, NJ: Princeton University Press, 1961), 98.

26. J. Y. T. Greig, *David Hume* (New York: Garland, [1931] 1983), 414.

27. Aristotle, *Nicomachean Ethics*, trans. Robert C. Bartlett and Susan D. Collins (Chicago: University of Chicago Press, 2011), 1166a32, 194; and 1169b7, 203.

28. This aspect of the *Letter* has been stressed in Eric Schliesser, "Obituary of a Vain Philosopher: Adam Smith's Reflections on Hume's Life," *Hume Studies* 29.2 (November 2003): esp. 347–52.

29. Strahan, xliii, xlviii.

30. Stewart, 273.

31. Adam Smith to Andreas Holt, 26 October 1780, in CAS, 251.

32. Hugh Blair to William Strahan, 10 April 1778, in *Letters of David Hume to William Strahan*, ed. G. Birkbeck Hill (Oxford: Clarendon, 1888), xl n. 1.

33. Samuel Jackson Pratt, *An Apology for the Life and Writings of David Hume, Esq.* (1777), in Fieser X, 11.

34. John Ramsay of Ochtertyre, *Scotland and Scotsmen in the Eighteenth Century*, ed. Alexander Allardyce, vol. 1 (Edinburgh: William Blackwood, 1888), 466–67.

35. See Rae, 312.

36. George Horne, *A Letter to Adam Smith LL.D. on the Life, Death, and Philosophy of His Friend David Hume Esq. by One of the People Called Christians* (1777), in Fieser IX, 390.

37. Ibid., 391, 390, 393.

38. Ibid., 395–96.

39. E. M., "Remarks on Dr Adam Smith's *Letter to Mr. Strahan, on the Death of David Hume, Esq.*," *Weekly Magazine*, vol. 36 (24 April 1777), in Fieser IX, 406, 408–9.

40. See *London Review*, vol. 5 (March 1777), in Fieser IX, 275; "Strictures on the Life of David Hume," *Gentleman's Magazine*, vol. 46 (March 1777), in Fieser IX, 385; and Agricola, "Observations on Mr. Hume's Life Lately Published," *Weekly Magazine*, vol. 36 (12 June 1777), in Fieser IX, 417–18.

41. James Boswell, *The Life of Samuel Johnson*, ed. David Womersley (New York: Penguin, [1791] 2008), 605.

42. Ibid., 585.

43. James Boswell, *Journal of a Tour to the Hebrides with Samuel Johnson, LL.D.*, ed. Frederick A. Pottle and Charles H. Bennett (New York: McGraw-Hill, [1785] 1961), 18.

44. James Boswell, *Boswell: Laird of Auchinleck, 1778–1782*, ed. Joseph W. Reed and Frederick A. Pottle (New York: McGraw-Hill, 1977), 135; see also 255.

45. William Johnson Temple to James Boswell, 21 March 1777, in *The Correspondence of James Boswell and William Johnson Temple, 1756–1795, Volume 1: 1756–1777*, ed. Thomas Crawford (New Haven, CT: Yale University Press, 1997), 433.

46. James Boswell, *Boswell in Extremes, 1776–1778*, ed. Charles McC. Weis and Frederick A. Pottle (New York: McGraw-Hill, 1970), 270.

47. John Wesley, "The Deceitfulness of the Human Heart" (1790), in Fieser IX, 426.

48. See the stories collected in Fieser IX, 319–32, 424–25.

49. Alexander Haldane, *Memoirs of the Lives of Robert Haldane of Airthrey, and of His Brother, James Alexander Haldane* (1852), in Fieser IX, 332.

50. John Marshall Lowrie, *The Life of David* (1869), in Fieser IX, 429.

51. Adam Smith to Andreas Holt, 26 October 1780, in CAS, 251.
52. Adam Smith to Alexander Wedderburn, 14 August 1776, in CAS, 203–4.
53. Greig, *David Hume*, 414.

1. See Ross, 5–8.
2. Adam Smith to Andreas Holt, 26 October 1780, in CAS, 252–53.
3. Stewart, 326.
4. See Rae, 335–36.
5. Adam Smith to William Strahan, 10 June 1784, in CAS, 275.
6. Adam Smith to Thomas Cadell, 7 May 1786, in CAS, 296.
7. François Xavier Schwediauer to Jeremy Bentham, 14 September 1784, in *The Correspondence of Jeremy Bentham*, ed. Ian R. Christie, vol. 3 (London: Athlone Press, 1972), 306.
8. Adam Smith to Andreas Holt, 26 October 1780, in CAS, 252.
9. See Ross, 406. Nicholas Phillipson sees this work too as being deeply influenced by Hume, writing that Hume's essays "Of Tragedy" and "Of the Standard of Taste" were "of as much importance in opening up Smith's aesthetic thinking as Hume's essays on commerce had been for his thinking about political economy." Phillipson, 249.
10. Adam Smith to the duc de La Rochefoucauld, 1 November 1785, in CAS, 286–87. In the advertisement that Smith added to the sixth edition of *The Theory of Moral Sentiments* in 1790, he admitted that his "very advanced age" left him "very little expectation of ever being able to execute" the work on law and government "to my own satisfaction." See TMS, 3.
11. Adam Smith to William Strahan, 22 May 1783, in CAS, 266; see also the advertisement to the third edition at WN, 8; and Adam Smith to Thomas Cadell, 7 December 1782, in CAS, 263.
12. Walter Bagehot, "Adam Smith as a Person," in *Biographical Studies* (London: Longmans, Green, [1895] 1907), 278.
13. See John Kay, *A Series of Original Portraits and Character Etchings*, vol. 1 (Edinburgh: Hugh Paton, 1842), 75; and Rae, 405.
14. For Smith's brief description of these changes, see the advertisement to the sixth edition at TMS, 3. For more complete summaries, see D. D. Raphael and A. L. Macfie's introduction in TMS, 43–44; and Ryan Patrick Hanley, *Adam Smith and the Character of Virtue* (Cambridge: Cambridge University Press, 2009), 82–83n1.
15. See, for example, D. D. Raphael and A. L. Macfie's introduction in TMS, 18, 20; Charles L. Griswold, *Adam Smith and the Virtues of Enlightenment* (Cambridge: Cambridge University Press, 1999), 28; and James R. Otteson, *Adam Smith's Marketplace of Life* (Cambridge: Cambridge University Press, 2002), 14.

16. See, respectively, D. D. Raphael, "Adam Smith 1790: The Man Recalled; the Philosopher Revived," in *Adam Smith Reviewed*, ed. Peter Jones and Andrew S. Skinner (Edinburgh: Edinburgh University Press, 1992), esp. 109–10; Laurence Dickey, "Historicizing the 'Adam Smith Problem': Conceptual, Historiographical, and Textual Issues," *Journal of Modern History* 58.3 (September 1986): 579–609; and Hanley, *Adam Smith and the Character of Virtue*, chaps. 3–6.

17. For a very different argument, according to which Smith *distanced* himself from Hume's outlook in the sixth edition of *The Theory of Moral Sentiments*, see Chad Flanders, "Hume's Death and Smith's Philosophy," in *New Essays on Adam Smith's Moral Philosophy*, ed. Wade L. Robison and David B. Suits (Rochester, NY: Rochester Institute of Technology Press, 2012), 195–209.

18. See TMS VI.ii.2.15–18, 232–34.

19. TMS III.3.43, 155–56.

20. See TMS I.iii.3.5, 63; and VI.i.6–13, 213–16.

21. See TMS VI.ii.2.3, 228–29.

22. TMS VII.ii.1.34, 287.

23. Samuel Fleischacker, *A Third Concept of Liberty: Judgment and Freedom in Kant and Adam Smith* (Princeton, NJ: Princeton University Press, 1999), 144. See also Emma Rothschild, *Economic Sentiments: Adam Smith, Condorcet, and the Enlightenment* (Cambridge, MA: Harvard University Press, 2001), 129–30 and 299–300nn78–79; and Emma Rothschild, "Dignity or Meanness," *Adam Smith Review* 1 (2004): 160–61.

24. It is worth noting, however, that the first softening of the religious overtones came in the third edition, which was published in 1767 and was thus the first to appear after Smith left his professorship and the religious duties and expectations that attended it. D. D. Raphael postulates that perhaps "the more cautious statements of edition 3 represent Smith's original views, the expression of which he felt would be injudicious as coming from a Professor of Moral Philosophy but which honesty obliged him to make clear after he had quitted his Chair." D. D. Raphael, "Adam Smith and 'The Infection of David Hume's Society': New Light on an Old Controversy, Together with the Text of a Hitherto Unpublished Manuscript," *Journal of the History of Ideas* 30.2 (April–June 1969): 246.

25. TMS III.2.34–35, 132–34.

26. TMS II.ii.3.12, 91. This revision has gained special prominence in recent years due to its being singled out for discussion in an appendix to the Glasgow edition of *The Theory of Moral Sentiments* (itself a slightly edited version of D. D. Raphael's "Adam Smith and 'The Infection of David Hume's Society' ").

27. For an overview of the controversy, see Raphael, "Adam Smith and 'The Infection of David Hume's Society,'" esp. 226–27, 245–48.

28. Ibid., 247. While this revision is widely viewed as an indication of Smith's increasing skepticism about religion—or increasing willingness to express it—

this view is not unanimous: see Hanley, *Adam Smith and the Character of Virtue*, 197–98n22.

29. For further gestures in this direction, see Ryan Patrick Hanley, "Hume's Last Lessons: The Civic Education of 'My Own Life,'" *Review of Politics* 64.4 (Autumn 2002): 682–83; and Eric Schliesser, "Obituary of a Vain Philosopher: Adam Smith's Reflections on Hume's Life," *Hume Studies* 29.2 (November 2003): 350–51.

30. TMS VI.iii.11, 241. That said, Smith does not regard self-command as an unalloyed good; on the contrary, he stresses the danger inherent in the fact that we tend to admire self-command even when it is employed for the sake of pernicious ends: see TMS VI.iii.12, 241–42; and VI.concl.7, 264.

31. TMS VI.iii.5, 238.

32. TMS VI.iii.5, 238; see also I.iii.1.14, 48.

33. This point is also made in Schliesser, "Obituary of a Vain Philosopher," 351–52.

34. TMS VI.ii.1.15–18, 224–25.

35. Stewart, 327, 329.

36. Samuel Romilly to Madame G, 20 August 1790, in *Memoirs of the Life of Sir Samuel Romilly, Written by Himself*, vol. 1 (London: John Murray, 1840), 404.

37. See, for instance, *Times* (London), 16 August 1790, 4.

38. *Times* (London), 4 August 1790, 2.

39. See *Scots Magazine*, vol. 52 (July 1790): 363.

INDEX

Page numbers in *italics* refer to illustrations

History of Scotland (Robertson), 107
History of the Decline and Fall of the Roman Empire (Gibbon), 182, 200
Hobbes, Thomas, 37, 90–91
Holbach, Paul Henri Thiry, baron d', 123, 125, 130, 138, 141
Home, Henry (Lord Kames), 8, 29, 32, 45, 54, 69, 87, 104, 106
Home, John (brother of David Hume), 19, 204, 207, 208, 215, 217, 218
Home, John (playwright), 5, 8, 10, 69, 79, 204, 208, 217, 227
Home, Joseph, 19
Home, Katherine (sister), 19, 117, 150
Home, Katherine Falconer (mother), 19
Horace, 150
Horne, George, 224–25
How the Scots Invented the Modern World (Herman), 8
Hume, David: attempted excommunication of, 1, 70, 77–81, 129, 202; death of, 1, 9, 155, 192, 199, 214, 229; economic views of, 13, 59–62, 154; Edinburgh residences of, 55, 117–18, 149, 151–52; factionalism decried by, 26, 157, 233, 273n53; free trade embraced by, 13, 59–60, 166–67, 168, 175, 178; friendship viewed by, 5–6, 20, 27; as Hertford's secretary, 119, 120, 127–30; ill health of, 183, 185, 199–200, 205–6, 210, 212–13; impiety of, 14, 16–17, 23–24, 26–27, 28, 30, 31–32, 39, 58–59, 74, 78, 82, 124–25, 127, 129, 152, 174, 187–88, 199, 206, 208–9, 222–28, 235; last will of, 186, 188–89, 191, 195, 200; as library keeper, 54, 64, 66–67, 69; in Paris, 121–25; physical appearance of, 21, 46, 47, 122, 135; professorships sought by, 28–29, 52–54; religious benefits acknowledged by, 74–75; religious hypocrisy justified by, 28–29; Rousseau's dispute with, 5,

133–45, 196, 201, 203; Smith's correspondence with, 4, 45–46, 63–66, 76, 83–84, 103–7, 110, 113–14, 116, 118–19, 121, 123–24, 126, 127–29, 137, 141–42, 148–51, 153–55, 156–57, 158–59, 180–82, 189–92, 194, 204–5, 210, 212–13; Smith's *Theory of Moral Sentiments* reviewed by, 107–9, 111–12; sympathy viewed by, 91–94, 110, 111; *Treatise* disavowed by, 24–25, 41, 87; as under-secretary of state, 146, 157; at university, 19–20; upbringing of, 18–19. See also *Dialogues Concerning Natural Religion; Enquiry Concerning Human Understanding; Enquiry Concerning the Principles of Morals; Essays Moral and Political; Four Dissertations; History of England; My Own Life; Natural History of Religion;* "Of the Jealousy of Trade"; *Political Discourses; Treatise of Human Nature*
Hurd, Richard, 83, 202
Hutcheson, Francis, 8, 24–25, 40, 50, 51, 53, 58, 125, 161; as empiricist, 22, 89; Hume's appointment opposed by, 28; moral sense posited by, 24, 89; Smith's studies with, 37
Hutchinson, Thomas, 157
Hutton, James, 8, 40, 230, 236
Huxley, Thomas Henry, 22

impartial spectator, 89–90
Independents, 177
inequality, 135, 172–73
"Irish Massacre," 76
Irvine, Peggy, 69, 117, 152

Jacobite Rebellions, 7, 9, 33, 38–39
James I, king of England, 64, 73
Jardine, John, 68, 79
Johnson, Samuel, 2, 52, 85, 190, 226; death of, 238; dictionary of, 77; Hume disliked by, 87, 116–17; Smith vs., 117, 156